GAIL BORDEN

Dairyman to a Nation

BY

JOE B. FRANTZ

UNIVERSITY OF OKLAHOMA PRESS

NORMAN

Copyright 1951 by the University of Oklahoma Press
Publishing Division of the University
Composed and printed at Norman, Oklahoma, U. S. A.
by the University of Oklahoma Press
FIRST EDITION

Foreword

Several years ago when I was preparing a study of the newspapers of the Republic of Texas, I became aware that the story of one Texas publisher, Gail Borden, carried more than ordinary interest and importance. Here was a man who had founded an industry, who had pioneered in sanitary handling of that most important of modern foods, milk, who had played a large behind-the-scenes part in the birth of free Texas, who had tried a dozen things before hitting on the one thing that made his name known to almost every housewife in the nation—and yet strangely he had been overlooked by biographers for seventy years.

Gail Borden's story, it was apparent, had the log-cabin-to-mansion quality which nineteenth-century Americans believed was their peculiar belonging—and which still appears with sufficient frequency, especially in the nation's newer regions, to evoke from hard-bitten, blues-imbued contemporaries the comment that "only in America could this happen." The Borden story was the story, again dear to us, of the humble tinker who developed something the world wanted and of the world's beaten path to his door. It was the story, so beloved, of man's finding immortality of a sort in this world, leaving behind a monument which, in Borden's case, has grown into a company that not only perpetuates his name and his memory, but annually sells six hundred million dollars' worth of goods, employs thirty thousand persons, and pays dividends to fifty thousand stockholders. How many of us would like to have such a legion remember our name generations after our death!

With these things in mind I began to collect materials on Gail Borden's life, to rediscover the man, to find strength and frailty. It has been an adventure, this search for Bordeniana, one that has carried me through most of the United States from Texas eastward. And since biography is more than compilation, since it is really a recreation of personality that makes a subject live and breathe and exult and sorrow and triumph and lose and respond to forces about him, I have tried to go back a century, to live in the eighteen twenties and eighteen fifties and the other decades with Gail Borden and to know him as well as any man ever knows another. Consequently, I have visited every place where Borden lived and worked, absorbing local traditions, seeking an awareness of conditions which might have affected Borden, developing a feeling for the place and the time, trying to get inside the man. The result has been what I sought. Gail Borden has become real to me, a member of my family—or perhaps I have joined his family.

The quest for the man has led to San Felipe, Houston, Columbia, and Galveston in Texas; to the red hills around Liberty, Mississippi; to the ghost town of New London, Indiana; to Covington, Kentucky; to Keosauqua, Iowa, to Norwich, Brewster, Wassaic, Albany, Amenia, and White Plains in New York; to Elgin and Chicago, Illinois; to Burrville, Winsted, Winchester Center, and Torrington, Connecticut; to Livermore Falls, Maine—out-of-the-way places mostly, where old-timers speak of Borden as a man who died yesterday rather than three-quarters of a century ago.

But there must be compilation. And that, too, has meant travel. The Rosenberg Library, Galveston, has the largest collection of Borden manuscripts, but considerable other material may be found in the National Archives, Washington, D. C., and in the Borden Company archives, New York, as well as in the University of Texas Archives and the Texas State Library Archives in Austin.

Naturally, in a search spreading over eight years and two-score towns I have received many favors and courtesies, so many, in fact, that a separate acknowledgment has been added. However, something special and personal is due to three persons who have contributed most—to Mr. Milton Fairman, who arranged that ideal situation whereby the Borden Company made available a grant with no strings attached, to Dr. Eugene C. Barker, who has essayed the rôle of elder statesman to this study, sparing me countless hours of tracking down fugitive facts; and to Dr. Walter P. Webb, who has stood by as guide and adviser and who has encouraged and inspired me in my desire to write more than a conventional, acceptable biography, to take the raw facts of a man's life and mold them into a clay that for several hundred pages might actually live.

JOE B. FRANTZ

Austin, Texas
March 10, 1951.

Acknowledgments

SINCE TO LIST ALL THE PERSONS who have aided in bringing Gail Borden to life again would almost dwarf in volume the text of this biography, some of the acknowledgments must perforce be collective. Without the assistance and interest of these groups this study of Borden would necessarily have been incomplete.

For their contributions I am grateful to E. R. Dabney, N. A. Cleveland, Jr., Miss Winnie Allen, Miss Helen Hunnicutt, Miss Julia Harris, and Mrs. Marcelle Hamer and their staffs at the University of Texas Library; to Miss Harriet Smither, Archives of the Texas State Library, to the Newberry Library staff, Chicago; to J. S. Ibbotson and staff, Rosenberg Library, Galveston, to Miss Mildred Lathrop, Gail Borden Library, Elgin, Illinois, to the staffs of the National Archives and the Library of Congress, Washington D. C., the New York Public Library, New York, and the New York State Library, Albany, to the late Miss Julia Ideson, Houston Public Library; to the late Ike Moore, San Jacinto Museum of History, Houston; to Mrs. W. O. Harrell, State Department of Archives and History, Jackson, Mississippi, to L. R. Elliott, Southwestern Baptist Theological Seminary, Fort Worth; to the Alamo Museum staff, San Antonio, to Miss Nora Schwab, Jefferson County Historical Association, Madison, Indiana; to the late John E. Pugsley, Brewster, New York, to John A. Sincerbox, Wassaic, New York; to Albert G. Milbank, Stuart Peabody, Miss Rachel Reed, and Henry K. Greer, the Borden Company, New York, to George Kienzle, the Borden Company, Columbus, Ohio, to Dr. N. S. B. Gras, Cambridge, Massachusetts, to Fred Schaper, Norwich, New York; to Gail Borden and Manley Munford, Chicago, to Elliott Bronson, Winchester Center, Connecticut, to John Burr, Burrville, Connecticut, to Dr. Thad W. Riker, Dr. Milton R. Gutsch, Dr. Charles A. Timm, and Dr. J. Lloyd Mecham, University of Texas, Austin, to O. A. Zumwalt and the late J. J. Mansfield, Columbus, Texas, to Mr. and Mrs. J. L. Lockett, Otway Taylor, Andrew Forest Muir, W. Glenn Oxford, Lester O. Weison, and L. W. Kemp, Houston; to Herbert B. Bisby, Galveston, to Dr. William R. Hogan, New Orleans, to Dr. John Cravens, Forsyth, Georgia, to Dr. G. C. Boswell, Ranger, Texas, and to James M. Cotten, Fred R. Cotten, and my parents, Mr. and Mrs. E. A. Frantz, Weatherford, Texas.

To Rosemary Carr Benét, for permission to quote from *Western Star*, published by Rinehart and Company in 1943; and to the *Bulletin of the Business Historical Society*, the *Journal of Mississippi History*, and the *Southwestern Historical Quarterly* for permission to quote from various articles by the author which have appeared in these journals.

To the host of county and district clerks and their staffs, especially those in Chenango, Dutchess, and Westchester counties, New York; Litchfield County, Connecticut, Amite County, Mississippi, Kenton County, Kentucky; Jefferson County, Indiana; and Brazoria, Galveston, Colorado, Guadalupe, Harris, Austin, Fayette, Bastrop, Fort Bend, and Wharton counties, Texas, I express my appreciation.

For a variety of reasons I owe even more than the usual thanks to Mrs. Martha Ann Zivley and Herbert Lang, Austin; to W. F. Carothers, Pat Tennant, and Herbert Fletcher, Houston, to W. H. Ewen, New York; to J. H. Parker, Liberty, Mississippi, to Miss Mary Hill, Madison, Indiana; to William R. Galpin, Norwich, New York; to Arthur G. Bacon, Bainbridge, New York; and to A. L. Heminger, Keosauqua, Iowa.

The Chapters

I. Ancestral Voices: 1066–1801   3

II. The Valley of the Chenango: 1801–1814   15

III. A Kentuck' of a Place¹: 1814–1816   24

IV. Scantling-thin and Stooped a Little: 1816–1822   39

V. Days along the Milk and Cider: 1822–1829   51

VI. Hotspurs and Bumbling Officials: 1829–1835   60

VII. The Alarm Is Sounded: 1835–1836   82

VIII. The Voice of Texas: 1836–1837   101

IX. The One-faced Janus of Galveston Island: 1837–1839   129

X. Setting the Crooked Straight: 1839–1844   150

XI. More Toil Than Honor: 1841–1849   175

XII. The Terraqueous Machine and Other Curiosities: 1845–1849   188

XIII. The Good Ship Meat Biscuit: 1849–1855   201

XIV. Door to Door: 1851–1857   222

XV. The Turning Point: 1858–1861   241

XVI. Infinite Pursuit: 1861–1874   256

Bibliography   277

Index   295

The Illustrations

Gail Borden's birthplace	*facing page*	18
Borden's first factory		34
Handbill advertising condensed milk		50
Henry Lee Borden		66
Map of Texas, 1840		79
First issue, *Telegraph and Texas Register*		98
Letter, Borden to Burnet		114
Borden's patent application		130
Borden's condensed milk wrapper		146
John Gail Borden		162
Borden's checks		178
Early handbill		194
Great Council gold medals		210
Gail Borden and Jeremiah Milbank		226
Jeremiah Milbank		242
Map of New York and Connecticut, 1870		249
Gail and Eunice Borden		258
Gail Borden		274

GAIL BORDEN

Dairyman to a Nation

For out of the old fieldes, as men saithe,
Cometh al this new corne fro yere to yere.
—Chaucer, *The Assembly of Fowles*

I

Ancestral Voices
1066-1801

OPPRESSION behaves like any spiral spring, absolutely intransigent at the source, still taut but slightly yielding a little further down its helical path, loose, almost elastic on the broad outermost fringe. And in England in 1637 Richard Borden found himself squeezed into the tightest portion of that spiral of oppression, so close to the source that individual freedom of action was virtually impossible, not to say dangerous.

For this was England when the Stuarts reigned, and the church ruled. And William Laud—"Little Will"—was the church, stalking England and Scotland as its most militant Archbishop of Canterbury, enforcing orthodoxy with a violence belying that delicately formed head which was itself to know the stroke of the sharpened blade in the Tower of London.

For a simple farmer like Richard Borden, who feared God but owned no church, merely to be in England at this time would have been tribulation enough. But Richard Borden lived in the parish of Cranbrooke, a scant fifteen miles from the very seat of tyranny in Canterbury. At those close quarters not even a man's thoughts were his own one tiny heresy and an avenging angel wearing an archbishop's purple robes would surely descend.

Richard Borden had no choice. No fanatical Puritan, no Papist either, only a man who loved his Creator, forty-year-old Richard Borden gathered his portable belongings, his wife Joan and his children, and started for the rocky wilderness that was New England.

Ahead, Richard Borden hoped, lay freedom—of expression and of worship. Ahead, he knew, lay uncertainty and privation.

Behind lay tradition and memory and association and family, reaching all the way back to 1066 when the Bordens had come over with William the Conqueror—*Bourdons* they called themselves then —to place their names on William's Great Roll.

The low, flat country of Kent looked good to those eleventh-century conquerors, and there they settled, not far from where Caesar's legions had marched, not far from later-famed Watling Street, near where the heathen Druids had worshiped, only a few miles from the city of Rochester. There grew the parish of Borden, eventually to include six hundred and fifty people within its bounds. For three hundred years Richard Borden's ancestors remained at Borden before moving twelve miles away to Hedcorn, there to live for two hundred and fifty years more until Richard himself shifted to Cranbrooke.

In the church of Hedcorn the Bordens left many records. In 1469 Henry Borden requested that a priest sing for his soul and that of his wife for two years after their deaths. Henry's son, Thomas, a yeoman, joined that bit of Irish temperament known as Jack Cade when in 1450 Cade led a rebellion against the excesses of Henry VI that succeeded in capturing London. After order was restored, Thomas was pardoned.

Years passed, and Bordens continued to be buried in Hedcorn churchyard. Meanwhile, the Bordens prospered until Mathew, Richard's father, a Hedcorn churchwarden, was able to leave Joane, his wife, £8 yearly from his farm, plus the rent from his houses in Hedcorn, another farm, and his tenement "wherein Roger Jones dwells." Daughter Amye received sixty pounds; William, forty pounds and house and lot at Smarden; and Richard, two houses and accompanying land.

These ties, this small prosperity, centuries in the gathering, Richard Borden forsook to go to America, only suspecting the way of life ahead, certainly not realizing that he was to be the root of an American family tree that would proliferate until today more than six thousand people in this country trace their ancestry directly to Richard Borden, nor that in a little more than two centuries his descendant, Gail Borden, would make discoveries which would make of that descendant a citizen of the world.

In America, in Massachusetts, Richard Borden found no freedom. True, William Laud no longer raged. But the Puritans did.

For them freedom of religion meant freedom for their religion only, and in this religion Borden did not share. This America, this haven, this was not the free world he had envisaged when he had felt the walls of intolerance closing about him in Kent. Elusory freedom must lie still farther into the wilderness.

The young firebrand liberal, Roger Williams, had chosen the head of Narragansett Bay to find religious peace. Richard Borden determined to seek the same locale. In the spring of 1638 he set out, following foot trails where he could, erecting temporary bridges, building rude rafts to cross the larger streams. Beyond Williams' settlement he passed, crossing to Rhode Island proper to found with others the town of Portsmouth. Here in May, before Richard had time to build a proper cabin, Joan Borden gave birth to another son, Matthew, the first child, some say, to be born on the island. He was the Bordens' sixth child; six more were yet to be born.

In Rhode Island freedom could be found, and Richard Borden made the most of it. Anticipating Gail Borden, he became one of the official surveyors of the town, helping to "mapp or plott" all the farming lands in Portsmouth. He prospered; he acquired considerable land—"ackers and lotts"—not only in Rhode Island but away west in Carteret's new colony of East Jersey, near Shrewsbury. His prominence increased: freeman of Portsmouth, 1641; member of eight-man committee to treat with the Dutch, 1653; assistant, town of Portsmouth, 1653, 1654, commissioner, 1654, 1656, 1657; treasurer of court of commissioners, 1654 (Roger Williams was president), 1655; freeman, 1655; and deputy from Portsmouth to the General Assembly, 1667, 1670.

And, in Portsmouth, Richard Borden at last found a church in which he wanted to worship—the Society of Friends, themselves persecuted in Massachusetts and disliked though tolerated by the Baptist Williams.

Thus then did the Bordens settle in America, planting their seed deep. Six generations later, Gail Borden was to show that same questing spirit, that same thirst for quiet adventure, that same perseverance that would make the name Borden known in virtually every home in America, and even beyond.[1]

[1] In his will Richard Borden left his wife, in addition to the house and other usual belongings, "firewood yearly, use of thirty fruit trees in orchard, . . . liberty to

Richard Borden's family grew, and like their father the children increased their stature in the community. Matthew, perhaps the least acquisitive of the children, turned to religion, and his home became the regular meeting place for the Portsmouth Friends. The pride of the family, though, was son John, Gail's direct ancestor, who so far overshadowed his brothers and even his father that for generations most of the descendants traced their ancestry to John only, forgetting or never knowing that Richard had started the family. While still a young man, John had employed his shrewd business acumen and his amazing energy to acquire large tracts in Rhode Island, New Jersey, Delaware, and Pennsylvania. Privately townspeople would mock his favorite sentence: "If any man has land to sell at a fair price I am ready to buy, and have the money ready at my house to pay for it," an offer which brought him Hog Island and lands at Bristol Ferry, Swansea, Tiverton, and Freetown.

But John did not confine his talents to business. He developed an intimate friendship with King Philip, that tortured Indian sachem who saw his people being pushed back farther and farther from their lands. In desperation Philip told John Borden, sent by Plymouth to forestall an Indian war, "I am determined I will not live till I have no country." When Borden failed to pacify Philip, Plymouth felt that the Rhode Islander had failed them.

John Borden incensed the Plymouth government further. Expanding Plymouth claimed that Hog Island, owned by John, owed its colony taxes, Borden paid only to Portsmouth, the upshot being that Plymouth had him arrested. Immediately John complained to the Rhode Island legislature, which, seizing his case as a cudgel to beat off any further Plymouth inroads, addressed a complaint to Plymouth's General Assembly charging extortion and informing its neighbor that it had issued orders to John Borden not to answer Plymouth's court.

---

keep fowls about the house not exceeding forty, . thirty ewe sheep, . . fifty other sheep, . . . three cows kept and their profit, and to have paid her yearly a good well fed beef, three well fed swine, ten bushels of wheat, twenty bushels of barley malt and four barrels of cider " The entire estate was inventoried at £1,572 8s 9d, including a Negro man and woman and three Negro children. H B. Weld, *Historical and Genealogical Record of Richard and Joan Borden*, 18. Unless otherwise noted, material for this chapter is taken from Weld, from T A Green, *Pedigree of Richard Borden*, and from J R. Bartlett (ed), *Records of the Colony of Rhode Island*, I–IV.

The Bordens moved on into the eighteenth century. A varied family they were. There was Mercy Borden, a man, so named because of a vow taken by his mother during an electrical storm. While she was sitting in her chair with her cat at her feet, a bolt of lightning struck the house, killing the cat. Already in advanced pregnancy, Mrs. Borden jumped to her feet, crying "The mercy of God has spared my life. . . . my child shall be called Mercy." Not even giving birth to a son deterred her, but then, strange names ran in her family —one of her brothers had lived and died bearing the name of Howlong Harris. Perhaps it was the influence of their father's having been captured by an Algerian pirate.

For that matter, piracy was not unknown on the Borden side. Moses Butterworth had just confessed to the court of sessions at Middletown, New Jersey, that he had sailed with Captain William Kidd on his last voyage when in rushed Benjamin Borden and his brother, Richard, with thirty other young hearties to rescue the prisoner. The two Bordens were arrested by the constables, only to be rescued in turn by their rallying comrades. The rioters then turned the tables by holding Governor Andrew Hamilton, the court, the attorney general, and the court officers for four days.[2]

Another Borden, Joseph, left Rhode Island for the "West," seeking a wife. So intent was he on success that he carried a letter from the Friends "concerning his clearness of entanglements as to marriage," but he returned to become a subject for town speculation: no wife, no engagement, no explanation. Five years later he went westward again, this time without either letter or statement of intention, and to everyone's surprise showed up again in a very few weeks with a blooming bride.

Following the great John Borden on our main highway to Gail Borden came another John Borden, the antithesis of his strong-willed, energetic father. On the death of his father this younger John Borden became so discouraged by the prospect of having to care entirely for his family that, in the words of Parson Seabury, he "pined away and died." Searchers for character strains in Gail Borden derive no comfort from this second John.

[2] Book of Minutes No. 1, Monmouth County Records, quoted in W. Nelson (ed.), *Documents Relating to the Colonial History of the State of New Jersey*, XXIV, 653.

Young John's brother, Thomas, seemed more his father's child. Seeing that salt meadows were coveted by most of the moneyed townspeople, he cut his hundred acres on Hog Island into ten-acre plots and sold them quickly at five hundred pounds a plot. Then he waited a year for the saline enthusiasm to cool and bought the lots back at three hundred pounds, a net over-all profit of two thousand pounds. It was the sensation of the day, and old-timers were still talking about the transaction when Gail Borden was born.

Still another brother, William, operated what is generally credited to be the first duck factory in America, the Rhode Island General Assembly helping along with a bounty on every pound of flax or hemp which should be raised for his factory, granting him exclusive right of manufacture and three thousand pounds in bills of credit without interest for ten years. The Assembly further provided that Borden must make 150 bolts of "good merchantable duck yearly" or pay back the three thousand pounds. But the Dutch, foremost duck manufacturers, need not have worried: at the end of his decade William Borden decided that America was not ready for domestic duck, closed his factory, moved to the vicinity of Beaufort, North Carolina, and became a successful shipbuilder.

The youngest of the children—father John had nine—left the Rhode Island fold early, settling in Virginia. Through a chain of circumstances he obtained the dubious honor of presenting the governor of Virginia with a buffalo calf, an animal not known around Williamsburg. Governor Gooch was so delighted that he promptly authorized Benjamin Borden to locate a half-million acres of land on the Shenandoah and James rivers—Virginia's famed Natural Bridge was once his property—and settle one hundred families there within the next ten years. Borden went to England for his emigrants, bringing back mostly Presbyterians from Scotland and Northern Ireland. So conscientious was Benjamin in fulfilling his obligations both to Virginia and to settlers that his name was perpetuated in a popular simile—"as good as Ben Borden's bill."

In the fourth generation of American Bordens the family continued to ramify its interests and expand its numbers. There were the sisters, Patience and Peace, who between them had twenty-six children. There was Samuel, like the earlier Richard and the later Gail, a surveyor of prominence. When the order came from England to replace the recently expelled French in Acadia with English colonists, Governor Shirley of Massachusetts named Samuel Borden to lead the expedition. In 1760 Borden went to Nova Scotia, stayed a few years, and returned to New England to live the quiet life of a farmer, leaving his son, Perry, to found the Canadian branch of the family that in time was to produce a prime minister, Sir Robert Laird Borden, Conservative leader from 1911 to 1920.

Another Joseph Borden, whose asthmatic father had founded Bordentown, New Jersey, transported mail and passengers between Philadelphia and New York and kept a house in Bordentown where his stage-boat passengers could obtain overnight accommodations. He was one of New Jersey's delegates to the Stamp Act Congress in October, 1765. And with revolution threatening, he became a member of New Jersey's committee of correspondence, later joining the American army after open fighting flared. A British officer who made the Borden home his headquarters during his station on the Delaware is reported to have threatened Mrs. Borden with destruction of her home unless she could get her husband to abandon the American cause, Mrs. Borden replying defiantly that "the sight of my house in flames would be a treat to me [since] I should regard it as a signal for your departure." The officer, it should be added, was a man of his word: the house was burned, the property laid waste, and the animals killed or scattered.[3]

Bumbling John Borden, who could not bear to live without his father's direction, lived long enough to have five children, the second of whom he named John also. This third John set up a forge on the Ponaganset River in Rhode Island for the manufacture of wrought iron, his ore coming from present-day Cranston and the surrounding forests furnishing ample charcoal. This John was Gail Borden's great-grandfather.

The fifth generation introduces Oliver Borden, who strayed from his Quaker background to become a Baptist exhorter in John-

[3] E. F. Ellet, *The Women of the American Revolution*, II, 305–306. Nelson (ed.), *Documents of New Jersey*, XXIV, 210, 654–55. The younger Joseph Borden was one of the promoters of the episode made famous by the Francis Hopkinson poem, "Battle of the Kegs" Kegs of gunpowder, equipped with a mechanism to fire them, were sent down the Delaware shortly before daylight on January 7, 1778, to blow up the British ships stationed in the river Unfortunately for the plan, the British hauled their ships into dock the night before

ston, Rhode Island. Parson Seabury said he lacked "intelligence, natural ability, or education," while Elder Wilson of Providence remarked, "There is a minister in Jonston . . . who preaches for nothing, and I think that is as much as it is worth."

But if Oliver was not held in much esteem, his cousin, Richard, over in Fall River, was at times held in even less. Although prosperous enough, Richard was really an ordinary fellow who showed enthusiasm on only one subject—the future value of Fall River property. Idlers about his mill were wont to bring up the subject just to watch his fervor mount as they baited him.

"Do ye see, neighbor," he burst out on more than one occasion, "do ye see, I tell ye, the time will come when every dam on the stream will be sought after by men who have the money to pay for it at a great price, and every stone and tree around Fall River will be wanted—yes, I tell ye, the time will come when the rocks on Rattlesnake Hill will bring the gould." Not even Richard knew how prophetic a half-century of the Industrial Revolution would make his words.

Out in New Jersey, Ann Borden, of the Bordentown Bordens, made a brilliant marriage to thirty-year-old Francis Hopkinson, lawyer, poet, musician, and composer, whose father had been an intimate of Benjamin Franklin. Francis Hopkinson had been the first student to enter the College of Philadelphia, had spent two years in England, and already possessed a small reputation as a writer and translator. After his marriage he settled in Bordentown in a house built in 1750 but known to this day as the Hopkinson House. Like his father-in-law, Joseph, whose home the British had taken over, Hopkinson was vehement in his antipathy to the British. He was a delegate to the Continental Congress at Philadelphia, where on July 4, 1776, he signed the Declaration of Independence; he penned several pamphlets satirizing the British political position; and then, in 1777, he became judge of the admiralty court for Pennsylvania, a position he held until Washington in 1789 named him a United States district judge. It was the son of Francis and Ann, Joseph Hopkinson, who wrote the words to "Hail Columbia" and became Joseph Bonaparte's legal adviser in America.[4]

[4] The *Pennsylvania Chronicle* carried an account of the Borden-Hopkinson wedding in the following eloquent language "On Thursday last [September 1,

Ann's sister, Mary, also married a signer of the Declaration of Independence, Thomas McKean, delegate from Delaware, who later spent nine years as governor of Pennsylvania. Joseph Borden's stage house, only a little way out of Billet Wharff in Philadelphia, was ideally located for a man with daughters¹

During this same period the first of three Gail Bordens appeared, this one destined to live only thirty-two years and to accomplish little in that time. However, his wife, Mary Knowlton, added new strength to the family line. She was a direct descendant of Gabriel Bernon, a wealthy merchant of Rochelle, France, who had been forced to flee France during the Huguenot persecutions, arriving in Boston in 1688.

In the year that this Gail Borden died, the summer before Washington's dreary winter at Valley Forge, another Gail Borden was born—on August 23, 1777. He was his father's second child and his only son.

Like his father, this young Gail grew up around Gloucester, Rhode Island, and about 1800 he met the twenty-year-old daughter of another old, old Rhode Island family, established also around the waters of Narragansett because of a desire to escape religious bigotry. The girl was Philadelphia Wheeler, whose mother was Esther Williams, the great-great-granddaughter of Roger Williams. The couple were married in 1800, fusing two blood strains with a centuries-old reputation for independence, perseverance, and tolerance. The union was to produce splendid results.

And so time moves nearer.

They came westward, bidding farewell to Rhode Island and its six generations of Bordens. For Rhode Island was a busy, crowded place occupied with commerce, and they were pioneers with dreams in their hearts.

Probably by land they moved into New York state. That was the usual way. Overland to Albany, up the Mohawk, not yet refined

1768] Francis Hopkinson, Esq , of Philadelphia, was joined in the Velvet Bands of HYMEN, to Miss Nancy Borden, of this place, a lady amiable both for her internal as well as external Accomplishments, and in the words of a celebrated poet
Without all shining, and within all white,
Pure to the sense, and pleasing to the sight."
Quoted in Nelson (ed), *Documents of New Jersey*, X, 427.

and made shapeless by DeWitt Clinton's canal, and on to Duanesburg, a bustling depot for people whose eyes were set toward the wilderness. From there the trail wound till it hit the north end of Otsego Lake, thence down to the southern end to Cooperstown, where less than four decades later the first game of baseball was to be played.

But baseball and other frivolity were far in the future then. Beyond Cooperstown, civilization thinned. In 1801 trails were beginning to be well marked and in some directions there were roads. Still, to be absolutely sure, one often traveled by compass and marked trees, now climbing hills, now threading through tangled forests claimed almost eternally by shadows, fording streams, toiling on until night overtook the tired traveler. Perhaps they packed their own baggage on an animal or two. Perhaps, as they drew nearer, they found Indians who would carry the baggage for them.

The next day the same weary scene would be re-enacted. And the next and the next days also until finally they crossed the Unadilla, climbed one more great range of stretching hills, and looked down into their valley, the valley of the Chenango, in whose flat lay Norwich—*Nor-idj*, its settlers pronounced it. This was home, the end of their journey—at least for a while. Here too they found people, hordes of people; the 1800 census said more than two thousand in their township of Norwich alone. But there was a difference in these people. Like Gail and Philadelphia Borden, these were newcomers, people uprooted from their past, people seeking a present and a future, but still people with their feet planted firmly on the good soil that was giving them their livelihood.

Straightaway the Bordens set about to make a home, for Philadelphia was expecting a child in the late fall and what was left of the year must be utilized in clearing land, putting in late crops, and erecting a house to see them through the first winter.

By the first of September, 1801, Gail Borden was legally a propertied man. He had located his ideal spot—right alongside the east bank of the Chenango in the middle of the valley. Looking north he could see his valley funneling into the distance, for all the world like a great cornucopia, its riches waiting to be plumbed by the man industrious enough, intelligent enough, and lucky enough to find the proper key. To the east and the west the valley crept upward till it fused with the giant hills which sheltered it.

And the pride of the twenty-four-year-old young husband must have mounted as he looked at the land—his land—ascending gently eastward. "Two hundred and fifty six acres one rood and two perches be the same more or less"—these were his. For it, he had paid Anthony and Mary Lamb "nine hundred and ninety-five dollars and sixty-two cents money of the United States"—nearly four dollars an acre, where a few years earlier he could have bought it for a dollar and a quarter; but it was his "TO HAVE AND TO HOLD."[5]

Gail Borden scarce had time to contemplate the wonders of his new station. Older settlers were still talking of the winter of ninety-three when a hard frost had come on the first day of September and a snow smack on top of that, leaving not a leaf on a tree by September 15. That was warning enough for Borden. While the weather remained mild, there was that house to be built. Building a house followed an almost invariable pattern: round logs laid one atop another, notched at the ends to lie as snug as possible. Each joint filled with small sticks, then plastered over with clay mortar. A temporary covering of brush; when time permitted, a permanent bark covering. Openings for doors and windows, part of the logs cut away at one end, and a few stones piled up for a back to the fireplace. The bare earth for a hearth and floor. A hole cut in the roof so the smoke could escape. Thus a house was built. Later the logs could be replaced by smooth boards from the sawmill—but that must wait.

It didn't take Philadelphia Borden long to make a home of this rough beginning. Gail would roll in a log four feet long, maybe longer, with a forestick to correspond, raise it on wooden firedogs, and then Philadelphia would take over. With the kettle adjusted on the top of the burning log, she would put in her pork and potatoes and set them to foaming and boiling. Sometimes there was more to it than that—an unbalanced kettle would overturn and dinner would be well peppered with ashes. For bread there was the Indian meal, cooked over the coals in a long-handled frying pan or in a short-handled spider. The dining room would be a large chest, or maybe

[5] Book C of Deeds, Chenango County, New York, 109

13

some rough boards supported at each end on boxes or old barrels. Heeding the dinner horn—a conch shell whose sound would echo throughout the woods—Gail Borden would come, undoubtedly on occasion looking as if he, too, had overturned in ashes, so blackened was he from working his fallow ground only recently burned over.

꙳ As the chill of fall succeeded mellow summer, Philadelphia's time came. On November 9, 1801, the child was born—a son. For a cradle it possibly had no better than a sap-trough; for a home, a rude cabin only a decade away from the wilderness; and for its inheritance, the liberal blood of Roger Williams and Richard Borden; but for its future it had the unbounded horizon.

*The wilderness and the solitary place
shall be glad for them*
—Isaiah 35 1[1]

II

The Valley of the Chenango
1801-1814

THEY named the child Gail Borden, Junior. And if Gail, the father, had felt any youth lingering, such feeling was dispersed now, for at a scant twenty-four he became Old Gail, and the child Young Gail, to most friends and relatives from that time forward.

Unlike his father, Old Gail Borden was not content with just one son. Two years later—on January 28, 1804, the year of the typhus epidemic—a second son, Thomas Henry, was born. Three winters later, December, 1806, Paschal Pavolo was born, to be followed on December 30, 1812, by John Petit. All the Borden sons were born in midwinter when icy blasts were frequent and the air was fresh from the English Lakes, so that by the time summer came with its dullness and its fevers they were hardy children, able to withstand preying summer diseases. Having babies was not expensive for either the Bordens or any other upstate New Yorkers. The doctor charged three dollars if the birth were natural, six dollars if instruments were used, plus traveling fees of one shilling sixpence a mile.

Young Gail Borden grew like any other child in a small semi-frontier town in the first decade of the roistering nineteenth century. He learned the woods, he learned household chores, and he learned self-reliance. Apparently he attended no formal school, though several did exist. His was the knowledge of practice. Meanwhile Old Gail's farm had confirmed his choice of location, and he sought to improve his position by a little trading. In October, 1805,

---

[1] From the text used by the Reverend Blackleach Burritt for what is reputed to be the first sermon delivered in the Chenango Valley. Joel Hatch, *Town of Sherburne*, 15.

he added five more acres running along Burdens [Borden's] Mill Brook—this for $230 in New York money. Two months later he sold Miriam Saunders thirty acres for $150 and a week after that nearly thirty acres for $327.50. Early in January, 1806, he sold fifty more acres for $225, after which he slacked off until just before Christmas of 1807, when he bought a half-interest in a sawmill and an extra half-acre of land for $140.[2]

Between selling and buying land and making crops, Old Gail had other work to do, work in which sometimes Young Gail could help. For one thing, four walls and a few rude tables were not good enough for a man of family. The blanket which served as a door must be replaced with a real door made of boards and fastened with wooden hinges, with wooden latch and handle and a string connected with the latch running through the door and hanging on the outside. He could smooth his door with a plane or leave it in its rough state, depending on his time and energy.

Windows must be carved out, substituting oiled paper for unobtainable glass. He would want a real floor, which again he could make himself by cutting some suitable tree, rending it with beetle and wedge, leveling it with a hewing ax, and, if he wished, smoothing it with the plane. Lay these boards over a few poles adjusted upon the ground and a man had his floor. He could not be careless, however, with such small objects as pocketknives lest they fall through a chink of the floor and disappear from sight.

As the boy grew, he could watch his mother at work in one corner of the house, occupied with the inflexible routine of meal preparation. He could perhaps investigate the shelf suspended from the beams overhead, a depository for almost every article not regularly needed. Or he could pry about the pantry, which, if like most Norwich pantries, consisted of wide boards, one above another, resting on long pins driven into the logs. Here also, between romps with his little brothers, the child could watch his mother, bred to New England neatness, tidying the house with her broom of hemlock boughs or small twigs of beech.

With the enlargement of the family the house can reasonably

[2] Chenango County, New York Book O of Deeds, 138; Book H of Deeds, 169, 252; Book I of Deeds, 75, Book S of Deeds, 122. The original deed in which Gail and Philadelphia Borden sold nearly thirty acres for $327.50 is in the Gail Borden Papers, Borden Company, New York.

be expected to have been enlarged also. Probably as soon as boards were obtainable, the roof was boarded over, while other boards were laid loosely overhead for a chamber floor for the children and any visitors who might happen in. Such a chamber was always subject to the caprices of the wind, for if the wind were just right—or just wrong—the sleeper would be smoked out of his chamber as if he were a troublesome mosquito. Children also meant that there were more clothes to make. No one had time yet to be wealthy, so the whole township wore the plainest kind of clothing. Every piece was home-manufactured, and every pound of flax, from the hatchel to the distaff, and every fleece of wool, from the cards and spindle to the loom, had to pass through Philadelphia Borden's hands. She too must make all their dyes, her husband, or her children when they were old enough, obtaining the dyestuffs for her in the surrounding forests. Butternut, soft maple, witch hazel, sumac, or if one could afford it, indigo—these determined the color.

Meals might lack variety, but never supply or wholesomeness. Since swine were easily fattened on acorns, beechnuts, and other "shack," pork in many forms was the most common meat. Etiquette was different then. The father cut the meat into small pieces, each the size of a proper mouthful, and placed it in the center of the table, from where each person, fork in hand, would help himself, mouthful by mouthful. To have taken an entire slice of meat on one's plate would have been nothing less than gluttonous, as bad a breach of good manners as a house-raising without rum.

Lamb and beef were not infrequent. Neighbors mutually arranged when each should kill his calf so that portions might be passed around to the other neighbors, thus assuring each of regular supplies of "fresh." Trout abounded in the small streams, and occasionally someone would bring in a deer.

Prominent in the diet were beans and Indian corn. Breakfast and supper usually consisted of hasty pudding, eaten in milk, or if milk were lacking, spread over with maple molasses. Bean porridge, flavored with salt beef or pork, also was commonly seen on the tables. At first, bread was prepared in its simplest style—as "Johnny cake," baked in a spider or on a board set up on edge before the open fireplace. If the mother had more time, she could bake loaves of Indian bread, compounded with pumpkins to make it moist and sweet and baked in a wrapper of cabbage leaves under a bed of burning coals. And as more land was cleared and wheat was grown throughout the community, wheat bread became the staple, even as it is today, though it was not the same bread, the flour of that time being well mixed with cockle, chess, smut, and other impurities. For baking soda, corncob ashes were the vogue.

If after such a meal the family's appetites remained unsatisfied, there was always the tin milk-pan or wooden bowl at the end of the table with its generous-sized doughnuts. A wide choice of coffee existed: sage, burned crust, roasted acorns, evans'-root, or parched corn. When all present were properly stuffed, they would rise while the head of the house expressed their thanks for the mercies and bounty received.

Visitors would drop in to see Old Gail Borden, and the child Gail would sit and listen wide-eyed to tales of Indians and great battles and politics. Only twenty years ago, until George Clinton had made his celebrated purchase in 1788, this had all been Indian country. Early settlers loved to retell the experience, apocryphal perhaps, of Governor Clinton soon after the treaty was signed.

As the Governor seated himself on a log to rest, an Indian chief nudged up to him. Courteously, the Governor moved down the log, but the chief closed the gap quickly. This was repeated and repeated until finally the Governor found himself edged off the log. Perplexed and with his dignity outraged, Clinton demanded an explanation. With characteristic deliberation the Indian is supposed to have replied: "Just so white man crowd poor Indian—keep crowding—keep crowding—by and by, crowd him clear off:—where poor Indian then?"

For years apparently Norwich had been a favorite resort of the Oneida and their adopted tribe, the Tuscarora, their headquarters being a short distance south of the confluence of the Chenango and Canasewacta Creek. The plain upon which Norwich is located is flat, dry, and spacious, and interspersed with springs of pure water, ideal from an Indian point of view. Even the name Chenango—or Chenengo, as literate Oneida insisted it should be—was an Indian name meaning "beautiful river." The coming of the white man brought only a gradual abandonment of the "beautiful river" coun-

18

Gail Borden's birthplace is still in use in Norwich, New York

The Borden Company

try by the Oneida, and young Gail Borden undoubtedly glared at many of them, wondering as he stared why they were not the same as he and picturing them as romantic warriors restlessly seeking new victims.

But the Oneida were a peaceable, inoffensive race by 1800. In the winter they built lodges near the settlers, manufacturing baskets and splint brooms to sell for provisions to sustain themselves until spring would allow them to take up hunting and fishing once more. Their brooms were usually made of black-ash staddles, two or three inches in diameter, pounded the length of the brush until the grains would separate, and then split into fine strands. If black-ash were not available, they would use water beech or birch, peeling off bark into fine shreds and binding it with strips of the same bark. The white children loved to give the Indians small presents whenever they brought in their brooms so that they could receive the Indians' thanks in an unknown, and therefore exceedingly amusing, tongue, or in a half-English, half-Indian dialect that to naturally merry children was almost side-splitting.

There was no privacy for the settlers. The Indian walked in or spied as suited his fancy, though he seldom lingered. Your door would open and a low voice would ask, "Want to buy broom?" The trade would be made, and the Indian would leave without ever changing countenance.

Men liked to tell how in the early days one settler's wife, alone with her small children, looked up to see an Indian staring squarely through a hole in the wall. Alarmed, she involuntarily shouted a very womanly "peek-a-boo!" at which the Indian quietly retired.

If the occasion demanded, the Oneida knew the wile of flattery. After the War of 1812, a young man was sitting doing nothing when a young Indian approached and seated himself close by, saying: "How do? how do? Don't you know me? Ain't you Colonel P.? Didn't you command me at the battle of Queenstown?"

"No, I never was in the army," replied the youth.

"Me thought you was Colonel P.—he brave warrior—he handsome man—you look just like him." Then, tapping the youth's shoulder, "Now treat—now treat."[3]

[3] Hatch, *Town of Sherburne*, 71–73

Along with his Indian lore the child Gail also learned wood-craft. He learned to shoot well, left-handed. There were still some bear and wolf and deer. And occasionally a traveler would tell how he had been stalked by a panther. In addition, for a boy whose lack of age kept him close to home, there were such small quarry as otter, foxes, raccoons, rabbits, squirrels, and once in a while a hedgehog or a skunk. The woods abounded in birds also—quail, so sought after that within a few years they would become extinct around Norwich; wild pigeons, passing overhead for hours at a time in successive flocks; wood ducks, whose nests could be found in the old, decaying trees; partridge, and purely for sport, hawks.

He learned his trees and shrubs, too. Beech, birch, hickory, ash, elm, and basswood; and standing here and there, large oaks, white, black, and red. Not all the pines had yet been cleared away. Looking into the hills from his valley home, he could see hemlocks interspersed with orchards of sugar maple, the chief source of sugar for many years.

And on a free afternoon, what better sport than to go chestnut or whortleberry hunting? Or to visit the sulphur spring on the Smiley farm, which old-timers said had been a popular deer lick, and to drink that terrible tasting water? Near the river could be found apples and pears and on the edge of the woods the bright yellow thorn-apple, less than an inch thick. There were meadow plums, gooseberries, currants, wild onions, ginseng, sweet cicely, and tallow roots, and more rarely, tiny wild potatoes. The undesired leek was numerous too, its sharp flavor spoiling many a youngster's appetite for milk whenever the cattle had been feeding off its tops.

There was also much to learn and to see within the town of Norwich. On his occasional visits into the village young Gail Borden could check the progress of the courthouse, the first one in the county. When finished, it was the pride of everyone—wooden, two stories high, square and solid. It had cost all of $6,500! Perhaps eleven-year-old Gail Borden attended the trial there of David Thomas, the state treasurer, accused of attempting to bribe a state senator from Chenango County. Everyone else in the county was there, and most of the state officials. Heading the prosecution was the state's attorney-general, Thomas Addis Emmet, a consummate logician with just enough Irish in his character and his speech to fascinate any jury. But though the crowd gathered to hear this disciple of Edmund Burke and to be swayed by his charm, the jury was unimpressed. After fifty hours the case was closed, and the jury acquitted Thomas. The great Emmet, victorious in more sophisticated cities, had met defeat in tiny Norwich.

Arousing a more morbid interest had been the trial up at the North Norwich meetinghouse in August, 1808, at which Rufus Hill had been convicted of murdering a child by throwing an armload of wood on it. If young Borden nourished any secret hopes of witnessing the much-anticipated hanging, he was doomed to disappointment, for the governor set aside the sentence.

In a country opened to white settlement only twenty years before, legends were already beginning to grow, and the boy must have listened greedily to their telling and wished himself back in those exciting times. There was old Avery Power, who had intruded into the valley in 1788 and cultivated his land on no one knew what terms from the Indians. Some said he paid his rent in whiskey. He had been more than a pioneer, for he brought his family to live with him in a land of savage sanctions beyond the white man's legal domain. He opened his house as a kind of inn for white and red alike, though he seemed to incline toward the latter. Then in the waning days of the eighteenth century tragedy struck—his three daughters died in as many weeks. After that Norwich depressed him, and in 1800 he sold out to seek happiness once more beyond the white man's limit, somewhere in the far, forested West.

Or young Borden could hear again the story of old Parson Blackleach Burritt, who in 1792 preached one of the very first sermons in the valley east of Sherburne village. A Yale graduate and an undying Whig, he had been imprisoned by the British in New York during the Revolutionary War, where he occupied himself by preaching British-baiting sermons to the prisoners on Sunday. When orders arrived for his discharge on Monday, he somehow obtained knowledge of them and prepared an especially biting philippic for the final Sunday. But the British, fearful of his intentions, released him on Saturday night instead, peremptorily refusing to consider his plea to be kept prisoner for just two days more!

Mystery was present in the story of the coal diggers. A blacksmith in Norwich had used pure anthracite instead of the usual charcoal, but no one knew the sources of his supply. Every Sunday the blacksmith and a man on jail liberties would go into the hills along Goodrich Brook, remain away about an hour, and return freighted with as much coal as they could carry on their shoulders. Others would try to trail them, but always lost the spoor. When the prisoner left town and the blacksmith died, many unavailing efforts were made to unearth this cache.

Young Gail Borden could join the other settlers, young and old, in marveling at a tale concerning the first bridge across the Chenango above Norwich. The bridge consisted of three large trees laid end to end and leveled on the upper side with a hewing ax. Stakes were driven a few feet apart near the outer edges and interwoven with withes to help maintain balance. A woman named Lathrop had crossed the bridge on her horse, with a child in her arms. When a Frenchman tried to emulate Mrs. Lathrop's feat, his horse slipped, feet dangling on either side, and it took every man in the neighborhood to lift the horse up and across the remainder of the bridge.

Stories of the *Ark* abounded, the same *Ark* that had come right down past the Borden farm on its maiden voyage in 1803. Its launching above Sherburne had been a gala affair, reminiscent of the original ark, with every man, woman, and child—and dog—trying to board her. Nat Austin had built her to float down the Chenango, on into the Susquehanna at Binghamton, and thence to Baltimore, where he would sell his lumber, he hoped, for an enormous profit. But underway the *Ark* proved difficult to hold to channel, Nat and his son, Seymour, caught yellow fever, and the *Ark* found its Ararat in hardly more than forty days and nights.

Nat Austin himself was living on borrowed time, for he had been sentenced to be hanged after Shays' Rebellion. But his wife had exchanged clothes with him on what was supposed to be her farewell visit, and he had walked out unsuspected. That explains their settling in Chenango County.

That young Gail Borden identified himself with any church is unlikely, since his baptism into the Baptist church in Texas three decades later was to be hailed as a not inconsiderable triumph for the religious forces. Norwich had the usual number of struggling congregations, and it was the custom to assemble all the children of members at the beginning of each year for personal conversations on their souls' well-being and to learn by heart their catechisms.

But whether he joined a church or not, young Borden apparently acquired moral values that were to shape his actions for the remainder of his life. In some ways Chenango was a strict county, the conservatives in near-by Sherburne going so far as to detain, by force if necessary, all persons traveling through their town on secular business on the Sabbath. On Monday the miscreant would be hauled before the magistrate and fined.

As the boy passed into the second decade of his life, his father began to grow restive. Norwich was continuing to enlarge and thrive, its population passing 2,700 in the 1810 census.[4] The county was losing its rougher edges: it had a carding machine, machine shops, woolen factories, and newspapers, though the price of a rough cotton shirt was still as high as the price of a fine linen shirt would be forty years later.

Perhaps then the town was becoming too large and neighbors too near and frequent for Old Gail Borden, or perhaps the lure of new lands farther west was too strong, or perhaps Old Gail's farming and sawmill endeavors had not proved especially profitable. If the last is true, he must have helped his position somewhat when on March 25, 1811, he sold thirty more of his acres to Peter B. Garnsey, donor of the site for the new courthouse, for $336.50.[5] Again, it may have been the sight of Norwich men moving off to fight in the War of 1812 while he stayed behind that made him eager to leave.

Whatever the reason, when the winter flaws of 1813–14 came blowing down from the English Lakes, Old Gail could stand it no longer. He had to go, and spring was a good time for moving. So on the thirty-first of January, 1814, he sold to Archibald Pellet his remaining 115 acres. The sale gave him $1,620 with which to seek happiness in a newer land.[6]

[4] The Third Census of the United States shows "Gale Burden's" household as containing four males under ten years of age and one female between ten and sixteen These totals, if accurate, must include persons other than Old Gail's children, since all other records indicate that the immediate family would have included three males under ten and no females Third Census, New York, I, 235.

[5] Book O of Deeds, Chenango County, New York, 211

[6] Book U of Deeds, Chenango County, New York, 380

Americans are always moving on
It's an old Spanish custom gone astray,
A sort of English fever, I believe,
Or just a mere desire to take French leave.
—Benét, *Western Star*
I have never seen a country to appearance
more fruitful in men, as well as corn
—Timothy Flint, *Recollections of*
the Last Ten Years

III

A Kentuck' of a Place!
1814-1816

Young Gail Borden had never seen the great ocean, but he might have imagined that it was like this Ohio country —stretching, always stretching on and on and on, never to end. To a boy who had lived his first dozen years walled in by hills and streams, that the great world should be this vast was inconceivable. For days—cold days, warmer days, wet days, dry days—the six of them had traveled on, the father hopeful and determined, the mother fearful and a little sad at leaving behind the home and neighbors she loved, the three older boys as playful and excited as young foxes, sobered only by the packs they sometimes had to shoulder, and the baby, John, disinterested, willing to be carried or held most of the time.

Several routes lay open to the Bordens as they worked westward. Most likely they packed what they could and set out in a flat-bottomed bateau down the Chenango till it flowed into the Susquehanna at Bingham's Patent,[1] then followed the meanderings of that magnificent river into Pennsylvania until they met its west fork, worked upstream along that branch to Sinemahoning Creek, and

[1] Present-day Binghamton. Other likely routes would have taken the Bordens on down the Susquehanna almost to Harrisburg, where they could work up the Juniata almost to Bedford, then portage across to Conemaugh Creek, which flows into the Kiskimenetas, which in turn joins the Allegheny about forty-five miles above Pittsburgh, or they could have gone on to Harrisburg and from there gone overland by wagon to Pittsburgh, a frequently used road [Z. Cramer], *The Navigator*, 16-17.

then ascended that stream as far as they could go. After that, a portage of twenty-three miles to Port Allegheny, where they could assure themselves that the worst though not the longest part of their journey was over, because from here on their route would no longer be "fernenst" the current.

Did Old Gail Borden know where he was heading? Probably not specifically. Just "out West," where there was game aplenty and virgin timber and black soil, where a man could work hard and trade and grow with the country. If he had a goal, it would have been Cincinnati, whence word had drifted back even into York state that it would one day be one of the larger wealthy cities of the world, the great inland port of America.

From its port the transparent Allegheny wound its gravelly way worse than a wounded deer's trail back up into York state, then down through the western part of Pennsylvania until it pushed its clear mountain waters hard against the slower yellow waters of the Monongahela to form the Ohio. It was wild country that the Bordens could see on that rushing stream, mountains to the east and mountains to the west and scarcely a cabin between.

Midway or better they might find the quiet places along the shore covered with a supernatant rainbow film. This film, they would learn, was the famed Seneca oil which seeped right out of the ground like a sulphur spring. They would learn, too, that people around Pittsburgh thought there was nothing finer for greasing body-aches and stiffness. Many years later other men would learn that by artificial means they could find enough oil in these mountains to run engines and lubricate motors, and they would start much of the world on a frenetic search for seas of oil to keep the wheels of industry turning. But that was far in the future.

Of the three jumping-off places for the West, Pittsburgh had it all over its two rivals, Wheeling and Brownsville. Situated in the right angle formed by the confluence of the Allegheny and the Monongahela, it offered at outrageous prices all facilities for the traveler faced with weeks of living beyond the reach of supplies.

Already in 1814 Pittsburgh had a measure of notoriety as a smoky city. Lying almost upon a bed of coal itself, it nurtured many small factories that were to expand into the industrial giants of the next century. Soon its six thousand people were to receive a charter as a city. Except for Cincinnati, it was the largest city the traveler would see until he reached New Orleans, two thousand miles downriver. Probably it was the largest city that young Gail Borden had ever seen.

Boats lined its shore. Boatmen, just returning from a body-breaking upstream pull from Orleans; or boatmen, about to take "down" a cargo—these and merchants and shopkeepers and emigrants tramped its streets, taking a last fling at the delights of a semi-civilized town, brawling, cursing, bragging, and drinking. Hard-living Pittsburgh was hardly a town that a daughter of Roger Williams could approve.

At Pittsburgh the Bordens would have needed to outfit themselves. It would be their last opportunity, acquaintances would tell them. First, something larger than their bateau would be wanted for the great river ahead. Most families favored the Kentucky flatboat, an arklike conveyance thirty to forty feet long, boarded on the sides and roofed to within less than ten feet of the bow. At $1.00 or $1.25 a foot, the usual price, a family could buy such a boat for $35.00 to $75.00. Their cable, pump, and fireplace would run another $10.00, and they were ready to start loading.

Several families might share one of these arks, or "broadhorns," as they were frequently called. The more the prosperity the worse the conditions aboard, for if one owned a cow or two, a horse, an ox, chickens, and perhaps a hound dog he might as comfortably have lived at home—in the barn. The Reverend Timothy Flint described the flats as hardly preferable to "a New England pig-stye." Scotch fiddle, or itch, was a common complaint.[2]

Once their plunder was aboard, the Bordens could shove off. Gingerly at first past the bar at the Allegheny's mouth, steering toward O'Hara's glass works, keeping the bow pointed ahead. Then with mounting confidence past Hamilton's Island, where hospitable Dr. Brunot maintained his reputation as a horticulturist; and then on to the West, as Pittsburgh receded from view and from memory.

To Gail, Tom, and Paschal Borden this was surely high ad-

---

[2] T. Flint, *Recollections of the Last Ten Years*, 13. L. D. Baldwin, *The Keelboat Age on Western Waters*, 136.

venture. Around each bend might lie danger; beyond each gap, excitement such as only children believe in. In each settlement and up each creek, who knew what wonderful thing lay in wait? It was a good time to be living.

Several days of being penned in by a water barrier, however, and the boys must have found their anticipation of adventure beginning to dull. There was that sameness of rations, varied only when someone hauled in a five-pound cat, or a buffalo or perch,[3] or shot one of the wild duck or brant that sometimes flew past. Then there was that terrifying tenseness of their elders when a dangerous riffle was being run. Besides, it was time for young Gail Borden to behave like a man. He may have been a romping twelve-year-old when he left Norwich, but for weeks now he must be depended on to look after his two next younger brothers, to carry a man's load on the trail, and perhaps even to keep a watch for the "sawyers" and "planters"[4] which could so easily overturn their boat.

Slowly they made their way, thirty miles today, forty tomorrow, the color of the sky getting lighter every day. From Pittsburgh to Limestone[5] was a two weeks' journey—at low water even longer. The Bordens were to go beyond there.

The Western country was filling as people drifted in faster than falling leaves. Thirty miles out of Pittsburgh was the first sizable settlement of Beaver, with its forty or fifty houses on a stony plain high above the river. Another day and they would reach Steubenville. "A nice place," Hulme was to comment five years later. "Has more stores than taverns, which is a good sign."[6] Already the settlers here had pushed back the dark forest, and the children could obtain their first view of pawpaw and persimmon.

---

[3] Audubon once devoted considerable space to the white perch of the Ohio· "The Ohio is one in whose pure stream the White Perch seems to delight. . . . No impure food will 'the Growler' touch. . . What beautiful fishes these perches are! So silvery beneath, so deeply colored above. . . . When poised in the water close to the bottom of the boat, it emits a rough croaking noise, somewhat resembling a groan [thus its name of Growler]." M. R. Audubon, *Audubon and His Journals*, II, 510-12.

[4] Sawyer—a tree loosely set in water, one of its ends bobbing up and down. Planter—a partly submerged tree with its roots firmly embedded.

[5] Maysville, Kentucky

[6] Thomas Hulme, *A Journal Made During a Tour in the Western Countries of America September 30, 1818–August 7, 1819* (in volume X of R. G. Thwaites [ed.], *Early Western Travels, 1748–1846*), 38

Away from towns and out on the river there were still people to be seen. Perhaps the Bordens traveled in company with several other arks, as many persons did. Certainly they would have met boats and have been passed by boats, for the Ohio was the broad, generally smooth highway from the old states to Ohio, Kentucky, Indiana Territory, and all the wild new regions of the Louisiana country.

Not too far out of Pittsburgh the whole family would have been intrigued to see a boatload of men apparently engaged in some solemn bowing ritual of obeisance to King Ohio. These were keel-boatmen, setting poles "fernenst" the stream, propelling themselves against the current with the most strenuous effort.

"Stand to your poles!" the patroon, or captain, would command, and the keelers would form into two files, one on each runway facing the stern.

"Set poles!" and the men would set their twenty-foot iron-tipped poles hard against the Ohio bottom. The other end of the pole, which had a button, they would place against their thickly padded shoulders, incline their bodies, and creep aft, apelike, on their hands and toes, until the first man reached the stern. Then, "Lift poles!" and the men straightened, turned, and walked forward, their poles trailing in the water.[7]

To the Borden boys these sturdy figures, straining their muscles beneath their flannel shirts and linsey-woolsey breeches for forty dollars a month, must have breathed the very air of romance. The king of the boatmen, Mike Fink, was in his fabulous heydey in 1814, and the Ohio country was his empire. Every settlement resounded with tales of his unerring eye with a rifle, his eagerness to fight any man in any fashion, his ability to consume prodigious draughts of the rawest whiskey, his wenching which made him the hero of every easy maid in the valley and the master of more than a few—yes, Mike Fink was a river god whom young boys could worship, however much their mothers might deplore such a disciple of Satan. The Borden children, taught to abhor sin though they were, could not have escaped his spell.

A different picture of the keelboatmen was presented by those

[7] Baldwin, *The Keelboat Age on Western Waters*, 62

who passed the slow arks heading downstream, for compared with its tedious upstream haul keelboating downriver was a pleasure cruise. Only when riffles or bars or snags appeared did the keelboatmen have much work to do. From the roof of his cabin the patroon steered with his long oar, pivoted at the stern and extending a dozen feet beyond the boat. Some of the men sat forward, gambling or swapping tall tales of conquest. Invariably there was a fiddler, whose almost sole concern was to entertain. Life was easy for these men in the long, slender crafts. And at the end, New Orleans and money in their pockets.

Then upstream again . . . .

Alongside the sleek keelboat the Borden ark appeared clumsy indeed. Outside of a bow that was raked forward somewhat, the ark had no more style than a packing box. Of oak, if it were a good boat, it was held together by wooden pins and tree nails. Its floor—*deck* would dignify it unduly—was about two inches thick, its width perhaps fifteen feet, its cabin six feet high, its length from twenty feet upward. Tonnage varied, usually being expressed in barrels. An average flat would hold four hundred barrels, or forty tons.

To ascend the swift Mississippi or even the placid Ohio in a flatboat was unthinkable. At the end of your journey you sold your boat to some man who needed the lumber, or, if you were going to an unsettled place, you lived in your flat after you arrived. So many flats came to New Orleans that even the plank sidewalks were made of old flatboats.

And so day succeeded day, and settlement followed settlement:

Wheeling, with emigrants, tradesmen, and roisterers flocking its one shoddy street.

Marietta, at the mouth of the Muskingum. Already Marietta had experienced floods, including the disastrous pumpkin flood of 1811 which brought pumpkin, squash, and other vegetables and fruits on its crest. Many more floods would pour their waters across the streets of Marietta in the next century.

Sixteen miles farther on, just short of two hundred miles out of Pittsburgh, is Blennerhassett's Island, where the poetic Irishman and his beautiful wife founded a western Eden, only to encounter a personal serpent known as Aaron Burr. By the time the Bordens passed, fire and militia had destroyed the lovely home, only chimney stacks rising from the surrounding apple trees to remind the traveler that once people had lived graciously here.

Two or three days later and the Bordens were past Leading Creek on their right. Here an idyllic scene—a small tavern with Lombardy poplars before the door.

Another half-day's run would bring them to the mouth of the Great Kenawha, whose warm waters poured in from deep in the Virginia hills. Here another straggling town, Point Pleasant, with its fifteen or twenty families, its log courthouse and jail, and its anachronistic pillory and whipping post.

Four miles farther is Gallipolis, its spelling since shortened by one letter. A quarter of a century earlier a hundred French families were settled here by speculators who had not bothered about clear titles. After untold confusion and suffering the emigrants were forced to leave heartbroken. Now sixty families of Americans had settled, building a brick courthouse.

On and on. Past sandbars, with pelicans and sand-hill cranes waddling across them. On either shore forests of giant sycamores, tops heavy with mistletoe. Following this same course a year later, the Reverend Timothy Flint was moved to write: "I have never seen a country to appearance more fruitful in men, as well as corn. From the cabins and houses tumble out . . . a whole posse of big and little boys and girls; and the white-headed urchins, with their matted locks, and their culottes gaping with many a dismal rent, stare at you as you pass."[8]

Now it was the Big Guyandot River on the left. Just below, an unbroken vista not to be seen for many hundreds of miles more—a breath-taking view of the Ohio winding ahead for nine miles like a casually tossed ribbon.

Nearly 350 miles out of Pittsburgh they passed the mouth of the Great Sandy, or Tottery, River. Now Virginia was behind. This land rising from the riverbank on the left was storied Kentucky, where already the men grew taller,[9] the women more beautiful, the

---

[8] Flint, *Recollections of the Last Ten Years*, 26, 29.

[9] Even Frances Trollope, who found little to like in America, thought that the men of Kentucky were "a very noble-looking race of men" with "extremely handsome" countenances except "when disfigured by red hair." *Domestic Manners of the Americans*, 36.

horses swifter, the huntsmen surer, and the whiskey finer. Kentuckians liked to tell how one pioneer preacher, pressed for a description of Heaven, silenced his auditors with, "Heaven, gentlemen? Why, Heaven is a-uh-why, Heaven is a Kentuck' of a place!'" Fine farms lined both shores of the river; this looked like excellent country. But it was not what Old Gail Borden was seeking.

Still afloat. Greenup, Ohio, newly platted. Portsmouth, three quarters of a mile up the Scioto. Here were thirty buildings and three taverns. Here, too, was the famous Watch Tower, a perpendicular cliff, its top dotted with pine and hemlock growths. From its summit Indians of a generation before had watched for the approach of their white enemy.

Another day's journey brought the travelers to Manchester, Ohio—twenty-five houses, some brick, scattered up and down the river's bank. When John Woods traversed this same route six years later, he noted that a Manchester woman was in such straits she could feed her pigs only apples and peaches.[10]

Then a half-day's journey and, suddenly, Limestone, or Maysville, on the lower bank of Limestone Creek. Here was the principal port for the traveler who wished to go into the interior of Kentucky by way of the Ohio. Overland travelers usually used the Cumberland Gap route.

Limestone Creek offered a sheltered harbor for boats whose owners wished to tie up to go ashore. Limestone displayed goods for sale. It had mercantile stores and public inns. Here was civilization again. Up the steep hill hugging close to the town's heels one found virgin forest again; downstream a few miles Limestone's refinements became memory. Civilization's line was that thin.

By now Old Gail Borden was getting where he wanted to go. Two days beyond Ripley on the right and Augusta on the left he would nose his boat in to the low, scraggly canebrakes along the shore of Licking River, and the Bordens would have found their home in the Great West. A thousand dangerous miles they would have come.

---

[10] J Woods, *Two Years' Residence in the Settlement on the English Prairie, in the Illinois Country, United States* (in volume X of Thwaites [ed.], *Early Western Travels*), 232

Why had Gail Borden subjected his wife and children to the rigors of a hazardous journey and uncertain prospects? Why were thousands of other men doing the same thing? Why indeed? The pioneers were not displaced, aimless wanderers. They had to go. It was as if the heavens had rent and some supernal nova had shone through, pulling, tugging irresistibly, drawing men out of themselves, making them seekers whose steps turned automatically westward. They did not think: they moved. It was a fever, a religion, a crusade, with the West as the Holy Grail. Few men could hope to attain it during a lifetime because it was forever receding, always a little farther on. A comprehensive term, the West, including everything that man with his imagination desired. The quest was perennial, perpetual. The West summoned, and men by the thousands obeyed as eagerly as young lovers, dragging in their wake uncertain wives and confused, tired little children.

Gail Borden, father and son, could no more withstand the call of the West than could any other restless, striving souls.

On the north side of the Ohio was Cincinnati, already calling herself the "Queen City of the West," even if her womenfolk did run around barefoot in the summer.

Opposite Cincinnati, separated only by the Licking River, were two small settlements. Newport, above the Licking mouth, actually carried the dignity of incorporation, dating from 1795. It had a two-story brick arsenal, a magazine, and barracks for several regiments.

The other settlement, however, lacked even an official name. Generally it was called Kennedy's Ferry, after Thomas Kennedy, who had run boats across to Cincinnati since 1790. His large stone house facing the river had been one of the section's landmarks for the past fifteen years.

The history of Kennedy's Ferry went back more than sixty years. Christopher Gist passed this way in 1751 en route to Big Bone Lick; Mary Inglis and another white woman, flying from Indiana on a forty-day wilderness nightmare, crossed five years later; Simon Kenton, one of Kentucky's immortals, placed his pioneering feet on its soft sod before the American Revolution was more than a dream in the hearts of the most radical Bay Staters; and

George Rogers Clark, implacable pursuer of Indians, crossed the Ohio here seeking his usual quarry, plus a few Britishers who were leading the Indians.

Then Thomas Kennedy took over the ferry that Francis Kennedy had just started. Three years later the Rittenhouse family moved in. Kennedy's Ferry was now considered a settlement.

The land was not thought to be worth much. In 1780 George Muse was granted the two hundred acres which eventually became the townsite, but along came St. Valentine's Day and he was thirsty and so, a man who knew the value of the present, if not the potentialities of the future, Muse traded his two hundred acres for a keg of whiskey. The new owner thought little more of it, but he wanted something more substantial in exchange: he sold his acres for a quarter of buffalo meat and tallow. Many exchanges followed, each man valuing the land more highly than his predecessor until Thomas Kennedy bought it in 1801 for $750, built his home, operated his tavern and ferry, and waited.

Here the Bordens landed in 1814 to seek their fortunes in the West. Kennedy's Ferry was little more than a bright cornfield, but there were signs that greater things were in store. Men were talking of laying out a town here, of its natural advantages as an inland port, of the trade regions of Georgia, Tennessee, and the Carolinas that could be tapped. Besides, a sizable town could live here if it did nothing more than profit from its neighbors: Newport, with its federal arsenal, must always be an important town; and Cincinnati might someday become the greatest city in the world. Old Gail Borden thought prospects were excellent.

The Bordens settled down to making a new home among the bluegrass and tobacco. Gail, Jr., was approaching thirteen years old. Since Norwich village had disappeared around the Chenango's bend, he had been nearly a man, doing a man's work and carrying a young man's responsibilities. He was shooting up, getting long and skinny and growing out of his clothes. Yes, Gail Borden, Jr., was now a man, as was any other frontier lad in his teens. But boyhood and joy in the seasons were not altogether lost. He could still enjoy a surge of animal enthusiasm as he foot-raced Tom to the smooth-stoned springs above the Licking mouth. Or in the fall, feeling the increasing tensile strength of his muscles, he could take both Tom and Paschal on for that favorite frontier sport of wrestling, twisting and bending and heaving and rolling about until the beaten brown leaves beneath the trio smelled like a tanyard. Come spring and he could frolic and frisk like any young colt, splashing wildly over the shapeless breccia at the Licking mouth, swinging on grapevines thicker than a man's body, climbing the giant oaks and sycamores.

Early on late summer mornings he could scamper up one of the hills that enclosed the three towns like the walls of a vast amphitheater, there to look out over an interminable, unruffled sea of fog in the valley below and feel an inexplicable lump in his throat as the sun ascended above, its rays dispersing the vapors to reveal the city, the two villages, the great river with its many varied craft, and the verdant forests on all sides. It was something like being present at the unfolding of Creation.

On still summer evenings young Borden could sit on a stump in the Borden clearing and think brave boy's thoughts as he watched the sky illumine with "broad obtuse flashes of lightning, unattended by thunder or rain." On bright Sundays he could cross to the Newport parade ground on the opposite shore of the Licking, there to see precision drills, hear band concerts, and enjoy the splashes of color of the soldiers' blue uniforms mingling with the suits and dresses of the picnicking Cincinnatians who arrived by the bargeload.

But when chores called, he had his full load to carry and, as the eldest child, his example to set to his own little trio of jealous hero-worshipers.

One day three Cincinnati men caught old Thomas Kennedy in a receptive mood. After papers were signed transferring 150 acres to these men, plans were announced for the founding of a city, which meant work for men who knew how to survey. Old Gail Borden knew how.

With Gail, Jr., helping for experience, the surveyors planned and began their work. Young Gail held chain, carried levels, and measured tapes. Good surveyors were the tradition in the Borden family from the days of Richard Borden himself, and this descendant must be no exception. On February 8, 1815, the proprietors an-

Borden's first real factory, at Burrville, Connecticut

The Borden Company

nounced the completion of their project: lots would go on sale in six weeks.

The name of the town would be Covington, after a hero of the War of 1812. In time it would become the second city of Kentucky.

The Bordens and their colleagues laid out their town with the Ohio for the north boundary, the Licking for the east, Sixth Street on the south, and Washington Street on the west. Five streets were named for Kentucky governors, and another was named for Thomas Kennedy. The town was so surveyed and platted that from the heights above Cincinnati its streets appeared to be continuations of Cincinnati streets.

Now, everyone felt, all that was lacking were more settlers and a bridge across the Licking to Newport.

About this time electrifying news filtered into Cincinnati. The War of 1812 was over! After three long years the British had signed a peace. Andy Jackson had shown John Bull how Western men could fight, and the British wanted no more of it.

At once Cincinnati began to celebrate. Undoubtedly the two Gails crossed over to see the merrymaking. And an impressive sight it was to any imaginative child. Up and down Main Street the procession moved, in its center a huge bull—John Bull—manacled and decorated to show who was master. When night came, the town lighted up and the celebration continued long after Gail Borden, Jr., was in bed. Even then, sounds of the jubilee could be heard in quiet Covington with its one tavern.

As in Norwich, indications point to an absence of formal schooling during Gail Borden's stay in Covington. Likely his mother or his father, or both, took on the task of teaching him his three *R*'s, though there is no record to indicate it. An academy had existed in Newport since 1798, drawing through its doors many students from Cincinnati, but Gail, Jr., was probably needed at home to aid with the many essential tasks of day-to-day living.

Also, as in Norwich, he seems to have escaped the arms of the church. Cincinnati had nearly a full quota of churches, Newport had both a Baptist and a Methodist church, and in 1815 the Methodists placed the Reverend Othniel Talbot on the Licking circuit,

35

which would have included Covington as one of his charges. But if Parson Talbot ever influenced young Gail, or any of the others of his family, there is no record.

In a sense this is surprising, for the West, and especially Kentucky, was just settling down from the greatest wave of religious fanaticism in the history of the United States. It started with the Presbyterians about the time Gail, Jr., was born, the excitement spreading as meetings were held which attracted thousands from hundreds of miles around to indulge in an orgy of singing, praying, exhorting, preaching, leaping, shouting, disputing, and conversing.

All sorts of exercises took place in the name of religion, and all sorts of religious sects sprang up, or broke away from the older denominations, many failing to last out the revival period. In addition to such lesser manifestations as falling, jerking, running, and climbing exercises, worship would take the form of, for instance, a group of people gathering about the foot of a tree, some praying, others barking, as they "treed the devil."

Or, acting on the admonition that "Except ye be converted, and become as little children," a group of men would go down on their knees in the midst of a meeting and play marbles or ride stick horses up and down the aisles.

One old Scotsman put his Scripture to even more literal application. As the minister, impersonating Satan tempting Eve, crawled about the congregation's feet, the Scotsman lifted his heel, then stamped it fiercely in the face of the hapless minister, calling out, "The seed of the woman shall bruise the serpent's head!"

After the excitement of living in a new town had subsided, Old Gail Borden began to wonder whether Covington was his answer after all. Cincinnati was running away with itself,[11] paving its streets, installing shipbuilding yards, and packing an average of ten persons to a house as the emigrants thronged in. Some guessed the population as high as nine thousand. Many of the social amenities existed: even Dr. Drake, proud as he was of his adopted city, deplored the

[11] Cincinnati's growth and progress from a handful in 1800 to the sixth largest American city in 1850 with 115,436 people is hardly to be matched during this period. In 1805 it was described by a booster as "one of the dirtiest little villages you ever saw." (E. D. Mansfield, *Personal Memories*, 19.) Fifteen years later it was the commercial and social capital of the West.

many balls and evening parties "so destructive to female health" that added to Cincinnati's gayety.[12] The distresses accompanying city-building appeared: a benevolent society was organized and a poor-relief tax was levied. A Bible society was formed. Choice lots sold for two hundred dollars a front foot.

But Covington grew little richer, and except for a more accommodating climate the Bordens might have been just as well off back in Norwich.

And so, after allowing Philadelphia time to give birth to her only daughter, Esther, Old Gail Borden and his family, totaling seven now, repacked their possessions and started west once more, leaving behind Covington and the Licking with its red maples and its chalybeate springs.

But they traveled not so far this time—only a little more than a hundred miles by land, and slightly more by river, to Indiana, which was rapidly filling until men were beginning to talk of statehood. Old Gail Borden decided he would like to be there at the start. '

Again the Bordens apparently moved by flatboat. Within an hour after shoving off, they were passing Ludlow, newly platted, and then The Landmark, a two-foot-thick stone building dating back to pre-Revolution days. By midafternoon they had passed North Bend, where General William Henry Harrison entertained the famous and near-famous who thrust themselves onto the Western scene. An hour and a half later they passed the mouth of the Great Miami—from there on the Indiana Territory lay to their right. Opposite the Great Miami was Tanner's Station,[13] named for the first Baptist preacher in that section of Kentucky.

Two days later they passed one of the great Southern highways, the Kentucky River, steering carefully and mightily to pull out of the countercurrent set up where the Kentucky disembogued its waters into the Ohio. A promising settlement known as Port William[14] was being established here.

Another half-day's journey brought the Bordens to a broad

[12] Daniel Drake, "Notices Concerning Cincinnati," *Quarterly Publication of the Historical and Philosophical Society of Ohio*, Vol. III (1908), 31. Drake also pointed out that the women dressed too thin, apparently another concomitant of civilization.

[13] Petersburg, Kentucky.

[14] Carrollton, Kentucky.

V-bend in the river and past the cottonwoods lining Madison's shore. Everyone must have stared with interest at Madison—perhaps the party even tied up briefly—for Madison was to be their county seat and business would be bringing them all in there not infrequently.

Five miles farther they passed Crawford's Bar, finding their six-foot channel near the center of the stream. Then, an hour later, eyes straining for a landing place, they pulled into New London, newer even than Covington. Here was to be their home.

but when I became a man,
I put away childish things
—I Corinthians 13 11

IV

Scantling-thin and Stooped a Little
1816-1822

THERE WERE FEW PLACES in the awakening West where an impressionable youth of nearly fifteen could have lived among as varied a background of intrigue and excitement as in New London, Indiana, in its first decade of existence. The town was raw and new, and it liked itself that way. Its speculators foresaw tremendous possibilities, and none of the deterrents of respectability were to block the path. Madison might have a head start as the county town, but its streets were filled with pious Baptists mouthing platitudes about law and order and decency. New London would have none of that.

Jesse Connell had laid out a town here in 1810. He tried again in 1812. Three years later another attempt was made: Benjamin Hunt drew a plan which was entered in the Jefferson County plat book on August 4, 1815.[1]

The next year the Bordens arrived.

An ambitious plan it was: First Street ran along the river for six blocks. Second Street paralleled it. Third, Fourth, and Market Streets were two blocks shorter. All were 60 feet wide except Market, which was 80 feet. For each block a careful system of 10-foot alleys had been devised. In the center of Market Street was a public square, 230 feet across at each corner. Each lot was 75 by 150 feet and was bound by either two streets or a street and an alley. The over-all appearance of the plan was that of an L, the direction of its base reversed.

Its proprietors seemed to have planned astutely. New London, agreed one early traveler, "is formed by nature for one of the most

[1] Plat Book, Jefferson County, Indiana, 59

pleasant situations on that river; presenting a gradual and gentle descent for 150 rods back from the river, the position of the ground affording a most excellent route for a good road to the back country, and exhibiting from a distance, a charming view of the broad expanse of the Ohio."

All that remains of New London today is the top of a cistern. Most of the very soil on which it rested has gone downstream to augment the banks of Illinois state, or the delta of the Mississippi, or the bed of the Gulf of Mexico. The last chimney disappeared in the flood of 1876. Some people accord New London the dubious honor of being the only town destroyed by the Ohio River.[2]

Tradition is strong that New London was a haven for river pirates, driven west by more stringent precautions upriver. New London is supposed to have been a principal rendezvous, where loot could be parceled and revelry indulged.

About a mile and a half upstream from New London was a settlement called Concord and near it a break in the river's contour known as Plow Handle Point, overlooking a bay. This small bay came to be designated as Dead Man's Pool from the number of bodies fished from its water during the nineteenth century, none of the dead being victims of accidental drownings. The peak year is believed to have been 1830, when twenty bodies were recovered.

Some say that New London also became the nesting place of an interstate gang of counterfeiters operating from Pittsburgh to St. Louis until one day when agents of the federal government dropped in, to leave New London hours later with twenty-two of its inhabitants in tow.

Unfortunately, neither pirates nor counterfeiters documented their activities, and reputable historians place the river pirates hundreds of miles downriver at this time. But the tradition remains.

Certainly New London was an easygoing place, zealous of parking as many keels, flats, and pirogues at its landing as at Madison's. Cordiality reigned; there was no jail, no local police, and a most obliging constabulary. Everyone was welcome.

[2] E. Dana, "Geographical Sketches on the Western Country Designed for Emigrants and Settlers," in Harlow Lindley (ed.), *Indiana as Seen by Early Travellers*, 206. See also Mildred Holsapple, "The Disappearance of New London," *Indiana Magazine of History*, Vol. XXXI, No 1 (March, 1935), 10–13.

Why Old Gail Borden with his strict Rhode Island sense of morality ever selected this site to rear his sons must remain one of the many inconsequential imponderables of history.

The Bordens chose their land in New London near the present location of Lee's Landing. On their property was a tanyard. In the vicinity were already a score of cabins, including a store, a warehouse, and two taverns.

At the outset it was the same story as in Norwich and Kennedy's Ferry—a feverishly busy first summer, planting corn, erecting and facing up a cabin for protection against the oncoming winter, and clearing land. When harvest time came, the grain was threshed with a flail, horses being used to tramp out the grain. The saw was hardly known in Indiana then, and like every other family the Bordens had to use an ax. After the land was cleared sufficiently, puncheons must be cut out of limbs and laid for a floor. Then after the round-log house was up, the ridge pole set in, and the chinks stuffed with mud mixed with straw to make it stick, attention could be paid to refinements. Perhaps the Bordens were able to bring some furniture with them. If not, tables had to be made of puncheons, and legs added from limbs of trees set in at angles. After dark, Old Gail, helped now by his stripling son, could work with his adz by firelight to trim off and level the limbs of his puncheon floor.

Meanwhile Philadelphia Borden would continue her same chores, caring for her baby daughter, spinning cloth, dyeing cloth—white walnut juice was the favored dye here—knitting sox, making candles from beef and mutton tallow, and generally busying herself around the cabin in her homespun dress and her soft, high-cut Nelson shoes, doing the thousand and one things called for by frontier homemaking. Now in her middle thirties, Philadelphia was considered almost an old woman, as the usual pioneer wife wore herself out early with childbearing and child-caring.

Here at last Gail Borden trudged through a schoolhouse door to put a formal polish on his heretofore informal education. Undoubtedly he already knew considerably more than the fundamental three *R*'s, for he was at the age when many youths were leaving, not entering, school, and his stay was short—the usual estimate is a year

41

and a half. There was not much need for his staying longer, as he was old enough to be productive and attending school would be a waste of profitable time.

Several schools existed in Jefferson County. As early as 1810 William Robinson had opened in Madison a school which became so popular that he had to rule against more than one member of a family attending at the same time. The best-known teacher was called simply "Old Father George." Sartorially unprogressive, he affected a queue, knee breeches, long stockings, and low shoes with large buckles. Old Father George believed in the dunce stool and the dunce cap, and over his head always hung a canopy of six-foot birch switches on two pegs. A moment's indiscretion by some student and the irate pedagogue could pull down one of the birches faster than a hunter could flush a quail.

As in Kentucky, there was plenty of fiery preaching to scorch the soul of young Gail Borden, but again he seems to have gone his way unattached. Ever since Elder Jesse Vawter, James Underwood, and other good Baptists had come down in their pirogues in the spring of 1806, the country for thirty-five miles around had been vehemently Baptist, although by now missionaries from other denominations were filtering in.

Church services held a place in the social as well as the spiritual lives of the nineteenth-century American far beyond any comparable activity today. A Holy Communion might be the most memorable event of any month, while a protracted meeting was often the most exciting experience of any year's calendar, an event in which emotions easily might run the gamut from joy to despairing grief. Thus an account by Isaac Reed, a New England Presbyterian missionary, tells how in 1818 he held in and near Madison a series of meetings which invariably drew larger crowds than could be accommodated and how during the sacrament many were in tears and made addresses that "were long and affecting. . . . Mr. C— gave an exhortation . . . a very superior one . . . animated and very pathetic."[3]

Not even severe weather could daunt the pioneer's quest for his soul's salvation. From early fall of 1816, when the Ohio began

[3] Isaac Reed, "The Christian Traveler," in Lindley (ed.), *Indiana as Seen by Early Travellers*, 464–65.

freezing sooner than usual, it was apparent that the winter of 1816–17 was going to be extreme (Older settlers blamed the influx of Yankees for bringing the cold weather from New England[1]), but when the Beverly Vawters decided it was time to be baptized, they could not delay a day longer. On New Year's Day, 1817, Vawter and his wife were immersed by John McClung on a day so bitterly cold that their garments froze as they walked from the stream to the nearest house.

Game in Indiana was the most plentiful of any place the Bordens had lived. With his long-barreled rifle in his left hand, Gail Borden must have squinted down the sights at many a wild creature. Bear, deer, squirrel, and wild turkeys were a downright nuisance to some settlers, eating away young grain despite the growers' most vigilant efforts. Deer even ate the green tobacco leaves, something the other animals refused.

For a while, squirrels became a community problem, collecting in such hordes that three or four times a day whole families, men and boys and women and girls, would chase through the fields to scatter the rodents, one of the party scaring the squirrels away with a noise-maker, usually a horse-fiddle, while the others stood by with their guns and dogs. Sometimes dozens of squirrels would be killed. These squirrel hunts served a double purpose: they rid the fields of a destructive invader and incidentally provided large quantities of meat. Hams of squirrels would be preserved, salted, and smoked in the wide-mouth chimneys, and the dogs could make a feast while growling over the remainder.

Wolves also were bad enough that in 1817 a bounty of one dollar a scalp was placed on them.[4] A crack shot like Gail Borden could enrich himself considerably through this means. In one day alone the county paid out fifty-eight dollars in wolf bounties.

Most of the deer hunting was done after dark. On the windward bank of a lick the hunter would place a bit of spongy rotten root of sugar maple or beech, known as foxfire,[5] which shone in the night. Concealing himself behind a blind of green boughs on the opposite bank, the hunter would steady his rifle in the crotch of

---

[4] Book A, Commissioners Record, Jefferson County, Indiana, [9].
[5] Probably a corruption of phosphor

two sticks, train it on the foxfire, and wait. Sometime during the evening the foxfire would be hidden from view, and the hunter would pull the trigger. Nine times out of ten he had himself a deer.

Night roaming was not encouraged, however, because of the wildcats. The earlier settlers still shuddered at the story of the Gowans woman who, caught out after dark, was followed by a panther. She took refuge in a deserted hut, only to have the panther claw on the makeshift door. Fearing that the beast might break in, she sought to distract him by climbing to the loft. Her ruse worked to the extent that the panther climbed to the roof and started clawing there. All night the race continued, the terrified woman climbing up and down and down and up, always followed by the panther, until dawn finally drove the animal away. A few days later Mrs. Gowans died as a result of her fright.

There were other reasons for coming in by nightfall. Old Man Neil, for whom Neil's Creek is named, stayed out too long one winter night hunting his cattle, became lost, had no means of kindling a fire, crept into a hollow log, and froze to death.

As time passed, New London increased in importance. On February 3, 1817, Jefferson County's three commissioners decreed creation of Saluda township with New London as the seat for elections. At the same time Samuel McKinley[6] presented a petition for a tobacco inspector to set up offices at the mouth of Great Saluda Creek. Joining the petitioners was Gail Borden, Sr. In April the request was granted—three commissioners, not just one, were named to inspect tobacco at McKinley's warehouse at Great Saluda and John Medcap's warehouse at New London.[7]

Gail Borden's elevation to full manhood in these river woods led him more and more away from New London on various missions. Usually when he had greased his Wellington boots and started forth,

[6] Samuel McKinley, whom the Bordens undoubtedly knew well, was somewhat of a power in Saluda township, where he arrived in 1811 to erect a still on Still Creek near Little Saluda Creek. His corn liquor became so famous that when he died in 1827 a Louisville newspaper announced that "1,000 gallons of that famous Saluda whiskey, made by Samuel McKinley," would be sold at auction to settle his estate, and readers were invited to send in their bids. Manuscript notes of Charles E. Heberhart, in Jefferson County Historical Association Archives, Madison, Indiana.

[7] Book A, Commissioners Record, Jefferson County, Indiana, 4, 23.

his goal was Madison, ten miles away, there to participate in the multifarious activities of a county seat. New London's ambitions to the contrary, Madison was fast becoming the most important town in Indiana. As a port it played an important part in distributing most of Indiana's goods. A census check in 1819 showed 821 inhabitants,[8] and more were arriving almost daily. So many of them came from Baltimore that a sunny day was spoken of as "Baltimore weather" and the slender three-storied houses as "Baltimore flats."[9] Madison citizens established a ferry across to Kentucky and set rates at one dollar for a two-horse wagon, 37.5 cents for man and horse, and 12.5 cents for a single passenger during the season from the first of December to the first of June. For the summer and fall, rates were one-fourth to one-third cheaper.[10] Since 1814 Madison had possessed a bank with a capital of half a million dollars. A traveler might write that "the aspect of this village is not imposing,"[11] but Indianans and their trade seemed to gravitate to its Main Cross, as the principal street was known. Its two-story courthouse of buckeye logs, with an outside stairway, had already surrounded itself with legends at the same time that the town was realizing a larger structure was needed as soon as possible. There was much discussion also about making Madison the capital of the new state; only its location down in a corner was against it.

The old Spanish dollar was universally used as the basis for exchange, being split as necessary into half-dollars, quarters, "bits" (12.5 cents), and "fips" (6.25 cents). Money which had been cut from larger pieces was usually known as "sharpshins," and John Hunt kept a block of wood and an ax at his tavern just for splitting change. By 1820, as evidences of stringent days ahead began to loom, all types of money were becoming scarce.

[8] Dana, "Geographical Sketches on the Western Country," in Lindley (ed.), *Indiana as Seen by Early Travellers*, 205. *Madison Weekly Courier*, January 3, 1877, quoted in letter from Mary Hill to author, March 6, 1946.

[9] Baltimore flats usually contained a basement of two rooms, the front one a cellar, the back one a kitchen, a first floor of two double parlors, the second floor of two bedrooms, and a third floor of two attic rooms with dormer windows

[10] Book A, Commissioners Record, Jefferson County, Indiana, 199, quoted in E. O Muncie, "A History of Jefferson County, Indiana" (unpublished master's thesis, Indiana University, 1932), 19.

[11] David Thomas, "Travels Through the Western Country in the Summer of 1816," quoted in Lindley (ed.), *Indiana as Seen by Early Travellers*, 47.

Election days rivaled protracted meetings for popularity, people throughout the county flocking to the courthouse square in Madison to make the days festive. On the courthouse corner near the public well would stand two or three barrels on end, heads out, full of whiskey. From the barrel would hang tin cups with the name of the political party chalked on the outside. Whiskey swayed as many elections, perhaps, as political policy. On election day the taverns were nearly as busy as the courthouse cups. Refreshment prices ran about the same at any of the taverns, whiskey costing 12.5 cents for a half-pint, peach brandy, 18.75 cents; and cherry bounce, 18.75 cents. Samuel Burnett's tavern, advertised as a "place for refreshment for man & beast," even doubled as county courtroom on occasion.

One day in June, 1816, Gail Borden could have looked up from his work to see an unfamiliar contraption go riding down the river. It was Henry Shreve's *Washington*, the first steamboat really adapted to river requirements. There had been occasional steamboats on the river since 1811, when Nicholas Roosevelt with his bride and her big Newfoundland dog had brought the *New Orleans* down the Ohio, its scape pipes screaming. The general desecration of nature's rights by the Roosevelt boat convinced the more superstitious that the end of the world must be near. Some blamed the presence of the *New Orleans* for the New Madrid earthquakes in Missouri that year.

But the *Washington* was unlike any boat heretofore built. Shreve had piloted both flatboats and steamboats before, and he knew that something radical must be done if the steamboat were to be utilized for more than mere downstream traveling. The result was a steamboat 148 feet long, with a 60-foot main cabin, three handsome private rooms, and a "commodious" barroom furnished in "very superior" style. The principal innovations were that the *Washington* carried her boilers on deck, set horizontally instead of upright, with her cylinders vibrating instead of stationary, and that instead of a hull plowing deep through the water the boat rode corklike almost atop the water. She had no balance wheel, and her hundred-horsepower engine weighed only nine thousand pounds. As usual, critics opined that the *Washington* would never find her way upstream.

46

After a winter's layover in Louisville, during which she ran excursions up to Cincinnati before the river became ice-clogged, the *Washington,* with Shreve, a quietly boyish Quaker who clung to his short breeches and broad hat, at the helm, left for New Orleans. Every preparation had been made to make the trip a holiday, something unknown in Western traveling. Meals were excellent, almost luxurious, service was formal, and the furnishings were in good taste. By moonlight there was dancing on the decks; by sunlight there were games. And always there was the exquisite Mississippi scenery with its contrasts of whites and pale greens and dark timbers against the reds and mud-browns of bank and bottom.

Forty-one days later—only twenty-four days upstream from New Orleans—the *Washington* was back in Louisville. The West was electrified! Distance, the great barrier, had been breached. Instead of one round trip a year, merchants could ship to New Orleans four, five, maybe six boatloads. And the goods that could be brought back to their shelves—all the exotic articles of the New Orleans market. For the West the *Washington's* success ushered in an era of development beyond contemporary conception.

By 1820 rates would be unbelievable. Where formerly a barge charged $5.00 a hundredweight from New Orleans to Louisville and required at least three months to make the hazardous journey, now the steamboat would carry the same goods for $2.00 and get it there in two to three weeks. Passenger fares were $150; within a few years they would drop below $25.[12] And all the while steamboats would be bringing in more and more goods to diminish the severities of life in the Western cities.

It was to require more than the introduction of practical steamboating, however, to ease life on the rim of the frontier. Away from the river highway, men would still have to live by ax and rifle.

Back in Gloucester, Rhode Island, Mrs. Mary Hopkins, whose first husband had been the original Gail Borden, opened a letter dated "New London May 28th AD 1820." It was from her son in the far West, the earliest personal record of the Gail Bordens extant:

[12] Baldwin, *The Keelboat Age on Western Waters,* 192. Florence L Dorsey's *Master of the Mississippi* gives the best treatment of Shreve's life.

Dear Mother

With Pleasure I can inform you that through the goodness of Divine Providence I am Blessed with good health Phil[a] is in tolerable health and still mending Gail's health is much the same it has ben for a year past Thomas left here the 5th April for New Orleans for hides in a steam Boat I expect him back soon. Paskal John & Esther are all in good health John goes to schol 7 miles from here he is a fine Boy to learn

. . . it would be verry agreeable to us if you & Amy [Old Gail's sister] could come and live with us Prehaps you may think the distance so great it would be imposible . . . it apears to me that you might injoy yourselves better here with us than where you are I think the Country is as healthy as that [of Rhode Island] and a very agreeable Climate we have had a few Day quite cold but no frost that I have seen Money is verry scarce with us that is good Produce low & plenty. . . .

I am with esteem your

affetonate son Gail Borden

Mrs Mary Hopkins

Pleas to write on the Rec.[t] of this G. B.[13]

The name of Gail Borden, Jr., first appears on a legal document in an indenture made only two days after Old Gail had written his mother. In it two other Hopkinses—no relation—agreed to sell to Gail for $200 two and one-half acres "including a tanyard" and taking in "All that tract and parcel of land lying and being in . . . the Bottom of the Ohio River. Beginning at a beech and ash stump at the foot of the hill directly on the south line of the one hundred acres purchased by Reed and Begain from George Monroe running east and said line seventeen rods to a stake. Twenty three poles[14] ten feet to a stake; thence west seventeen poles to a stake thence north twenty three and ten feet to the place of beginning." Richard Hopkins signed it, and Mary, his wife, made her mark.[15]

In other ways young Borden was becoming a man of substance in Jefferson County. It is believed that he made at least one round trip to the New Orleans country, working his way as supercargo for a flatboat. Apparently he continued to do some surveying, and

[13] Gail Borden, Sr., to Mrs. Mary Hopkins, May 28, 1820. Collection of Mr. and Mrs J. L. Lockett, Houston, Texas

[14] A pole is equivalent to 16 5 feet.

[15] Book C, Deed Record, Jefferson County, Indiana, 78–79.

the legend persists that at one time he taught in the district school of Saluda township.

Although the War of 1812 was long over and General Harrison had disposed of the Indian threat in that region for all time, each county boasted a volunteer organization of militia rangers for the sake of preparedness and, if necessary, to combat such other evils as banditry. Gail Borden, Jr., with his keen rifle eye and his steady hand, was a natural choice for a militiaman, eventually becoming a captain and doing excellent work.[16]

Gail Borden was growing like an Indiana poplar, scantling-thin and stooped a little. But the long, cold winters and the river vapors in summer were impressing themselves on his spare frame. At first, it was an occasional cough, but as he approached official manhood the cough became more frequent and annoying. Catarrhal troubles were not unusual in the region, and already settlers were speaking of "Valley throat" as an indigenous and unavoidable product of the river bottoms.

There was but one choice: leave the valley. It would mean parting from his family and striking out alone, but he must go to a less rigorous climate. By night he and Tom would discuss the venture, winnowing localities and setting and resetting departure dates. For Tom, a robust lad of eighteen, was going too, not for his health but for adventure and fortune, the Southwest promising greater wealth than Indiana, where the market had scraped bottom in 1821. The two boys were too far away to select an exact destination. Instead, they decided, they would go to New Orleans, a city of fabulous opportunity, and choose there.

Before he left, however, Borden became involved in one last episode which prefigures the character of the man to be. His action risked whatever social standing he may have attained, and undoubtedly it jeopardized his life.

16 Manuscript notes of Charles E. Heberhart, in Jefferson County Historical Association Archives. The 1820 census reveals three persons in Old Gail's household as engaged in manufactures of an unknown nature. Probably the three were Gail, Sr., Gail, Jr., and Thomas. The census also indicates that there was a girl between ten and sixteen years old living at the Borden house, probably to help Philadelphia with her work. Fourth Census, Indiana, II, 277.

Somewhere in the historical pattern between the cattle rustler of the Anglo-Scot border and the rustler of the later Far West appeared the Negro rustler, ruthless, powerful, and often desperate. He operated from the Gulf coast to the borders of the free country, the thorn in the slaveowners' flesh and the terror of the freed Negro.

In February, 1822, David Jones, supposedly a fugitive slave, was seized by rustlers, who had only to prove he was a fugitive to make their venture pay handsomely. They could claim the reward, usually about $250 for a young buck, or they could shoot him down the river to the slave markets where the increased price usually more than justified the trouble and expense.

Apparently Gail Borden heard of the seizure and forced the rustlers' hand, for the case went to court and Gail trudged the ten miles into Madison to rescue the man. On February 12, Borden made an affidavit that six days earlier, while in "New Castle," Kentucky, he had seen in the hands of the jailer there a freedom certificate signed by a half-dozen people certifying that "David Jones a yellow man who was born of a white woman by the name of Jones had served the term of thirty one years and now was free and at liberty to go anywhere in the United States and that he had always conducted himself soberly" and "that he was a regular member in the Methodist Church."

Borden testified further that Jones' certificate "was wrongfully taken . . . by persons living in the State of Indiana who pretended that the said David Jones was a slave who had absconded from his master" and that "it is his belief that the said David Jones is a free man."

After Borden's testimony had been considered, the justices examined Jones, found that the Negro "is generally very correct in his statement," and declared him "a free man."[17]

Having struck this small but concrete blow for the freedom of man, Gail Borden was ready to leave Indiana and his family behind and set out with Tom to recover his health and to make his fortune. His immediate goal: New Orleans; his ultimate home: a matter of fate and chance.

[17] Book C, Deed Record, Jefferson County, Indiana, 262.

CONDENSED MILK,

MADE BY BORDEN'S PROCESS,

Patented 19th August, 1856, Re-issued 13th May, 1862, and 10th February, 1863,

Is pure Milk reduced in quantity 75 per cent. It is used by thousands of families in New York and Brooklyn.

CONDENSED PRESERVED MILK,

MADE BY BORDEN'S PROCESS,

Is the same as the above, further concentrated with the addition of the best refined sugar. Made with integrity, this milk will keep for years, and for all purposes in which sugar is used with milk, is, in every respect, equal to fresh milk, to wit: COFFEE, CUSTARDS, PUDDINGS for CREAM, CREAM SYRUPS, etc. [See directions for using.]

Tens of thousands have testified to the superiority of "Borden's Condensed Milk," which is manufactured under his superintendence, in Dutchess and Putnam Counties, State of New York, now amounting to several tons each day.

THE "ELGIN MILK CONDENSING COMPANY,"

AT ELGIN, ILLINOIS,

Organized under the general Act of the State, has procured a license under the above patent to manufacture the **PLAIN CONDENSED** and **PRESERVED MILK**, and offer the same to the public for sale at the Factory, where all persons are permitted to call and see the works.

The Company invites a comparison of its Milk with any other made.

"GAIL BORDEN'S CONDENSED CREAM."

Condensed by his vacuum process, is a superior article, hitherto unknown. It is not subject to deterioration, like other cream, so frequently rendered unhealthy by exposure. Cream is procured from new milk, set in running spring water, in vessels made for the purpose, combined with the best refined sugar, and the watery portions evaporated. It will be found unsurpassed, in quality and cheapness, for ICE CREAM, CREAM SYRUPS, for STRAWBERRIES, PEACHES and other RIPE FRUITS. [See directions for using.]

NOTE.—As a Dairy District, ELGIN is not equalled by any other place in the State for tame grasses, and fine running springs for cooling milk.

Depot and Office—53 LaSalle Street, Chicago.

JULY, 1865

S. T. HINCKLEY, Agent for Company.

The above for sale at Elgin, Chicago, and other Western Cities. Also, for sale, Borden's Products, Extract of Coffee, combined with Condensed Milk and Sugar, a superior article, Extract of Meats, Condensed Fruit Juices, etc.

O. C. SABIN, Traveling Agent.

Handbill advertising Borden's condensed milk.
The notation at the upper right is in
Gail Borden's handwriting

The Borden Company

I have need of the sky
I have business with the grass.
—Hovey, *I Have Need of the Sky* .

V

Days Along the Milk and Cider
1822-1829

H AVING DISPOSED of cargo and boat at New Orleans, flat-
boatmen could choose one of several routes as they
turned their steps northward. One of the most popular
was to cross the lakes out of New Orleans, clamber
aboard some kind of water-borne conveyance at the mouth of the
Amite River, and help paddle upstream, for the Amite was frequently sluggish enough that even a barge could be pushed up its
torpid waters and its rowers hardly notice the pull of a current.

Just after crossing the boundary into the new state of Mississippi, the river divided at Fort Hazard, which was not really a fort
at all, but only a tavern and a grog shop where a "flatter" could
fortify his insides against the trail and the weather ahead, the "hazard" being more internal than mortal. Once Fort Hazard was behind, the traveler struck out, usually afoot, for a straggly collection
of huts known hopefully as Elysian Fields, replenished there, and
continued on to Natchez, where again several routes, especially the
Natchez Trace, lay before him.

If, as seems probable, Gail Borden had made a trip south prior
to his coming to stay, he likely had returned from New Orleans to
Natchez by this route. And when he had sat in his Indiana cabin
talking soberly with Tom of settling in the southern regions, his
thoughts would naturally have turned to the grass-green freshness
of this country he had crossed earlier.

It is likewise possible that while Borden was in New Orleans
trying to decide whether to take root close by or to be swept up in
the flame of Texas fever which was being fanned by young Stephen
F. Austin, he met Dr. William Lattimore, scholarly Mississippi con-

51

gressman whose Green Valley plantation was only a few miles from Fort Hazard, and that Dr. Lattimore helped persuade the stooped young Yankee to locate in the Amite River region.

 Whatever his reasons, Gail Borden did choose Amite County on Mississippi's southwestern border, arriving there in the spring or early summer of 1822.

 At twenty-one Borden found himself facing one of those periodic crises that arise to plague the soul and thoughts of men, particularly young men, whose ambitions are limitless but whose prospects resemble more those of a virgin field from which the stumps of youth have only been cleared and whose soil might be fertile or barren, yielding a harvest rich and full from one type of seed but poor and pinched if another type be planted. So much can depend on the selection.

 For his almanac of augury Borden could provide these facts concerning himself. He was twenty-one. He knew some surveying. He had attended school a little and he had taught a little. He could shoot straighter than a Choctaw's arrow. He had saved a Negro's freedom. And he had a cough that circumscribed his area of choice because it meant he must have a proper balance of sunshine and hard work, not too little of one or too much of the other. Not altogether rich soil from which to grow a full and flowering life.

Other young men of vision were turning to the law and politics, to commerce and power, and to speculation and wealth. Borden's health forbade the first, his inclination the second, and his particular morality the last.

 What then to do? It was a decision which had to be made alone. Old Gail was a thousand miles away where some people still thought of Mississippi in terms of the Spanish territories. Brother Tom was by now halfway up the Mississippi, bitten by the Texas bug and making plans to strike out for that Mexican veldt as soon as possible.

Gail Borden narrowed his field. Really, he knew only surveying, schoolteaching, and farming. Surveying was out, because with his cough he could not afford the daily exposure in a country where the rain could come down like Eternity until a man forgot what day he last wore dry boots. He might survey some, but he could not chance six days a week.

Farming? That meant land and Negroes, and they in turn meant money, which eliminates most young men. To hire out would be socially unthinkable: Mississippi had slaves for that.

Only schoolmastering was left. There was no money in the profession, but he could remain indoors when the weather was bad, and on other days he need stay in only part of the time. He could get all the hot sunshine his underheated lungs required without risking excessive exposure. And when school dismissed for planting and harvesting seasons, or just for Saturdays, he could survey. Gail Borden did the unavoidable: he taught.

He was not the ordinary schoolmaster, fierce of mien and lonelier than Genius. He was simply a young man who taught school because he seemed to have a gift for it, because he needed to conserve his health, and because he liked people.

In the cool of the morning you could see him. He seldom rode to school astride a shuffling horse, and unlike the traditional teacher, he seldom walked either, oblivious to surroundings while he strode along, his thoughts as deep in abstruse recollections as his ankles were deep in Mississippi mud. Gail Borden ran to school. That chest of his needed wind to breathe, and he provided the wind, jogging along over road and path like a bare-knuckle fighter training for a promised purse.

Imagine the picture. Now as he runs along, he overtakes a little fellow, one of his beginners. Pollard Butler, perhaps. With a greeting to Mrs. Butler in the front yard, he stops momentarily, bends low, and scoops up the delighted and expectant Pollard somewhat like an excavating machine sweeping a load of dirt into its cavernous maw, hoists the youngster to his left shoulder, and trots off again, for all the world resembling a man carrying a sack of corn to the miller and already an hour late for his milling-time.

Another quarter of a mile and he reaches the Webb place, where young Charlie Webb is waiting. The ceremony is repeated, and there on the opposite right shoulder perches little Charlie, so proud of his seat of honor that generations later Charlie Webb—now old Charlie Webb—will be telling cousins, nephews, grandchildren, anyone who will listen to an old man talk, how Mr. Borden used to let him "ride" to school.

Down the Webbs' long meadow and across Lazy Creek and up the defile, and Gail Borden would let his riders dismount. A few deep breaths to decelerate to normal breathing, perhaps a fire started in the schoolhouse stove, a quick dash to the cold spring a hundred yards away, and a slower trot back with the pail, a "good morning!" to all the less fortunate students who were so big that they had to walk or ride just a horse, and Gail Borden was ready to ring his school bell.

School had to commence briskly, or else the sleepyhead would nod. Mr. Borden's school quickly established a reputation for early convocation. No ten o'clock scholar was he! No sooner did the Mississippi sun begin to send its morning beams flirting with the clearing on which stood the Bates schoolhouse than Borden rang his bell. By the time the sun had topped the pines to the east and waxed warm enough to send the traces of morning frost scurrying for the deeper, cooler earth, Gail Borden had school so far along that the students had forgotten their sunrise hopes that maybe Mr. Borden would be ill today and wouldn't come and were concentrating instead on what they were going to trade Mattie or Cy out of their dinner sacks.

Borden taught two schools in Amite County; in which order there is no way of knowing. The one at Bates was located in the present Cold Springs community, four miles north of Liberty, the county seat. The other, and probably the later, school was at Zion Hill, eight miles farther north, already an established community built around a Baptist church.

While teaching at Bates, he boarded with Kinchon Webb and his wife, Rebecca, who lived on a slope within sight of the schoolhouse chimney-smoke. Whether he continued to live with them when he taught at Zion Hill is not known. Invariably, however, he spent week ends in Liberty, enjoying the company and the advantages of a town of several hundred people whose chief social activities hinged around the church and the courthouse. In this he shows himself to have been no more than a normal young man of any generation seeking week-end bright lights, only in his case the lights were dim lanterns burning smoky pine-oil. In odd moments he surveyed a little.

Teaching school did for Gail Borden what he had hoped it would. His cough improved and his prospects brightened. Apparently the people in his community liked him, and he must have made good contacts in Liberty, for shortly after his twenty-fourth birthday the following order was written into the Amite County probate records: "Ordered, that Gail Borden be recommended to his Excellency the Governor as suitable person to fill the Office of County Surveyor, in place of Charles Davis resigned."

The order was executed, the governor was willing, two men were brought forward as security for bond, and on March 6, 1826, "Gail Borden Esqr. appeared in open Court & took the necessary oaths to qualify him to act as County Surveyor." Not only that, but the court allowed the new surveyor to borrow the county map for two months and to make a copy for his own use, and it entered his name as "Captn." Gail Borden.[1] Captain of what or whom was never specified.

An appointment as deputy federal surveyor augmented his income still more, and Borden began to know Amite County from one end to the other—from the heavy pine forests of the Homochitto in the northwest through the region of Milk and Cider Creek, which ran between the Zion Hill and Bates schoolhouses, to the plantation country along the Tangipahoa in the southeast, where Negroes drenched in sweat and song raised four-hundred-pound bales of white Mexican cotton from every two acres; and from now-forgotten Elysian Fields in the southwest, where the Baptists clustered thicker than wet rice, to Mars Hill, where Andrew Jackson reputedly had borrowed the steed that saw him through the battle of New Orleans; and beyond to the extreme northeast where simple oxen pulling Carey plows cleft light, broad furrows.

Not too long after settling in Amite County, Gail Borden undoubtedly became aware that there were almost enough Mercers in the county to hold the balance of power in any contest. Elder Thomas Mercer, brother of the galvanic Jesse Mercer who more than any other one man made Georgia a continuing Baptist stronghold, had helped found the Mississippi Baptist Association, had been its moderator, and had compiled Mississippi's first collection of hymns. When Borden arrived, Thomas Mercer had been dead a

[1] Probate Record, 1823-33, Amite County, Mississippi, 55, 57.

short enough time that people marveled yet at his spiritual stature. Still around was Brother Asa Mercer as one of the Association's five missionaries; in one year his work netted him the overwhelming stipend of $37. At various times both he and Thomas Mercer held the Zion Hill pastorate.

Not directly associated with the church was Eli Mercer, kinsman of Thomas, who lived down in the old Spanish grants off Wagoner Creek and who had been prominent as farmer and useful citizen ever since Gail Borden had entered the county. He had been a juror in the much discussed trial of Summerset, a slave charged with murder, and had voted that the Negro be hanged, while his accomplice, a slave named Phillis, was to be branded on her right hand with an "M"—for "murder." Again he had been a juror at the trial of Rose, another Negro woman charged with murder, this time voting that Rose be taken to the public whipping post and given thirty-nine lashes "on her bare back well laid on—." He had been a commissioner of roads in Captain Butler's company and several times an inspector of electors at Noble Johnson's. And when Gail Borden's bond as surveyor had been approved, it had been Eli Mercer, along with William Bates, who had stood as security for the young man.[2]

That was in the spring of 1826, when John Quincy Adams was president because of a timely assist from Henry Clay, when Andrew Jackson was plotting to succeed to the presidency come next election, when the Monroe Doctrine was still too new to carry much international weight, when the Missouri Compromise supposedly had set the limits of slavery extension, when John Jacob Astor was turning from furs and the China trade to New York real estate, and when shortly two great Americans, John Adams and Thomas Jefferson, would die within a few hours of each other. In that spring Eli Mercer's daughter, Penelope, was fourteen, too young to marry but not too young to think about it.

And Gail Borden? There is no record when he began to notice that this young daughter of his friend was more than just another young woods-filly going merrily about her work and play, or a pleasant child to be treated as a child and a child only.

---

[2] T C Schilling, *Abstract History of the Mississippi Baptist Association for One Hundred Years*, 35–36, 44, 46, 72. Probate Record, 1823–33, Amite County, Mississippi, 8–10, 57, 61. Orphans Court Record, I, 252, 259–60, 292.

One story is that Borden fell desperately in love with Susan Vance, daughter of aristocratic, land-owning Colonel Robert Vance, but that Colonel Vance objected to his daughter's receiving calls from an impecunious schoolteacher who was in addition a Yankee. Hearing of the objection, Borden, always hypersensitive, instead of fighting, withdrew. Then it was he turned his attention to Miss Vance's young friend, Penelope Mercer. Nearly a half-century later a youth who had heard the anecdote asked Borden about it: "There is just enough truth in it to build a romance on, nothing more," he replied. "I knew Miss Vance and admired her but that is all. I married the only woman I ever loved."

Meanwhile Penelope Mercer was maturing, and, either slowly or suddenly, the awareness of her was developing within Borden's heart. And so in February, 1828, when Penelope was sixteen and he was twenty-six, Gail Borden went into Liberty, pledged the two hundred dollars required by Mississippi law to prove that a man was financially able to marry, and received his license.

Earlier, in January, he had further guaranteed his ability to care for his bride. With his Negro body-servant, Tom Rowe, he had gone to the slave block, which stood near the new pillory and whipping post a few feet in front of the present Amite courthouse, instructing Tom to select a likely-looking Negro girl for his wife. Tom chose Ellen, and Borden paid the sheriff $170. Penelope now had someone to watch over her.

Everything being set, on March 18 a minister—Asa Mercer perhaps—"celebrated the rites of Matrimony Gail Borden of Penelope Mercer." The same minister is believed to have married Tom and Ellen.[3]

Out in Texas, Tom Borden was enthusiastic. Oh, there were hardships aplenty, but the soil was fresh and rich and the game had not been beaten off and cattle could feed on the grasses the year around. The government at Mexico was benevolent—and careless —and land was to be had almost for the asking. Tom had gone to

[3] Manuscript of an address by Sam Houston Dixon, Houston, Texas, December 13, 1927, in San Jacinto Museum of History, Houston, Texas Gail Borden to J. H Parker, March 8, 1939 Conveyance Record, Vol. 2, 298. Marriage Record, Vol. 2, Amite County, Mississippi, 223. The marriage document is signed by the performing minister, but his signature is illegible

Texas early, in 1824, to become one of Stephen F. Austin's locally celebrated "Old Three Hundred." Like Austin, he was convinced that the possibilities of Texas knew no limits, that all Texas lacked to become the wealthiest state in the whole United States of Mexico was time and settlers and work.

Tom Borden's optimism spilled over, into Indiana, into Mississippi. First, Old Gail in Indiana succumbed to Tom's fervor, selling his river-bottom land in 1828 and heading south. Then the younger Gail began to teeter, spending spare hours and minutes discussing with Penelope and Mr. Mercer the latest letter from Tom or the reports of some passing traveler. He hardly knew what to do. He was well liked here, he had his school and his county work, and he had excellent prospects. But seven thousand people in one county left little room for many more. Now, in Texas, where a man could get in at the near-beginning . . . .

The discussions must have run on until finally Penelope Borden herself was glad to see her husband leave for a visit to Texas, hoping probably that Texas would be everything he thought it wasn't—and nothing that he thought it was—and that he would return cured of the Texas fever.

In June, 1828, he came home, having been one of seven passengers aboard the schooner *Hope* when it debarked in New Orleans. He was not cured, however. Tom had been right. Texas was the place for an ambitious man. But though impulsiveness was one of Gail Borden's traits, he bided his time, working, thinking, and planning. Soon Penelope must have known that any fight to remain in Mississippi could at best be only a delaying action, for now her father was also smitten with the fever.

For months the indecision dragged on, and then for months more preparations went slowly ahead. It was decided to leave for Texas in the late fall, when the fierce summer heat there would be past and the danger of disease lessened. Finally on September 17, 1829, the commissioners of Amite County met and took official notice that their surveyor, Gail Borden, had resigned, naming in his stead Angus Wilkinson, distant cousin of eloping Calista Wilkinson, who had lost her stocking fording Milk and Cider Creek and had to

4 Probate Record, 1823–33, Amite County, Mississippi, 118. J. H Parker to author, April 11, 1947.

honeymoon with only one stocking in her trousseau.[4] But Calista's embarrassment happened years later, while this was near the end of 1829.

The Mercers set out westward, going overland to Natchitoches on the Red River and on into Texas. Shortly afterward Gail and Penelope Borden bade permanent good-bys to their Mississippi friends, reversed the trail to New Orleans that Gail had traveled seven years earlier, and caught a boat for Texas. They could not go overland, for Penelope was carrying a child and her time was short. But time and nature were gracious, and not until the day after their boat touched the foreign Texas soil did little Mary Borden make her appearance on wind-swept, wave-leveled, treeless Galveston Island, once the lair of the pirate Lafitte, now the stopping place for immigrants and the home of no one. The date was December 24, 1829, the day before Christmas.

It is an interesting time in Texas.
—Gail Borden to S M Williams, 1835

*Earth is here so kind, that just tickle her
with a hoe and she laughs with a harvest.*
—Jerrold, *A Land of Plenty*

VI

Hotspurs and Bumbling Officials
1829-1835

To GAIL BORDEN the future had never looked more encouraging. Here in Texas he could satisfy his urge to grow with a country, for people had barely begun to enter. Introduced to real immigration less than a decade before by Stephen F. Austin, Texas by the time Borden arrived had hardly two thousand Anglo-Americans in a region as large as continental France. And what governing power could be more generous than Mexico, which granted him and his father-in-law a *sitio*—4,428 acres—of land each? Here was truly the land of opportunity.

Here, too, Gail Borden was reunited with his family—his father, with Paschal as his helper, already mending skeins and repairing "waggon toungs" and axletrees as a blacksmith in San Felipe; Thomas H., married now to Demis Woodward and an important landowner and a surveyor for the *empresario* Austin himself; and John, a strapping six-foot lad nearing twenty. For the first time Gail could actually realize that two members of his family were beyond his grasp —his mother, left behind in a shallow grave somewhere on the Choctaw bluffs of the Mississippi near Memphis; and his little sister, Esther, whose death in 1826 had temporarily blighted young Borden's pleasure in being named Amite County surveyor. Only the men of the Borden family had survived the wilderness road.

At the outset he turned to farming and stock raising. The soil was virginal and the climate pure magic. All the attention cattle needed was an annual branding: the grassy prairies and the mild weather took care of their feeding and housing, and the instincts of bovine nature provided for their increase. Farming was nearly as automatic. The growing season was nine months long, there was small danger of late freezes in the spring, and as the country filled with immigrants, the market was assured. With a whole *sitio*, or league, of land as his very own, it was only a question of time until wealth followed. Or so it must have seemed to Gail Borden.

The Reverend Rufus Burleson, whose thoroughgoing Christianity induced him to try to speak charitably of at least all fellow-Christians, wrote that unlike his father-in-law, "a prince among farmers," Borden was not a successful agrarian and that he became discouraged and quit. Certainly he seems to have devoted less and less time to farming and instead to have spent more time taking orders to survey in the vicinity of San Felipe, Austin's headquarters a score of miles up the Brazos River from Borden's upper Fort Bend County farm.

Between surveying and watching his cattle increase and hoping that his crops would thrive, he may have taught school awhile, as one early writer asserts. Whatever the case, it is true that he did not wait long to begin surveying. Six weeks after he landed in Texas, Gail Borden assumed Tom's surveying duties when the latter left Texas for four months. *The Texas Gazette*, San Felipe's hard-pressed newspaper, carried the notice on page four of its January 30, 1830, issue:

SURVEYING.—Being appointed Partition Surveyor, by the Ayuntamiento of this Municipality, for the Surveying land, belonging to individuals; and having business to call me away for a few months, I have appointed my brother GAIL BORDEN, JR. Deputy Surveyor, who is hereby authorized to do any surveying that may be required in my absence.

Persons wishing work done, will give ten days notice at the office of the Texas Gazette. Cattle will be received in payment.

Jan. 30—   THOS. H. BORDEN

For the next two years life for Gail Borden followed a pattern of farming, stock raising, and surveying. Through his surveying he became known over a considerable portion of the colony, and he in turn acquainted himself thoroughly with the country and the people who formed the solid tissue of Austin's colony. When it became apparent that surveying meant more to him than the produce of his land, he moved his family into San Felipe, an often dusty, often muddy village on a bluff in a bend of the Brazos with slight excuse for existence beyond its fairly central location and its selection as Austin's capital.

There he might have continued a reasonably tranquil career—as tranquil as any career in a frontier community can be—gradually adding to his stature as a conscientious God-fearing neighbor, prospering as the colony prospered, perhaps in time becoming a political or commercial figure of some importance simply because he was honest and sober in an era when the proportion of honest and sober men was no greater than it is in any age.

But, as it usually does for fortunate men, history intervened, slightly at first but gathering momentum until it hit Gail Borden with an impact that spun his life around until he forgot entirely the old known paths and struck out in unfamiliar directions, blasting his own new trail as he progressed.

Most Americans who emigrated to Texas in the eighteen twenties arrived with an earnest desire to get a fresh start or to achieve a security they did not possess in the United States. They came prepared to live with Mexicans under Mexican rule, and the Mexicans welcomed them, for these men from the north populated a vast territory which native Mexicans were little disposed to colonize themselves. If Mexico was to continue to hold its Texas lands, it must have people on those lands who could defend them against the United States or England or any other prowling nation, and Mexico knew this. So Mexico made generous terms to Austin and the other *empresarios* who came, scheme in hand, asking for permission to bring in colonists. And the people came.

But Mexico was a volatile, young nation, unsure of itself, faced suddenly with governing its millions with leaders who were more revolutionists and patriots than good administrators. Administration followed administration, each so busy disposing of its predecessor and guarding against its intriguing successor that Texas became a neglected child, growing in its peculiar, undisciplined fashion.

This is what happened. One day the Bustamante government paused long enough from its duplicities to notice that the Texas half of its dual state of Coahuila y Texas was getting out of hand. Anglo-

Americans were arriving at an alarming rate. To be sure, it was only a trickle, but the trickle was steady and promised an eventual flood. And these Americans were getting the best land and adding to their estates, while the few Mexicans in Texas were a submerged group, living as a rule from hand to mouth, showing little ambition and making little progress. If this state of affairs continued, it was foreseeable that one day Mexico would have an Anglo-American cancer menacing its eastern arm and that the United States, not Mexico, would play the dissecting doctor.

To obviate such a situation, Mexico on April 6, 1830, passed a law forbidding further emigration from the United States to Texas. Thus the hopes of all Texans, from the handful of *empresarios* to the hundreds of simple settlers depending on normal immigration to increase the value of their holdings and enhance their prospects, were dashed, and their protests went unheeded.

However, through the use of various subterfuges emigration did not cease, and in the spring of 1831 William Hunter was able to write a friend in Missouri that "Emigrants are coming in verry fast it is thought that more will come in this year than has in any before there has been several vessels in this trade, no one has come in without a N°. of passengers, a number of negroes have been brought in this spring, a vessel is now in the river that brought 70 passengers, she brought word that another would sail for Matagorda Bay in a few days with about 100."[1]

Most of the citizens, like Hunter, were about as well satisfied with their outlook and with their government as any citizens ever are, and open friction might have been avoided, or at least delayed, if Mexico had not chosen two unfortunate officials to send to Texas in 1831. The first, George Fisher, a Serbian adventurer and former United States citizen, followed a completely unrealistic customs-collections policy for the spoiled Texans, who heretofore had enjoyed customs immunity. But of more immediate importance was the appointment of Colonel John Davis Bradburn, a Kentucky renegade, to head the military detachment at Anáhuac, a hundred miles east of San Felipe. Bradburn's bullheadedness led him to antagonize some local firebrands, especially William B. Travis, later

[1] William W. Hunter to James F. Perry, March 21, 1831, in J F. Perry Papers, University of Texas Archives.

the Alamo commander, and Patrick Jack, who played practical jokes on Bradburn until that irate individual arrested both Travis and Jack, along with other citizens, and refused to turn them over to civil authorities. When the news of Bradburn's action reached San Felipe, William H. Jack hurried to Anáhuac to obtain the release of his brother, Patrick. Unsuccessful, he returned to San Felipe to whip up sentiment for attacking Bradburn. Although most of San Felipe opposed such a move, Jack persevered. By early June, 1832, he and others had raised 160 men, who were waiting before Anáhuac for cannon to arrive from Brazoria when the quarrel was called off. Meanwhile, the Mexican commander at Velasco refused to allow the Texans to pass his fort with their cannon, the groups exchanged fire, and the fort surrendered.

/This was no less than war and rebellion—or it could have been if politics in Mexico City had not favored the Texans. There Santa Anna was in open opposition to Bustamante's tyrannical government and was ostensibly fighting to restore the federal constitution which Bustamante had tossed to the winds. Accordingly, the Texans at Turtle Bayou outside Anáhuac announced in a group of resolutions that Santa Anna's fight was their fight and that they were fighting Bustamante's officials, not Mexico. On learning this, the older, more conservative settlers were in a dilemma. They wanted no quarrel with Mexico and heretofore had remained meticulously aloof from the Mexican struggles for presidential power, but now they were committed by a handful of hotspurs and two bumbling officials. Action—quick action—was necessary.

It was advertised as a "Citizens' Meeting," and quite a gathering from the Navidad, Karankawa, and Lavaca settlements turned out at Thomas Menefee's place to learn what had already taken place and to help decide what should be done next. Major George Sutherland was called to the chair, and Gail Borden was named secretary.

First William Menefee read a history of the Anáhuac disturbance, then an account of the situation at Brazoria and Velasco. After that, he read the Turtle Bayou resolutions, commented briefly on the movement of the volunteers who had endeavored to take the cannon down the Brazos, and finally explained the purpose of the meeting.

/ A committee of six, among them Gail Borden, was named to draft resolutions. When the committee reported back, its resolutions were adopted unanimously.

"We still desire to be governed" by the Mexican government, the resolutions read. And, the document continued, "having emigrated to this colony, to share the liberality of government, and to acquire a living by an honest and steady pursuit of business; it is with deep regret we hear of the necessity of repelling unconstitutional encroachments of any officer of government."[2]

It was then suggested that a standing committee of inquiry and correspondence be named "to quiet the minds of the people" by keeping them informed authentically. Three men—Major Sutherland, John C. Caldwell, and Gail Borden—were named to the committee, which was also charged with creating similar committees in other settlements and to press for a convention of the entire colony.[3]

In the uncertain months ahead these three men were to link the Texas chain into a tight, strong bond with both utility and purpose.

It began to look as if the insurrection of 1832 were going to accomplish what its instigators had hoped. The attitude of Santa Anna, who was rapidly gaining power, was most conciliatory. Events began to settle down again to the same routine of living that had been achieved in 1831 when Moses Lapham, fresh out of Miami University, could write his parents of no more important matters than "I am living at a Mr. Bordens. It appears to be a very clever family," and to complain of San Felipe society as being "such as to preclude all satisfaction; drinking, gambling, swearing & fighting are the chief amusements."[4]

Beneath this complacent exterior Texas was looking forward eagerly to its first convention, called by the *ayuntamiento* of San Felipe to meet there on October 1, 1832. Fifty or more delegates attended. Eli Mercer came in from Mina (Bastrop) with two other delegates and between convention sessions enjoyed a visit with his

[2] C A Gulick and others (eds), *The Papers of Mirabeau Buonaparte Lamar,* I, 125–26 (referred to hereafter as *Lamar Papers*).

[3] *Ibid* , 126–27.

[4] Moses Lapham to Amos Lapham, July 13, 1831, in A. L. Heminger Papers, Keosauqua, Iowa.

daughter and granddaughter and obtained his first view of his eight-months-old grandson, Henry Lee.[5]

The convention lasted six days. After reaffirming their loyalty to the Mexican government and constitution, convention members dealt primarily with two requests: repeal of the anti-immigration clause of the decree of April 6, 1830, and admission to the Mexican confederation as a state separate from Coahuila. These petitions never reached the state or the federal governments, and Mexican officials from the local political chiefs to Santa Anna himself expressed their distaste for this independent attitude of the colonists.

On the other hand, Texans were jubilant. They had come together and visited with folks they had not seen in ages and had met a lot of new ones; and between times they had shown the officials in Mexico that they both respected and insisted on their constitutional rights as good Mexicans. In such a mood Tom Borden wrote his friend, Moses Lapham, that "Our times is much better than they was a month or so ago the war is over in these parts . . . . We have whiped all the troops out of Texas and I am in hopes that we shall have no more of them."[6]

A warm winter followed—the warmest, old settlers said, since they had come to Texas, but made disagreeable by so much rain that the creek flooded the floor of Tom Borden's north room. Immigrants were arriving regularly—six vessels were tied up in Brazoria at the same time. McNeel and Woodson established a store in Brazoria with $30,000 worth of merchandise, and money was plentiful on all sides. Tom Borden splurged to the extent of a forty-dollar gun—"had it a month shot it once"—and Mr. Queen opened a school in San Felipe to forty scared "schollars." But although everyone's health was "tolerable good," spirits began sagging as time wore on and no relief came from the Mexicans. Still, felt Tom Borden, "I had rather belong to Mexico than to the U. S." Enthusiastically he wrote to Lapham: "Times in Texas is better than I ever saw them."[7]

By January, 1833, however, most Texans had decided that if

---

[5] Since no doctor was available at Henry Lee Borden's birth, Gail Borden had to serve as both delivering physician and nurse Statement by Frank Wells, Brewster, New York, May 25, 1918, in Arthur G. Clark Papers, Borden Company, New York

[6] T. H Borden to Moses Lapham, October 18, 1832, in Heminger Papers

[7] *Ibid*, February 1, 1833.

Henry Lee Borden, eldest son of Gail Borden
and third president of the New York
Condensed Milk Company

The Borden Company

"times" could not be improved, politics could. Their first convention, they had to admit, had been inconclusive. Another was necessary. The call was sent out for April 1 at San Felipe. Gail Borden was a delegate.[8]

The more than fifty men who gathered in San Felipe presented a study in contrasts to be found only where men live on the fringes of society. There was wealth and poverty, brilliance and mediocrity, probity and whispered scandal. Although the same districts were represented, only one-third of the men who had attended the October consultation were returned. This time Texans meant to go a step further in seeking redress, and they sent as their representatives men of steadfast courage, some more radical than their predecessors.

There was Austin, truly the spirit of Texas. There was David G. Burnet, bombastic in action and florid of expression, but withal a man around whom others rallied. There was James Bowie, one of those rare persons who become legends in their own lifetimes. There was Nestor Clay, a college graduate with an incisive tongue and a taste for liquor which may have been inherited from his Kentucky kinsman, Henry Clay.

And Jared Groce, who had brought so many wagons and slaves to Texas in 1822 that the government had granted him more than forty thousand acres; and Robert M. Williamson—"Three-Legged Willie"—who John Henry Brown claimed could outsing any amateur vocalist in either Texas or the United States. Eli Mercer came again. But the most interesting person of all was a large forty-year-old newcomer whose reputation had preceded him to Texas—Sam Houston, late governor of Tennessee, late United States congressman, late Indian agent, and, no one knew for sure whether late or present, favorite of President Jackson. Had Jackson sent him here now?

As before, petitions were addressed to the Mexican government praying for repeal of the anti-immigration law and the passage of a law for the separation of Texas and Coahuila. This convention, though, went further, taking a step that offended completely the

[8] Borden represented the district of Lavaca, which translated means "The Cow," an interesting foreshadowing, perhaps, of his later important work in the field of milk

Mexican sense of political propriety. Without waiting for approval of its separation petition, the convention proceeded to frame its own state constitution, the first of Texas' several constitutions, and to approve it. Anglo-Americans, Gail Borden among them, had written the document; consequently its more important features embodied Anglo-American rather than Roman concepts of law and government.[9] It should have been no surprise then that the Mexican government received the news of this impudence with little pleasure.

With the close of the convention of 1833, Texas set itself for a long period of waiting and hoping. Austin had been named by the convention to carry the new petitions and the constitution to Mexico, a thousand-mile journey through a land of uncertain roads. It was a several weeks' journey each way, and, once there, Austin had no possible method to obtain speedy action from a Mexican government torn by revolution and counterrevolution. Austin might not return for a year.

Meanwhile Texas waited. And the Brazos and the Colorado overflowed their bottom lands, making replanting necessary and crops correspondingly late; and cholera came to the coastlands, taking Henry Smith's second wife along with several others at Brazoria; and the price of land rose in the San Bernard bottoms to $2.00 an acre, while a mainspring for a man's watch cost $4.00; and Father Muldoon, "the old rascal" who was reputed to own eleven leagues of land, made his belated rounds, legalizing, for $25.00 or $30.00 each, marriages long since celebrated in fact and baptizing the results of those marriages for $2.50 to $5.00 each; and two slaves, Polax and Caster, were given Christian names by their master, Tom Borden, who "wished a hundred times . . . they had broke there necks the time that they run a way"; and Paschal Borden, still blacksmithing, took "a little sick" but soon recovered; and Moses Lapham up in Ohio learned that chances for a wife in Texas "is pretty good . . . since the new crop has come in"; and most men continued to

[9] E. W. Winkler, "Membership of the 1833 Convention of Texas," *Southwestern Historical Quarterly*, Vol. XLV, No 3 (January, 1942), 255–57 Hereafter the *Southwestern Historical Quarterly* and its predecessor *Quarterly of the Texas State Historical Association* will be cited as *The Quarterly*. See also J. H. Brown, *History of Texas*, I, 227.

prefer Mexican rule if only because under Mexico Texas was a "bright star . . . whereas in the U. S. it would be dim."

Spring rains poured themselves out and summer came, and with summer good health generally. And then it was the fall of 1833, and rumors out of Mexico City indicated that Austin would at least obtain repeal of the law of April 6, 1830, before he started home. Tom Borden got caught in a driving rain sixty-five miles from home —"Such a rain I never saw before this is the fourth day since it commence"; and the *Sabine* arrived with forty more immigrants, partially fulfilling the prophecy of "more new comers this faul and winter than has come the last 3 years before."[10]

And while Texas waited, Gail Borden was busier than he had ever been in his life. Before Austin left, he turned over the administration of his many colonial duties to Borden and to Samuel M. Williams, his colonial secretary since the early eighteen twenties. But Williams had land fever and was gone frequently, so that much of the work devolved upon Borden, who sought in his painstaking, conscientious manner to straighten out confusions of titles, to locate likely lands for persons back in the States who wanted to move to Texas, to keep land-office records straight, and to answer the tremendous correspondence with persons merely seeking information about this new country. Between times, he surveyed. And although Texas in the summer of 1833 was enjoying its healthiest season, the Gail Borden family could hardly share that enjoyment. On August 28, little Mary, their first-born, died. She would have been four in December.

In midwinter word reached Texas that Austin, en route home, had been arrested in Saltillo on January 3 and was being returned to Mexico. But even this news failed to ripple the smooth surface of Texas affairs. The state government was making concession after concession to the Texans, repealing the law prohibiting any but native-born Mexicans from engaging in retail merchandising, permitting Texas to send three of the twelve deputies composing the state congress, recognizing the English language for official pur-

[10] T. H Borden to Moses Lapham, May 19, June 20, September 4, November 7, 1833, in Heminger Papers. Undoubtedly Thomas Borden's two slaves were named for the Greek twin heroes, Pollux and Castor, but with a slightly original spelling approach.

poses, granting religious toleration, and overhauling the court system. Colonel Juan N. Almonte, in Texas to learn how soon Texas would revolt, wound up instead in mid-July of 1834 as guest of honor at a San Felipe banquet and returned to Mexico recommending almost the same reforms for which the colonists had been clamoring. Except for a small group of firebrands, Texas was content with Mexico, and for the nonce Mexico was too occupied with internal struggles to be anything other than content with Texas.

The scene then in Texas was that of people in the usual unending pursuit of happiness. In October, 1834, John P. Borden, now twenty-two years old, reached Goliad on his way to San Antonio to study Spanish, writing his father of "The rud and *cuasi* savage construction of the houses some of which are as destitute of mechanism as the blackest Mexican is of gachupin blood."[11] A young man named Joseph Baker, called "Don José" because of his facility with Spanish, was happy as he wrote out a receipt to Samuel M. Williams for "tuition of two scholars 5-½ months" at two dollars a month—Williams had owed the bill for more than a year.[12] And Williams, reputedly a one-time private secretary to Andrew Jackson, was spending his time in Monclova or Saltillo, wherever the state government happened to be, pushing land schemes designed to make him wealthy and distrusted.

Gail Borden was so busy around the land office that in December, 1834, he had to write his good friend, John P. Coles, that he could not undertake the surveying Coles had requested but that he would send another man. "Should come myself," he wrote, "but am unable."

Requests seemed to drift in from everywhere. From William B. Bridgers: "I want you to enter Wm. Gold on your Books he has a wife and three children. . . . Likewise I want you to entry the name the widow Lily Barbary Tiley her name age is about 64 years age. . . . Bin four years sence come to this Contry . . . . PS Capt I want you to attend the Business of Mr Peake Land . . . . PS Mr Borden

[11] John P. Borden to Gail Borden, Sr., and P P. Borden, October 25, 1834, in Austin Papers, 1834–35, University of Texas Archives. Unless otherwise noted, all letters quoted in this chapter are from this manuscript collection or from E. C. Barker (ed.), *The Austin Papers*, III

[12] Receipt, Joseph Baker to Samuel M. Williams, November 2, 1834, in S M. Williams Papers, Rosenberg Library, Galveston.

this Mr Gold is Poor but onest good Citisen . . . I want you to write to me as soon as Possible whether he git it or no."

From Elisha Flack: "I wish you would send me . . . the survey or field nots of they survey your Brother John made for me." From G. B. Jameson of Orozimbo, Texas: "I further apply to you in the name of Samuel Damon for a survey of a League of Land."

Out in Gonzales, Andrew Ponton wrote that his father had made Williams a first payment on a league of land but that no deed had been forwarded. "Now sir," wrote Ponton, "if I cannot have the deed I wish you to give me information of the cause. . . . I have become somewhat suspicious of intreague in the matter."

Letters came from his helpers in the field, reporting and seeking instruction. From Peach Creek came word from W. Cave: "I have got through the Jackson Job." From Bastrop, Bartlett Sims asked for more plotting paper and a sketch of the headwaters of "the Navordad and Buckners Creek." And from Sims again: "I send you by Mr Caruthers A Map of the work have done below the San Antonio Road and West. of the Colorado River. An alteration is made in League No. 31." Jesse Bartlett wrote that "the Survey of the River leagues will be of much value in straiting up things and enable you to give a true map of the country." And Jameson assured Borden that "Should you . . . authorize me to make the survys I will give you the ordinary price for entering them in the office. The question you gave me to work I have done."

Gail Borden's nose, however, was not plunged so deep in his work that he could not look up and smell opportunity in the air. Texas was growing and growth meant wealth. How was he to obtain his portion? In March, 1835, he wrote Williams that he had "many things to say" to him: "Had I $5000 now, I would not fear but what I could make it $10000 in one year. More stir of Emigrants now than have ever seen all pushing round for land."[13]

If he could arrange his work, Borden knew what he wanted to do. He and John P. and "Don José" Baker had discussed a plan several times before John Borden had gone to San Antonio. The first glimpse of the plan appears on January 29, 1835, in a letter to W. C. White and James F. Perry at Columbia: "The bearer Mr. L. Ab-

13 Gail Borden to S. M. Williams, March 4, 1835, in Williams Papers

botts[14] will present you with a letter addressed to you and others," the letter read, "containing an application for assistance to establish a press at this place—." Dr. James B. Miller, soon to become political chief of the Brazos department, Alexander Somervell, a San Felipe merchant, and Samuel M. Williams had offered their assistance, the letter explained, adding that a further helping hand from White and Perry would be "gratefully acknowledged."

The news of the proposed newspaper spread, and in March a printer named John Gordon wrote from Brazoria inquiring about employment. John Rice Jones wrote in April that without waiting for authorization he had gathered eight subscribers, for which "I shall claim one copy of the Telegraph gratis." Everywhere the response was gratifying, and the field was wide open, for Texas had only one paper at the time, *The Texas Republican* at Brazoria.

But John Borden was in San Antonio paying his twenty-two dollars a month for board and tuition, Baker had other work at the moment, and Gail Borden was inundated with the details of Austin's office. If only Austin could come home. Or if only Williams would stay home!

Besides, as time passed, conditions seemed less propitious for founding a newspaper. Only one previous newspaper, genial Godwin Brown Cotten's *Texas Gazette*, had achieved anything akin to permanency, and it had lasted less than two years. It was too early to predict the life span of the *Republican*. True, Texas had more people and more wealth as month followed month and could therefore support a paper better, but supplies were still short—"This is the last sheet of good paper I can find any where," Borden confessed to Williams in March—and political difficulties were lowering. From Monclova inflammable Frank W. Johnson was sending home such dire predictions as:

"*Hell* to pay and no pitch.—

"*Wars* and rumours of *War*.—

"Want help from Tejas—Keep your guns in good order." Such a letter was not calculated to soothe.

So the plans for a newspaper continued in suspension, and though Tom Borden might write Moses Lapham in March that

[14] Abbotts was later press foreman for the Bordens' newspaper, *The Telegraph and Texas Register*.

"Gail John and one Baker will start a paper shortly,"[15] no news-paper was to issue from the press of "Baker and Bordens" until spring and summer had passed and the exciting days of October had arrived.

One day in Mechanicsburg, Ohio, Moses Lapham opened an uncommonly thick letter in which his friend and former employer, Thomas H. Borden, recounted a detailed chapter of his recent life. During these days Tom Borden was living in the big bend of the Brazos in a community he had named Louisville, today a part of the town of Richmond, Texas. He was raising cotton and some cattle, doing some surveying, and trying to interest late settlers in Louisville.

Across the Brazos lived Jesse Thompson, a man of "onusual size," considerable wealth, and in Tom Borden's words, "a man of a good deal of adress." According to Borden, his farm was "presisely" in Thompson's way, "for he is compeled to come on this side of the river in a high time of water." Apparently Thompson coveted Borden's land, and Borden refused to sell.

For several months the two men quarreled, and, again according to Borden, Thompson even sent his sons to annoy his neighbor. At length the two men agreed to leave their dispute to a board of honor, signing a pledge before a witness that "We agree that as our dispute is about to be left to gentlemen we will cease hostile movements towards each other as also the members of our respective family."

Despite the agreement Tom Borden always traveled well armed and apparently so did Thompson. For what happened next there is only Borden's word, for Thompson left no record and the account of the trial, if one were ever held, is lost.

"I had business at one of my nabours," Borden explained, "and went past Thompsons and on my way back one of his sons shot at me with a rifle   Thompson the old man was below he came home in a day or two he made no apology what ever to me   I started to go to Sanfelipe with a two horse wagon Mr. James Cochran with me. . . . I had proceded about two miles when we were supprized by

<hr />

[15] Gail Borden to S M Williams, March 4, 1835, in Williams Papers T. H. Borden to Moses Lapham, March 8, 1835, in Heminger Papers.

Thompson and one Dr. Erwin coming up to me with a large pistol in his hand and says I have got you d——m you."

At that moment Borden was about to clamber into the wagon after having been on the ground to tend a trace.

"I had a small pistol in a side pocket," Borden continued, "(the rest of my arms was in the wagon) I drew it and fired at the old hellion he fired at the same time but missed me he wheeled and pursued Cochrane fired his pistol at him."

With all this disturbance breaking around them Borden's horses took to the timber about three hundred yards away, Tom Borden following after to get his "big pistols and double barrel shot gun." Then he went back to see about Cochrane, who was "in a cuffle of a fight I fired an other pistol but C had hold of the muzel I ran up and shot the old rascal strange as it may appear to you in the land of steady habits."

Unlike tradition, which has man shooting in anger and repenting later, Tom Borden felt no remorse. "I am glad that I gut shot him that he may have the pangs of as hard a death as possible," he observed. "Thus the great Maximin fel he lived 3 hours I went to town gave my self up produced my proof am now bound to the superior court in a penalty of $2500 only David G Burnett was the judge."

That is Thomas Borden's story. Thompson, of course, left no record of the affray. Handed down in the Thompson family is the belief that Borden deliberately murdered Jesse Thompson, but only Borden's statement to the contrary is in evidence.

The letter which Moses Lapham read so carefully cost him fifty-two cents postage.[16]

Gail Borden attained no such heights of excitement and provocation. Instead, he continued cautious preparations for a newspaper, kept his ear to the political ground, and worked more long hours as Austin's surveyor. Requests poured in. His brother-in-law, Reason Mercer, wrote from Louisville, Texas, for a copy of a

---

[16] T. H Borden to Moses Lapham, March 8, 1835, in Heminger Papers On the credit side of Thompson's character is Noah Smithwick's statement that an escaped Negro slave belonging to Thompson returned voluntarily to his master, "preferring slavery under Thompson's lenient rule to freedom in Mexico." *Evolution of a State*, 37.

deed; a Major Norton dropped in from Boston to have Borden spend a day helping him select lands; and Samuel Williams apologized for his negligence in not aiding Borden, agreeing to make partial amends by writing Thomas McKinney to "further your Views with regard to the press &c. I am pleased to hear of your promised success in that enterprise."[17]

And more land matters. From Matagorda: "Please inform me . . . whether I can get [a league] . . . please inform me what is necessary for me." From S. Rhoads Fisher: "I want you to point out to Mr: Baker a league of land, which is valuable, and which I know a stranger or one who has not influence at the office cannot obtain—." From a man in Anáhuac: "Give me the necessary information of Conveyance etc my means of Traveling is so limited I cannot go to Sanfelipa." From Frank Johnson. "Use your best exertions."[18] From a Mr. Dooley: "I would Inform you that I am an applicant for Land." From Daniel Yeamans, Live Oak Landing: "I am about selecting land . . . where you would clear out one."

And disputes—between land claimants, between assisting surveyors. From Fayette Copeland in Brazoria: "I am informed that I have [been] imposed upon." From Thomas J. Gazley, who was disputing with a Mr. Harman: "And it is now reported here that Harman has written a letter to you, and has obtained a promise . . . I cannot give credit to this report." From Elias R. Wightman: "I understand Mr. Ingram has been surveying there, but my surveys must stand . . . if you will act as my agent please to inform me."

And sometimes, collections. "In the Town of San Felipe de Austin on the sixth day of May One thousand eight hundred and thirty five [appeared Gail Borden, Jr.] who declares that he has this day received of James F. Perry Two hundred and twelve dollars and ten cents the full amount due the State."[19] From Henry Austin: "I have arranged for a loan of 3000$ which will enable me to close my acct of fees with the office."

In June came a letter from Henry McDowell, owner of an engraving shop at No. 7 Chartres Street, New Orleans. McDowell

[17] S M Williams to Gail Borden, April 1, 1835, in Alamo Museum

[18] F. W Johnson to Gail Borden, March 18, 1835, in Alamo Museum.

[19] Certificate in Perry Papers

had met a Major Smith from Texas who had informed him that Gail Borden was the most qualified man in Texas to help McDowell engrave and publish a map of the Mexican subprovince.

"[I] beg that you will take the trouble to compile for me a Pocket Map from the Best information now on record in your office and others. I want one better than any extant in the U. States of the North, which I am told by Gentleman from Texas are bad enough." Payment, McDowell added, would be in finished engraved copies, "or in any other way you wish." The map need be "only plain, intelligible, and the words correctly spelled."

Some biographers credit Borden with compiling the first topographical map of Texas. In absence of positive proof in the form of a dated, signed map, McDowell's letter provides at least a clue.

Slowly, very slowly, the Bordens and Joseph Baker inched their way toward their newspaper. The need for a press was evident, and the people were ready. But materials were not. By June, 1835, a press had been ordered.[20] When it would arrive was as uncertain as the Texas weather.

Advertisements were circulated informing the country that a new paper would be issued soon. The response was immediate and pleasing. From Lavaca, James Kerr hurried to send in his subscription: "On Receipt of first copy—I will send you $5.00." In Brazoria printer John Gordon was more than ready to start work. "I will inform you that I am not engaged for any particular time, and shall leave this place some time in July. . . . I will come at any time if you thought me competent."

Now only the press and the paper and the type were still lacking.

In San Felipe in the summer of 1835 agitation was at fever pitch. No matter on which side of the political fence you stood, you could not ignore events of the past few days. With most people clinging to their belief that Mexico eventually would grant Texas the rights implied under the federal constitution, the fact remained that the

20 Mrs. Mary Austin Holley, quoting a Mrs. Eberly, says that Borden purchased his press from Godwin Brown Cotten, *Texas Gazette* publisher Notes made by Mrs. Holley, in University of Texas Archives There is no other evidence to support this claim.

war party had seized a messenger from General Cós, had held a quick but highly inflammatory meeting, and under William B. Travis had sent a force of thirty men and one cannon to capture the Mexican garrison at Anáhuac. And, whether you approved or not, they had done just that on the morning of June 30 without a shot being fired.

It was the story of 1832 all over again: lack of uniformity in customs collections on the one hand, hotheads on the other. Again the trouble centered in Anáhuac, where in January, 1835, Santa Anna had sent a small detachment of soldiers to enforce the collections there and at Galveston. That action would have been approved by most Texans, but the collector over at Velasco on the Brazos collected tonnage duties only, while the officers at Galveston and Anáhuac were insisting on payment of all duties. When an Anáhuac merchant refused to pay any more duties until collections were enforced equally at all ports, misunderstanding followed misunderstanding, and a Texan was wounded while two of Anáhuac's better citizens were imprisoned.

Hearing of the difficulties, Santa Anna's brother-in-law, General Martín Perfecto de Cós, sent word to the Anáhuac commander, Captain Antonio Tenorio, that reinforcements were on the way. En route to Anáhuac, Cós's messenger on June 21 stopped over in San Felipe, which was crowded by court week. There the war party took over.

Elsewhere in Texas, however, conciliatory forces immediately asserted their superior strength. Seven communities met and condemned the action of the firebrands. In San Felipe general gatherings were held on July 14 and 15, and the political chief, who a few weeks earlier had been chairman of the radical meeting which chose Travis to lead the march on Anáhuac, even wrote a letter of apology to Cós. After that, committees from Columbia and Mina met with a San Felipe committee for four days, in the end sending two emissaries of peace to Matamoros to see Cós.

But letters of conciliation did not satisfy the Mexican leaders. Cós demanded the arrest of Lorenzo de Zavala, a political refugee lately arrived in Texas; of Frank Johnson, long prominent around Monclova in land speculations; of "Three-Legged Willie" Williamson, who had implied too broadly that the words *liberty* and *Mexico* might not be exactly synonymous; of Travis, naturally enough; and

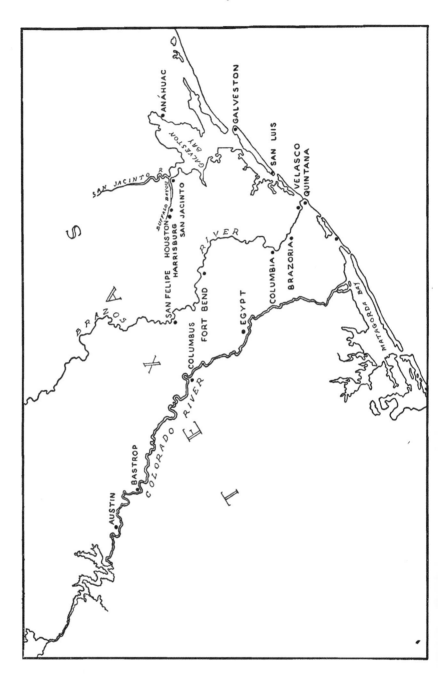

of Samuel Williams. Once apprehended, these men were to be turned over to the military for trial. Until this was done, Cós refused to see any peace commissioners.

This demand was too much for the Texans. Although most of them might be loyal to Mexico, they would never see members of their own race turned over to a Mexican military tribunal. They would fight first.

But Texas was not yet ready to fight, and before it would fight, its people would meet again and hold another consultation to sound general sentiment and to try to work out a peaceful solution. Each jurisdiction was instructed to send five delegates to Washington-on-the-Brazos on October 15. Their instructions: "Secure peace if it is to be obtained on constitutional terms . . . prepare for war—if war be inevitable."

On September 1, 1835, Austin arrived by boat at Velasco, more than two years after he had been sent to Mexico by the convention of April, 1833. He returned to find a country plunged deep into uncertainty, wanting peace but fearing war. He found, too, that another consultation had been called, although many people opposed it. A wave of relief swept Texas: Austin would know what to do. A stage manager couldn't have gauged better the moment to re-enter the Texas scene.

"At the time it was known at San Felipe that Austin had arrived on our shores," wrote Gail Borden later, "both the war and peace party hailed the event as one which would unite the people and produce one course of action whatever that might be—They said 'if Col Austin is for peace, we are for peace, if he is for war we are for *War.*'"

One uncertainty Austin dispelled almost at once. At a dinner tendered him at Brazoria a week after his landing, he spoke unequivocally for the consultation. There and there only, he said, could Texas decide what it wanted.

On his return to San Felipe, Austin threw himself into the snarled affairs of Texas, striving to achieve the best possible representation for the October consultation. Disillusioned by the continual rebuffs and delays in Mexico City, he had returned with strong doubts whether Texas could continue to live under Mexican rule.

Under Santa Anna federalism was dying—Texas was almost the only spot remaining in the Mexican nation that had not succumbed to the oppressive arm of the military. Stability in Mexican affairs seemed possible only at the expense of liberty.

During the summer the old committee of correspondence had been resurrected in San Felipe, as well as in other Texas municipalities. On September 12 the committee called a public meeting at Johnson and Winburn's tavern in San Felipe and chose Austin chairman. Resolutions were passed recommending the consultation, pledging adherence to the constitution of 1824, and urging the committee of vigilance and safety to superintend the election of delegates and to correspond with the committees of other jurisdictions. Once again, Gail Borden was a member of the local committee.

On the following day the committee issued a long statement favoring the consultation. One point in its report reveals that at last the long-looked-for printing press had been delivered. Discussing the site of the proposed consultation, the committee observed that it preferred San Felipe because "there is a printing press here."

On September 19 the committee of six men—aging Wily Martin, William Pettus, John H. Money, Randal Jones, Austin, and Gail Borden—met again. Borden, thirty-four years old, was the youngest. Not a one of the six was a firebrand, that is, a member of the war party. Except for Borden all had entered Texas as members of Austin's Old Three Hundred, and their loyalty had always been to Mexico.

But the news that Cós and his army had landed and were marching on San Antonio changed outlooks and loyalties. If Cós succeeded, Texas might become a military camp with soldiers dominating and individual liberties disappearing. His success would mean the end of the proposed consultation: choice of action no longer would lie with the Texans.

The six men knew what to do—what they *must* do. They drafted a proclamation, and Austin signed it and sent it to the Texas *Republican* to be printed. Soon riders were distributing copies throughout Texas.

"WAR is our only resource," the proclamation declared. "There is no other remedy but to defend our rights, our country, and ourselves by force of arms."

Events moved swiftly. Within a fortnight Ugartechea's demand for the cannon at Gonzales had been refused, a clash had developed, and on October 1, 1835, the first shot was fired in the Texas revolution. This really was war!

Here shall the Press the People's right maintain,
Unaw'd by influence and unbrib'd by gain.
—Motto of the Salem, Massachusetts, *Register*

We have endeavored to present facts . . .
believing that a community composed of Americans
would draw just conclusions, and act correctly
when in possession of all the evidence.
—[Gail Borden] *Telegraph and Texas Register,*
February 20, 1836

VII

The Alarm Is Sounded
1835-1836

ANY TIME a man attempts to be two people, holding two jobs and working two places, he is likely to find himself an exceedingly busy and a partially confused person. In the early days of October, 1835, Gail Borden was just that. On the one hand he was helping San Felipe particularly and Texas generally to prepare for war, holding postmidnight meetings with the local committee of safety, drafting appeals for aid and co-operation, trying to rally men and money for defense against the Mexicans. At the same time he was starting a new business, one to which he brought no experience, at a time when labor, supplies, and money were short, in a place where daily people were becoming more concerned for their personal safety than for anything else.

But if Texas in unrehearsed turmoil did not seem to portend the financial success of new enterprises by inexperienced entrepreneurs, the troubles of Texas did permit a vision of service to rise in Borden's mind. No time to start a newspaper when money was scarce and people were scared? Nonsense! Just the opposite, he must have thought. Think of the cohesive force that a newspaper can be, the unifying appeal it can make, the rallying point it can become! Instead of presaging gloom, the omens in the clear, autumn Texas skies must have spoken of success and service and position and prosperity to this sometime surveyor, farmer, and teacher.

Position now, prosperity later perhaps, but in the fall of 1835

82

Gail Borden was a curious mixture of the patient and the impatient —patient and persevering where unfulfilled promises, redeemable only by increased knowledge, dangled just out of reach; impatient and even testy where man-made obstructions alone deterred. These qualities were to be peculiarly his for the remainder of his life, continually refueling his ambition, spurring him to go ahead when he no longer knew where he was going or how he was going to get there, driving him later from a life of comparative comfort into a life of loneliness and disaster, keeping him striving continually like some cave-trapped person searching ceaselessly for an opening that would let through the light.

How hard he worked, how much he worried, how anxiously he waited in those October days can only be imagined, though the swirl of events about him gives some idea. The first copy of his newspaper was due on October 10, but the Mexican timetable could not await the birth of a new publication. On the Mexicans pressed, determined to quell the Texas menace, and with each beat of a Mexican boot Texan leaders became more apprehensive and more insistent in their efforts to rouse the populace and steady the troops.

In San Felipe five men prepared a determined circular, under which they scrawled bold signatures. They had met the night of October 8, the committee of safety from San Felipe plus one member each from Matagorda and Harrisburg.

The time has now arrived when it behooves every friend to his country to be up and doing. . . . Colonel Ugartechea is on his march from Bexar [San Antonio] with 500 men. . . . They come to fasten down upon our necks the yoke, and to rivet upon our hands the manacles of military servitude. Gonzales is doomed to the sword and flame. Colorado will next be the theatre of blood and rapine—then the Brazos. . . . Shall we give up without a struggle, the fruits of so many years of danger, difficulty and unparalleled suffering? . . . Can we let a military despot reap the harvest after we have sown the seeds? This Committee are ready to answer for their countrymen, and they answer by calling upon them to come, and come quickly. . . . three hundred . . . are already on the field. . . . These have to contend with the whole of the Mexican army. . . . they will dispute every inch of ground.[1]

[1] Barker (ed), *The Austin Papers*, III, 165–66 This appeared in *The Telegraph and Texas Register*, October 10, 1835 (hereafter cited as *Telegraph*)

At twelve o'clock that night the circular was finished. The first to sign was Gail Borden.

Leading the volunteer army was Austin—Colonel Austin now. Having left San Felipe in a hurry, only now did he have sufficient time to collect an idea of his needs and the needs of his people: "Write by every opportunity to Nacogdoches and Ayish bayou—Lead—Lead we want Lead," he wrote Borden on October 8. "You might get some one from Coles' settlement to go for the Cannon at Tenoxtitlan. . . . I want the proceedings . . . of all the other meetings in every place where they have resolved to support the constitution of 1824." And a postscript signed "Mosley": "By request of Austin you will send his shoes they are in his room."[2]

On the same day Borden as chairman pro tem of the committee of safety wrote Austin that he was elected a delegate to represent San Felipe in the general consultation convening October 15. Two days later he sent Thomas F. McKinney an urgent command in Austin's name to send to San Felipe all the powder and lead McKinney could spare.[3] But the rôle of Gail Borden was not to be that of leading an army, provisioning a colony, or managing a campaign —nor even that of merely acting as middleman or clearing agent for orders from and to Austin. His function was to be the voice of the revolution, a voice sometimes of moderation, a voice other times of quick, aggressive action. Almost at once he was destined to assume this rôle.

There was nothing startling about the newspaper that appeared late Saturday evening from the press of "Baker & Bordens." No innovations, no blaring typography, no thundering editorials. It was simply a small journal of eight pages, modestly written, not much better or much worse than other frontier newspapers in the second quarter of the nineteenth century. Trumpetings and paeans neither preceded nor followed its first appearance in San Felipe that tenth day of October in the year 1835.

But *The Telegraph and Texas Register*, the tenth newspaper to be attempted in Texas since 1813, proved to be the first to last longer than two years, for more than forty years were to pass before

[2] Barker (ed), *The Austin Papers*, III, 167.
[3] *Ibid* , 165, 186.

its distribution would cease, forty years that were to include two more wars after this one. From such an unprepossessing beginning, then, came the first really permanent newspaper in Texas. Before its demise its columns would know some of the best journalists of early Texas, including one editor-publisher, Francis Moore, whose biting invective and heated convictions would help make the nineteenth century the golden age for American editors.

Nothing in this first edition, however, foreshadowed the meatier days ahead. "Baker & Bordens" had no axes to grind, no enemies to thwart, no causes to espouse save the defense of Texas and constitutional liberties. Their firm held no illusions that the establishment of a new press in San Felipe would change morals or politics or folkways in either the world at large or in Texas round about. "Baker & Bordens" merely wanted to print a faithful record of events and to help Texas whenever possible.

Only four advertisements appeared in this first issue, and they were relegated to page eight, where they could hardly offend. At the top of column one, page one, was a box, announcing that the paper would be published every Saturday and giving terms of subscription and advertising. If paid in advance, the price was five dollars a year, about usual for a weekly newspaper in Texas in the eighteen thirties. The price rose to six dollars if not paid for six months, and seven dollars if the purchaser waited a year. No subscription would be accepted for less than six months, and none would be terminated within that period, except at the proprietors' option. For advertisements requiring eight lines or less, the charge was one dollar for the first insertion and fifty cents for each subsequent appearance. Longer advertisements were charged in the same proportion.

Completing the left-hand column of the first page was one-fourth of a column—twelve lines—of poetry, entitled simply "From the Italian":

> *Lady, not for her we sigh,*
> *Loving only fashion's dye,*
> *And her charms to every eye*
> > *Revealing;*
> *But we love the bashful maid*
> *In sweet modesty arrayed . . . .*

After that came two columns on the life of Robert Morris and a half-column culled from the Troy, New York, *Sentinel*, headed "A Good Story." That was all of page one. No news of an incipient revolution, of an invading enemy, or of the hopes and fears and desires of a people aware that their future, whether for better or worse, was dangerously uncertain.

On page two the publishers abandoned their detachment to give their readers the history behind the name of *The Telegraph and Texas Register*. Originally, they explained, they had intended to name the newspaper *Telegraph and Texas Planter* because at that time "the engrossing object was the accumulation of wealth and consequent aggrandizement of the country." But now *Register* had supplanted *Planter*, for "the all absorbing question is how to protect ourselves, and what we already possess. We shall therefore endeavour to make our paper what its title indicates, the organ by which the most important news is communicated to the people, and a faithful *register* of passing events."

Conditions in Texas were discussed on page three in an unsigned article that probably was staff-prepared. Commenting on speculators and fraudulent holders of land titles, the writer proposed "that commissioners be sent to examine the land titles of the colonists, and that those [lacking authentic titles] be driven across the Sabine by an armed force." Strong talk this—of raising an army to chase people eastward when the Mexicans were marching from the west[1]

However, the writer was aware of the presence of the Mexicans. "It will be seen that the blow has already been struck," he concluded, "and that success has attended our arms in the first engagement. The alarm is sounded, and the friends of the Constitution, and of constitutional liberty, are called upon to rally for the defence of their families, their homes, and their possessions."

Such, briefly, was the character of *The Telegraph and Texas Register*. Probably every man has dreamed at one time of owning a newspaper, and here were three tired men realizing that dream—Gail Borden, teacher; Thomas H. Borden, surveyor; and Joseph Baker, translator. None of the three brought any practical newspaper experience to their new post, which certainly is no recommendation for founding a successful publication. But each was a man of diverse talents, each was a young man barely in his thirties, and each was a man adaptable to the requirements of any particular situation.

The normal reaction of most young men who had just fingered the damp, inky fruition of months of planning and hoping and waiting would have been to seek escape from the tension through excessive merriment or through complete relaxation—Lord Northcliffe slept twenty-four straight hours after the first issue of his *Daily Mail* appeared. But it is doubtful whether these three men were swept with a feeling of sufficient relief to indulge such reactions, for other problems remained—personal problems. What Gail Borden did that evening is known. He wrote Colonel Austin a long letter which must have kept him at the office until Penelope despaired of his ever coming home. He told Austin of the war effort at San Felipe and asked his advice about publishing certain letters. He told Austin how Colonel Ward, who was to have distributed the *Telegraph,* refused to wait when it became evident that the paper would not be issued by midafternoon and how the partners had to hire an express to overtake Ward's carriage with the papers. And he told Austin that although he felt that his first duty belonged to the land office, yet "I am willing to contribute what I can."

But it was wartime, and young men are the sinew of war, and war furnished the gravest problem of all; for young men who have not answered the call to war lose standing with the other young men who have, with their wives and mothers, and often with themselves. This problem, then, faced the partners, sobering their natural elation over their printed offspring, as Gail Borden's letter indicates:

Mr. Baker says he ought to be in the Camp brother Tom says he also should be with you but indeed if they leave we never can get along with the paper which is of more importance than their services can be in the Camp

They say it will be said, we do not turn out. But we work night and day—Mr Toy has scarcely slept for two night.

You can represent the matter if you hear anything said. I shall endeavor to prevent their going, for my maxim is Do the best for my country, praise or no praise.[4]

[4] *Ibid*, 170–71

87

As time passed, more and more of the work of continuing the paper seems to have devolved upon Gail Borden. Both of the younger partners soon found the call to arms irresistible and were absent for long periods, and after the beginning Thomas Borden looked on the *Telegraph* as a secondary enterprise, perhaps the more so because he was shoved in as a partner in a last-minute substitution for his youngest brother, John.

Except for the early days of *The Telegraph and Texas Register*, Gail Borden gave himself completely to the fledgling paper, nursing it, pushing it, fondling it as one would a reluctant child. From time to time he accepted other chores, but apparently the newspaper always came first. The tone of much of the writing in the *Telegraph* during the spring and fall of 1836, the turn of phrases, and the thought processes certainly mirror the style and the moral flavor of this transplanted Yankee with the high-geared mind and the restless body.

San Felipe now became an extremely animated town. On the Friday following the first issue of the *Telegraph* the Consultation of all Texas opened there with thirty-one delegates from eight municipalities and towns, and shortly afterwards six more delegates came from the town of Liberty. It was the delegates' duty to decide how far this revolution should be prosecuted, and it was San Felipe's chore to absorb this influx of visitors. Every moment might well be precious, and even such conscientious Sabbath observers as Gail Borden found themselves attending Sunday meetings to form patrols against midnight intruders into horse lots and poultry yards or to elect permanent officers to represent the town at the Consultation.

But none of this activity must prevent the publication of a newspaper, and one week after the first issue appeared the second number of the *Telegraph*, containing an apology for having "been somewhat delayed" because documents and communications were not contributed in time to be set in type.

There were other problems for the new publishers. Texans were on the move, some to the west to join the army, among them *Telegraph* subscribers, leaving the puzzled publishers to admit "we know not where to direct their papers." Because of the uncertainties of travel, exchanges from the United States were also delayed, so that the *Telegraph* was forced to substitute a promise "to serve [its readers] up a collation of the products of different climates" next week in place of any foreign news this week.

Meanwhile, however, there was plenty in Texas to report, and the *Telegraph* tried to publish its share. It told how Gail Borden relinquished his post as secretary of the Permanent Council to C. B. Stewart in a Sunday meeting held in the windowless, floorless, cheerless "Council Hall," a hewn-log cabin whose builders had been content to erect four walls, a roof, and nothing more, leaving the cracks unchinked to catch and amplify the roar of the fall winds until even Sam Houston's impassioned oratory might not be heard.

As its contribution to shaping public opinion the October 17 *Telegraph* ran an editorial headed "Texas patriotism," testifying to the singleness of purpose of all progressive Texans:

> We know one man who has taken the leaden pipes out of his aqueduct to furnish ammunition for the army; and a number of others who have melted up their clock weights (thus stopping, as it were, "the wheels of time"). . . . Even the ladies, bless their souls, [would] enter the ranks, and fight *manfully* for the rights of the country. In short, but one spirit pervades the whole population, and that is a determined resolution to free themselves from military usurpation and tyranny, or perish in the attempt.

It is doubtful whether the proprietors suspected how prophetic were those last words, for many Texans were to "perish in the attempt" before the enemy would be driven from the soil and the whole of San Felipe itself would be one of the victims.

Issue succeeded issue, now on time, now late. Because there was almost no other means of learning what was happening on the battlefield, each issue must have been received greedily. And with Gail Borden for a publisher the *Telegraph* held an additional advantage. Close always to Austin, Borden could receive letters from the commander-in-chief himself which would be not only authoritative but up to the minute.

At least one San Felipe citizen, however, felt that the editor did not always exercise proper discretion in quoting Austin. On October 21, R. R. Royall, president of the Permanent Council, complained to Austin that the commander's discouraging letter of the week previous had found its way into the *Telegraph.* "I had no intention of Publishing that Letter. . . . Mr. Borden . . . borried your letters under promise to examine them and with hold from the Press such as was Improper for publication when I found it had gone out in the Paper, it was too Late to recall it."[5]

Not all news was bad, and when it was "flatering" Baker and Bordens broadcast it. In their October 31 issue under a headline of "VICTORY! VICTORY!" appeared the account of an action near Bexar between four hundred Mexicans and ninety "colonial troops" under James Fannin, in which the Mexicans lost "about fifty men" and the Texans "one man wounded."

"Almost every day brings with it cheering intelligence from some quarter," trumpeted another article in the same issue. Great excitement had arisen in the United States when news of the Texas revolt reached there. Sixty-five volunteers, "well armed and equipped," had arrived from New Orleans; "seventy or eighty" more had started overland, and "many more" were about to start.

And though few persons considered independence for Texas the *Telegraph* gave its readers a rallying song if they should need one. It began like this:

NEW YANKEE DOODLE.
St. Ana did a notion take, that he must rule the land, sir:
The church and he forthwith agree to publish the command, sir.
In Mexico none shall be free—
The people are too blind to see;
They cannot share the liberty
Of Yankee Doodle Dandy

And so on for seven more verses. No author was listed.

But the breakup of the revolutionary government, the massacres at the Alamo and Goliad in March, the "Runaway Scrape," and the advance of Santa Anna beyond the Colorado and the Brazos across four-fifths of Texas lay ahead, so that the jubilation of Texans and of the *Telegraph's* proprietors proved premature. Although the early progress of the war was eminently satisfactory from a Texan point of view, especially after Cós capitulated at San Antonio in December to a volunteer force under Milam,[6] Santa Anna had only begun to fight.

[5] *Ibid*, 199

A month earlier, on November 14, the *Telegraph* had sensed some of the danger: "Should this expedition [against San Antonio] fail, our enemy will take courage, and the theatre of war may be in the heart of our country, and instead of our troops [being] fed at the expense of the enemy, the whole burden of supplying our own forces, and those of the enemy will fall upon our citizens. But by meeting the enemy in their own country, we avoid the devastating effects of the war, we preserve our dwellings from the flames, and our families from the unrelenting cruelty of an unprincipled and infuriated soldiery."

But the expedition against San Antonio did succeed, and to most Texans its success signified an early conclusion to a brief war. At home, despite a spring drouth which had extended into early summer, crops were excellent. To harvest them, men began to drop out of the army and return home in wholesale numbers. Seemingly unmindful of the war clouds lowering on the horizon, daily routine went ahead, as people's active interest in the war grew or fell away in direct proportion to their actual participation in its events.

Something of this attitude is reflected in the *Telegraph*, which found time to deliver disquisitions on all sorts of unrelated subjects having nothing whatsoever to do with the war.

About seven o'clock on Sunday night, October 11, citizens of San Felipe looking to the northwestward could discern an intense light in the sky. When nearly a week later it could still be seen, the *Telegraph* decided to inform its patrons of the nature of this phenomenon:

This is probably the [comet] predicted by Dr. Halley to make its appearance this year, and approach very near the earth. . . . We know not what are the superstitious notions of the Mexicans upon this subject, but we recollect that, at the time of the last great eclipse of the sun, we asked one who appeared to be a man of some intelligence, what he thought of it. He answered that he considered it a harbinger of war, and he was apprehensive that this country would be involved in it. His prediction is verified, and he, no doubt, confirmed in his own superstition.

⁶ After Milam was killed in the storming of San Antonio in one of Texas' most dramatic incidents, Gail Borden, John Rice Jones, Governor Henry Smith, John H Money, and James Cochrane were named on December 27, 1835, to erect a monument to the warrior's memory G. Talbot, "John Rice Jones," *The Quarterly*, Vol. XXXV, No 2 (October, 1931), 148.

The advent of a new town on the tidewater of the Neches was noted favorably. "It has received the name of Beaumont, which strikes our fancy as very appropriate." Like newspapermen of all ages, the proprietors of the *Telegraph* were civic and national boosters, taking obvious pride in their country and its men, as for example their boast that "No country offers greater inducements to industry, or promises a surer reward"—an assertion that could have been lifted from almost any twentieth-century Texas daily newspaper.

The *Telegraph* believed in its function to instruct. Regarding Irish potatoes, generally thought to thrive only in the early part of the season, the *Telegraph* stated flatly: "This is a mistake. We have specimens taken from the garden contiguous to our office, weighing one pound each." In the course of its moral instruction, the *Telegraph* warned that drunkenness might well lead to "spontaneous combustion of the human body. . . . The constant drinking of ardent spirits saturates the whole fabric of the body, making it so highly inflammable, that under certain circumstances, where a flame is contiguous, the catastrophe of burning to death ensues." No professional prohibitionist ever conjured a more horrible fate! Perhaps it was Gail Borden's reaction against a cold and stormy November.

Running throughout the columns of the *Telegraph* are commentaries on the political scene which would indicate one of two things: either Gail Borden had devoured the writings of Thomas Paine or had been considerably exposed to their teachings, or else he possessed a remarkably similar method of thinking and of stating the results of his ratiocinations. Perhaps the answer is neither—under similar conditions patriots may merely respond in the same manner; or again the writings of Paine may have been so generally familiar as to become the platitudes of the day, with Borden lacking a sufficiently original mind to coin his own phrases. Whatever the answer, sufficient reason does exist to refer to Borden as the Tom Paine of the Texas Revolution. If he be accused of being a lesser Paine, the reply may be that the Texas Revolution was only a small-scale American Revolution, requiring therefore a writer somewhat less than grand though every bit as simple and direct in approach.

In *The Crisis*, Paine warned that "We are a young nation, just stepping upon the stage of public life, and the eye of the world is upon us to see how we act." Gail Borden's version is somewhat longer: "At this time . . . when Texas is beginning to act for herself, extreme caution, prudence, and moderation should characterize every step that is taken; and the wishes of the citizens should . . . be consulted, so as to perpetuate that harmony which now so fortunately prevails, in the cause of liberty, and the rights of man. . . . Texas is now placed in a situation where one imprudent measure might involve her in entire ruin. The eyes of the world are upon her."

Again in *The Crisis*: "Not an ability ought now to sleep, that can produce but a mite to the general good, nor even a whisper to pass that militates against it." Less eloquent but equally earnest is Borden's call· "This is a time which requires the exertions of every man. . . . We must do what we can for ourselves."

Files of the *Telegraph* furnish an excellent account of the difficulties of newspapering in a pioneer community, for the proprietors were never reticent about discussing their problems. It was a land where money was tight, labor scarce, materials hard to procure, and transportation uncertain and hazardous. *Telegraph* policy did not include concealment of any of these impediments to success.

Coyly the *Telegraph* reminded its readers of the money situation in its October 26 issue: "Every one must be aware that the expense of an establishment of this kind is considerable, and that funds are necessary to carry it on properly. . . . we hope that those of [our subscribers] who have money for which they have no other use, will bear us in mind."

In the same issue the labor problem is hinted by an advertisement calling for "An active and intelligent boy, as an apprentice to the printing business." Seven weeks later, in the issue of December 12, the advertisement was still running. No boy was available.

By November 21 the newspaper was commanding enough attention that its entire eighth page was composed of advertisements. Such a condition was still a long way from prosperity, as included in these advertisements were a number originating with the business office of the *Telegraph* itself, while the inside pages contained no advertisements at all. One-eighth advertising space and seven-eighths editorial matter does not approach the 40 per cent–60 per cent ratio that most modern newspapers consider a necessary minimum for their financial success.

Delays being unavoidable, apologies were frequent. On December 12, 1835, the lateness of the *Telegraph* was attributed to "a press of public printing" and a dwindling stock of printing materials. The quantity of paper used had been so much greater than had been anticipated that the publishers were forced to reduce their newspaper to four pages. Until a new stock of paper arrived, the readers "must content themselves with such as we find it in our power to give them."

Two weeks elapsed before Baker and Bordens found it in their "power to give" the public another edition. Again it contained only four pages. Shortly after, three weeks passed without an edition, the explanation being once more a "want of hands" and "want of paper."

With all these troubles overhanging, Thomas Borden and then Joseph Baker elected to join the army. Thomas went first in October, remaining until almost Christmas, when he returned "quite poorly ... from exposure and cold."[7] In camp Tom Borden spent part of his time writing "pressingly" for Gail to join him, but the elder brother believed his duty lay in San Felipe—"If I should go, the business could not go on," he wrote Austin.[8] Expenses were $250 a month, yet less than $75 had been collected from subscriptions and nothing for public printing. Again he sought out Austin's aid:

I have written to brother Tom, that without we had more materials in our printing establishment, it was impossible to do work to any extent that it was all important, as well for ourselves as the interest of the Country to send an agent immediately to N. Orleans for the purpose of getting what articles we want, and extend our subscription list, without a great patronage, can not stand the heavy expense of carrying on the office—We have sufficient weight of type, but not proportion Mr. Baker can not be spared, because he is our only translator—I can not go for the reasons of my pressing business, as well of other things, as the improvement of the printing office. This is, therefore, to request you give Thomas a furlough so soon as you think he can be spared that he may go to the U S for the purposes above named .... I discovered from his last letter he was determined not to come home till after the campaign; and unless you thought he could better serve the country by

[7] Moses Lapham to Amos Lapham, December 26, 1835, in Heminger Papers.
[8] Barker (ed.), *The Austin Papers*, III, 228.

forwarding our printing establishment, he would not consent to come from the field.[9]

No possibility for raising operating funds was overlooked. Tired of waiting for the impecunious provisional government of Texas to pay for its public printing, the harried *Telegraph* operators petitioned the Permanent Council, Texas' real governing body, to come to their aid. They presented the government a bill for $593.75 for printing from October 3 through November 19, including fourteen separate items, among them five hundred copies of the governor's message for $60.00. Accompanying the bill was a petition explaining the situation facing the proprietors:

Because of the present unsettled state of the country the publishers could not realize the benefits they had anticipated, the petition began, pointing out the heavy expenses, the complete lack of pay for job work, the almost total absence of subscriptions collections, and the necessity for paying workmen "at the highest rates known in the United States" in order to hold any labor at all. In some instances, the firm claimed, it had been so zealous that it had even neglected its paper to execute promptly state printing. If pecuniary assistance were not forthcoming soon, it promised, the firm must discontinue. Cognizant of "the great expense of maintaining the war &c.," Baker and Bordens nevertheless felt that "the burden should be equally divided." Money would not be necessary: an order on Hotchkiss and Company or the Committee on Texas Affairs of New Orleans would serve as well as money.[10]

But no relief from the government was immediately in sight, and before long the *Telegraph* would be suggesting means of raising money for the government rather than asking the government for funds for itself. Meanwhile the proprietors would have to struggle along on an overextended credit, doing the best they could, which sometimes meant doing without. The newspaper which a New York man assured Austin might "easily do more for your cause, *than a park* of Artillery"[11] would have to limp along unaided, to live alone or to die alone.

[9] *Ibid*, 239
[10] Baker & Bordens to Governor and Council of Texas, November 24, 1835, in Public Printing Papers, Archives of the Texas State Library, Austin, Texas.
[11] H. Meigs to S. F. Austin, November 27, 1835, in Austin Papers

The art of newspapering as understood by Baker and Bordens received its share of attention in the early numbers of the *Telegraph*. Style and method were of secondary concern to politics and free interchange of opinion. So far as the former were concerned, the only demands were that contributions "should at least be written in a hand which can be deciphered by the printer, and if intended for English, should not transgress the rules of grammar so widely, as to leave room for a doubt whether they are written in a foreign language or not."

Borden considered the press "one of the greatest and most important inventions of man," while recognizing that unbridled it "may be rendered a curse instead of a blessing." While its powerful influence could be employed to improve the lot of man, the press could also be diverted from its enlightening course to become "a scourge of mankind. To render the press useful it should never be prostituted to misrepresentation, slander, and vituperation."

Twentieth-century scandal sheets, tabloid and full size, would have made no appeal to Borden. "Private quarrels can never be interesting to the community at large," he wrote. "It would be an unjust taxation upon [the readers'] patience, to trouble them with the private concerns of others.

"The columns of the Telegraph are at all times open to the free and impartial discussion of political subjects; but can never stoop to low and scurrilous abuse of private character." This policy was not mere theory on Borden's part, to be cast aside in the interest of circulation and expediency. On December 12 he asserted that a "number of communications have been received, which are too personal to be interesting to our readers in general, and which, consequently, cannot be admitted." Two weeks later he warned correspondents again that no abuse of individuals would be permitted· "If 'Julius Caesar' wishes to publish his views through the medium of the Telegraph," he wrote, "he must be more decorous in his language."

During Borden's connection the *Telegraph* scrupulously avoided taking sides or giving advice, a policy which was abandoned with a vengeance after Dr. Moore assumed the editorship in 1837. Even on such an important subject as a declaration of independence, Borden tried to remain aloof, although he himself had favored separation from Mexico long before Austin and other moderates had conceded the necessity for such action.

"It has never been the object of this paper to forestall public opinion, and to crowd upon the people our *own* views in a matter so important as that touching a change of government," Borden wrote only eleven days before the Texas Declaration of Independence was signed. "We have endeavored to present facts, and the publication of public documents, believing that a community composed of Americans would draw just conclusions, and act correctly when in possession of all the evidence. To have advocated a declaration of independence, before understanding the true situation of the Mexican government, and without any assurance of assistance from the United States, would have been a rashness to which others as well as ourselves might have fallen victims."

He went on: "Few have doubted the right to declare independence [but] The expediency of such a measure, many as well as ourselves have doubted." Independence? Desirable, yes, but be certain it is what you want and what you can obtain. Gail Borden refused to be stampeded, or to stampede.

However heavy his responsibilities, a man before the public almost invariably receives first thought when a new position is created. "He has handled his job well; let's reward him with more work," the appointive powers seem to reason. So in late October when the governing body of Texas decided that the depleted public coffers must be replenished by enforcing collections of land dues, stamped paper, and so on, Gail Borden—newspaper publisher, keeper of the land office, chairman pro tem of San Felipe's committee of safety, etc., etc.—found himself with another title and another position—collector for the Department of Brazos. Pay—unspecified. Duties—onerous; or if not onerous, then unrewarding.

The appointment was made on Wednesday, October 21, 1835. On the following Monday the *Telegraph* carried Borden's notice that he was prepared to receive and receipt all land dues. Texas needed money, and quickly. Whether this expedient would prove sufficiently large and timely, no one, except perhaps Austin, knew. Certainly funds materialized slowly. At the end of ten days Borden could send Austin only $70—"all I have collected." Previously he had turned over to the Permanent Council $58.30 from land dues.

From then on until he relinquished his post in 1837, Borden collected for the government of Texas. Not infrequently performance of his duties puzzled him, sending him to the governmental heads for advice, as on January 13, 1836, when he asked the General Council to decide whether a man could pay all installments of his land dues at once. When sometimes the authorities failed to satisfy his requests, Borden stubbornly refused to pursue his collections. In the *Telegraph* of February 27, 1836, he advertised his attitude: "The operation of receiving public dues on land . . . is so complicated . . . that further payments will not be received, till I can obtain, from the authorities, more definite instructions."

Borden's report of July 31, 1836, shows that he had received less than $800. His total might have been larger, he explained, but he had heard from only one deputy and many persons had neglected to endorse the treasury orders with which they paid their debts, so that he could not include their dues as paid. Five months later his report reveals a total collection of $6,836.32, which probably includes the amount reported in July.[12] Not a considerable sum when compared with the cost of the war, but still important to a government fighting that war and then operating an administration on a shoestring.

But if the war brought an increase in Borden's responsibilities on the one hand, on the other it compensated in part by a lessening of other duties. Business of the land office fell off to a whisper, while Borden's corps of surveyors found it more profitable or exciting to join the army.

Privately, he continued his interest in land matters. On November 17 he purchased five hundred acres for himself on the east bank of the Colorado above Bastrop, land that indicates his faith in the country as fully as any words could have, since the land lay on the far frontier, exposed alike to Indian depredations and Mexican invasions. For Austin he assumed the rôle of attorney, in place of Father Muldoon, to complete the sale of eleven leagues of land to Peter W. Grayson. He further served the Texas leader as "special

[12] Petitions, Archives of the Texas State Library. Barker (ed), *The Austin Papers*, III, 200, 228 See also Barker, *The Finances of the Texas Revolution*, 614, 625. Although appointed October 21, Borden did not post his $25,000 bond until December 31, 1835. William Menefee, Thomas F. McKinney, and Charles B Stewart were his securities Bonds and Oaths, Republic of Texas, Archives of the Texas State Library

TELEGRAPH,
AND TEXAS REGISTER.

VOL. I. San Felipe de Austin, Saturday, October 10, 1835. NO. 1.

PUBLISHED EVERY SATURDAY, BY
BAKER & BORDENS,
SAN FELIPE DE AUSTIN.

TERMS OF SUBSCRIPTION

POETRY.

FROM THE ITALIAN

LIFE OF ROBERT MORRIS

Page one of the first issue of "Baker & Bordens'"
Telegraph and Texas Register

University of Texas Newspaper Collection

agent to collect any debts due" Austin when the latter relinquished his army command in late December to go to the States to raise money for Texas.[13]

Gail Borden's newspaper then may have been his first interest, but it was not his only one. It was never to be his nature to concentrate on one thing to the exclusion of all others, because one endeavor suggested another; or if not that, his very considerable energy left him unfit for idleness, even in his declining years when his goal had been reached and success and affluence were his. In this period when he was still only thirty-four years old, it was to be the same story. In this respect his last year as a Mexican subject was no different from the next year when he would become a Texas citizen, or from a decade later when he became an American again.

But now he and Texas were in their last weeks of pretended Mexican allegiance. Very soon, and quite abruptly, he and other Texans would become an independent people, forming their own sovereign state to govern themselves, to rise or fall, to prosper or withdraw—without aid from either an aggressively expanding United States or a "forever revolutionizing" Mexico.

A revolution which had begun as a protest against government by military decree had outgrown a mere desire to return to the principles of the constitution of 1824. Everywhere in Texas sentiment was swinging to complete severance of the Mexican tie, to nothing less than independence. News that Santa Anna was returning with six thousand troops, instead of frightening Texans, made them more resolute to stand alone.

Once Santa Anna arrived before San Antonio on February 23, 1836, to begin his siege of the Alamo, there was no turning back. The outcome must be decisive: complete victory—or complete defeat. How nearly it was disaster and how triumphantly it became victory form an indelible chapter in the saga of America, showering sprinklings of vicarious glory on twentieth-century office-bound Texans, ease-seeking Californians, and ancestor-worshiping New Englanders alike.

To the individuals caught in the vortex of blood and conquest and confusion there was no glory, only enduring anxiety and per-

---

[13] Barker (ed.), *The Austin Papers*, III, 238-39. Deed Record Book, A, Bastrop County, Texas, 493-95. Record Book, P, Galveston County, Texas, 190-92.

severance commingled with alternating flashes of fear, hope, and despair. Two men trying to keep alive a newspaper knew nothing of glory, especially when successive blows threatened to flatten their very last hopes of a decent survival. However, man is a tenacious creature, holding on most strongly when his line is tenuous and his grasp desperate. And the Bordens, Gail and Thomas, were men, and like distressed men everywhere they held on and endured despite their buffetings, because they knew nothing else to do. How they persisted, how they surmounted the successive shocks of war provides part of the Texas drama of the next several weeks.

*We promise the public of our beloved country,
that our press will never cease its operations til
our silence shall announce   that there is no
more in Texas a resting place for a free press.*
—[Gail Borden] *Telegraph and Texas Register,*
April 14, 1836

VIII

The Voice of Texas
1836-1837

ALL OVER TEXAS, talk of independence was in the air, mothered by desperation as much as by enthusiasm. Daily it was becoming more apparent that the Texans walled up in the Alamo were caught in a deathtrap and that only the unlikely mercy of a sanguine Santa Anna could save them. If the expected annihilation at the Alamo did occur, it would behoove all Texans to the eastward to ensure that such sacrifice should not prove futile. Santa Anna's insistence on reducing the Alamo defenders before pressing onward meant that other Texans would have one, two, three, no one knew how many weeks to prepare for the inevitable advance of the Napoleon of the West.

Texas stiffened. The hastily formed Texas government, split hopelessly for almost two months, called a convention for March 1 to meet at tiny Washington-on-the-Brazos, twenty miles up the Brazos from San Felipe, to form a positive provisional government. It was almost predetermined that the convention would declare for unequivocal separation from Mexico, thus hoping to whet American appetites for Texas land and thereby obtain men, money, and arms that otherwise might not be forthcoming.

Companies of militia were formed, provisioned, and dispatched westward. On the last Saturday in February such a company under the captaincy of Mosely Baker was organized at San Felipe, with John P. Borden, who had served Texas earlier around Goliad, as its first lieutenant. Two days later the company was mustered, ready to march to the front, waiting only for the ceremonial presentation of its colors.

Gail Borden made the presentation. It was one of the first flags of Texas, including in its design an English jack showing the origins of the Anglo-Americans, thirteen stripes recognizing that most Texans came from the United States, one star representing Texas—"the only state in Mexico retaining the least spark of the light of liberty"—and three colors representing recent membership in the tricolored confederacy of Mexico. It was, said the *Telegraph*, a "flag of Texas and of independence . . . the whole flag historic."

Besides presenting flags, Gail Borden had other things to do. There was, in fact, plenty of work for everyone. On Sunday before the flag ceremony a committee had been formed to procure arms and provisions. Two days later the first wagonload was rolling westward, while a second wagon was being loaded. " 'Go ye (every town in Texas), and do likewise,' " urged the *Telegraph*. "Nothing but promptness and the greatest energy will now save Texas."

Three of the *Telegraph's* printers joined the army, but the San Felipe standing committee obtained their release that they might keep the press operating. Edward Gritten, an Englishman who had come to Texas as Almonte's secretary, was taken on as translator. Proudly the proprietors announced that "having procured a sufficiency of hands," they were prepared to execute any order, "either at night or day."

But the issue of March 5, 1836, which had carried the jubilant announcement, contained more electrifying news. At the bottom of the right-hand column of the last page was an arresting headline:

TEXAS HAS DECLARED HER
INDEPENDENCE.

Apparently news of the declaration was received barely in time to shove it into the March 5 edition, for only the briefest excerpt was printed, including, of course, those pregnant words: "We therefore . . . do hereby resolve and declare, that our political connexion with the Mexican nation has forever ended, and that the people of Texas, do now constitute a FREE SOVEREIGN, and Independent Republic . . . and conscious of the rectitude of our intentions, we fearlessly and confidently commit the issue to the decision of the Supreme arbitor of the destinies of nations."

Brave words these, and to contemporary Texans and sympathetic Americans, thrilling words.

Simply declaring independence, however, irrevocable though it was, proved nothing beyond a desire to be free of Mexico's overlordship. The declaration confirmed Santa Anna's belief that the whole issue was one of separation and that devotion to constitutional principles was but a thin disguise which he had penetrated from the beginning; so that instead of weakening his pursuit of the Texas forces, the declaration strengthened his determination to humble these arrogant intruders who would dare to wrest land from his country. If Texas wanted to be independent, she would have to prove her right by blood. The hardest fighting—and the greatest tragedy—lay close ahead.

When news first reached the Bordens that delegates were proposing meeting at Washington to form a new government, they considered moving their press up the Brazos to that town, dropping the idea only after hearing that a press had already been established. However, this report was erroneous, and the early days of March, 1836, found the *Telegraph* proprietors wishing they had followed their February impulse. In addition to the newspaper they had broadsides and circulars to print and distribute, delayed always by the government's being in one place and their being in another. Colonel Travis's last impassioned plea from the Alamo, ordered printed on a Sunday morning, was not received at the *Telegraph* office until eleven o'clock Tuesday morning. The afternoon was spent setting it up and a thousand copies were run off that night, but then "we could get no person to carry it to Washington till Thursday." There were similar occurrences almost daily.

It was too late to move to Washington, as the transfer would lose a week or more when minutes were so valuable. "We have already labored under disadvantages to be met with in a place so far removed from mercantile and mechanical transaction" without hauling away to a smaller, more remote village, Gail Borden observed. The *Telegraph* could suggest only a partial solution—employ an express to work full time carrying documents from and to the convention. Before this or any other plan could be placed in operation, however, the convention had adjourned and the governing officials it had established had flown south and east in the van of the advancing enemy.

In their haste to meet the government's printing demands the Bordens made one mistake that must have been most embarrassing. On the handbill containing the Declaration of Independence and its signers, they omitted the names of two of the signers, the two men being the generally credited authors of the document, George C. Childress, and one of Texas' most important *empresarios*, Sterling C. Robertson. In the *Telegraph* the Bordens explained: "We feel unable to atone for [the omission]; and have this only to offer as an apology, that it was executed in too much haste, and principally done in the night."

The charge that the Declaration of Independence had been adopted too quickly (it was adopted unanimously on March 2, the second day of the convention) was dismissed airily by the Bordens —"Despatch of business unparalleled in legislative bodies," the *Telegraph* noted approvingly. "The alarming situation of our country admitted of no delay. Some may think more time should have been employed on the instrument which is to sever Texas from the body of a great nation. . . . we think '*that* point is reached at which forbearance ceases to be a virtue.' "

The Bordens were willing to implement their written support of an independent government with action. Gail proposed that landowning Texans "hypothecate" one-half their holdings to bolster the fading Texas credit. He and Thomas would start the movement, Gail pledging one league and Tom four leagues. This was no sacrifice, Gail Borden explained, because if Texas received no financial and military relief, her lands would be worth nothing anyway.

A few nights after the March 12 issue a lone, grim messenger came riding hell-for-leather into sleepy San Felipe, whose usually unadorned harshness shone soft and pleasant in the relaxing reflection of the bright spring night. The messenger brought tidings that soon shook San Felipeans from their uncomfortable houses like ants being brushed off a picnic spread. From one house came a scream— "Miss Cummings!"—and everyone knew. She was Colonel Travis's fiancée, and now she, too, had learned that Travis and almost every other defender of the Alamo were dead.

All night long men talked in groups in the dusty streets, while women shivered in doorways as the chill March wind made light of their heavy nightclothes. This news was catastrophic, the worst of the revolution. Men tried to recall the whereabouts of absent relatives and friends. Could they have joined the Alamo band?

One implication was distinct. The fall of the Alamo would not satisfy Santa Anna's desire for revenge. On he would move, as inexorably as a Brazos flood. If God or the badly organized Texans did not intervene, he would reach the Colorado soon—and, after that, the Brazos. That would mean San Felipe.

That night many men resolved to pack what they could, take their families, and flee. When close behind the messenger came terrified householders from the west, urgency strengthened their resolve, and San Felipe began to depopulate as if the Asiatic cholera had struck. To be safe, Gail Borden sent his collector's papers ahead to his father in Fort Bend, but he preferred to remain in San Felipe, explaining, "My presence [is] so essential here."[1] For the panic of others he had only scorn: "Some of us who could not find it in our power to leave home to go to the field, can with much despatch strike tents and move easterly," he wrote. The Alamo defeat was "lamentable," he conceded, "yet so glorious to Texas . . . that we shall never cease to celebrate . . . the Thermopylae of Texas."

Hearing that Houston's army had dropped back to the Colorado, burning as it retreated, the *Telegraph* was approving and defiant: "We do consider that it was the only safe course . . . . The laying waste of all the property which could not be removed will convince our enemies that if they overrun our territory they will get no booty."

In the afternoon of March 17, Houston reached the Colorado. Nine days later he resumed his retreat, his plan being apparently to avoid direct contact with Santa Anna until he was forced into an encounter or until the Mexican was caught in an error. In the meantime the Texas government, quaffing great draughts of the pervading panic, had taken flight from Washington to Harrisburg, a small hamlet long since consumed by present-day Houston. Here the

---

[1] Gail Borden to B[ailey] Hardeman, March 24, 1836, in Comptroller's Letters Customs, 1836–45, Archives of the Texas State Library (hereafter cited as Comptroller's Letters).

officials found few facilities, and no printing press to publish their hasty proclamations.

The newly elected president, David G. Burnet, decided that Harrisburg must have a press, and he knew the man he wanted to bring it. To F. C. Gray, who had recently suspended his Brazoria *Republican*, he promised the government's entire business. Gray answered promptly: "I am ready . . . at any moment you will send."[2]

But something happened, and in the end it was *The Telegraph and Texas Register*, not the Brazoria *Republican*, which set up in Harrisburg. Why Gray was dropped has never been explained. An undated letter from Gail Borden, scrawled hurriedly about the same time as the Burnet-Gray exchange, announced that the Bordens would move but revealed no official encouragement of such a move: "It has become necessary to remove our press I shall endeavor to put it over the river to day—If the government can send a team for it we will set it up in Harrisburg—It will require a large waggon & team—I have none—.... If no team comes, it must lie in the bottom— Our Army consists of upward of One thousand.—"[3]

The story of these last hectic days in San Felipe, of the Bordens' determination to remain in San Felipe when everyone else was deserting, is told at some length in the *Telegraph* of January 18, 1837:

All these things passed and were noticed in our paper; and pursuing, undismayed, our duties, and prosecuting our labors at San Felipe, believing that so long as a paper should be printed *west* of the Brazos, the people *east* of it would not take the alarm. And though deprived of the services of Mr. Joseph Baker . . . we endeavored to cheer and encourage our countrymen to the contest. . . .

Our army, on its retreat, reached San Felipe on the 27th, at night; till now we had no intention to cross the Brazos with our press, which with the aid of Capt. Baker's company, left at that place, we effected on the 30th March, but not without the satisfaction of being in the rear guard—the last to consent to move, we were resolved not to be in front.

On the 1st of April our main army at Groce's. All Texas, west of the Brazos, deserted and a prey to the destroyer—San Felipe burned—a

[2] D. G Burnet to F. C. Gray, March 25, 1836, in Executive Record Book, March–October, 1836, Archives of the Texas State Library. F. C. Gray to [D. G. Burnet], March 26, 1836, in Domestic Correspondence, 1836, Archives of the Texas State Library.

[3] Gail Borden to D. G. Burnet, n.d., in Public Printing Papers.

dismal smoke arising from a bed of ashes, heightened the gloom.[4] At this juncture, we were irresolute, whether to attempt, for the present, the publication. The destruction of our buildings, and with them much of the valuable furniture which we could not remove, the great difficulty of procuring teams, and the preparation of new buildings, after having expended most of our means in putting up the establishment, the payment of journeymen, having received but little from our subscribers, and nothing for the public printing, we felt for a moment discouraged in carrying on the further publication of the paper.

About them the two brothers "could see nothing but ruin." But while pondering this cheerless contingency the Bordens received an invitation to remove their *Telegraph*—"the last and only medium of publication [the Texas government] could possibly obtain"—to Harrisburg, and the Bordens accepted, "determined to spend the last dollar in the cause we had embarked: we believed, the people must have information, without which no concert of action could be had.

"The difficulty and labor of removing so heavy an establishment, were not the greatest inconvenience," the lugubrious recapitulation continued. "The team employed in conveying it to Harrisburgh, being detained to haul public property to the army, our families were compelled to flee from Fort Bend . . . without the means of taking even their necessary apparel."

And so the Bordens, impoverished by the destruction at San Felipe and Fort Bend, prepared to issue their newspaper from another town. Because of the widespread confusion, delays were inevitable. Neither Sam Houston nor Santa Anna aided in allaying the situation, Houston forever withdrawing and the Mexican Napoleon following implacably. But despite the disorder of a half-heroic, half-scared populace, despite the clutter of frightened refugees indulging themselves in one last stop to catch their breath before fleeing eastward for a Louisiana haven, and despite the jumble caused by inadequate facilities and the erection of new buildings, the Bordens had issue No. 22 ready for printing on April 14. Although on the day before the ad interim government of Texas had designated *The Telegraph and Texas Register* its official press, the paper's increased prestige was not reflected in the four-page, adless edition.

[4] The building housing the *Telegraph* was the first San Felipe building to be put to the torch.

However, buried on the last page of the undistinguished issue was a ringing statement that modern newspapers would have emblazoned in red type: "We promise the public of our beloved country, that our press will never cease its operations til our silence shall announce to them that there is no more in Texas a resting place for a free press, nor for the government of their choice."

No statement of patriotic intention ever met more immediate fulfillment. Before the paper could be struck off, the alarm—"Mexicans!"—was sounded. Archives were grabbed in bunches by startled officials, portable belongings gathered by everyone. There was neither time nor means for removing a bulky printing press. Thus, after only two weeks' residence, Gail Borden, laden with land records, and Thomas H. Borden had to leave Harrisburg, bound probably for Galveston aboard a small steamboat which fortuitously was waiting at Harrisburg.

Before they left, the Bordens instructed their newspaper force to remain, put the paper to bed if possible, and preserve as many numbers as they could. Loyally the three printers stuck to their jobs, the only persons left in deserted Harrisburg, but before the seventh paper could roll off the press, the enemy had arrived and the printers were held for Santa Anna, who himself writes the next paragraph:

"I entered Harrisburg the night of the 15th, lighted by the glare of several houses that were burning, and found only a Frenchman and two North Americans working in a printing shop. They declared *that the so-called president, vice-president,* and other important personages had left at noon for the island of Galveston . . . [and] that the fire had been accidental, they having been unable to put it out; that the families had abandoned their homes by order of Houston, who was at Groce's Crossing with 800 men and two four-pounders."[5]

Historians—and the Bordens—neglected to record the names or the fates of the three printers who continued at their posts in the best journalistic tradition, but to the anonymous trio Texas owes a debt. In the days of disquieted peace that followed, the six copies of the *Telegraph* that the printers doggedly ran off in the face of cer-

[5] A. L. de Santa Anna, "Manifesto Relative to His Operations in the Texas Campaign and His Capture," in C. E. Castañeda (ed. and trans.), *The Mexican Side of the Texan Revolution,* 74.

tain capture were found to contain the only evidence extant of the authority for the ad interim government's existence.

For Santa Anna, capture of the press had only a negative meaning. He could have used it to issue proclamations propagandizing an already distracted people, but instead of turning the press against its sponsors, he merely muzzled it. The silencing was most effective. Into the somber waters of near-by Buffalo Bayou, tumid with spring rains, the Mexicans lowered the heavy machinery, watching the brown current eddy and plash about it, strolling away to town once the swashing waters had adjusted their flow to include this new obstruction planted deep in their bed.[6] The free press of Texas had been stilled.

In six days it was all over. While a four-piece band blared away on a popular love song, "Will You Come to My Bower I Have Shaded for You?" Houston's army of nearly one thousand men at midafternoon on April 21 made an incredible advance to within two hundred yards of the Mexican forces before being spotted, surprised the numerically superior Mexicans, and in eighteen minutes killed 630 and captured 730 of the enemy.[7] It was a complete rout from which only a handful of the Mexicans escaped. The next day, April 22, Santa Anna himself was taken.

With the battle of San Jacinto came peace. But at what a dear price! It was well into May and farmers along the Brazos and Colorado still had to plant their spring crops. Complicating late planting was the further difficulty that barns had been burned, implements stolen, and families scattered—some families did not return from running away until the summer's end. And there remained the threat of roving Mexican forces, some of whom were slow in removing.

For the Bordens peace brought other perplexities. Their press was gone, a casualty of the final week of the war. San Felipe and Fort Bend were destroyed.[8] Santa Anna had burned Harrisburg.

[6] The issue of April 14, 1836, carried the announcement, dated April 5, that Joseph Baker's connection with the paper had been formally severed

[7] Among the participants at San Jacinto were Gail Borden's father-in-law, Eli Mercer, and his two youngest brothers, Paschal and John P. Borden, the latter being the last surviving commissioned officer in the San Jacinto Veterans Association.

[8] San Felipe never recovered When William Bollaert visited it seven years later, he found "it is now a 'deserted Village.' One or two families reside here only,

There was nothing to which to return and no means, but a beginning had to be made somewhere. "I have lost all of my personal property buildings fenceing all burned and I did not even save my own clothes," Tom Borden noted ruefully.

Gail Borden went first to Colonel James Morgan's[9] plantation at New Washington to leave his family and then to Velasco, where, according to Borden, President Burnet and his cabinet on May 9 agreed to advance enough money "to purchase in New Orleans or New York an establishment equal in value to the one destroyed, and pay all charges for freight and insurance to Velasco," this advance to be applied against the Republic's indebtedness to the Bordens. The agreement cannot be found. Certainly it was never made operative.

Borden assembled his notes of indebtedness, obtained a letter of credit from President Burnet, borrowed clothes, and with Thomas shipped to New Orleans to buy a press on credit, but the Texas agent there lacked money and New Orleans merchants placed no faith in the new Texas government.

The people of New Orleans were more helpful: when the Bordens "candidly declared" their plight, their New Orleans subscribers, "notwithstanding the uncertainty of our ultimate success," paid their subscriptions in advance.[10] But it was not enough.

Gail Borden returned to Velasco, where the Texas government had now moved, to present its auditor a bill for $982.50 for public printing for the five weeks prior to March 25, 1836. Included in the itemization were some of Texas' most treasured documents—the Declaration of Independence, 1,000 copies, $97.50; Travis's letter from "Bejar," 1,000 copies, $65.00; fall of the Alamo, 150 copies, $10.00. But the Texas government had no funds, and the Bordens' bill was laid aside.

---

the weeds & bushes have grown up in the streets & unoccupied lots, so that one has a difficulty in tracing his way to the main road on the opposite side of the town " W. Bollaert, "Notes on Texas, 1843-1844," 5, in Ayer Collection, Newberry Library, Chicago.

[9] Morgan's mulatto girl, Emily, is supposed to have been in Santa Anna's tent when the Texans attacked and to have detained the General so long that he emerged from his tent too late to restore order. W. Bollaert, "Texas in 1842," II, 34, in Ayer Collection.

[10] T. H. Borden to Amos Lapham, August 9, 1836, in Heminger Papers.

From New Orleans, Tom Borden turned north, prepared to trade on the brothers' one last asset. He went to "Cincinnaty," mortgaged his and Gail's lands, for speculators would always take a chance on good Texas land, and bought a printing establishment—press plus fonts, paper, ink, and other materials.[11] By June 18 a New Orleans resident was able to write: "Mr. Borden has just arrived . . . with a press; Type &c &c. and no time will be lost in getting down and at work."[12]

The capital of the Republic of Texas was for the time being in Columbia, another inconsequential village sixty miles southwest of present-day Houston. In its position near the west bank of the Brazos and only twenty-five miles inland, it had lain south of the route of the main contending armies, managing thereby to avoid the torch that had been applied to other towns farther north. Its escape, plus its proximity to the port of Velasco at the mouth of the Brazos, were almost its only qualifications. But then, Texas contained no real towns in 1836.

Anticipating the coming of the first Congress of the Republic of Texas to Columbia in October, the Bordens moved there in July. On August 2 they brought out their first issue, ending a 110-day news drouth during which Texas had no medium for disseminating information. Henceforth, the publishers said, their motto would be, "We go for our country."

Between issues Gail Borden occupied himself with land matters and with politics. Houston and Austin were running for the presidency, and Borden, although an admirer of the victorious general, was supporting his long-time friend, Austin. Friendship, however, did not dim his critical eye, and on August 15 he wrote Austin, "I wish to tell you, that from the sign of the times you can not be elected." Suspicion of complicity in earlier land speculation schemes

[11] Public Printing Papers T. H Borden to Amos Lapham, August 9, 1836, in Heminger Papers *Telegraph,* January 27, 1837 Gail Borden to J Pinckney Henderson and Henry Smith, May 23, 1837, in Alamo Museum.

[12] W. C Binkley (ed.), *Official Correspondence of the Texan Revolution, 1835–1836,* II, 797 Why the Bordens did not fish their old press from the Buffalo Bayou and use it has never been explained. Later, another publisher did this very thing, printing the Houston *Morning Star* for several years on the resurrected press. D. C McMurtrie, "Pioneer Printing in Texas," *The Quarterly,* Vol. XXXV, No. 3 (January, 1932), 184.

was the barrier, Borden said, urging Austin to "make a positive denial of having anything to do with . . . land speculation. . . . I would give my life, if at any time it should be found that you were engaged in the affair." Austin, who undoubtedly did not care whether he was elected and who permitted his name to be entered only to avoid an allegation of shirking public responsibility, complied with the suggestion in a long open letter to Borden, which was printed and distributed as a handbill. But Houston had the charm and the reputation and the mystic personality that draws worshipful hosannas from devoted flocks, and his triumph in the election was overwhelming.

Back at newspapering, Gail Borden found that living in a free republic had, if anything, intensified his problems. Money was hard to find, credit had diminished, and vexations were with him daily. The distributor for the *Telegraph* at Brazoria, Velasco, and Quintana slipped off to New Orleans, carrying along one whole week's edition intended for those three towns. In Petersburg, Virginia, an agent for the *Telegraph*, "a man of plausible appearance," had collected money for *Telegraph* subscriptions—and no one had heard of him since.

Since nearly everyone in Texas was moving somewhere or other, keeping track of subscribers' addresses was nearly impossible. Living unsystematically, men naturally neglected to pay subscription bills. In vain the Bordens opined "how thankful we shall be [if the subscribers] will . . . *pay their subscriptions in advance.*"

Still, their faith in the Republic never wavered. Together, Gail and Thomas Borden pledged their land to the value of $5,000 to help contract a loan for Texas, and Thomas pledged an additional $5,000 by himself. Pointing out that corn brought $1.50 a bushel and butter 25 cents a pound in Texas, Gail declared that there was "no country under the sun" where labor was rewarded better than in Texas.

In September, 1836, real misfortune appeared. First, Gail Borden became ill and at least one public document was issued without having been properly proofread. One of the printers died. An article intended for one week's issue was mislaid and not found until after the paper had been put to press. A highly interesting defense of the patriotism of Juan N. Seguin, written in Spanish, had to be omitted for lack of a printer able to compose in Spanish.

The prevailing fever was not through, and though the *Telegraph* was spared further loss among its staff, Tom Borden on September 15 lost his wife, Demis, who left behind two young sons, aged five and three, in addition to her husband. With her death Tom Borden lost his taste for newspaper publishing, and in the October 19 issue the brothers announced their inclination to sell—Gail because of ill health, Tom because of his recent loss. The announcement said further that their business was "in the most prosperous condition [with] more than seven hundred subscribers, and the list rapidly increasing." In addition, there were contracts to print for Congress and other government agencies, so that business was "abundant." "[The] establishment . . . has become a matter of profit; and [the owners] flatter themselves, [of] incalculable advantage to the community."

Actually, Gail confessed later, he and Tom wanted to sell for two other reasons. Many people believed the Bordens were making "enormous profits . . . when our books and the facts admonished us to the contrary," so that the brothers felt it was a good time to sell. In the second place they were just plain tired: "We did not wish to toil so hard, & bear so much responsibility."[13]

However, the right offer was slow in coming. It was the following March before Thomas Borden severed his connection, and even longer before the "senior proprietor" sold his interest.

Columbia, Texas, in October, 1836, assumed many of the characteristics of a Texas oil-boom village of a century later. The influx of the first Congress brought vitality—and problems—to a town that heretofore had lacked any distinctive elements to set it apart from any other frontier community. But now! It was the first capital of an independent nation—the Republic of Texas—and it meant to enjoy its new fame to the fullest. Detractors the world over could point out that the Republic was an uncertain something whose stability, leadership, and credit might be discounted heavily in other

[13] The quotations above appear variously in these sources. Gail and T. H. Borden to D. G. Burnet, September 16, 1836, in Public Printing Papers; Moses Lapham to Amos Lapham, October 1, 1836, in Heminger Papers, and Gail Borden to J. Pinckney Henderson and Henry Smith, May 23, 1837, in Alamo Museum.

nations' capitals and money centers (not even the United States, which had the most to gain by Texas' independence, had recognized Texas), but they could not discourage the citizens of Columbia. Right now, they felt, they were the hub of the universe, the brightest, latest star in the Western firmament.

As always in a boom town, the immediate problem was immorality. "Although I make myself as much at ease as possible with the society I am compelled to associate with," wrote Moses Lapham, "yet their principles and morals are ... most disgusting." The *Telegraph* complained of the "midnight uproar and shameful ... squabbles both by day and night." Loafers filled the public houses. Discharged army volunteers—"the most miserable wretches that the world ever produced"—flocked in, many remaining only long enough to sell their bounty-land scrips for a few nights of gambling and wenching. Housing became critical, and Borden, member of a four-man committee to prepare buildings for the new Congress, accomplished that chore only after "considerable difficulty." Seven weeks later the columns of the *Telegraph* carried a letter threatening the removal of the government to Brazoria or some other unspecified town unless the citizens of Columbia adopted some measures to relieve the housing shortage.

When problems overwhelmed, however, the discontented could always be diverted by staging a fresh scene in the continuing show. Perhaps it would be the arrival of an important personage. On Sunday morning, October 9: "Major-general SAM. HOUSTON, the President elect of our republic, and suite, arrived." On another day it would be an important professional man setting up offices· Dr. T. Leger, late vice-president of the New Orleans Medical Society, is now ready for general practice, "including midwifery, surgery, &c. ... He will keep a general assortment of medicines, perfumery, &c. constantly on hand."

The social side was not neglected. Celebrating the anniversary of the battle of Concepción, Mrs. Jane Long, who had been in Texas longer even than Stephen F. Austin, threw a ball at her Brazoria home downriver. Participating in "that brilliant atchievement" were the President, the former President, members of Congress, and many officers in the battle of San Jacinto. A steamboat left the Columbia docks on Friday afternoon, taking everyone who did not want to

His Excy D. G. Burnet

Our army
having retreated from the Colora
—do it has become necessary to
remove our press, I shall
endeavor to put it over the river
to day — If the government
can send a team for it we will
set it up in ~~Harrisburg~~ — It
will require a large waggon &
team — I have none —
I send Mr Magruder to inform
you — If no team comes, it
must lie in the bottom here

Our army consist of upwards
of one thousand. ——

Your ob't hum Sert.

G. Borden jr

Gail Borden to President Burnet of Texas
in early April, 1836

Archives of the Texas State Library

travel horseback, tied up at Brazoria overnight, and brought back the tired dancers the next morning. Even Congress adjourned for the affair.

Next to dancing, the favorite amusement was horse racing. P. R. Splane was willing to match his horse against "any horse, mare, or gelding" that would be brought to his farm, the Gin Place, "six hundred yards or one mile . . . for any named sum of ten thousand dollars, or under." In November, Jacob Eberly, John Chaffin, and George Brown opened a race track for a three-day meet to be "guided by the Nashville rules and regulations."

In the midst of this glittering, unaccustomed excitement Congress sat for its first session, trying to establish a workable plan to sustain itself and the new Republic. The day after Congress convened Gail Borden abandoned his usual neutrality to point out to Congress in particular and to Texas at large the needs of the Republic. It was a comprehensive article, composed of sober reflections and high aspirations, that might well have served as a framework for the Congressional agenda:

Never was an era more auspicious than the present for commencing a course of legislation. . . . Our country is free from an invading foe. . . . The weather has suddenly changed to a temperature which braces the nerves, and disposes the mind and body to action. There is even something auspicious in the . . . names of the place where the "first Congress of Texas" meets. In the East, the significant appellation of the river (Brazos de Dios—Arms of God) would have furnished in Roman times a good omen for the foundation of an empire; whilst the derivative Columbia has its moral worth, and suggests to us reflections which may not be out of place. . . . The new world did not present to Columbus and to Spain . . . a field more vast . . . than does our infant republic (assailed and *de juris* unacknowledged) to its actual law-givers and executive!

We shall take the liberty of throwing out a few ideas for consideration.

First. Our army should be placed on a respectable footing for warfare—offensive and defensive. . . . The corps of Rangers should be made efficient. . . .

Encouragement, with a fostering hand, held out to our navy. . . . But this arm of our national defence and attack, should be cautious not to infringe on the rights of neutrality; it is at present all important for us to avoid creating enemies to our cause.

The opening and organization of the Land Offices . . . .

Forfeited lands . . . . Legal investigations should be instituted . . . to ascertain who . . . have gone over to the enemy, or have rendered to them any assistance. We suggest that [their] lands, when adjudicated, be put up at public sale . . . ; they would thus sell to immense advantage, and a considerable part of the national debt would be redeemed. . . .

A vigorous prosecution of the war is necessary, in order to compel Mexico, . . . to acknowledge our independence. . . . peace can be procured only by forcing that republic to manifest her utter inability to subdue us, or rather by forcing her, *feelingly*, that Texas can be a thorn in her side during war, and can even endanger the further integrity of her territory. . . .

Indian Affairs: To check the depredations of the hostile tribes, and to secure the neutrality and alliance of those disposed to be friendly. . . .

In the disposition to be made of general Santa Anna's person, we fervently hope that the result will be one most conducive to the welfare of our country.

Fortifications and line of defence . . . .

Public Debt . . . .

It is now time to create a permanent revenue. We shall not always have vacant lands to dispose of. . . . Duties should be assessed and levied on the importation of certain articles of merchandise. . . .

The General Post Office and its ramifications should be put in operation. . . .

Our courts of justice, need organizing. . . . it may be expedient to change the styles of Alcalde, Regidor, &c., for others of English origin.

Establishments of education are much required. . . .

The present department of accountability is in good hands. . . .

The respective offices of the Cabinet are without their functionaries. . . .

Thus, O, People of Texas! have we ventured to point out some of the subjects which . . . will call for legislation in the First Constitutional Congress of our infant Republic.[14]

Congress continued in session until late December. During that time a disproportionate amount of consideration was given over to discussion of petitions from the Bordens asking financial relief, some of which were scrutinized as distrustfully as if they had been applications for loans from the Mexican government.

The Bordens were despairing. Payment on their mortgaged lands was due on December 10, and although the brothers at last may have been profiting from their business, the margin was too thin to meet the mortgages. Minimum running expenses were $144 a week—five printers at $18 a week each; house rent, $8, wood and devil work, $10; and salary to the two brothers, $18 a week each. The thousand dollars' worth of paper bought in the summer was running out. Subscription collections were haphazard; advertising revenue, insufficient. And, instead of retrenching, the Bordens had expanded their operations, making the *Telegraph* a semiweekly and increasing their mechanical force to take care of additional public printing.

Since current resources provided revenue too slowly, the Bordens turned to the one agency that could help them immediately— the government. For a year the Bordens had been printing for the government and its predecessors until now they had a collection of unpaid bills, some due immediately, some long overdue. Early in October the brothers started their financial assault.

To insure against any future financial misunderstandings, they proposed a contract which the new Congress soon accepted. The journals of the two houses were to be published free in the *Telegraph*, but in pamphlet form were to cost according to a graduated scale. At the lowest the charge would be $3.50 an octavo page for two hundred copies or under, advancing until $4.50 a page would be charged for one thousand copies, "The foregoing Printing to be done in small Pica type." All laws, proclamations, and notices in the *Telegraph* were to cost $10 a column. Handbills also were placed on a sliding scale: $15 for the first hundred copies, if the printing ran a column or less, plus $5 extra for each additional hundred copies; $30 for the first hundred copies for material between two and three columns, plus $7 for each additional hundred. One-half the payment must be made in sixty days, the balance in four months. "Any arrangements made by which our Accounts will be cashed . . . by the merchants of this country, or the Agents in New Orleans" would be acceptable.

Specific new statements to the Texas government supplemented the earlier, still unpaid statements submitted by the *Telegraph* pub-

14 *Telegraph*, October 4, 1836.

lishers. One petition, buttressed by certifications from such leading Texans as Houston, Austin, and Thomas J. Rusk, pointed out the number of copies of the *Telegraph* contributed to the government and the army since the paper's birth. Another statement, presented October 28, stated that 1,982 copies, the equivalent of thirty-eight subscriptions, had been provided the government, plus a "large number" to postmasters and influential individuals in the United States. "For this gratuitous distribution we feel ourselves compensated in the consciousness of having done much good in keeping *that* people informed of the proceedings of this country," the Bordens added.

In two weeks another statement of services followed, summing up the complete bill from the beginning to November 5, 1836 —total, $2,238.27, but a month rolled by with no relief from Congress. On December 9, after Congress had been in session two months, Gail Borden presented a memorial showing the unfeigned desperation of the publishers: tomorrow was the last day for redeeming their lands—at the minimum they must have $1,200. "Even now the sacrifice of our land is inevitable," wrote Borden.

This hopeless plea awakened the dawdling legislative conscience to an attempt to speed relief, but to do so by December 10 was out of the question. Led by Mosely Baker, the legislature rushed through authorization, only to have its action checked temporarily by the insistence of the Republic's treasurer, Henry Smith, that "the government was open to be defrauded" unless he could obtain access to the Borden accounts. Others claimed that the Bordens were charging the government an "extravagant price," to which Gail Borden replied: "If the printing has cost the government high, it has been dear to us."

Five days after the December 10 deadline the legislature by joint resolution ordered the payment of $2,238.27 to the Bordens to satisfy past accounts. Further, another $2,662.56 was to be paid them in satisfaction of their October contract, the first half of which was not due for another sixty days. President Houston approved the bill promptly.[15] It was such a windfall to the harassed proprietors that in their elation they ran the full resolution three times in two issues of the *Telegraph*.

[15] Proposals ... for executing Printing, October 5, 1836, Acceptance, October 11, 1836, Statement, G & T. H. Borden to Republic of Texas, October 28, 1836—

Their delight was premature, however, for Smith delayed authorization. Once more, on December 27, Gail Borden submitted a petition: "[The publishers] are reduced to the unavoidable necessity of either sacrificing their land upon the one hand, or denying to the operative printers their weekly wages if some available appropriation . . . can not be immediately effected."[16] But still no funds.

Once the government authorization was obtained, a new obstacle arose—the brothers could not contact David White, the Texas agent in Mobile who was to furnish the actual funds. Destitute, the Bordens gave drafts on White for badly needed supplies and continued their work. But a few weeks later the drafts returned, "and to give a relish to the matter, the seller of the goods came with them, and was hot upon us. It was in vain to put him off, and not likeing to have our credit damed, we offered to return the goods . . . at 5 per cent less than cost." Meanwhile the Bordens had presented the government another bill for nearly $2,500 for printing from December 15, 1836, to February 21, 1837, which likewise brought no action.

In March, Tom Borden went to Mobile to collect from "Uncle Davy" White the money due on the two authorized drafts. It was a disappointing journey. Tom fell ill, losing valuable time. Well again, he could not raise enough money to start home. Since his letters to Gail were highly unfavorable, the elder Borden issued instructions to do no more public printing until the government made payment, which left Congress complaining. But, Gail explained, the government had not extended to the Bordens "that protection which a citizen has a right to expect. . . . we are . . . compelled as well as justified in refusing to risk any further liabilities."

By April 19, Tom Borden had obtained $3,000, sufficient only to meet three-fourths of the New Orleans demands.[17] Two months later when Gail Borden sold his interest in the *Telegraph*, the financial situation was unchanged: a dozen years were to pass before the government caught up with its monetary obligations to the two brothers.

in Public Printing Papers G & T H Borden to Speaker of House of Representatives, October 27, December 9, 1836, G & T H Borden to Joint Committee on Claims and Accounts, November 5, November 26, 1836—in Petitions, Archives of the Texas State Library.

[16] G. & T. H Borden to Senate, December 27, 1836, in Petitions

[17] Public Printing Papers, February 21, 1837 Gail Borden to J. Pinckney Henderson and Henry Smith, May 23, 1837, in Alamo Museum

Aside from their disheartening financial struggle, Gail and Thomas Borden found the fall and winter at Columbia an exciting one in which they shared the triumphs and tasted the sorrows. As publishers of the only newspaper in the capital city of Texas, they were men of importance, and because of their paper they were able to spread abroad their views on all sorts of subjects—and know that they would be heard, if not heeded.

Gail Borden abandoned his former careful neutrality to suggest, lead, grumble, and even rebuke. Some of his remarks are naive; others, shrewd. Commenting on a possible reinvasion from Mexico, he suggested that Texas prevent further war by laying waste the country between the Río Grande and Guadalupe rivers. Surely, he said belligerently in a later issue, Texas had enough free men to "crush the abject race," which he likened to "the musquetoe, . . . easier to kill, than endure its annoying buzz."

On the subject of a national loan he counseled Texas to look past the United States, which was hampered by "the queroulous whinings" of the Mexican minister in Washington, and apply instead to England. Such a procedure, he promised, "opens a new market, excites the jealous pride of the United States, obtains from them her immediate recognition, and by her minister, proclaims herself a nation." He made it sound automatic.

Borden advised a new commander-in-chief for the Texas army, "one whose thrilling war cry would be heard from the Atlantic to the Sabine." His choice was James Hamilton, leader of the South Carolina forces during the Nullification controversy—"in reality, a general politic, prudent, brave and energetic." And of minor importance, a more analytical Gail Borden might have added. Another South Carolinian was less admired. This was Governor McDuffie, who had stated that Texans were pariahs who had deserted the United States to revolt against a sheltering government. If the American colonies could revolt over a threepence tax on tea, retorted Borden, then surely Texas could revolt when her constitution and representation were removed. When news reached Borden that two Kentuckians, former soldiers in the Texas army, had impugned the patriotism of revolutionary Texans in an article in the Lexington *Intelligencer*, he launched a philippic that lasted through almost two months of *Telegraphs*. One of the men, he said, was at best a "VIL-

LAIN" and at worst a "LIAR" while the other was little better; and he intended to say enough to make the couple's fame "stink in the nose of all succeeding time."[18]

But if Gail Borden were scorching within, outside he was cool. The weather in early December was "remarkably fine"—white frost in the morning, sunshine in the afternoon, with occasionally a light dry norther—tonic weather, good to work in. But then, as the issue of December 17 was ready to go to press, winter struck. The walls of the rough cabin where the *Telegraph* was composed proved about as effective in shutting out the north winds as a rail fence, so that when the printer's devil wetted down the paper for publication, the paper froze! Despite the cold, an amused Gail Borden took time to insert a note: "[It requires] devil's fingers, to handle the type and paper [in] such weather, and doubtless, our diabolical cognomen must have been conferred in frosty weather."

By the close of the year Congress had adjourned. Gail Borden spent a large part of Christmas night, 1836, penning an appreciation to this first Congress. As a citizen of Texas, "jealous of her honor and interest," and as a publisher of "a press which should ever be as a sentinel on the watch-tower," he was happy that Congress had possessed the enlightened leadership necessary to launch a nation on a positive, righteous path. When Congress had first convened, Texas had existed "literally in a state of nature," but now Texas knew unity and direction.

As if the end of the first year of freedom, the closing of the first Congress, and the near completion of the administrative organization of the Republic of Texas signified that he could be released from his days and nights of amazingly selfless service, Stephen F. Austin died at the house of Judge McKinstry at twelve-thirty in the afternoon of Tuesday, December 27. In the *Telegraph* the inside pages were bordered with heavy black ink, and a simple headline told the profound loss which Gail Borden must have felt at the death of the forty-three-year-old "Father of Texas":

THE PATRIARCH HAS LEFT US.

[18] For a full treatment, see *Documents Connected with the Late Controversy between Gen T J Chambers, of Texas, and Messrs. Wilson & Postlethwaite, of Kentucky.*

Twenty-three guns were fired, one for each Texas county. When the body left Columbia at nine o'clock on Thursday morning, a long procession followed it to the Brazos landing where it was placed aboard the steamboat *Yellow Stone* to be borne downriver to Peach Point, Austin's nearest approach to a real home.

Toward the last of the procession walked Gail Borden, who had known Austin as employer, mentor, and friend. He had been faithful to Austin's friendship, for which Austin had written one paragraph that could have served as Borden's epitaph. The previous October, Austin had written James F. Perry of his desire to go to the United States but that he hesitated to leave. It was an agonized letter, composed by a man whose friends of earlier days had played him false. "Who can I trust to close the land business? . . . who can I trust? I know of no one but Gail Borden. He *can be* trusted for he is conscienciously an honest man."[19]

The New Year found three of the Borden brothers living in Columbia, Paschal having opened a store with H. F. Armstrong which dealt in a broad assortment of "Petersham overcoats; . . . blue and green blanket overcoats . . . martin caps . . . fine and potmetal boots . . . good and superior fur hats, 200,000 percussion caps . . . rectified whiskey, wine and porter." But the family group was not to exist long, for both Gail and Thomas were becoming restless.

Neither Gail nor Thomas Borden had entirely given up surveying, finding time here and there between issues of the *Telegraph* to sandwich a few days in the field. Back in August, 1836, A. C. and J. K. Allen had announced in the *Telegraph* their intention of founding a new town eight miles up Buffalo Bayou from Harrisburg, to be named after the hero of San Jacinto and first president of the Republic, Sam Houston. A month later Gail and Thomas Borden and Moses Lapham began laying off the town lots. But with Congress opening in Columbia, the change of the *Telegraph* to a semi-

[19] Barker (ed.), *The Austin Papers*, III, 439 Evidently Gail and John P. Borden classified and indexed the Austin archives, for which they were paid $2,500 to $3,000, probably by the Perrys. Such a work would have been enormous, consuming at the minimum six months. See Clarence Wharton, *Gail Borden, Pioneer*, 131, S. F. Austin to Gail Borden, September 18, 1836, in Alamo Museum, Barker (ed), *The Austin Papers*, III, 431, 482–84, Gulick and others (eds), *Lamar Papers*, I, 534. See also the *Telegraph*, May 16, December 2, 1837, and the Galveston *Daily News*, August 20, 1873.

weekly, the continuing fight for funds, and the sixty-mile ride from Columbia to Houston, the work progressed very slowly. Lapham, the only member of the team who could devote full time to the survey, added to the distress by coming down with chills and fever.

But the work did get done, and in late November the brothers were able to announce: "We have at length, and almost without the use of mathematical instruments, completed a plan of the City of HOUSTON which can be seen at the senate chamber."

The plan contained some unique features. Instead of laying out Houston on a north-south axis, as is done with most first plats, the Bordens surveyed the town on a nearly northeast-southwest axis in order, according to tradition, to obtain full benefit from the Gulf breeze which blows in from the southeast. There may have been a topographical consideration also—a ridge running along Buffalo Bayou may have induced the brothers to alter their axes. All streets were eighty feet wide and straight, with the exception of Water Street, which was one hundred feet wide and followed the twistings of the bayou. Six streets ran from east to west, eleven streets, north to south. Five squares were set aside for public purposes: courthouse, congress, schoolhouse, commerce, and church. The center street, Main, ran southwesterly from the confluence of the bayou with its White Oak fork. The entire town was placed south of the bayou.[20]

On March 9, Thomas Borden sold his interest in the *Telegraph* to Dr. Francis Moore, Jr., until recently a surgeon in the regular Texas army. Now the publishing firm was to be known as Borden and Moore, Gail Borden remaining the senior proprietor. With the advent of Moore the *Telegraph* altered its personality, despite the publishers' promise that the "slight change which has been made in the firm . . . will not materially affect its character." But Moore was militant and ambitious, a crusader by nature. During his long editorship the *Telegraph* presented an unbroken front of quarreling and sharpshooting on almost every issue—local, state, or national—that interested Dr. Moore. In his calmer moments an invincible logician,

[20] Moses Lapham to Amos Lapham, October 1, November 21, 1836, in Heminger Papers A lithograph of the original plat with the endorsement, "Surveyed by G. & T H. Borden," is in the possession of the Houston Title Guaranty Company, Houston. Additional information from interview with W. F Carothers, Houston, July 17, 1947.

Dr. Moore too often subordinated logic to captious spite or senti-
mentality. Some of his fights, such as the one against extending railroads west of Houston or his running duel with General Houston,
are classics in vitriol. He was not the ideal partner for a nervous
Gail Borden, who usually strove for at least superficial serenity.

The first noticeable change in the *Telegraph* was its removal
from Columbia. Even in its early flushing pride as capital, Colum-
bians had realized its inadequacy as a permanent site for the government of the Republic of Texas. The greatest bar was its location—
inland on a silty river and off-center of the settled areas. To succeed
Columbia, Brazoria, Washington, Nacogdoches, and Groce's Retreat were all considered and rejected for one reason or other, Houston emerging as favorite.

In choosing Houston, the selectors had been swayed more by
potentialities than by actualities. There was almost nothing there,
the Bordens having laid out the town in the previous October and
November. But the extravagant terms of its prospectus proved the
Allens to be better, albeit unexpected, prophets than most promoters
when they proclaimed that the location of Houston was at "a point
. . . which must ever command the trade of the largest and richest
portion of Texas [and which] will at this time warrant the employment of at least ONE MILLION DOLLARS of capital. . . . Vessels
from New Orleans or New York can sail without obstacle [and]
steamboats of the largest class can run down to Galveston Island in
8 or 10 hours . . . . It is handsome and beautifully elevated,[21] salu-
brious and well watered."

Almost nine months after the first issue in Columbia, the *Telegraph* was moving again. In Columbia its proprietors had seen history made—and had contributed their portion. There they had done
the first public printing of a new nation, including two printed
documents, *An Accurate and Authentic Report of the Proceedings
of the House of Representatives. From the 3d of October to the 23d
of December,* 220 pages long, and the *Journals of the Senate of the
Republic of Texas*—two early Texas imprints that today have become collectors' items. But with the government gone, Columbia
had no more attraction for Borden and Moore. For them, the cry
was "On to Houston!"

[21] General average twenty-five feet above sea level.

As the two proprietors pulled out of Columbia aboard the *Yellow Stone*, their anticipations were mounting. It was April 16, 1837. Within a week they would issue their first number from Houston, where, they had been promised, a nearly completed building awaited them. Rather than risk the boggy roads, they were sending their gear aboard the steamboat, down the Brazos, across to Galveston Bay, up the bay, and then to the head of Buffalo Bayou, where sprawled the new town of Houston.

But a week later they were still on the Brazos—or more literally, on the bar in the mouth of the Brazos, opposite Velasco. After fretting out that delay, the proprietors moved forward again, only to lose another day when the tide deserted them as they were crossing Clopper's Bar. Ten days out of Columbia they reached Lynchburg, across Buffalo Bayou from the San Jacinto battleground. From there, "a great part of the ensuing day was spent in groping (if a steamboat can grope) at the rapid rate of one or two miles an hour, to the very *crown* of the 'head of Navigation of Buffalo Bayou.'"

Debarking at Houston, Borden and Moore hurried to their "nearly completed" building to find, "like others who have confided in *speculative things*, we have been deceived: no building had ever been nearly finished . . . intended for the press." They rented a shanty, the only convenient building obtainable, described by Moore in the couplet:

> *Without a roof, and without a floor,*
> *Without windows and without a door.*

Their troubles continued: "The shanty is falling about our ears," wrote Moore; "the massive beams have dropped upon the stands, made a most disgusting *pi*, and driven the workmen to seek safety outside, the *devil* alone looks smiling on the mischief." But though the quality of their reception was dubious, the proprietors liked Houston.

The *Telegraph* first appeared on Houston's mud streets on May 2, 1837. It was the fourth town in which Gail Borden had published, and in three of them—Harrisburg, Columbia, and Houston—his was the first paper on the scene. With Dr. Moore contributing the editorial fire, the *Telegraph* launched at once into a forthright, fearless program that was to make it a leading influence in Houston and the dominant newspaper of Texas until after the Civil War.

Borden spent little, if any, time around the *Telegraph* office.[22] Only once did he even seem to want to interfere with his partner's editorial policy. In a much interlined, marked-through draft of a letter to J. Pinckney Henderson and Henry Smith that illustrates how painfully he composed some letters, he revealed his reaction to Moore's comments on an address by President Houston:

[I] am gratified that the (favourable)[23] *Telegraph* made the just remarks which the importance of the message (deserved) called for— The word "great" in the second sentence I would have left out, because it should not be used in speaking of *any* living man present. it is affected adulation towards the man that we (only) wished to give deserved praise, and thereby (give) render him that support which his (acts measures) acts merit and which it is due to the Chief Magistrate of Texas. I have ever endeavoured to give him that support (and) and am glad to see that Dr. Moore is disposed [illegible] hope the Telegraph will always (and shall ever call the) give support to all (of Genl) of our President's wise meas[ures] and let o[th]ers infer that the man is "great"   (Then) This if I am not mistaken is the true notion of the motto
"Measures & not men."[24]

In June, 1837, Gail Borden returned to Houston where he found a buyer for his share of the *Telegraph*, a soft-spoken young New Yorker named Jacob W. Cruger, who in his seventeen years had already been copartner in a mercantile business, postmaster at Houston, and assistant secretary of the Texas Senate.[25] No details of the transaction exist. The *Telegraph* noted the transfer in an advertisement headed "Dissolution of Copartnership," informing its

---

[22] On May 24 Borden was in Quintana, attending the birth of his second daughter, Philadelphia, in a warehouse. A second son, Morton Quinn, had been born in Aunt Mina Heard's house at Egypt, Texas, on September 10, 1834.

[23] All words enclosed in parentheses were marked through.

[24] Gail Borden to J Pinckney Henderson and Henry Smith, May 23, 1837, in Alamo Museum

[25] Cruger remained as business manager of the *Telegraph* for fourteen years, a perfect foil for the hard-driving Moore Together, they became Texas' first real newspaper magnates, at one time owning the *Telegraph* and the *Morning Star* in Houston and the *Centinel* in Austin.

readers that the firm of Borden and Moore was "dissolved by mutual consent." Apparently the transfer, which is dated June 20, surprised no one, for from far-off Pittsburgh came the inquiry of a traveling Texan asking whether Borden had "closed the business he is ingaged in."[26]

The last issue of *The Telegraph and Texas Register* which carried the Borden name on its masthead was in character. Its front page announced its date as June 13; its inside flag, as June 20. On page two appeared the explanation:

NO INK, NO INK.—The want of this *black* article has kept our subscribers in the *dark* as to news for the last week, and enabled the *devil* for once to appear with a white face.

It was the end of Gail Borden's newspaper days. For twenty months—including gaps—and seventy-four editions he *registered* the important events of a momentous era. If at times his leadership appeared long on stenography and short of exegesis, it was characteristic of the time and the man. He believed in a free press, but also in a free public. Only when the public faltered should the press lead, but first the public must have its chance, for to Gail Borden the mere physical act of occupying an editor's or a publisher's chair did not provide the sitter with the omniscience to know always what course is best. Instead, he would maintain a policy of attentive deliberation, applying his whips when sluggish Texas needed prodding, braking hard when Texas tried to run away with itself. And when Texas needed a voice, Gail Borden, through his paper, tried to provide it.

Now all this was behind and would remain there. He had helped to play midwife at the birth of Texas, and the infant had outgrown the nurses. As the years passed, the servants of Texas would not forget the crisis of the accouchement, but their recollections of the rôles of some of the lesser nurses would dim until a half-century later a Baptist minister-turned-historian, after asking, "Who can ever estimate the power of Brother Borden's press in that dark and trying hour?" would regretfully observe, "How strange how few editors or historians of Texas ever even refer to it."[27]

26 Emily M Bryan Perry to James F Perry, July 22, 1837, in Perry Papers.
27 *The Life and Writings of Rufus C Burleson*, 724 When in 1838 some

Even in his later, mellower days Gail Borden himself seldom reminisced about the period of the *Telegraph*. It was a chapter in his life that, when he had turned the last page, was closed. If ever again he felt any desire to own a newspaper, he left no evidence.

editors referred to Francis Moore as the "patriarch" of the Texas press, Moore disclaimed the title in a sincere though somewhat florid tribute to Gail Borden Wrote Moore· "We assure the gentlemen, that we are not entitled to the high honor. It belongs rather, to that patriotic and indefatigable man, who, when the clouds of tyranny were beginning to lift their terrific forms in the western horizon, boldly launched the Telegraph upon that sea of troubles, whose tumultuous waves threatened to overwhelm every vestige of Texian liberty, though it sunk amid the general desolation, he survived the wreck, and returning sunshine found him again at the helm of a new and stouter bark ... may we ever keep in view those lofty landmarks of virtue and freedom, which were to him a solace and a guide." *Telegraph*, May 16, 1838.

There's but the twinkling of a star
Between a man of peace and war
—Butler, *Hudibras*

The very essence of a free government consists
in considering offices as public trusts, bestowed for
the good of the country, and not for the benefit of
an individual or a party
—John C Calhoun, February 13, 1835

IX

The One-faced Janus of
Galveston Island
1837-1839

THE SIX-YEAR-OLD BOY crept cautiously up to the door of the one-room frame building, lifted himself bravely until he measured a full three feet or more, and looked in, his arms resting on the low doorsill. With one glance he took in the whole interior—the furniture, a dry-goods box for a desk and an empty barrel for a seat; the floor, gray beach-sands soft-packed and shifting; the foundation, two-foot timbers placed laterally beneath the sills; and the occupants, two piratical looking men perching on the sills for seats.

The lad was Billy Parker, later to be known as Captain William E. Parker, United States marshal for the eastern district of Texas, and the time was a few days before the battle of San Jacinto. What Billy was looking at so intently was John Davis Bradburn's old customhouse, the first "permanent" building on Galveston Island, soon to be the office of Gail Borden, first collector of customs for the Republic of Texas stationed at Galveston.

When Borden alighted at Galveston at the beginning of the summer of 1837, he found it little altered from the bleak island where he had first landed in Texas more than seven years earlier. Half-wild goats provided the milk supply. Green turtles abounded on the beach, laying their eggs in the sand. There were alligators in the ponds, snakes in the sand, and deer on the grass. When Audubon hunted there, he saw twenty-five deer, four of which his party killed. A few fowls, a pig, and a dog composed the domesticated population. Not even the house rat had landed yet, and the ants did not show up until the first shipment of coffee had been unloaded.

The several families lived in houses of wire-grass sods brought in from the bay shore. To be out of the reach of snakes, everyone slept in hammocks. Windows were almost unknown. Cooking was primitive, the women using ovens of oyster shells mixed into bricks that were baked in a pit till hard. A few half-blood Indians, leftovers from the days of Lafitte, roamed the island, thoroughly pacified and even dispirited, preferring the easy tedium of their camp at Eagle Grove, six miles from Galveston, to the uncertain independence of life beyond the white man's reach.

No town was Galveston, only a settlement, lacking even the vulgar culture and hard-come-by refinements of such new-fashioned towns as Columbia and Houston. Tom Borden might boast that "nature has designed [Galveston] as the New York of Texas," and for the next forty years Galveston might rank as the foremost city in Texas, but geography and nature and the enterprising city of Houston in combination restrained its ever endangering the position of New York or even of New Orleans.

For the next fourteen years Galveston was to be Gail Borden's active home and for the remainder of his life his sentimental home. More than any other place in which he lived, he left his imprint on Galveston and Galveston left its marks on him, neither ever entirely surrendering the other.

Unwittingly, since his early days in Texas, Gail Borden had been serving an apprenticeship for his new position as collector of the port of Galveston. As a surveyor he knew Texas, and more important, Texans knew him. As the wheel horse of Austin's land office he had shown himself a faithful public servant. During the revolution he had been a scrupulous collector for the Department of Brazos, gaining much practical experience in the tribulations of a financial middleman between citizens and government. And his editorship of the *Telegraph* had, of course, established him as one of the patriots of Texas to whom the awarding of a political prize was justifiable, if not actually due.

Gail Borden Jr. Concentration of Sweet Milk and Extracts. Patented Aug. 19. 1856.

Nº 15.553.

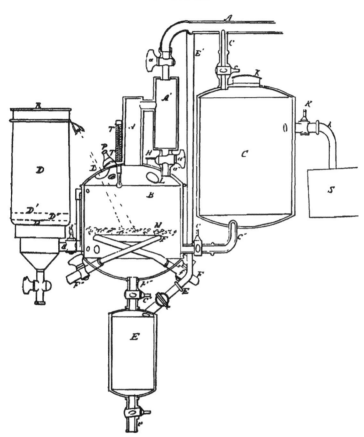

A copy of the original drawing of Borden's
application for patent in
concentration of milk

United States Patent Office, Washington, D C

There is no evidence that Borden or his friends importuned President Houston concerning an appointment to the most important customs post in Texas. None may have been necessary. That the post was destined to become a cornucopia for the Republic was undeniable. That fact had been recognized a year and a half earlier by William P. Harris, who had been sent to the deserted island by the provisional government in January, 1836. Wrote Harris: "The Island is the only place the duties can be secured with any kind of certainty as it is the Key to the many Rivers, bayous and Landing places in the bay where goods could and would be landed to avoid the duties notwithstanding all the vigilance of the Collector."[1] Galveston Island might appear unprepossessing, but its position athwart the best water-entrances to Texas assured its supremacy as a collecting station. For the next dozen years the port of Galveston was to furnish Texas a large portion of its meager finances. It was vital that the Republic station there a man on whom it could rely.

In a secret session on May 19, 1837, the Senate confirmed Houston's appointment of Gail Borden, ten to one, the lone dissenter giving no reason. When Borden went to Houston to dissolve his newspaper connections, he dropped down to Harrisburg to make $25,000 bond to Henry Smith, the secretary of the treasury, naming Thomas F. McKinney, John K. Allen, and W. B. Aldridge as his securities.[2] On the same day, June 13, he affirmed his intentions to "support the Constitution . . . and faithfully discharge the duties of Collector to the best of my skill and ability, as I will answer under the penalties of purgery."[3]

The next afternoon Borden arrived in Galveston to take up his new duties. About the same time three ships hove to offshore, and the master of one of them, the schooner *New Orleans*, came ashore to give Gail Borden his first chores as customs collector. The schooner, incidentally, was principally laden with lumber from Mobile intended for Thomas H. Borden.

Immediately effective collection was out of the question. The

[1] William P. Harris to Henry Smith, January 19, 1836, in Comptroller's Letters
[2] E W Winkler (ed.), *Secret Journals of the Senate, Republic of Texas, 1836–1845*, 48 First reported publicly in the *Telegraph*, May 30, 1837
[3] Bonds and Oaths, Republic of Texas, Archives of the Texas State Library.

law establishing customs rates had not been published. Amasa Turner had repaired and occupied the old cypress customhouse as a residence. Borden had no "suitable room for doing business—destitute of paper, ink, and the necessary blanks and books." Tom Borden, just returned from New Orleans, brought Gail a table and a large writing desk to use until he could obtain furniture from the Republic.

Where he could, Turner helped. He provided Borden with office room, and in turn the collector urged that the Secretary of the Treasury permit Borden to name Turner as his assistant. Borden's chief clerk had failed to show up, and anyway, the collector felt, the port of Galveston would not require permanent appointments in the subordinate positions. It would be wiser to engage local personnel who would work only when called upon.

The shortage of supplies convinced Borden that outside aid was essential. He went to Houston to establish a public store, appointing a storekeeper and deputy collector there. Returning to Galveston in an open boat, he was caught in a storm and was forced to fight headwinds and current for twenty-five hours, with much water damage to his books and papers resulting. In July the chief clerk, David Murphree, arrived, and with his assistance and that of "Mr. [C. H.] Van Winkle, . . . (late from New York)," Borden began to feel as if he might soon have business in good order. Already he had received $1,088, of which he had sent $300 to New Orleans for supplies and "an iron chest, which we are in much want of."[4]

As the first collector for the Republic he was aware that most of his activities would establish precedents for his successors. Accordingly, he proceeded with more than the usual admixture of Borden caution and recklessness whenever occasions arose for which the skeletal customs law of Texas did not specifically provide solutions. When one man landed twelve trunks of clothing and eighteen boxes of furniture, plus such extraneous items as a box of sausages, an organ, and five boxes of preserves, all of which he claimed was family baggage, Borden ordered the shipment to the public store to

[4] Gail Borden to Henry Smith, June 15, June 18, 1837, Borden to Asa Brigham, July 1, July 8, 1837—in Galveston Custom House Record Book. (Unless otherwise noted, all letters quoted in this chapter are from the Galveston Custom House Record Book.) Additional data from Frances Harwood, "Colonel Amasa Turner's Reminiscences of Galveston," *The Quarterly*, Vol III, No 1 (July, 1899), 46.

await appraisal for impost duties in the belief that no Texas family could possess that much personal baggage. Since his first statement of returns might be the model for future statements, Borden wrote several letters to the Treasury Department, enclosing sample forms and asking advice. In the absence of notaries he permitted Murphree and Van Winkle to assume notarial duties and to make entries in the record, in defiance of technical regulations.

Late in July a small sloop with three men aboard arrived in Galveston. After waiting a reasonable time for the master to report, Borden sent for him. The captain explained that he had no papers, that he had intended to spend the summer on Grand Tier Island fishing and hunting, that he had been blown off the coast, and that Point Bolivar at the entrance of Galveston Harbor was his first contact with land.

Suspicious, Borden directed Van Winkle to board the sloop, where, under orders, he unbent her sails, unshipped her rudder, and announced that the sloop was seized for examination. The sails—a main, square, and jib—were placed in the customhouse and the vessel was beached under the lee of a schooner. Borden then wrote Asa Brigham, the acting secretary of the treasury: "As our law is entirely silent on this subject [I concluded] to refer the matter to you." Whatever disposition was made of the case is unrecorded.

Up at Red Fish Bar, near the mainland, Borden placed another deputy to serve as inspector and discharging officer for ships stopping there. His selection, a man named Lee, had come recommended "as a good man, and . . . I found that his competency was equal to what it had been recommended." Not included in Lee's recommendation was the information that he was an excessive drinker. As soon as Borden learned of Lee's alcoholism, he sent for his new employee, determined to dismiss him. Probably aware of the collector's intentions, Lee went instead into Houston to complete business, indulged himself in one last long spree, and died as a result. His employer's reactions were more self-righteous than sympathetic:

"Knowing my sentiments on the subject," Borden wrote, "he was uneasy on account of his conduct, and probably dreaded being replaced. I am myself mortified, that any officer . . . should have drank to excess and bring discredit on me, and ruin to himself. . . .

I trust it may be the last appointment which I may make, which shall prove so unfortunate."

He found himself getting more short-handed. Murphree had to go to San Antonio for six weeks. Van Winkle received an offer elsewhere of $1,500 a year, and Borden could not hold him. Borden himself needed to go to Houston but could not leave, having to press Thomas Borden into making the journey for him.

One reason that he had to remain close to Galveston was to cope with smugglers. Without consulting their geographies, the Texas officials had designated the eastern boundary of Borden's district at Point Bolivar, just across the entrance to Galveston Bay. The next district to the east extended to the Louisiana border, its headquarters centering around the Sabine River boundary. That left at least seventy-five miles of unprotected coastline, most of whose expanse fortunately was too marshy to provide easy access to the interior.

But Point Bolivar was at the end of a peninsular stretch resembling a tenuous finger whose connection with its base has almost worn away. This narrowest spot, only three to four hundred yards wide, separates the Gulf of Mexico from East Bay, an adjunct of Galveston Bay. Borden saw it as the most likely spot for smugglers since only a short portage would be required to transfer a cargo from a ship in the Gulf to small boats in the bay. But it was out of his territory.

However, when the sloop *Rein Deer* sailed into Galveston with a cargo transferred from a schooner stranded at the "rolling over place," as Borden christened it, he decided that district lines did not matter. The authorities had not known of the foundered ship, and neither had he. If a ship could founder there, unload her cargo, reload it on another ship, and the entire transfer take place without the knowledge of any customs official, the situation was serious. He hastened to write Brigham for permission to extend his authority over any ships and goods found "on the Gulph side of the rolling over place." The area might not be his responsibility, but he wanted no smuggling in his vicinity.

At the end of September he submitted his first quarterly report as collector. It showed that in his first three months he had collected $2,718.81 in "duties paid in," $20,913.21 in duties bonded, and

$698.75 from public sales of seized goods. The total: $25,530.77.[5] It was not a staggering amount, but it was more than he and most of the Texas government had anticipated, and it was going to grow.

During the summer and fall of 1837, Galveston strove mightily to become a town. McKinney and Williams moved their extensive jobbing business from Quintana to a new large warehouse and store-room on Twenty-fourth Street. Peter J. Menard and Medard Menard opened a small merchandising establishment on the north side of Strand, with J. S. LeClere as their clerk. Shortly afterward, Paul Bremond, who later became a Texas railroad magnate, began his mercantile operations in the same block.

In the midst of the building excitement Gail Borden decided that he needed more working space than Turner could provide. In August he wrote Brigham of his need, revealing, however, that he had not waited for Brigham's authorization but had forged ahead with his own plans. The work would cost $500, the materials $150 at minimum. He had an offer from Fred Cook and B. Houghton to erect a new customhouse for $700, which he thought was reasonable. "I am anxious the President should appoint a person to desig-nate the Square upon which the Custom House is to be erected," he wrote, adding guilelessly, "The workmen are expected to day."

A month later he wrote Brigham that progress with the custom-house was too slow and that he had engaged another builder, a man named Caffrey. On October 4 Caffrey handed the keys to the new customhouse to Collector Borden, who began evacuating the por-tion of the Mexican customhouse that Turner had granted him. The new establishment was a full two stories, set back a short distance from the street in the middle of a square between Twenty-third and Twenty-fourth Streets, with Avenue A on the north and Strand on the south.[6] Borden was proud of his structure, and all Galveston shared his pride.

Two days later Galveston forgot pride as it fought desperately

[5] Quarterly Return of Duties for the Quarter ending 30 Sept. 1837 by Gail Borden, in Galveston Custom House Record Book.

[6] G. W. Hayes, "Island and City of Galveston," 269-70, 276. This work, com-piled from contemporary sources no longer extant, progressed as far as the proof stage but was never published. The page proofs are in the Rosenberg Library. The San Jacinto Museum of History, Houston, has a typescript

to hold on during the battering of the first of a series of great storms that have marred its century of existence. Six days earlier the wind had begun to blow, coming out of the southeast steadily for three days, then shifting slightly to the east, filling Galveston Bay with water and causing a four-foot rise as far away as Houston. On the sixth day the wind veered to the north and began to blow in earnest, sweeping water inland and threatening to inundate the island. At anchor in Galveston Harbor were perhaps twenty-five foreign ships, most of them from the States. Just before the wind shifted northward, the privateer *Tom Toby* parted her chains and smashed ashore near Virginia Point. A short time after, the soldiers' camp surrendered to the gale, and soldiers dragged themselves into the old customhouse.

By nine o'clock that evening Turner's place had taken on the appearance of a refugee camp. In addition to the eighty soldiers standing packed in the twenty-by-thirty-foot first story, Turner had given refuge to two other families chased from their homes by high water. Turner tells the story in detail:

With three families above, numbering about fifteen in all, and ninety below, if the house should fall, the consequences would be dreadful. I had taken the precaution, before dark, to request Captain L. M. Hitchcock, who was then a pilot on the bar, to anchor his boat near my house, and asked him, if the storm increased, or the Island should be all overflowed, if he thought his boat would live to reach the mainland. He informed me that he had rigged his mainsail into a mutton-leg sail, and he thought with it in that condition he could perhaps reach the mainland at Virginia Point. The water rose rapidly, striking the siding of the house with great force, causing it to slide from its blocks on which it stood and settle on the ground. I then determined to knock off the siding on the north and south ends of the house, and let the water rush through. This eased the house some, but the number inside prevented the water from having free passage, which made the pressure still very great.

About ten P. M. Captain Hitchcock suggested that his boat be brought to lee of the house, and we put mattresses on the thwarts of the boat two three deep, put the ladies and children on them, and cover all with quilts and blankets, and take the boat up on the island and ground her, and as the water rose, move the boat until we could find no land, and when the water had completely submerged the whole island, he would then do the best he could to make land. We loaded the boat with our treasures, and after putting on board a full supply of the creature comforts, we run her hard aground about one hundred and fifty yards from the house, took the anchor further landward, and planted it as securely as possible, and detailed two men to bale the boat and keep the precious cargo as dry as possible.

. . . The Captain had no occasion to move his anchor again. It seemed the storm had spent its fury soon after we had effected this removal. In about an hour and a half, the Captain reported to me that the water had fallen, he thought, about six inches.[7]

About one o'clock in the morning the storm began to abate, and by sunrise the passengers were able to disembark. The scene which met their salt-strained eyes brought no cheer. Before them Galveston lay prostrate. About the only building left was the Mexican customhouse they had abandoned during the night, for which Turner would always credit the ballast provided by the eighty soldiers on the first floor.[8] Gone was the fine new warehouse of McKinney and Williams. Gone, too, were Galveston's two curiosities, a pair of China trees planted ten years earlier near the wine-pipes and wells that once had belonged to Lafitte. The trees, almost the only ones on the island, had grown to a ten-inch diameter when the storm broke them off just above the ground, too old to sprout again. Not gone but removed more than a half-mile from its lot was the new customhouse, roof caved in, foundation destroyed, and sides battered.

Fortunately, because of the high winds preceding the storm, Borden had not moved much of his gear and records from Turner's house, so that beyond being water-stained, they were secure. No documents were lost. But the iron chest, which had been moved and stored with papers, was almost worthless. For temporary quarters Borden moved aboard a large brig, the *Perseverance*, which had been beached, and worked there almost a year. Near by another ship, the *Elbe*, had also been grounded, and it was converted into Galveston's first hotel and then, in a dubious sort of evolution, into a jail.

[7] Harwood, "Colonel Amasa Turner's Reminiscences of Galveston," *The Quarterly*, Vol III, No. 1 (July, 1899), 46–47.

[8] Hayes, "Island and City of Galveston," 276–78 The same story is told in less detail in Harwood, "Colonel Amasa Turner's Reminiscences of Galveston," *The Quarterly*, Vol III, No 1 (July, 1899), 46–47

Feverishly Galveston began rebuilding. Gail and Thomas Borden erected residences, while Amasa Turner constructed a real hotel near the Mexican customhouse, a two-story, nine-bedroom building which he finished in the spring of 1838. Gail Borden decided that the customhouse should be rebuilt on the same plot as before, characteristically starting his plans and then writing the Treasury Department for its opinion. To tear apart the wrecked house he hired Joseph Ehlenger,[9] who had worked for him in pre-Republic days, for five days at twenty dollars. At the end of the five days Ehlenger offered a recommendation which has influenced Galveston architecture to the present day:

He says [wrote Borden] that if raised only four feet from the ground the late storm would not have effected [the customhouse], that if the Blocks of the first had been set into the ground and one foot higher, the house would have stood, and I have not a doubt but the present distinction of houses at Galveston will prove an advantage to the place in ten years hence, for houses will now be built four feet from the ground which is six or seven feet above ordinary high tides.[10]

To Smith, Borden suggested that he be permitted to rebuild the house at five dollars a day. When Smith agreed, the new construction began.

Although Galveston was growing more important in the commercial and financial affairs of Texas, it remained without any local civil government throughout the fall and winter of 1837. The Texas government had representatives there—the customs collector and his staff, a garrison of soldiers, and a few naval officers, usually in transit. No courts, no judges, no police officers or administrators had been provided, however. And Galveston itself stayed too busy rebuilding and expanding to indulge in the luxury of an organized city government.

Into the breach stepped Gail Borden, whose eagerness to cor-

[9] In September, 1837, Ehlenger, or Ehlinger, came from interior Texas to Galveston on his way to France to get his family. Eight days out of Galveston his ship sprang a leak and returned in distress. Ehlenger, being ill, remained on the island till after the storm, after which he decided to remain in Galveston to build the customhouse. Certificate by Gail Borden, January 23, 1838, in Domestic Correspondence, 1838.

[10] Gail Borden to Henry Smith, October 24, 1837.

rect apparent wrongs undoubtedly caused some people to regard him as a nuisance. Whether he busied himself with affairs that were none of his concern is debatable, because almost every phase of life touching Galveston was a matter that could concern him, sometimes to the discomfiture of others.

Up and down the settled east end of the island he tramped, advising here, superintending there, guarding the insular entrance to Texas like some odd Janus, except that Borden had only one face to watch the doors. Being able to see in only one direction at a time merely increased Borden's vigilance; he peered into the navy yard, the army fort, and any place on the island that might belong to the government—and therefore to the people—of Texas, to protect its public property.

After the storm the scattered lumber had been gathered and stacked until possibly 100,000 feet lay unattended in the tall grass covering the higher ground of the island. Exposed, the lumber represented to Borden a fire hazard, and he spent most of one day going about warning everyone who used fires out of doors, which meant almost the entire population—"for it is all *out of doors* with us here." Despite Borden's cautionings, on October 27 a fire did break out, only to be quickly extinguished. When search disclosed that the fire had been set accidentally by a careless cook carrying coals for his stove from a neighbor's house, Borden warned the man that any future slackness would result in his apprehension—by Gail Borden, of course, who had no such authority. "This I did," Borden explained, ". . . as a caution to others who . . . should be guilty of a like dangerous offence."

He was determined to play sheriff. After Christmas he wrote Henry Smith, who was more interested in financial returns than in law and order in Galveston, that "I expect in a few days to attempt to arrest a man . . . for Stealing, which he has practiced for some time—Indeed we are infested with a parcel of abandoned creatures and without some appearances of civil authority at this place we are not safe." In other ways he gathered authority, sometimes in the line of duty, more often in the line of tying up someone else's loose ends. He made elaborate plans to defend Galveston against a Mexican attack from the sea; he perfected plans to place two buoys in the entrance to Galveston Bay, and as soon as he had determined his positions and selected his workmen, he sought Smith's advice—but not until arrangements were already underway; he hired smiths to reclaim rifles damaged by the storm; and he concerned himself with the pay of pilots—two dollars for each foot of water displaced was too low, he thought. He sent Smith a copy of a new pilotage provision to be proposed to Congress, along with an indisputable argument: "Should the first large vessel from England get wrecked on our bars (even if she had nothing but ballast on board) it would injure Texas thousands not to say a million."

Toward the close of the year Borden began to find himself increasingly weighed with customs responsibilities and with less time to reflect on matters of more general interest. His letters to Smith, though, became longer, as he poured out to that harassed official all his problems and almost all his dreams. On December 27 he wrote Smith two unusually long letters. In one of them he made a statement which would have brought a tongue-in-cheek smile to a less earnest person than the humorless Secretary of the Treasury: "I have not written half what I wish to say, nor previously communicated half what I should have done, had I found time to write."

The year 1837 closed on Gail Borden, public servant. The six months just terminated had brought unaccustomed obstacles, but by now work was assuming more and more the appearance of routine. Easier days, he could hope, lay ahead. Meanwhile he could continue working, reassured by his own self-satisfied observation: "[I] am rewarded in the consciousness of having done some good."

Contrary to expectations the early months of 1838 brought no respite to customhouse workers. In December an amended customs law had been enacted, lifting duties from such items as sugar, coffee, tea, pickled pork, bale rope, lumber, and farming implements intended for the importer's use. Since no effective date was set by the bill's framers, Borden continued for several weeks to collect duties under the original customs act, his year-end report containing such collections in his totals. As soon as they learned of the new law, importers and immigrants clamored for a return of their duties, confusing Borden's bookkeeping and sending him scurrying by mail to Smith for advice.

Complicating the situation were an unprecedented and unexpected increase in traffic and the coldest February in the history of Anglo-American Texas. In 1836 Galveston had felt rewarded when one ship a month arrived. By February, 1838, when it had become fairly established that Texas would remain independent and not join the United States, vessels were arriving daily, and one morning, within an hour, five ships entered the harbor to increase the burden of an already overworked customs staff. The fact that the weather was "cold as Ohio"—16 degrees below freezing on February 2, 22 degrees below on the sixteenth, and snow and ice on the ground in Houston—did not hamper shipping at all, though business of all other kinds suspended and the less fortunately housed lay "dying in their little bivouacs & shanties."

Cold weather finally went away, but customers did not. By March 23 duties for the spring quarter had reached $40,000, to collect which, Borden claimed, required five times the labor necessary to collect a similar amount at New Orleans or New York because of the many small consignments and the fact that nearly one-half of the immigrants were doubling as importers. In addition, Galveston's wharfage was such that ships could not be docked compactly, and since most of the ships coming from New Orleans provided no means for securing their hatches, Borden had to maintain watch day and night to prevent unlawful unloading of cargo. At one time Borden was employing fifteen discharging officers, three of them permanently.

Holding workers was a continuing difficulty. No sooner did a clerk become acquainted with customhouse routine than he was off to another position and a new employee was being broken in. Although Borden felt that higher wages would attract men who would remain longer, he received little official encouragement. His own remuneration was determined by a fixed commission—2.5 per cent of receipts until his total reached $2,000; after that, one-half of 1 per cent.[11] Under this arrangement his annual pay probably never exceeded $2,800.

On the first day of May, 1838, Gail Borden found himself in one of those rare moments when he had caught up with his backlog

[11] Gail Borden to Henry Smith, April 9, 1838 W. Roberts to James Harper Starr, August 1, 1839, in Comptroller's Letters E. T. Miller, *A Financial History of Texas*, 33 H. P. N. Gammel, *The Laws of Texas, 1822–1897*, I, 1313.

of customhouse work. Tomorrow ten ships might arrive and he would fall behind again, but right now he was idle. And he never learned to enjoy leisure.

He wrote his friend James F. Perry, in Brazoria, that he planned to re-enter the cattle business and wanted Perry's aid. Did Perry have any "gentle cows" to sell? Borden would like twenty to thirty cows and as many bulls. The range at Galveston was excellent. Already he had "engaged with a gentleman to deliver a full blooded Derham bull and a Cow & calf of the like breed."[12] Being collector of customs at the most important port in Texas was not enough. Gail Borden was itching to expand. He would begin by becoming a cattleman on the side, anticipating, perhaps, his destiny.

The big guns at the navy yard on Galveston Island began booming. One, two, three—sixteen times.

The President had arrived!

All Galveston turned out at high noon, Saturday, May 5, 1838. From another part of the island, where the military garrison was saluting also, came sixteen more guns.

Galveston watched the famous excursionists debark. First came Sam Houston, impressive as always. Next the vice-president, scholarly Mirabeau Buonaparte Lamar. Then the chief justice, members of Congress, the American chargé d'affaires, and the chiefs of the Cherokee delegations who were visiting President Houston at the time. Along to report the excursion was Dr. Francis Moore, still editor of *The Telegraph and Texas Register* and still trying to collect money from the Texas government for bills going back to the Bordens' ownership.

Uptown moved the party—to the navy yard, to the garrison, and then aboard the brig-of-war *Potomac*. At two o'clock there was an interruption. The steamer *Columbia* was unloading passengers. Off stepped three of Texas' most distinguished citizens, just back from the United States, William H. Wharton, A. C. Horton, and Dr. Branch T. Archer. After greetings and inquiries regarding President Van Buren's disposition toward annexing Texas, the inspection tour continued.

At the door of the new customhouse Gail Borden met the im-

12 Gail Borden to James F Perry, May 1, 1838, in Perry Papers.

posing party. With quick carefulness Houston looked about the premises, while Borden's voice undoubtedly ran away with itself in a staccato of observations and explanations and recommendations. When Houston said that he was highly pleased, Borden perhaps found partial compensation for months of toil and worry.

Instead of explaining to Houston, however, Borden should have been concentrating on the quiet, dark-haired Vice-president. Houston's presidential term was running out, and Lamar was his heir apparent—apparent, at least, to almost everyone but Houston. When trouble came to Gail Borden, Lamar would be the instigator. Borden could not know that Lamar's silence bespoke more pregnancy than Houston's well-meant but sterile blessing.

As the party moved on, Borden joined it. At four o'clock hosts and guests sat down at the "Messrs. Biggs' " hotel to enjoy "a sumptuous dinner prepared . . . in handsome style." After dinner, "wines and sentiments were drunk—'the feast of reason and the flow of soul' prevailed." The day's festivities ended with a ball.[13] Gail Borden retired happy: he had passed inspection.

Ashbel Smith was a wiry thirtyish Connecticut Yankee who stood only slightly over five feet tall. He had studied medicine in Paris, he held a Phi Beta Kappa key from Yale, he had practiced medicine successfully in North Carolina, and he had written authoritative medical studies. He possessed the polished suavity that develops from proper education and intelligent travel. He had spirit—once he struck a Texas senator in the Senate chamber and stood poised, bowie knife in hand, to follow up his attack, when the incipient struggle was broken up. And he had an annoying facility for being invariably correct, as Gail Borden was to learn.

In the year 1838 Smith was surgeon-general of the Texas army, stationed in Houston, where he shared residence with the President himself, having forsaken a bright future in settled North Carolina to come to raw Texas in search of a still brighter medical practice,

[13] *Telegraph*, May 12, 1838 One member of the party was unimpressed by the week-end jaunt of the "*great* men in *high* life If what I saw and heard were a fair representation, God keep me from such scenes in the future   . On our return . ' about one-half on board got mildly drunk and stripped   to their linen and pantaloons. Their Bacchanalian revels and blood-curdling profanity made the pleasure boat a floating hell." Dora Fowler Arthur, "Jottings from the Old Journal of Littleton Fowler," *The Quarterly*, Vol II, No 2 (October, 1898), 82

frontier adventure and service, or escape from an unfortunate love affair. Perhaps in varying degrees all three reasons figured. He may have met Borden on one of the collector's flying trips to Houston or on one of Smith's visits to the island. They became acquainted by mail. A dozen years later the acquaintanceship, unpromising at the outset, was to develop far-reaching effects.

In May, 1838, Borden stored two sealed boxes intended for Smith at Houston until Smith should consent to breaking the seals for inspection or until Smith should send an affidavit of the boxes' contents so that customs duties might be assessed and collected. In compliance Smith instructed Dr. J. Wilson Copes, his island assistant, to open the boxes, at the same time assuring Borden that they contained only medical supplies for the Republic and some personal gear. But Borden wanted an affidavit that nothing in the boxes would be sold.[14] Three weeks passed. Borden held the boxes, Dr. Copes all the while insisting that they be forwarded immediately. Why could not Borden take the word of McKinney and Williams, who along with Copes had been given authority to speak for Dr. Smith concerning goods reaching Galveston? Smith's impatience boiled over: "I was told that you intimated the suspicion that I was receiving free of duties articles that were dutiable— . . . inform me *specifically* and *distinctly* whether you expressed such suspicion."[15]

That left the next move to Borden. Dr. Copes records that the collector promptly permitted Smith's goods to be released.[16] At the first quiet opportunity, Borden covered his retreat with an explanation to Smith: "On seeing [your] Box I find it is directed to you in your official capacity. . . . I have made a rule not to permit packages, the contents of which is not Known [to be forwarded] even to the president." But Smith would be an exception: "I never have intended to convey an Idea that You were receiving dutiable goods free of duty. . . . [Hereafter] the instructions in your communication will be strictly attended to."[17]

Borden's reply, Smith acknowledged, was quite satisfactory.

[14] Ashbel Smith to [J W.] Copes, *ca* May 28, 1838, Smith to Gail Borden, *ca* May 24, 1838—in Ashbel Smith Papers, University of Texas Archives.
[15] Ashbel Smith to Gail Borden, June 14, 1838, Smith to [J. W.] Copes, *ca.* May 28, 1838—in Smith Papers
[16] J. W. Copes to Ashbel Smith, June 13, June 15, 1838, in Smith Papers.
[17] Gail Borden to Ashbel Smith, June 15, 1838, in Smith Papers

He had "felt no small degree of mortification on the subject," but in the future he wanted everything opened and forwarded to Houston.[18] When three weeks later Smith instructed Copes to superintend another shipment's arrival, Copes answered that the shipment had already passed customs and that "Mr. Borden told me, had there not have been some person to superintend your interests, he should have apprised me immediately."[19]

At first glance the contest between Smith and Borden appears inconsequential. As customs collector, Borden was involved in continual wranglings with some importer or other. Such incidents became daily routine in his life. The importance of the Smith-Borden interchange lay in the future. Each man had tested the other and found him disposed to be fair and dependable. Each had shown spirit, and each had dropped his mantle of mulishness when shown his mistakes. More than a decade later the two men would seek each other as partners. The 1838 incident would serve to show each that he need not hesitate.

During the year that Gail Borden had been customs collector at Galveston, the office had grown into one of the most important public posts of Texas, as well as one of the busiest. It had grown helter-skelter. Borden had met some needs as they had arisen; others he had anticipated. He had started from nothing and built as a man who had never built before might build a house—without organization, without unity, and without any real conception of what his house would resemble on completion.

A year's experience had taught him that if the customhouse was to enjoy an orderly second year, it would be better to have some definite, written rules. So in June, 1838, he drew up his "Rules for doing business at the Custom House at Galveston," forwarding the document to Henry Smith for amendment and approval. The rules included the following:

The office will be opened at 9 oClock A. M. and closed at 4 P. M.

Clerks . . . will attend the office at 8 oClock . . . and remain till 5 oClock, with a respite in the summer from 12 to half past 2 P. M. [Undoubtedly Borden approved the Mexican practice of the midday *siesta*.]

18 [Ashbel Smith] to Gail Borden, June 26, 1838, in Smith Papers
19 J W. Copes to Ashbel Smith, July 15, 1838, in Smith Papers

Inspectors and descharging officers will be ready for duty at any time between the rising and setting of Sun.

. . . Care will be taken not to interupt a Clerk while making a calculation. . . . no person will be allowed to go into the Cashier's room without his permission.

All Invoices or bills of dutiable goods [exceeding] two hundred Dollars, shall pass the inspection of the Collector. . . .

All permits for goods must be signed by the Collector or Deputy and attested by the Manifest Clerk.

All orders to send goods to the Public Store and all permits to take them out shall be attested by the Pub Store Repres.

No Money will be paid by the Cashier . . . except approved by the Collector.

Any Clerk or officer wishing a leave of absence during office hours shall obtain permission.

Secretary Smith kept the rules for six days before signing them without change on June 21, 1838. Apparently the Treasury Department was satisfied with the conduct of its Galveston customs.

Mirabeau Buonaparte Lamar, soldier, poet, and visionary, became the second constitutional president of Texas almost by default. Since the constitution forbade a president's succeeding himself, Sam Houston was eliminated. His friends, not liking Lamar any more than had Old Sam, solicited Thomas J. Rusk, who refused. Next they tried Peter W. Grayson, who killed himself in midsummer. Attention focused on James Collinsworth, the attorney general. In July he was drowned in Galveston Bay. Lamar won an almost unanimous decision.

Borden had known Lamar for perhaps two years. On the surface their relations seemed friendly enough, although Borden never tried to conceal his admiration for Houston. For the rift which developed, however, Borden should perhaps assume major responsibility. In the spring of 1838, a meeting was held in Galveston at which Lamar was named as Galveston's choice for president. On June 9, *The Telegraph and Texas Register* carried a column-long protest signed by eleven Galveston citizens. Fourth on the list appeared the name of Gail Borden. The signers claimed that the Lamar meeting had not been public, that those present had not resided in Texas long enough to vote, and that none of the signers had been

146

CONDENSED MILK

Is simply *Pure Milk*, from which, when perfectly *new* and *fresh*, nearly all the water has been evaporated in *vacuo*, and to which *nothing whatever* is added

Manufactured by BORDEN CONDENSED MILK Co, Winsted, Ct

FOR SALE BY THE

NEW YORK CONDENSED MILK CO.

34 & 36 Elizabeth Street,   **NEW YORK.**

One door from CANAL ST,

ALSO FOR SALE,

EXTRACT OF COFFEE,
Combined with Condensed Milk and Sugar;
A SUPERIOR ARTICLE

CONDENSED MILK.
(PRESERVED,)
BORDEN'S PATENT.
Patent Issued August 19th, 1856;
" Re-issued May 13th, 1862;
" " Feb. 10th, 1863;

Is the CONDENSED MILK, combined in due proportions with best Refined Sugar   Prepared in this form, it will remain perfectly sound

For use in Tea and Coffee, and for Ice Creams, Custards Puddings, and all other articles of cookery requiring both milk and sugar, it will be found excellent   It cannot when diluted, be distinguished from the best country milk sugared

Sugar of Milk may appear granulated or crystalized in lumps   It dissolves in warm or hot water   This proves the milk is pure and not having undergone a change before or during the process   the crystals should be dissolved

---

DIRECTIONS.

The Cans should be opened at the bottom by cutting the tin nearly round, and let it remain open, or partially covered

In removing the Milk from the cans, use only a DRY spoon and let the can remain open

For Custards, Puddings, &c , add water in the proportion of three pints to the pound to suit the taste   it can be used in Tea and Coffee without diluting

For Custards about four eggs may be used to the pound of milk   a less quantity will answer for Puddings   none are required for Rice Puddings

For Ice Cream   dilute with water, in such proportions as to suit the taste, and it is ready for the Freezer

---

Wrapper from an early can of Borden's condensed milk

The Borden Company

informed of the meeting. They wanted Grayson and other Texans to know that Galveston was not solidly in the Lamar camp and that Grayson "will be supported at this place, by others, as well as the undersigned." The protest was not designed to make Lamar feel any particular amity toward the eleven men.

Lamar assumed the presidency on December 10, 1838. His supporters had already determined their choices among the various political prizes which the former Georgia newspaperman could dispense. John Rice Jones wanted the customs post at either Matagorda, Velasco, or Galveston, "if new collectors are to be appointed."[20] That was the question: Would the President dismiss those officials who had served faithfully? Another applicant stated the prevailing opinion:

> I would not wish it thought, that I was willing, in the least, to contribute to the removal of the present incumbant, for whom I entertain great personal respect, yet I have so frequently heard it said, that Mr Borden would be required to give place to some one of Gen Lamars political friends.[21]

Gail Borden could only rest on his record: Texas' income during 1838 totaled $367,013.02, of which more than $235,000 derived from customs collections. Half the customs receipts had been collected in Galveston.[22]

Three days after Lamar's succession, the answer was known. "[Lamar] will turn out Gail Borden," Thomas F. McKinney wrote from Houston; "that will give him some trouble." Or as Hayes put it later: "Honest Uncle Gail Borden's head was among the first to drop into the basket."[23]

Other changes occurred. Toby was replaced as agent at New Orleans. Samuel M. Williams lost his navy agency at New York and Baltimore. Instead of to Jones, Borden's office went to Dr. Willis Roberts, a late arrival from Mobile, whom Lamar said he had known

[20] John Rice Jones to James F. Perry, December 9, 1838, in Perry Papers
[21] J. M. Bowyer to B E. Bee, November 15, 1838, in Domestic Correspondence
[22] R. E L Crane, "The Administration of the Customs Service of the Republic of Texas" (unpublished master's thesis, University of Texas, 1939), 232–33
[23] T. F. McKinney to S M Williams, December 13, 1838, in Williams Papers. Hayes, "Island and City of Galveston," 397

for twenty-five years "as a man of science, literature, and unblemished reputation."[24] McKinney apprised his partner, S. M. Williams, of the "general decapitation":

The Senate and in fact the whole country are indignant. . . . Gail Borden had a resolution offered of thanks to him and although not a member of the Senate was unfriendly towards him it was rejected because they are determined to place you in a more elevated position than any other man.[25]

Deserved or not, it was the way of politics in all ages. The new broom had swept, catching Gail Borden in its swath. He was collector no longer. Dr. Moore bade him farewell with a long eulogy:

Dr. Roberts . . . has been appointed Collector for the port of Galveston in place of Gail Borden, Jr. *removed.*

We feel a pleasure in declaring that this appointment has not been made in consequence of any neglect or misconduct of the late Collector. Mr. Borden has discharged the duties of this office with a degree of ability and integrity that has entitled him to the esteem and lasting gratitude of his fellow-citizens. His was the task of organizing and establishing a new department of government. No predecessor has smoothed his path and distinguished it by land marks. But, with indifatigable industry and perseverance, he surmounted every obstacle, and introduced system and regularity where all was chaos and confusion. During the whole term of his service, he has been distinguished by the most untiring vigilance and assiduity, and in consequence, has frequently elicited the admiration and praise of even prejudiced foreigners. As a proof of his disinterested zeal . . . we will here state that he has been so particular in collecting duties, that an amount of several hundred dollars had insensibly accumulated in his hands in consequence of his requiring the exchanges even for pennies and shillings, to be in favor rather than against the department. Yet he has paid in every farthing thus received . . . although it could not be claimed by the government. . . . During the

24 T. F. McKinney to S. M. Williams, January 1, 1839, in Williams Papers. Winkler (ed.), *Secret Journals of the Senate*, 119 S. R. Armstrong, "Chapters in the Early Life of Samuel May Williams, 1795–1836" (unpublished master's thesis, University of Texas, 1929), 15

25 It is typical of Borden that he harbored no permanent ill will toward Lamar. As one traveler wrote to Lamar more than two years later, "I am at present stopping with my friend Gail Borden.—you have *many* worse enemies than him." Gulick and others (ed.), *Lamar Papers*, V, 476.

period of the disastrous overflow of the island in the year 1837, he laboured with unremitting exertions to protect and secure every article of the property belonging to the government, and succeeded in preserving from destruction an amount of property far exceeding in value . . . the amount of his salary; and yet his services thus rendered, were entirely gratuitous, as they did not come within the sphere of his official duties. Such zeal and disinterestedness are seldom exhibited by those who obtain official stations only by favoritism. [Mr. Borden] will bear with him the confidence, gratitude and esteem of his fellow-citizens, who know well how to appreciate his worth and will award to him the tribute due to his merits.[26]

Gail Borden, public servant, had surrendered his title. Like nearly everyone else he was now a private citizen. For the first time in four years he could work entirely for himself, and he must be up and doing, for there were a dozen tasks awaiting his attention. He could not know, but his goal was drawing nearer.

[26] *Telegraph*, January 2, 1839.

*A man is a bundle of relations, a knot
of roots, whose flower and fruitage is
the world*   —Emerson

X

Setting the Crooked Straight
1839-1844

THE WORLD that was Laprairie was too small for Michel Branamour Menard. Having spent his first fourteen years in that tiny French-Canadian village across the St. Lawrence from Montreal, he decided that he could wait no longer to learn what lay beyond. Like other youths, most of them not so young, he traveled westward, roaming the great Northwest by land and by river, sometimes alone, sometimes with trappers, and sometimes with Indian traders.

When he was nearing eighteen, Menard dropped into Kaskaskia, St. Louis's rival as the most important settlement on the upper Mississippi. There he lived with his uncle, Pierre Menard, an Indian agent. There he learned to speak English of a sort. Pierre sent the wandering Michel to the unsettled Arkansas area to trade with the Shawnee, with whom he did more than just trade, entering into Indian life with such gusto that the tribe soon made him a chief. When the Shawnee migrated to Louisiana, Menard went along with "his people."

From Louisiana, Menard stepped easily into Texas in late autumn of 1829 to trade with the Mexicans and Indians around Nacogdoches. He liked Texas, and after a three-year visit to Illinois he returned to remain until his death, making friends on all sides and representing Liberty municipality at the signing of Texas' Declaration of Independence.

On December 9, 1836, Menard paid the Republic of Texas $50,000 to quitclaim a league and *labor* of land on Galveston Island that had been granted him by the Mexican government. Sizable doubts existed whether the Republic could guarantee clear title, but in 1836 the Republic was willing to take chances when the hook was baited with $50,000.[1] The sale met a notable lack of popular approval. Resentment died slowly, and nearly three years later an incensed county grand jury returned a true bill in the case of *Public Weal* v. *Inconsistent Legislative Acts*, charging that "the bargain and sale to Mr. Menard was indeed a *bargain* by which the Government *chiselled* itself out of $2,000,000, Minus $50,000."[2]

However, the development of "that wild project of Galveston" could not have been undertaken by more energetic hands than those of the thirty-one-year-old Michel Menard. At once he set about organizing a company of fellow promoters, including therein such astute men as Samuel M. Williams, Thomas F. McKinney, Mosely Baker, and the two practical dreamers who founded Houston, John K. and A. C. Allen. In the States, banker Nicholas Biddle, of national bank fame, bought stock valued at $44,000. The Galveston City Company resulted,[3] a firm that fostered and controlled Galveston's growth for the next three-quarters of a century. The company laid off the streets, advertised the advantages, encouraged prospective residents, and with some exceptions originally sold all the lots that all the residents and all the merchants and all the speculators and all the other categories of men necessary to a city bought and sold and traded and mortgaged.

When Gail Borden entered upon his duties as customs collector, the island had a population of two families, a sea-worn customhouse, and a few shacks. At the end of the Borden term Galveston was pushing toward the 1,500 mark, and hardly a day passed without the boom of cannon announcing arrival of another boatload of eager immigrants. When a city election was held in 1839, 520 more or less qualified voters turned out.

Immigrants came from everywhere, one traveler observing that though English-speaking persons predominated, "*'Buenos dias'*

[1] L W. Kemp, *The Signers of the Texas Declaration of Independence*, 215–16. Gammel, *The Laws of Texas*, I, 1130–31. Miller, *A Financial History of Texas*, 54. Hayes, "Island and City of Galveston," 177. Patent, Republic of Texas to Michel B. Menard, January 25, 1838, Galveston City Company Records, in possession of Stewart Title Guaranty Company, Galveston (hereafter cited as Records).

[2] District Court Minutes, A–C, Fayette County, Texas, 19

[3] Hayes, "Island and City of Galveston," 177 Armstrong, "Chapters in the Early Life of Samuel May Williams," 21. Nicholas Biddle to James Love, October 26, 1839, in Records.

'Bon jour' 'Bon giorno' 'Guten tag' 'Ya! Ya!' &c. &c.—and an occasional jabbering of the Lipans & Coshattas" were often heard. Included in the assortment were some of the world's less savory inhabitants, causing Mayor J. M. Allen, at least, to mount a six-pound gun in his front yard as a precaution.

Ships choked the harbor—sometimes thirty at one time. One hundred and fifty tons of ice arrived from Boston, three thousand miles away. There were two hotels, three warehouses, fifteen retail stores, an oyster house, two printing establishments, artisans' shops of all descriptions, and six licensed taverns. Proudly a local newspaper proclaimed in 1839: "It is no longer a misnomer to call this the *City* of Galveston."[4]

Houses seemed to spring full grown, as from the sea. The British consul wrote of having seen a house containing $20,000 worth of stores, the timbers of which had been growing in Maine only thirty days before. Stephen Southwick stepped ashore with the frame of a residence he had brought ready-made from New York. It soon became Galveston's first two-story house. Other buildings were so constructed that even a three-story house could be moved across town "at pleasure."[5]

Out toward the Gulf beach near the eastern arm of McKinney's Bayou, Gail Borden built himself a home complete with observatory and flagstaff. Just southwest was Williams's residence, and west of that, brother Tom's house and windmill. A block north were the homes of Michel Menard and J. S. Sydnor. Good neighbors all—men Borden liked and respected.

Here at the corner of Thirty-fifth and P Streets, Gail Borden prepared for a life of private citizenship. He had assets: Penelope, his wife; two sons and one daughter;[6] property scattered over half of Texas; experience as a farmer, teacher, surveyor, editor and publisher, and government official; a reputation for honesty and painstaking attention to duty; and an impulsive but purposive mind.

On the other hand, he was nearing forty in an era when many men burned their candles with more speed than wisdom. At the age of twenty-nine Austin had founded the colony that became Texas;

[4] Quoted in Hayes, "Island and City of Galveston," 376–77.

[5] S. B. Southwick in the Galveston *Daily News*, June 11, 1906. W Bollaert, "Residence and Travel in Texas, 1842–1843," 29, in Ayer Collection

[6] A third son, Stephen F. Austin Borden, was born June 5, 1839.

Houston had been governor of Tennessee at thirty-four and president of a pocket republic at forty-three. In the States the pattern was identical. In politics, Henry Clay had been speaker of the United States House of Representatives at thirty-four, and his colleague John C. Calhoun, acting chairman of the foreign relations committee at thirty. About 1836, twenty-two-year-old Samuel Colt had patented a pistol with a revolving breech, thereby contributing a foundation stone to the later development of the trans-Mississippi West; and in 1831 twenty-two-year-old Cyrus Hall McCormick, like Borden the son of a sometime blacksmith, had demonstrated the successful reaper that opened the vast stretches of Western plains to profitable agriculture. Probably in 1839 Gail Borden had heard of neither of these two inventors, but the knowledge was not necessary for him to realize that he was living in a young man's world—and that he was nearing middle age.

But he was adrift, swept along by a changing political current. It brought cold comfort that within three months after Lamar had taken office, defection was splitting his administration, prompting one onlooker to write that "Lamar is sinking like a plummet [and] could not be elected a constable."[7]

Borden had been in Texas nearly ten years, and now the continuity of those ten years had been snapped. He had worked and worried and arrived nowhere. He was a tinker at heart, and looking back, it seemed all he had done was tinker—with teaching, surveying, farming, publishing, and collecting. That was no life for a man whose head was in the stars.

When he turned over his books and keys to Dr. Roberts and walked away from the distractions of the customhouse, what relief must have flooded his heart as he realized that at last he was free to dream his dreams—dreams unhampered by details and complaints and manifests and entries and weekly reports to Henry Smith.

But always would come those searching moments of self-criticism when he must ask himself, "Where have those dreams brought me?" and could find only one answer: "Nowhere."

You have another answer, Gail Borden, but you still aren't prepared to receive it. Impatience comes easy to men who would

[7] Henry Austin to James F. Perry, March 24, 1839, in Perry Papers.

set the world ablaze. You are nearly forty, and your flint is hardly scratched. You must learn patience. You must learn it plodding a path whose milestones spell sorrow and affliction and adversity and disappointment and ordeal and separation and renunciation . . . and humiliation. By the end of that road you will be an old man, by your standards and by the standards of the times.

You couldn't know William Morris—he was only five years old when you lost your collectorship—but years later Morris would write two lines that in 1839 would have fit your thoughts like a cog in a mortise:

Dreamer of dreams, born out of my due time,
Why should I strive to set the crooked straight?

Yes, Gail Borden, your dreams are ahead of their time. Yours is to be a longer apprenticeship during which you will stretch your wings many times before you find them ready.

So, go back to your house and your wife and your children, go back to the gusty, gritty sandbar that you call an island, go back to your tinkering, go back to drawing absurd plans in the soft sand with your stick of sugar cane, go back to your dreams. Go back—and wait.

Dr. Levi Jones had all the medical practice he had time for, especially when one considered the hours consumed by his being agent for the Galveston City Company. Therefore, when he and Menard fell into a rather vague argument over financial procedure and Menard in his best broken English informed Jones of his disapproval, Jones walked out of the company, his back stiffened by the reassurance that his medical practice would support him more than adequately. He would, he announced, remain as a director of the company so that he might continue to share in any profits.

The outcome of the argument left the Galveston City Company without a pilot, for that was the agent's rôle. Dr. Jones had been secretary, business manager, and salesman. His successor must be a man who could assume equivalent responsibilities. Obviously, in labor-short Galveston such a man could not be plucked off the next schooner that tied up alongside McKinney and Williams's wharf. He must be a man of proved abilities and of integrity.

At his home on Thirty-fifth Street, Gail Borden had been fussing around his fig orchard and his sheds ever since President Lamar had replaced him as customs collector. He was into this and into that, until no one knew exactly what to expect of him. According to one report, any morning his gangling figure could be seen astride a placid bull, all saddled and bridled, the two of them making their way to market. The picture presented by the pair would be interesting if it ever existed, but other, more reliable evidence points to Thomas H. Borden as the bull-riding marketer.[8] Certainly a bull's pace would have dragged on Gail Borden worse than an anchor.

When in May, 1839, he learned of the Galveston City Company vacancy, he must have decided it was time to come from behind the high board fence around his residence and re-enter Galveston life. He may have needed the money. Regardless of financial considerations it was the type of position he would have wanted. To some degree he would be able to set his own hours of work. Part of the time he could spend out of doors. Seldom would he be required to work at being agent to the exclusion of other endeavors. Plenty of time would be left to tinker. And plenty of time to dream.

Borden held the Galveston City Company agency for twelve years, during which Galveston's population grew from about 1,300 to more than 4,200, becoming the largest city in Texas. By 1851, when he resigned, Galveston contained more than seven hundred residences and a proportionate number of business houses.[9] And almost without exception each dwelling and each commercial establishment had been erected on property purchased from the agent of the Galveston City Company. Along the east end of the island the company's holdings stretched for more than four miles, with an average width of more than one and one-half miles. Present-day Galveston with its population of 65,000, lies largely within that area.

Two reports issued during Borden's agency typify the company's operations. The first shows that by October, 1841, 1,543 lots had been sold for an aggregate of $1,218,911.18, Texas money. The second report, covering the seven months prior to May, 1846,

[8] Agreement, February 13, 1839, in Williams Papers. S. B. Southwick in the Galveston *Daily News*, June 11, 1906.

[9] Hayes, "Island and City of Galveston," 377 Seventh Census, Texas, II, 492. *Telegraph*, May 8, 1839.

reveals that 196 lots were sold for nearly $35,000; with a total since 1838 of 2,197 lots for $1,240,124.07, this in sound United States currency.[10]

Borden left no record of his financial arrangements with the company. A straight commission of 6 per cent would have grossed him between $50,000 and $60,000 for the first seven years. Possibly he received a salary and bonuses in addition, and undoubtedly he must have obtained concessions in purchasing land for himself, for the Galveston County records contain more than ninety deeds of private purchase involving him during his agency and the 1850 census shows him owning $100,000 worth of real estate, the second highest holding in Galveston.[11]

That the company directors were pleased with him is evidenced by their granting him seven lots and a 380-foot wharf privilege "in consideration of the valuable service rendered" at the time he resigned to devote full time to his meat biscuit.[12] He served the company well, and he was appreciated.

During Gail Borden's first summer in Galveston fresh water became so scarce that McKinney and Williams's team had to haul it from Robinson's place six miles down the island in order for the island population and ships' crews in port to be able to drink and cook. Solicitous of the comfort of his family and his island neighbors, Borden spent "no little time and . . . some expense" searching for water. On the sandy ridge back of Newel's residence he sank two wells which yielded good water in limited quantities. So long as the demand was small, he could save Galvestonians from sending to Robinson's.

Later, after building at Thirty-fifth and P, Borden decided that even Newel's was too far away. He prospected the ridge near the Gulf beach, just a few hundred yards from his house, but found the water was no good. He tried other places in the vicinity, discovering insufficient amounts of water to carry through the hot dry-season.

[10] Report, *ca* December 20, 1841, in Smith Papers. Extract of Report, Gail Borden to Stockholders, May 1, 1846, in Records.

[11] Seventh Census, Texas, II, 492.

[12] Report, *ca* December 21, 1841. Gail Borden to Ashbel Smith, April 22, 1851, in Smith Papers. Record Book, J, Galveston County, Texas, 404.

Toward the end of summer, 1839, such a shortage existed in Galveston that its citizens arranged to send by boat for water from the San Jacinto River, fifty miles away. (In Houston, complained the *Telegraph*, water was so bad that its rats had taken to drinking gin and were cutting all kinds of antics.)[13] At this juncture Gail Borden came hurrying into town with the announcement that he had discovered "sufficient water . . . to supply an immense population" out near the Gulf beach. Up and down the streets of Galveston he went, knocking on doors and stopping pedestrians to tell them where and how they could get water. Thereafter Galveston never wanted for fresh water.

In thus contributing to the convenience of life in Galveston and therefore in part to the town's prosperity, Borden disclaimed any credit for having done more than "any enterprising citizen should have considered it his duty to do." Since, however, the Galveston City Company stood to profit from his discovery, he petitioned the directors to show their appreciation by granting him a lot and a fraction near the Gulf shore, about four acres in all.

In return he would erect a bathhouse for both sexes. His idea was to enable the women to bathe in private by making the bathhouse portable. When it was in use, he would move it out into the surf; when bathing hours or season had terminated, he would bring the house ashore. He proposed that the machinery for moving the bathhouse should be located permanently in the yard of his residence. Ruefully, Borden noted on the back of his petition the company's reaction to his petition: "Not acted upon G. B. Jr."[14]

It was not the end of his bathhouse scheme, for although he had to insist for five more years that his portable bathhouse scheme was practicable, in the end he won. Among his taxable property listed at the close of 1846 is included one "Locomotive Bath House."[15] Thanks to Gail Borden, Galveston ladies had their "source of convenience and enjoyment."

[13] Report, Gail Borden to Directors of the Galveston City Company, *ca.* 1840, in Borden Papers, Rosenberg Library. *Telegraph*, August 7, 1839.

[14] Report, Gail Borden to Directors of the Galveston City Company, *ca.* 1840, in Borden Papers, Rosenberg Library.

[15] Tax Receipts, Galveston County, Texas, December 31, 1846, in Borden Papers, Rosenberg Library.

Having taken on the appearance of a full-grown city, Texas style, Galveston decided to dignify its position by organizing a city government. On March 14, 1839, the first city election was held, with John M. Allen being chosen mayor, James McKnight, recorder, and Peter J. Menard, treasurer. Included in the list of eight aldermen was the name of Gail Borden. The eleven men constituted Galveston's first city government.

A week later the eleven met in a partially completed house on Avenue E near Nineteenth Street that was being erected for M. de Saligny, French chargé to Texas, whose later experiences with Austin pigs led to one of the more hilarious episodes in Texas history. In this half-finished structure the board of alderman, profoundly impressed with the gravity of their municipal responsibilities, seated themselves on nail kegs around a slightly littered carpenter's workbench to take their oaths of office and to deliberate on the needs of the embryonic city.

A more suitable meeting place constituted the agenda. John Derrick, W. B. Nichols, and Gail Borden were named as a committee to contract for a council room, furniture, and stationery. On the following Monday the group convened to hear the committee apologize for having located no council room. But the committee reported on what it had found: "One large table, not finished; two chairs, seven inkstands, six sand boxes, two papers of sand, two cards of steel pins, two quires of paper, two blank books, and one box of wafers."[16]

At this meeting Borden was given membership on a committee to draft a code of government for Galveston. At the April 2 session the committee reported that it had drafted no bylaws but that it considered it had planned even better: it had arranged to obtain copies of the form and ordinances of the cities of Houston and Mobile. When on April 9 Mayor Allen summoned an extra session to consider the committee's report, the committee announced its inability to report because Houston and Mobile had not sent copies of their laws. The council would wait no longer, resolving to adopt the ordinances of Houston, whatever they might be, so far as they could apply to Galveston.[17]

[16] Hayes, "Island and City of Galveston," 330–31.
[17] *Ibid.*, 332–33.

In the three months that Borden served as alderman he labored to improve the morality of his island city. In this object he met with more success than he had in drafting a code of ordinances. He helped draft regulations whereby every barroom, grocery, "tent, recess, and every establishment of whatever description, where ardent liquors" were sold should be closed each night after eleven o'clock, to remain closed until five o'clock the next morning on penalty of a ten-dollar fine.

Borden turned next to the gamblers. Toward the close of 1838 and continuing through the spring of 1839, gamblers from New Orleans had flocked into Galveston to victimize the unwary immigrant who frequently landed with all his worldly goods converted into the cash he had in his pocket. The gamblers contributed more to the picturesqueness than to the respectability of Galveston by pitching tents and equipment in vacant lots along the main streets, spreading gold and silver coins with studied carelessness about their entrances. They flourished.

Emboldened by success, the gamblers began to swagger about Galveston's powdery streets, behaving rudely toward many conservative residents who clung to the moldering belief that hard work was the keystone to financial success. Among these citizens was Gail Borden.

The ordinance which Borden introduced stated flatly that the city council regarded gambling as a practice "having the most pernicious and demoralizing influence" and that the council was prepared to rid the city of its gamblers. To do this, Borden recommended that Mayor Allen appoint twenty men as special constables to co-operate with Galveston's existing authorities to suppress the activities of these undesirable gamblers. The ordinance was quickly adopted.

Although the gamblers were lawless men in a land where the law was nearly always behind, the twenty men accomplished the cleanup with surprising ease. With hardly a scowl the gamblers packed their belongings and left Galvestonians to enjoy, along with the salt breezes, the blessings of law and civic morality. With this victory Gail Borden resigned as alderman, his resignation being accepted on June 18, 1839.[18] By that time he had assumed his post with

18 *Ibid.,* 335, 345–46, 350.

the Galveston City Company, and besides, a dozen other matters clamored for his attention.

The Galveston setting in which Gail Borden lived presented scenes that shifted as steadily as if the island had been a kaleidoscope. In addition to the constant changes caused by Borden's multiplicity of interests, the growth in size and importance of a mushrooming community meant that almost daily something different turned up. It might be nothing more than the laying of foundation stones for another house or the arrival of another cordwainer or armorer or even a barber. Or it might be such a stirring event as took place when the French fleet appeared off the harbor entrance in May, 1839, to exchange salutes before entering. Then everyone in town quit work to view from the docks the French frigate that carried sixty-four guns, or the fleet flagship *Phaeton*. The greatest wonder of all was Commodore Baudin of the scarred forehead and missing right arm.

Always there was more than enough for Gail Borden to see to and do, since by nature he would try a little of everything. Thus he could be seen on June 21 tendering an invitation to Moses Austin Bryan to be guest of honor at a public dinner. He platted Pelican Shoal, a diminutive island in Galveston Bay. He began to buy more land and to try to sell land.[19] Others found work for him. At the end of January, 1840, the Texas Congress named him one of the land commissioners to detect fraudulent land claims. A Connecticut woman proposed that he or Thomas be named administrator for her late husband's Texas estate, since the Bordens were well known as "business men and women of integrity." Ashbel Smith had him experiment with planting Rohan potatoes, which, along with mulberry trees, broomcorn, Merino sheep, Berkshire hogs, and shorthorn cattle, were being fancied by farmers in the States as means to solve farm problems.[20] From all sides Borden's opinion was sought. And always the man had an opinion.

[19] Gail Borden and others to Austin Bryan, June 21, 1839, in Moses Austin Bryan Papers, University of Texas Archives. Gulick and others (eds), *Lamar Papers*, II, 204 Records, A, Galveston County, Texas, 309–11. *Telegraph*, September 4, 1839.

[20] *Texas Sentinel*, February 5, 1840. Ann W. Burritt to Ashbel Smith, September 15, 1839, [Ashbel Smith] to Gail Borden, January 21, 1840—in Smith Papers.

Occasionally visitors crowded his house, although the dietetic regimen and the pell-mell routine observed by their host usually discouraged a return call. Alexander Somervell, former secretary of war, was less fortunate than most—he dropped in for overnight and remained for days with an attack of fever.

When James Perry's children arrived in Galveston in 1842 aboard the *Neptune,* Borden, serving his second term as customs collector, was in such a furious rush that he forgot his intentions of caring for them until they could be sent on to Peach Point. His apology to Perry is illuminating:

I intended to take them to my house, and for that purpose sent for my carriage—but the day they came in my deputy and book-keeper both were sick and absent; Three vessels besides the Neptune were entering and discharging go[ods]   I was also engaged in directing the workmen on the fortification of the east end of the Island, and night found me with a load of unfinished business—Guy [Bryan] will remember the Jam of business in and about the Custom House. The next day I was on board of the Neptune at 4 O'clock in the morning,—and did not stop to rest till one in the afternoon—My wife regretted she could not see them.[21]

For nearly a year after leaving the collector's office Borden worked at clearing away details arising from his administration. In November, 1839, he took all of his customhouse vouchers and other papers to Austin to arrange a final adjustment of accounts with the Treasury Department.[22] In the meantime scandal had been growing around his successor, Dr. Roberts, the Galveston newspapers charging inefficiency and laxness. After an inspection Lamar removed his friend, but if Borden hoped to return to the post, the President dashed such hopes by naming A. A. M. Jackson.[23] Borden would have to await the re-election of Houston.

---

21 Gail Borden to James F. Perry, June 12, 1840, November 5, 1842, in Perry Papers.

22 Lamar had moved the capital to the frontier settlement on the banks of the Colorado which was named Austin At the time of the move, Austin's chief attraction lay three miles away at beautiful Barton Springs, where Mr. Barton lived with his two pretty daughters. Barton liked his solitude On one occasion when the government sent troops to the region to protect him from Indians, he sent word to the troop commander that if he did not evacuate his men immediately, Barton *"would let the Indians kill them "* C R Williams (ed), *Diary and Letters of Rutherford Birchard Hayes,* I, 260.

23 Gail Borden to James H. Starr, October 1, 1839, in Comptroller's Letters Winkler (ed.), *Secret Journals of the Senate,* 140 *Telegraph,* October 2, 1839.

In September, 1839, the first serious siege of yellow fever visited Galveston, more than three hundred persons dying before December frosts purified the island air. Though half the city fled, Borden and his family remained. Galveston was his home now, and it would take more than yellow fever to drive him out. In a few years, however, he would regret his decision to remain. But in 1839 and 1840 Borden was beginning to like Galveston and to feel that here he could work and prosper. And in a modest way he was prospering, as his tax receipts for 1840 reveal. He owned at least eight lots on the island, plus such personal property as three Negroes, one work horse, a "mettle" clock, a wooden clock, a silver watch, and a four-wheel carriage.[24] It was not much, but he had plans for an increase.

After the cuffings of its first three years of existence, Galveston enjoyed a reasonably unruffled twelve months during 1840. The city was free of fever. Texas currency was valued at 76 per cent. The British established a cotton export agency. J. P. Nash opened a school, and the navy shot two deserters at its yard. On everyone's tongue was talk of the proposed connection with the mainland by shell embankments and bridges on piles. Talk of annexation to the United States resembled talk of rain by Texas farmers during August drouths, still a possibility but not really expected soon.

Gail Borden was "garnisheed" to testify in the case of *Albert C. Horton* v. *William Christy*. In the fall Thomas H. Borden made $5,000 bond to become Galveston County's deputy surveyor. In Austin, John P. Borden was named to a committee of vigilance to protect the capital against surprise. Later in the year he resigned as the first commissioner of the Republic's General Land Office after a highly successful administration under both Houston and Lamar.[25]

It was a year in which Gail Borden and his wife, Penelope, experienced an increased feeling of peace, the serenity that comes to all persons who believe in the immortality of their souls. Behind Borden was a centuries-long tradition of simple trust in the doctrines of the Quaker and Baptist faiths. On Penelope Mercer Borden's side the Baptist connections held even stronger.

[24] Hayes, "Island and City of Galveston," 387. Tax Receipts, April 28, 1841, in Borden Papers, Rosenberg Library

[25] J O Dyer, "Early History of Galveston, Texas, 1518–1861," in Rosenberg Library. Records, A, Galveston County, Texas, 609 *Texas Sentinel*, June 13, 1840. *Telegraph*, December 23, 1840.

John Gail Borden, his father's favorite child,
succeeded as second president of the
New York Condensed Milk Company

The Borden Company

Penelope Borden's great-grandfather, a strict Episcopalian, had wept gall when he learned that his son, Silas, had attended a Baptist meeting. But Silas Mercer was undeterred. Baptist doctrine gripped his soul until in 1775 he completed the apostasy by transferring his membership to the Baptist church. On the baptismal day, the story goes, Silas Mercer "rose from the water . . . a minister of the gospel; for before he left the stream where he was immersed, he ascended a log and exhorted the surrounding multitude." He preached until he died. During a six-year period of the American Revolution he stumped North Carolina as an itinerant minister, preaching more than two thousand sermons.[26] When he was done preaching, he left behind eight children, one of whom, Jesse, outstripped even his father in the spirit he brought to the pulpit.

But Gail Borden, his wife, and his father-in-law, Eli Mercer, a cousin of Jesse Mercer, had deserted their Baptist community to go to barbarous Texas, where only Roman Catholics were allowed. Until 1836 Mexico had required all Texas immigrants to embrace the Catholic faith. However, since Mexico did not possess sufficient priests to minister to Texas' Catholic needs, the requirement was unenforceable. Some communities saw a priest about once every three years, which generally was not often enough to insure devotion to Catholic precepts.

Texans then were nominally Roman Catholics, but the profession was seldom followed in practice. Probably none of the Bordens or Mercers ever embraced the Roman Catholic church, but under the circumstances merely remained content to stay beyond the pale of organized religion. To a soul-concerned person like Gail Borden such a situation was far from satisfactory. To crusading Jesse Mercer back in Georgia the situation called for direct action—it created, to use a minister's favorite word, a challenge.

When Texas freed herself from Mexico, Jesse Mercer responded to his challenge by donating $2,500 to be used in maintaining a Baptist missionary in Texas. Considering the self-abnegation which missionaries were supposed to practice, the sum was enormous —enough to keep one man in the field for ten years. Texas Baptists awaited the choice of the man who was to direct their salvation.

---

[26] Jesse Mercer, *A History of the Georgia Baptist Association*, 389. C. D. Mallary, *Memoirs of Elder Jesse Mercer*, 14

An extensive prairie fire to the north sending dark clouds to obscure the winter sun brought early darkness to Galveston on the afternoon of January 24, 1840. Before darkness set in, however, several people had spotted the *Neptune* out at the harbor entrance, and when the steamer docked at seven o'clock the usual large gathering waited on tiptoe at the sixty-yard wharf to see who and what was aboard.

The person destined to play a leading rôle in Galveston's spiritual life in the next decade did not, however, come ashore that Friday night. For the Reverend James Huckins, a lean, handsome man with a thin strong face, keen black eyes, one of which danced about independently of the other, and black unruly hair, planned to continue to Houston, believing that Galveston contained no Baptists.

But when he stepped ashore the next morning in his high white collar, black scarf tie, and dark coat with black velvet lapels, he encountered almost immediately a man he had baptized only two years before. This friend introduced the Reverend Huckins to others who had been Baptists back in the States. All of them urged that he stay over one more day to preach, for some of them had waited years to hear a sermon.[27] In his journal Huckins noted the effect of his decision:

> About eleven o'clock public worship commenced. The congregation numbered 200, and many were forced to leave for want of room. A deep solemnity marked the scene. The countenances of male and female indicated deep interest, mellowness of feeling, and with many, very many, the indications of a crushed spirit and fallen hopes were too clear to prevent deception. When home, or native land, or kindred afar off . . . were referred to the tears would gush forth. Never did I preach to a company to whom the gospel appeared more grateful.[28]

That afternoon and again that night Huckins preached to overflow crowds. Galveston was starving for the gospel. When the night service closed, twelve regular Baptists and a dozen more who were Baptist in principle clustered around Jesse Mercer's missionary to urge Huckins to stay and organize a church. Wrote Huckins: "So

[27] J. M. Carroll, *A History of Texas Baptists*, 143. *The Life and Writings of Rufus C. Burleson*, 384.

[28] *The Texas Baptist*, November 14, 1855.

I shall stop for a few days."[29] Here was the man who could feast Gail Borden's soul.

Six men and five women gathered at the home of Thomas H. Borden the following Thursday night. Six brought letters of withdrawal from churches in the States. Among them were Mrs. Louisa R. Borden, Thomas's second wife, and her brother, Lewis Graves, who presented letters from the First Baptist Church of Seneca Falls, New York.[30] As soon as the organization had been completed, Gail and Penelope Borden stepped forward. Huckins wrote Jesse Mercer:

> One of the most reputable men in the republic, accompanied by his wife, came forward and desired the ordinance of baptism. The wife of this brother was a Mercer. . . . This brother and his wife . . . have been waiting and praying for more than ten years for some servant of Christ of their own faith to come and preach to them the word of life and to baptize them, and I was the first they had seen or heard. For five years they never saw a minister of Christ, or had the privilege of attending a religious meeting. . . . Though they could not find a single individual to join them, yet they have been accustomed to spend their Sabbaths in reading and prayer; to consecrate the day most sacredly to the Lord, and to maintain prayer in their own family. . . .
>
> "Oh," says the sister, "how long have I prayed for this, and hoped for this, and now the Lord is giving it!"[31]

Baptismal day—Tuesday, February 4—dawned fair and fine. By three o'clock fifty persons had assembled along the Gulf beach to witness the ceremony. The setting was perfect. To the north, prairie and sky as far as the eye could see. To the south, the waters of the Gulf of Mexico reaching to the horizon. All about, cream-colored sands packed as smooth and hard and gleaming as a concrete highway. And the participants: a humble, earnest man—described by a Virginia witness as "a man who . . . stands as high as any in the republic for sterling integrity, high-toned morality and the active interest he takes in every measure calculated to advance the moral and religious improvement of society"—his twenty-eight-year-old wife, and her sister. "I have never witnessed a scene like this," wrote one of the fifty.

[29] Carroll, *A History of Texas Baptists*, 143.
[30] *Historical Sketch of the First Baptist Church of Galveston, Texas*, 3
[31] *The Christian Index*, February 27, 1840.

Brother Huckins opened with a prayer. Next followed the hymn:

Jesus and shall it ever be,
A mortal man ashamed of Thee?

Gail Borden gave Huckins his hand as the two waded out into the waves. After immersion Borden strode out as "professor and non-professor pushed forward with streaming eyes and feelings too deep for utterance to give him their hands."

Penelope Borden followed, and then her sister. Penelope rose from the water, her face "radiant with joy and devotion." As the three returned to the beach, "a brother by blood, who had just tasted of the love of Jesus, came forward weeping and praising God, while shouting,

" 'My sisters! My sisters! I rejoice with you! My sisters!'

"And all three embracing each other, stood weeping, not able to vent their feelings but by tears.

"O my Father, there was not an eye present . . . but filled; not a heart . . . but began to melt."

Following the ceremony, the witness records, "The congregation dispersed in too solemn a mood for conversation, disposed to commune with their own hearts."[32]

Thus, with almost too-poetic good fortune Jesse Mercer's benevolence had realized its first success. With the Reverend Huckins as intermediary, the first fruits of Mercer's gift had brought none other than the Georgia preacher's own kinsmen into the fold.

And thus, too, the brown waters of the Gulf of Mexico around Galveston Island, only three decades before the highway for the pirate Lafitte, had parted for the first time to receive a soul in baptism.

It was reputedly the first baptismal service in the Gulf west of the Mississippi River. It was an important day in the history of Texas Baptists. The memory of this day would sustain Gail Borden through many difficult days ahead.

[32] The quotations and material above are taken variously from these sources *Historical Sketch of the First Baptist Church of Galveston, Texas*, 4 Carroll, *A History of Texas Baptists*, 144, 146–47, 148. *The Life and Writings of Rufus C. Burleson*, 671, 724–25. *The Christian Index*, February 27, March 26, 1840.

Another year. 1841. Heavy rains fell in January, as Buffalo Bayou rose forty feet. Count de Narbonne passed through, leaving boarders at the Tremont Hotel holding fifty dollars in counterfeit bills. Leeches, bloodthirsty from being starved in sugared water, sold three for a quarter. Ice cream brought three dollars a gallon. Galveston had nearly all the ice it wanted, shipped in by schooners to be kept in thick huts whose walls were packed in sawdust. William Sandusky and his mother visited the Bordens for several days, and Gail and John became executors for the Peter W. Grayson estate. John and Gail also teamed with James G. Burnham to buy fourteen lots (42 by 120 feet) from the Galveston City Company. In August a dancing school opened—culture was creeping up on Galveston. Good Spanish mares were bringing ten dollars each.

In October, a week after Penelope Borden had given birth to a daughter, Mary Jane, Gail Borden made a short trip to Clear Creek in Fayette County to attend the second annual meeting of the Union Baptist Association, which now included nine churches. Before the convention adjourned, it set up the Texas Baptist Education Society, which was to found, among other things, Baylor University and Baylor Female College. Among the first officers of the society were James Huckins, R. E. B. Baylor, Z. N. Morrell, all ministers, and Gail Borden. Borden was a manager, or trustee.[33]

In the States William Henry Harrison had hardly sat down in the president's chair after winning his "Log Cabin and Hard Cider" campaign when death replaced him with John Tyler, nominally a Whig but a Democrat at heart. Three years of frustration lay ahead for the Whig administration.

In Texas at the end of 1841 Sam Houston returned to the presidency. On the day before Christmas the Senate confirmed unanimously his appointment of Gail Borden for the Galveston collectorship.[34] Borden held the appointment for less than two years, but he required nearly ten years to dispose of the disputes and misunderstandings.[35]

About the same time that Gail Borden's father was marrying

[33] *The Life and Writings of Rufus C Burleson,* 186
[34] Winkler (ed), *Secret Journals of the Senate,* 211–12
[35] Borden's second term will be treated separately in the next chapter

the widow Catherine Carson,[36] trouble with an altogether too familiar visage reappeared. Angered by President Lamar's expedition against Santa Fé, Santa Anna sent an army into Texas which captured and held San Antonio, Goliad, and Refugio long enough for some West Texans to enact an 1842 version of the runaway scrape of six years before.

In September the Mexicans began a second invasion, General Woll holding San Antonio for nine days before retiring. President Houston instructed Borden to keep Galveston alert—unnecessary advice, for by this time Galveston had begun to be alarmed. Sitting apart from the remainder of Texas as it did, it felt itself vulnerable from the sea. What if the Mexican navy decided to bombard the city—or, worse, invade?

On October 6 the people of Galveston met to adopt measures of defense. Twenty-four of the town's "most active citizens" were named a committee for action. John S. Sydnor, L. M. Hitchcock, and Gail Borden prepared an address to be promulgated throughout town, outlining the seriousness of the situation and the measures to be adopted. The address, it was reported, "aroused an ardor of patriotism that made every man emulous to out do his neighbor. Every man was alert."

Citizens began erecting a fort at the east end of the island, pulling down the old icehouse to use its planks and timbers in building platforms for gun carriages. Companies were formed and drilled daily. Vedettes patrolled the beach west to San Luis Island. Congress appropriated $7,000 for the protection of Galveston Harbor, to be administered by James H. Cocke, Oscar Farish, and Gail Borden. In November, Borden wrote that despite an attack of dengue fever he was directing the work of fortification—and that he was "expecting the Mexicans here for a certainty."

Spring and summer followed, and the Mexicans had not come. A rumor that President Houston would appoint Borden and Samuel M. Williams as commissioners to negotiate with Santa Anna proved groundless. In late 1843 the fortifications were completed and a garrison maintained until annexation.[37]

[36] Record of Marriage Licenses, I, Brazoria County, Texas, 99–100

[37] Amelia W. Williams and E. C. Barker (eds), *The Writings of Sam Houston, 1813–1863*, IV, 146 John P. Borden joined the South-Western army at Camp Leon as a second lieutenant *Telegraph*, December 21, 1842.

The Mexicans never did come. But Galveston had tried to be ready.

Emeline Brightman was still in her teens when she landed in Galveston with her father and mother in the spring of 1843. Since the Brightmans were Baptists, it was natural they should meet Gail Borden, clerk of the First Baptist Church, who told them where services were held. In his precipitate fashion Borden offered Miss Brightman a Sunday-school class almost as soon as introductions were concluded. Before she could agree—indeed, before she could even consider—he had moved on to other subjects. Miss Brightman had been to high school? Good, he would come over and "parse" with her. Miss Brightman was terror-stricken: "I was too much of a stranger in a strange land to be disposed to vaunt my attainments in the presence of a gentleman who impressed me as being thorough." But she need not have worried, for "fortunately . . . other matters of more importance caused him to forget it."

The girl did accept Borden's invitation to Sunday school. Since her mother was rheumatic and her father "too proud to expose the poverty of his apparel by displaying himself in an urban congregation," Miss Brightman went alone to the meeting house on the Strand.

I reached the place with a feeling of timidity approaching fright, having to run the gauntlet of longshoremen, sailors and marines and other idlers, all of whom were unoccupied on account of its being Sunday. When I arrived . . . I found but little in the surroundings to reassure me. I have attended religious services at log schoolhouses, in the woods under the groves and many other places where both convenience and comfort were lacking, but to me I have never been anywhere on such a mission where the prospect was so uninviting not to say disgusting. The meeting was held in the garret of a dingy old storehouse, reached by a narrow, winding stairway almost enveloped in darkness. It seemed to me like a veritable prison.

Gail Borden showed her about. Everyone was congenial, and she was given a prealphabet group of children to teach. But the setting was too austere· "I visited the place but a few times before I became afraid to go alone, and so I quit."[38]

[38] Emeline Brightman Russell in the Galveston *Daily News*, October 20, 1901.

If the First Baptist Church of Galveston hoped to attract any but the most hardy Christians, it was going to have to build itself a church. But Gail Borden had been planning toward that for years.

Despite threats of invasion, storms, and inadequate facilities, life went ahead in Galveston. The firm of Perry and Johns opened a cotton press operated by horses on McLean's wharf. The *Star of the Republic*, a clipper, sailed in from Portland in seventeen fast days. The Galveston *Daily News*, today Texas' oldest continuous newspaper, was born. Monsieur Alphonse opened the San Jacinto Hotel. In Houston the former capitol building was converted to a hotel. The first slave was set free on the island. J. J. Davis advertised that he had porcelain teeth for sale. And Sam Houston called Commodore Moore of the Texas navy a pirate while most of Galveston seethed, for Moore was a local favorite.

Two venturous abolitionists named Andrews and Lee fled Houston ahead of a mob. On their way through Galveston they were met by Gail Borden, Sydnor, and others—most of them slaveholders—who guaranteed them a public hearing. But the "glorious Sovereign mob" promptly broke up the meeting, sending the hapless pair packing.

A new jail to replace the successor of the *Elbe* had to be built. The second jail had been constructed of homemade brick, but the absence of hard clay in Galveston's soil became glaringly apparent when a prisoner dug his way to freedom with an ordinary spoon.

Gail Borden paid taxes on eleven town lots, four Negroes, twenty cattle, and two "pleasure carriages."

In 1844 the best steamer in the United States—or so everyone said—arrived, and Galvestonians crowded the dock to see the *Union*, which had, of all things, a propeller instead of paddles. Prince Carl of Solms-Braunfels arrived in July to help found several German settlements, one of which, Fredericksburg, would produce Admiral Chester Nimitz of World War II naval fame. In the prince's entourage were twelve trunks and four servants. Gail Borden in 1844 increased his herd of cattle to 237, and John P. Borden opened a law office in Richmond.

The Episcopalians received an organ, Galveston's first, from Antwerp. The "picayune" system of bartering gave way to "*good cash trade.*" P. Victor established the first tree-nursery. And in addition to standard mint juleps and whiskey the Tremont bar featured such potations as Moral Suasion, Fiscal agent veto, *Ne plus ultra*, and Citronella Jim—each for "one bit a glass."

On San Jacinto day Captain Howe with a battalion of militia paraded the main streets with drum, fife, and glittering guns. At the conclusion of the parade, the battalion divided into companies to engage in a sham battle. "The culmination of this bloody contest," wrote one onlooker, "was the charging of a brush fence, which they utterly demolished."

At the beginning of July the French frigate *Brillante* tied up, but Galveston people stayed away from the docks, for yellow fever was aboard. Four days later, despite a quarantine, it was ashore. Before long, doctors had the disease under control, but by then the district judge, the district clerk, and a host of private citizens had fallen prey.

On January 4, 1844, Penelope Borden presented her husband with his last son. The child was named John Gail after his uncle and father. Because he was the youngest, or because of circumstances arising soon after his birth, John Gail Borden soon established himself as his father's favorite, a status he never relinquished.

Soon, however, Gail Borden's joy at having a fourth son gave way to overtones of grief. In mid-March Stephen F. Austin Borden, not quite five years old, came down with an ailment which the doctor diagnosed as yellow fever. On March 24, more than three months before the *Brillante*'s arrival, the child died. In the words of pious Job: "The Lord gave, and the Lord hath taken away; blessed be the name of the Lord."

One day late in August, Penelope Borden went downtown to shop for her family. It was warm, sleepy weather, but to a woman tied to her house by a baby, it was stimulating just to be among the smells and sights and flourishes of the Galveston streets and to hear merchants say, "Good morning, Mrs. Borden"; "You're looking well, Mrs. Borden"; and "How's the infant, Penelope? I hear he takes after you." Down along the dock Penelope strolled. To get to one wharf-side shop she had to pass through a huge stack of bales from Cuba being unloaded by shiphands who, it turned out, were going to collapse with yellow fever before the day's end.

Home she went, tired but full of the day's events. The next day she was still tired and a little queasy in her stomach. When she failed to improve, Gail sent for the doctor. Black vomit, said the doctor, and gave her some medicines. But her strength did not return. Instead, her back and shoulders began to ache intensely, her nausea increased, her eyes reddened. On his second visit the doctor changed his diagnosis.

Yellow fever!

Helplessly the family stood by as the orange tint spread from the eyes to the face to the body, until she became a heat-ridden, distorted, saffron image.

Mercifully the yellow fever worked with its usual swiftness. On September 5, 1844, Penelope Borden died.

She was only thirty-two years old, but middle-aged by the standards and conditions of her time. She had been married sixteen years and had borne seven children, of whom five still lived. She had left comfort of a sort back in Mississippi to go with this devoted eccentric who was her husband to a life in Texas that was crude and exposed and opposed to all things feminine.

In Texas in the eighteen thirties Penelope and other women could think sadly of homes and friends left behind, beyond all reach, it seemed; they could consider the privations and dangers; they could care for the children and for their husbands; but they could do little else to help them forget. Few were able to bring spinning wheels, few lived in houses large enough to require much keeping (most lived in wagons till land was cleared and cabins were erected), few had enough variety of foodstuffs to demand much time over the stove. Usually there existed "no poultry, no dairy, no garden, no books, or papers . . . no schools, no churches—nothing to break the dull monotony of their lives, save an occasional wrangle among the children and dogs."[39] They could only wait out the present, recall the past, and hope for the future. And Penelope Mercer Borden first knew this sort of life when she was a girl-wife of seventeen.

She learned what it was to experience the death of one's children. She learned to know the terror and sorrow of fleeing from an avenging enemy. And she learned to know the numbness of begin-

[39] Smithwick, *The Evolution of a State*, 15–16.

ning again that pervades when one returns home after the enemy has gone to find the work of years in ruins.

In Galveston she knew storms and plagues and more lack of facilities. But in Galveston she found peace of soul and a spiritual and material haven. For once, she felt, here was a place where her husband might remain content.

In Galveston, too, she experienced the triumphs and defeats of her husband's career—his importance as the first collector, his dismissal for political reasons, his being chosen collector again, and his defiant yet humiliating resignation from his second term. She knew, too, his growing prosperity. His homespun inventions that never quite worked. And his overnight enthusiasms for causes and gadgets that died with the Gulf breeze the next morning.

She had a woman's love of seeing familiar faces and of exchanging small talk. She would have loved more company, but her husband was not an ideal host—if gripped by a fresh inquisitorial ardor, he was too preoccupied to know or care that there were guests in the house. She would have been pleased to have read a letter in which Samuel Williams advised his wife to visit Galveston:

Take Mother along with you, and stay a few days . . . with Mrs. Borden—And a few with every *lady* on the Island. . . . I shall really expect to hear of your being at the Island—And visiting all those . . . worthy of . . . your esteem.[40]

Occasionally a careless word or phrase must have reached Penelope's ears that hurt cruelly, for townspeople considered her plain-spoken, eager husband Galveston's leading curiosity. And wives are more sensitive of husbands' reputations than they are of their own.

Some Galvestonians considered Gail Borden a genius; but more would have called him "peculiar." Almost all liked him. One resident observed that when it was not his own business that was concerned, Borden had "the longest head" of any person he knew. Another called him the "craziest" man in town. Said another: "He has dozens of inventions, and he is the most wonderful of them all himself."

[40] S. M. Williams to Sarah Williams, July 16, 1838, in Williams Papers.

But a local artist with whom Borden often disagreed called him the perfect model for a Sadducee and said she derived her idea for a portrait of a frenzied Judas from watching Gail Borden's "desperate hurry."

Some obliging tongue would bring such remarks to Penelope, and she would know that Galveston was laughing at her husband; then the joy she felt in her comfortable home would sour, leaving her to resent the town and its people.

To all this her husband was oblivious, for he never doubted that he was right in any cause or invention. If one failed, he did not regret, for by then he had a new idea, the largest one yet: "As fast as you drop one thing, seize upon another," was his advice to a friend. And after almost a lifetime he would see himself and his faith in himself vindicated, while every doubting Galvestonian who had called Gail Borden visionary would forget that he had despaired of the bizarre goings-on at Thirty-fifth and P and instead would remember only that he had always liked Gail and had always known that his inventions would succeed.

But Penelope was not to share in the triumph, except in Gail's memory. The girl from the Mississippi woods had poured sixteen years of faith and encouragement and courage into her husband's search for success. From now on he would have to supply those qualities entirely by himself.

XI

More Toil Than Honor
1841-1849

F OR GAIL BORDEN, returning to the Galveston collectorship
was almost unavoidable. His original successor, Dr. Willis
Roberts, had been dismissed before the termination of a year,
a victim of the Galveston *Civilian*, which had screamed mal-
feasance, overdrafts of salary, and general public dereliction until
President Lamar had sent an inspector to inquire into the official
conduct of the hapless doctor. Out went the doctor and in came the
inspector, Alden A. M. Jackson, a man of some military attainments
but generally undistinguished. Being a Lamar appointee, Jackson
could not survive Houston's return. With his usual flourish Old Sam
gave back to his good friend, Gail Borden, the position from which
politics had removed him. That the appointment placed Houston in
the political guise of a redressing knight did not detract from Borden's appreciation of the appointment. To him it was a vindication.
The Senate's unanimous confirmation on December 24, 1841,[1] only
heightened the pleasure.

At the outset Borden's hopes for a peaceful administration
seemed likely of realization. Quiet routine ruled. In tranquil fashion
a month passed. Then two, three, . . . six months. Nearly every
evening Borden could return from his dual job of collector and
Galveston City Company secretary with enough strength of body
and enough repose of mind to devote another half-dozen hours
pottering about his sheds among the fig orchards at his home. He
never slept more than six hours at night, and he never napped in the
gently soporific Galveston afternoons. Later, he claimed that he had

---

[1] Winkler (ed), *Secret Journals of the Senate*, 211–12 *Telegraph*, January 5,
1842. Unless otherwise noted, all material for this chapter is taken from Comptroller's Letters Customs, 1836–45, Archives of the Texas State Library.

learned to condense sleep along with his other condensations so that in six hours he received more refreshment than most people did in ten. Small wonder that Galveston whispered—up at four or five in the morning to burst into a long trot that carried him full tilt until ten or maybe midnight. Besides his customs, his company, and his church, what was he doing all that time? Since Galveston could see no results, it could only wonder.

During the three months preceding April 30, 1842, Borden collected a little less than $29,000; but for the next year he predicted collections of $200,000 or more. At Houston, which again was the Republic's capital, the Treasury Department was uninspired by his surge of confidence, responding curtly that he had overpaid his clerks and ordering him to correct his accounts accordingly. It was the first of several chilling responses which soon indicated to Borden that he would have been happier out of the government's employ.

With his retirement of "exchequer bills," as the virtually unsecured paper money issued by the Republic was known, the Treasury Department expressed more pleasure. In his first six months Borden retired almost $38,000, leaving about the same amount in circulation. In two more months they would be all gone, it was thought.[2] But that is not what happened.

In July, 1842, the Texas Congress stepped into the financial scene by passing a law calling for all duties to be paid in exchequers and for all collectors to receive the bills at their market value, which at that time was about thirty cents on the dollar.[3] Borden thought the act discouraged trade and placed a burden on importers. Elevate the standing of the government's paper, he urged, by crediting it at nearly full value. Eighty cents on the dollar should be the minimum. He proposed to proceed on that basis.

To reconcile Borden's nonobservance of the law from July until his resignation the following spring requires a well of understanding. The law was not his to interpret but to execute. But Borden's conscience was inelastic: it would not bend, even to comply

[2] Harriet Smither (ed.), *Journals of the Sixth Congress of the Republic of Texas, 1841–1842*, III, 140.

[3] Gammel, *The Laws of Texas*, II, 812. Crane, "The Administration of the Customs Service of the Republic of Texas," 26.

with the law of the land. When everywhere else in the Republic of Texas exchequer bills were being received at a third of their stated value, the Galveston customhouse was accepting them at nearly full value. If it was Houston's idea to force upward the value of the exchequers, Borden would not wait on a slow market. He would set their value high arbitrarily, leaving the market to close the gap or not. Thus every exchequer that Borden accepted meant a loss of approximately fifty cents on the dollar to the government. And with one government agency observing one price and another agency observing another, the inevitable happened—speculators began to deal in exchequers, in some instances withholding them entirely and gambling on a further price rise; in other instances withholding them from the government agencies which followed the market that they might be cashed at the Galveston customhouse. The flow of exchequers to retirement slowed measurably.

In vain the Treasury Department railed. The acting secretary, M. P. Woodhouse, ordered Borden to wait for the market to rise before advancing his own rates: "Take them strictly within the meaning of the law—'at their Market value.' "[4] But Borden took no heed of this advice. When he knew he was right, argument was useless. That he could be wrong was inadmissible, at least until his error should strike him full in the face.

Borden knew what to do. He wrote Woodhouse two letters. In the first, marked "private," he reiterated his stand: "I will never sacrifice principle to interest   The grounds which I have taken in this matter . . . can not be shaken   Time will . . . show." The second letter was official: "I can not consistently comply with your directions in putting down the price of Exchequer Bills. . . . discussion is no longer proper or expedient." On September 22, 1842, he resigned.

Now the government was concerned. The day he received the resignation the President himself wrote Borden.

"My Dear Gail," began Houston. "I regret that you have any thought of resigning. It is far from my wish that you should. This, I know; you have as much interest in the country as I have, and if you think the country can dispense with your services, every useful officer may think so too; and I will come to the same conclusion

---

[4] Williams and Barker (eds.), *The Writings of Sam Houston*, III, 149–50, IV, 155.

as to myself. What will be the consequences? Anarchy!!" . . . we have the law to govern us, and all we have to do is *to obey it*."

Houston could hardly have been more conciliatory: "You know how I estimate you as a man and as an officer," he continued. Since it might inflict "mortification" on Borden to lower his price standard, Houston promised not to wound his feelings by exacting "anything but what may arise from an imperative sense of duty. I do hope you will let the *actual rise precede* an advance on your part."

Bluntly but affectionately, Houston refused Borden's resignation. Instead, he announced that he was sending Secretary Woodhouse to Galveston to see the collector in the hope that he would continue to hold his post. If Borden would only alter his course, before long, promised Houston, "A dollar will be a dollar."[5]

Borden stayed on.

For some time Gail Borden had been seeking permission to employ a revenue cutter to aid in collections for goods landed at places other than Galveston. By September, 1842, his campaign was beginning to bear fruit, and on September 20 Woodhouse directed him to select his cutter, so long as expenses did not exceed $1,200 a year. Before he could choose a vessel, however, an interruption appeared in the form of a September storm, which tossed parts of Galveston about like pieces of a toy town. Although the customhouse stood, its foundation washed away, necessitating its removal. The customhouse boat was destroyed, and seventy barrels of sugar in the public warehouse were ruined.

In the weeks following, the threatened Mexican invasion brought business to a standstill, leaving Borden free time to think of matters other than exchequers and cutters. He devoted himself to putting Galveston in a state of defense, and as usual, in odd moments he wrote letters.

By December conditions were looking up. Exchequers rose to fifty-five cents, Borden obtained a cutter, the *Santa Anna*, and he apprehended a group of silk smugglers. Outside customs, he busied himself with many tasks, for he was more than just collector. Borden worked for every department, and it was estimated—by him—that he had rendered greater service in Galveston for the Department of

[5] *Ibid.*, IV, 147–49.

Borden's checks are distinctive for the milkmaid and cows at the left

The Borden Company

War and Marine than the island's naval agent. He felt that his salary, which had been cut to $1,200, was incommensurate with the services he rendered. During the first forty days of the winter quarter of 1842, he had collected more duties than the collectors at all the other customs districts during the first nine months of the year. Yet, Borden pointed out, their salaries aggregated $4,600, while his remained at $1,200. Rather than an increase in salary, however, he sought a right to the perquisites of office. Why not let him have the fees collected on vessels and permits, which would amount to another $1,200 in a good year? From the government came no comment.

Ever since the law had been passed for their retirement, exchequers had been climbing slowly in value. By spring, 1843, they had reached sixty-five to seventy cents, nearly as good as Gail Borden's price. Sometimes the customhouse price was no better than the market price, for the collector was trying hard to obey a law in which he did not believe.

But staying in line did not come easy for Borden. Consequently when William Henry Daingerfield, secretary of the treasury, dropped into Galveston, the collector tried to convince the visitor of his views. There is no record of the conversation, but Daingerfield must have made some remark that led Borden to believe his old policy of raising exchequer rates was a wise one. For up went the rates again.

Borden's defiance of orders was obvious and admitted. "I am however upon the scene of Action," he insisted, "and believe that I have Acted in Accordance with the best interests of the country." Daily, though, he grew more weary of the struggle. Was it worth its toll on his time and disposition? His attitude concerning exchequers was inflexible; the government's, equally so. On March 29 he wrote the Treasury Department that he could no longer remain in a post that had given him "more anxiety than honor, more toil than profit." To submit to the administration's views would violate his sense of "right, Justice and good policy," as well as endanger the revenue structure. Would the government find him a successor by the first of May?

While the government considered, Borden pursued his chores conscientiously. He helped the Treasury choose an inspector for San Augustine's customhouse, became involved in a dispute concerning the brig *Archer*, and arranged for the opening of a new customs district at Corpus Christi, at the moment held by Mexicans.

The earliest clear-cut indication that Borden's resignation would be accepted came from the collector himself. On March 29 he wrote James Shaw at the Treasury, proposing his cashier, Major James H. Cocke, as his successor. His praise of Cocke was unstinted: "A gentleman in every way qualified . . . in whose honesty all his acquaintances have the fullest confidence . . . , capable and worthy." Two months later he might have been less enthusiastic.

At first Houston did not reply to Borden's latest resignation directly, but let Acting Secretary Shaw, an Ireland-born University of Dublin graduate who had resided in Texas since 1837, accept for him. In an attempt to make the parting painless, Shaw drafted several unsatisfactory statements before telling Borden gently that his service was at an end. The soothing of the collector's pride posed no problem for Sam Houston. On April 22 he wrote a long letter characterized by its brusqueness. Gone was the familiarity of the "Dear Gail" or even the "Dear Borden" days.

"My Dear Sir," this one began. "Your resignation will be accepted. At one time I looked upon it as an unfortunate occurrence, and opposed it," but not now.

You say you feel proud and conscious of having executed the laws according to their provisions. . . . That you have acted with integrity of heart, I have no doubt, but that you have carried out the "provisions" of the law I cannot agree. You were not required to give any construction to the law. It was plain and required none.

. . . I do not comprehend your meaning in relation to [shifting] duty and responsibility upon you. I thought in all cases in which you had been called upon you had tendered your services, and as such they were accepted with pleasure. . . .

I perceive that your inveteracy to the law still exists. You cannot be reconciled to it, and deem it as "impolitic as it is unjust." It is, nevertheless, the law, and we will have to obey it whether we are in or out of office.[6]

Plainly Houston's patience was exhausted. And as plainly it was the end of Gail Borden, public servant. No Houston adherent would want him now.

[6] *Ibid*, IV, 186–89, 202–204.

But Borden was not to hand over the customhouse keys and walk away unfettered. For another five years he would be answering charges and making countercharges until finally time alone would cause all the old participants to weary of the contention. For continuing the bitter dispute, Borden himself must bear a large portion of the blame.

His successor, James Cocke, was told frankly that a principal reason for his appointment was the favorable recommendation of his late employer. Under those circumstances a high regard for Borden might have been expected. But if Cocke held his former employer in such esteem, he never revealed it.

Houston's attitude was too positive to be mistaken. In a letter of advice to the incoming collector, he delineated Borden's character tellingly. The letter follows in part:

You will assume the duties of the office under several embarrassments. . . .

. . . You have the errors of your friend, Gail, before you He is a good man, I think, but not a man of action. He lets too many influences enter into the discharge of his immediate duties. Instead of pursuing his instructions, he must consult with everybody, and whoever does that, never acts for himself. He canvasses in his mind the propriety of a law, and never once reflects that *it is a law*, and *that he is sworn to execute it.* He talks of its injustice and impolicy. . . . Some of its provisions he is willing to carry out—others he postpones or qualifies. . . . Gail's nervous excitability is too great for a station of the kind. Sometimes he talks about liberal and equitable constructions of the law, when he was perfectly aware that a construction had been given to the law and that it admitted of but one. . . . He was always pledging himself that he would have [exchequers] at par directly, and his success reminds one of a recent occurrence between two armies in South America. They encountered each other, and shortly after the action commenced each party began to retreat and each thought itself whipped. When they were apprised of their true situation they were forty miles apart. So as Gail advanced to the point of one hundred cents, the combination to depress the Exchequers had succeeded in pursuing another direction until they were as far apart as the antipodes.[7]

Nor was Houston through yet. The day before Borden's term expired, the President heard that he was still taking exchequers at

[7] *Ibid*, IV, 190–93.

eighty cents. "If he has done so," he wrote, "it will become a matter of very serious consideration. . . . Gail is a great enthusiast, and so far as this is confined to his private relations, 'tis all well; but when he blends it with his official duties, it is an unpardonable offence against the obligations which he owes to his station, both morally and officially. . . . I have always believed Gail an honest man; [but] if this [report be true] and it is decided that he is a sane man, I will canvass my belief and see if it has not [been] erroneous."[8]

Into office swept Cocke. Promply he lowered the customhouse exchequer rate to fifty cents, promising that if the exchequers became "dull in the market" he would go much lower. He assured Shaw that he would blot out all precedents and adhere strictly to the law. Already he had decided that Borden employed too many helpers, and he dismissed five men while promising still more retrenchments. He intended, he said, to undo all the wrong Gail Borden had committed. On the other hand Borden had his supporters, Francis Moore charging editorially that Borden's resignation represented the culmination of a serious evil which could only turn away trade from Galveston and Houston.[9]

Time proved, however, that Houston's view was better than Borden's. By October, 1843, exchequers had risen to seventy-nine cents, leading Shaw to comment that "It must be now apparent to *all*, that the law of July 23[d] has more good for effect than injury."

If Gail Borden had been content to rest his case at this point, the entire affair would have passed as just another political difference. But that "nervous excitability" of which Houston had complained took charge of Borden, compelling him to follow a course both bold and rash, whatever its justifications. He refused to turn over the customhouse funds in his possession!

Why? There were two reasons. For months merchants had been threatening to sue him for the disparity between face value of the exchequers and the amount at which he rated the bills, even though he valued them higher than anyone else. Fearing that such a suit would prove the exchequer law unconstitutional and that he might then have to make up the difference between customhouse

---

[8] *Ibid*, IV, 194–95.
[9] *Telegraph*, April 26, 1843. *The Northern Standard*, June 8, 1843.

and face values, Borden resolved to protect himself. If one suit succeeded, others might follow, leaving him to pay judgments running into five or six figures. He did not have that much money, and although his securities, McKinney and Williams, did, the least he could do was to try to protect them also. Actually, he probably reasoned, any judgment against him should rightfully be paid by the government, but previous experience had taught him that Texas finances were too shaky to be dependable. To him the solution was obvious. hold out enough government funds to protect himself and his securities.

The second reason was relatively minor—and less excusable. Borden had always believed that the government should reimburse him for the time spent working for the other departments. A settlement of $2,000 he would have considered more than generous By withholding the government's funds for a while, he might induce the Treasury Department to see his point of view. Certainly he could collect more easily if the money were already in his possession.

Regardless of reasons, he was withholding money that belonged to the public treasury. In any interpretation he was guilty of violating the law.

About the possibility of suits Borden was correct. The first one was brought by H. H. Williams and Company[10] in June, 1843, in Houston's district court. In a sense Borden's stand was contradictory: victory meant that the law of July 23, 1842, was constitutional and therefore should have been observed, which he certainly had not done; a losing decision supported his theory that the law was bad, but it meant that he could be liable for whatever judgment the court assessed.

The court decided for the defendant, Gail Borden. The law was valid. H. H. Williams and Company appealed to the Texas Supreme Court, which placed the case on its June, 1844, calendar, a year's delay during which Borden held to his customhouse funds, resisting all efforts by the government to collect. In November, 1843, Shaw requested him to send in all government money in his possession, about $27,000,[11] important money to an impoverished Texas

[10] In addition to being head of a Houston mercantile firm, H. H. Williams, a brother of Samuel M Williams, was Texas consul at Baltimore.

[11] Williams and Barker (eds.), *The Writings of Sam Houston*, III, 482 Certificate by A B. Shelby, December 28, 1849, Archives of the Texas State Library

treasury. Borden's reply of November 25 gives some insight into his reasoning:

I endeavored to pursue that course which seemed to me pointed out by my duty, and my situation, regarding alike the interest of Government, and the rights of the merchant. . . .

Deeply do I regret ever having accepted an office which may involve and perhaps ruin me and entail a debt upon my children. . . . I must therefore, decline . . . paying over the money in my possession . . . until I am fully released from my liability to third parties.

A month later a new charge had arisen to plague "Poor old Gail," as James H. Cocke dubbed him. Rumors were afloat that Borden was reissuing many of the exchequers which he held. This he denied, but Cocke was not certain: "I have made a proposition to his friends," said the collector, ". . . that in case he was innocent of the charge . . . he should choose two of his friends & I would go with them and count the money; if correct give him a certificate to that effect, & would say that he had been slandered   I am told . . . that he was greatly offended at the proposition."

In June, 1844, the Supreme Court handed down its judgment in *H. H. Williams and Company* v. *Gail Borden, Collector*. Because of the enfeebled condition of several judges and because additional arguments delayed the decision, the court was unable to detail reasons for its opinion upholding the district court. Gail Borden had won, with only one judge dissenting.[12]

With the case settled, Borden could release the public funds which he held. Or so the government thought. But still he refused.

His resoluteness threatened to develop into a national issue. In his farewell address to Congress in December, 1844, Houston spoke of the "defalcations of the late collectors" having cost the Republic nearly $30,000. *The Telegraph and Texas Register* pronounced its astonishment that Gail Borden, "this long tried public servant," was now facing impeachment as a public defaulter. Both houses of Congress considered acts of settlement.[13]

---

12 J W. Dallam, *Opinions of the Supreme Court of Texas from 1840 to 1844 Inclusive*, 350–51 Williams and Barker (eds.), *The Writings of Sam Houston*, IV, 286–87 Case No 15–D, District Clerk's Office, Galveston County, Texas.

Efforts to find the decision in a suit brought by the Republic in the spring of 1844, *President of the Republic of Texas* v. *Gail Borden, Jr, and others*, have been abortive.

Out of patience, the new secretary of the treasury, William B. Ochiltree, visited Galveston in December, 1844, to make a "fair, equitable, and *honest* settlement" of all Borden accounts which were "*tinged* with equity." Was Borden willing to settle? The gesture pleased Borden, who wrote on December 28:

I have no desire to retain in my hands, One Dollar that belongs to the government. . . . Imputations have gone abroad touching my conduct . . . and "the Defalcation of the late Collector of Galveston" has been sounded by functionaries in high places; all which have injured me greatly, and which are unjust & untrue.

In my humble station in life, with my feeble abilities, I could but poorly contend with so illustrious an individual as his Excly. Sam Houston, who possesses in so eminent a degree, the power of sustaining himself *right* or *wrong*. . . . I desire most expressly, that my conduct should be . . . scrutinised by a few, who are capable of understanding it, and disposed to do justice, and I am willing to stand or fall by their decision.

Though settlement was in sight, there was one hitch: Borden no longer possessed the money. He had turned over to Thomas F. McKinney and Samuel M. Williams almost the entire $27,000.

His action indicates a sort of loyalty rather than bad faith, for he believed that he must protect McKinney and Williams against any suits which might involve them as his securities. In return, McKinney and Williams had assumed the responsibilities and expense of his recent suit. And now when Borden desired to surrender the money to the Republic, the pair refused to refund what Borden had given them, alleging that they had a "good offset in law & equity" against Texas. Borden was helpless.

Ochiltree was outraged, informing Borden that he had certainly expected a different course of conduct and that he knew no code of law or morals which would justify the late collector's action. Borden retorted that neither his words nor his sentiments had been understood by Ochiltree:

It really seems to me that you are desirous of entering into a lengthy lawyer like, sort of correspondence, for what purpose I am unable to

---

[13] Williams and Barker (eds.), *The Writings of Sam Houston*, IV, 395. *Telegraph*, December 11, 1844. *Texas National Register*, December 28, 1844

understand. I am no lawyer . . . but in all business transactions I endeavor to make myself intelligible, and hoped you would have understood a plain and frank statement of facts, if you do not, or will not, it is not my fault.

With that the interchange ended.

Borden's actions continued to be debated, however, even on the floor of the Texas House of Representatives, where opinion was divided. Said one congressman: "We have . . . had our collections well and promptly attended to at Galveston." Another disagreed: "It is not my opinion that a eulogy upon the Collector [at Galveston] would be in order, or very strictly in accordance with truth [since] all the frauds which have been complained of in regard to finances . . . have been very materially assisted and accelerated by the action of that Custom House."[14]

Nearly three years elapsed before the next documented reference to the controversy was to appear, this time in a petition to the legislature of the state of Texas from Thomas F. McKinney. In it, McKinney stated that the $15,000 he had received from Borden had been "appropriated to his individual purposes" and could not be refunded to Texas. Would Texas permit McKinney to settle by placing the $15,000 as a credit upon the audited claims which he held against the Republic and thereby spare everyone the necessity of raising the money confided to him?[15]

A later document, dated January 24, 1848, reviews the controversy and the services to Texas of the three central figures, Borden, McKinney, and Williams. In the adverse days of early Texas independence McKinney and Williams had loaned the Republic approximately $150,000, a godsend which had never been repaid. Without the loan Texas independence might not have been realized. Therefore, recommended a special joint committee of the Texas legislature, in view of important past services rendered, Texas should call the case closed. As for Borden, his rôle in the dispute had become purely nominal anyway.[16]

[14] *Texas National Register*, January 18, February 1, 1845.
[15] Gulick and others (eds), *Lamar Papers*, IV, 190–91.
[16] Report to the President of the Senate . . . of the State of Texas, January 24, 1848, in Alamo Museum. In 1873 McKinney was still trying to obtain relief from the Texas government. Included in his petition was a deposition from Borden. State Papers, File Box 128, Senate, Archives of the Texas State Library.

Nevertheless, as late as 1849 Borden was preparing duplicate vouchers in an attempt to obtain final settlement of his accounts. Although he still believed his procedure had been correct throughout, none of the activities had been worth the effort and he would not repeat the experience for any amount. He felt bitter about the situation, writing McKinney that Major Cocke had grown rich as collector while he had become steadily poorer, laboring "like a wheel horse to take the government carriage out of the [bog]."[17]

With that disclosure Gail Borden drew the curtain on his career as public servant for Texas. In his defense it can only be said that he had done what he considered right and that he had shown courage and tenacity. But the courage was misguided and the tenacity could have been stubbornness. Administrative officers must execute the law or they breed disrespect for their government. Gail Borden, private citizen, had the right to believe the exchequer law was bad, but Gail Borden, public official or private citizen, had no right to take that law into his own hand. Courage and tenacity—or foolhardiness and stubbornness—can pay dividends when applied to other causes. And they were qualities Gail Borden possessed in abundance, qualities he would need in the years ahead. But when he placed them in opposition to the organized government of Texas, he was squandering two of his very best assets.

[17] Gail Borden to T. F. McKinney, December 28, 1849, in Claims, Archives of the Texas State Library.

*Produce! Were it but the pitifulest infinitesimal
fraction of a product, produce it in God's name*
—Carlyle, *Sartor Resartus*

*No-wher so busy a man as he ther nas,
And yet he semed bisier than he was*
—Chaucer, *The Canterbury Tales*

XII

The Terraqueous Machine
and Other Curiosities
1845-1849

YOUNG WILLIAM MUMFORD BAKER, new assistant pastor of the Galveston Presbyterian church, was breathing in the romance of Galveston on an island street corner, savoring its enchantment, resolving perhaps to write a book on it some day, when for the first time he saw Gail Borden, striding along "very rapidly." Borden, he observed, was "quite a tall man, very shabbily dressed, with a singularly narrow but high forehead. He had . . . an unusually long nose. I never saw a person drive along at such a swift pace, his head bent forward, his eyes on the ground. He caught sight of me in passing, but was under such headway, that he was a rod beyond me before he could turn and come back. Then he was in extreme hurry. I could not keep up with him in what he said, at all. He shook me by the hand very cordially indeed, welcomed me [and] asked me . . . a dozen questions without giving me time to answer one. Who is he? for he forgot to tell me his name."[1]

When a quarter-century later Baker wrote a book recounting his year in Galveston, he gave Borden a central position, and nowhere can one find a better picture of the man Gail Borden had become. In the late eighteen forties he seemed to be everywhere and part of everything in Galveston. No one on the island was sure

[1] W M Baker, *A Year Worth Living*, 56. In this work, a thinly veiled account of his year in Galveston, with historical incidents and characters easily recognizable, Princeton-educated Baker paints a portrait of an eccentric inventor and realtor who is unmistakably Gail Borden The University of Texas has the only known copy of this book

which moved faster or oftener, Borden's body or his tongue. Even his prayers, commented one minister, were rapid. Speed and condensation had taken hold of him. "Condense your sermons," he advised Baker.

In the winter Borden showed Baker his establishment at Thirty-fifth and P. About the cluttered yard the pair wandered, past the fig trees and the orange trees and the lemon trees, all now bandaged with straw against a possible norther, past enormous iron kettles, empty hogsheads, and wrecks of machinery.

"That was one of my ideas," the inventor explained as the two walked along. "Just then I was full of hydraulic pressure. I would put in water, half a hogshead of sugar, and a cartload of fruit, figs say, into the kettle. Then, while hot, I would press the preserves into ten-pound canisters. . . . But I learned better. I never drop an idea except for a better one—never!

"You can do almost any thing with every thing," he continued. "If you plan and think, and, as fast as you drop one thing, seize upon another. . . . The world is changing. In the direction of condensing."

He gave examples. If he were advising an absent son how to live, he would eschew long lectures and refer him merely "to a chapter of the New Testament for his theory, and to the proverbs of Solomon for his practice. Even lovers write no poetry, nor any other stuff and nonsense, now. They condense all they have to say, I suppose, into a kiss." Condensation had spread to the act of eating, he believed. "Time was when people would . . . spend hours at a meal. Napoleon never took over twenty minutes . . . · *I* am through in fifteen. People have almost lost the faculty of fooling away their time."[2]

On and on Gail Borden would walk and talk, changing subjects and changing directions as he was wont to switch ideas when the old ones had lost their appeal. That was Gail Borden as he neared his fiftieth year. It was past noon in his life, but he was finally getting started on the work for which he was intended—experimenting, trying this and failing in that, but forever striving. Lacking the benefits of education and scientific training, he could attack his problems by the only remaining method of trying and failing and trying again.

[2] *Ibid*, 104–105

After Penelope Borden died in September, 1844, Gail Borden found himself bound about by loneliness and confusion. After sixteen years of her balancing presence, he suddenly came to the knowledge that hereafter he had to find his way alone at a time when the world seemed to be mocking him. Penelope had gone. Sam Houston had lost faith in him. His own government was suing him. And whatever he might try to do was hampered by his having to care for five children, of which Henry Lee at thirteen was the eldest. Girls that age can sometimes mother the others, but a boy—never!

Under such conditions it surprised few Galvestonians when on February 15, 1845, the Reverend I. J. Henderson of the local Presbyterian church married Gail Borden and Mrs. A. F. Stearns. Not much is known of Mrs. Stearns. Even her first name is confused, appearing sometimes as Augusta and again as Azuba. One source describes her as round and rosy-faced, but drops the picture there. She was Borden's age and she was born in Maine.[3] It is uncertain when or where she died, although a reasonable guess would be about 1856 in Texas.

Borden always introduced her as his second wife until one day, with feigned annoyance, she challenged him· "Why will you always say I am your second wife?"

"Oh!" replied Borden, diplomatic for once, "I am such a dry old stick. . . . I don't want people to think that you are old."

For several weeks before their marriage Borden had worked on a homemade wedding present, another of his inventions. It was a table with a fixed rim the breadth of a plate, inside of which was a revolving center so that dishes could be pushed to whoever desired them.

"You have no idea . . . the expense he went to in making . . . it in time for our wedding," the second Mrs. Borden is quoted as saying. "I had a good cry over it. There was a large company, and he had forgotten that you could not use a tablecloth on such a thing. I was too afraid of him then to say one word! I could only cry."[4]

Augusta Stearns Borden soon lost her terror, however, so that afterward, whenever guests ate at the Borden home, she would keep

[3] Marriage License Records, 1838–50, Galveston County, Texas, 57. Seventh Census, Texas, II, 492.

[4] Baker, *A Year Worth Living*, 110–11.

up a laughing attack on her husband throughout the meal, deriding his habits and his tinkerings. Through it all Gail would eat abstractedly and "somewhat enormously, his long body bowed down over his plate, leaving the entertainment . . . to his wife."

"Don't misunderstand me," Mrs. Borden told Baker, "I do *not* believe in his inventions . . . but I do believe in his motives. . . . I don't think, myself, he will do anything but lose . . . but he does as *he* pleases, and lets me do as *I* please."[5]

That was the woman Gail Borden had taken for his second wife. That it was a marriage of convenience in which Borden was free to come or go may be inferred from his actions in the years ahead.

Time in passage. James K. Polk, the president of the United States, elected on a dubious slogan of "Reannexation and reoccupation"—reannexation of Texas and reoccupation of Oregon. Texas no longer a struggling republic but a member of the United States by treaty.

In Galveston, jury duty at the spring term, 1845. Gail Borden sworn in but excused. Work for the Galveston City Company, buying, selling, collecting; buying and selling for Gail Borden also. A director now.[6]

Work at home. A blackboard in the house where plans could be sketched and figures scrawled. And then erased for something newer, but no better.

A plan to convert all Roman Catholics in fifteen years by furnishing Catholic children with Protestant tracts attractively bound —"a glorious plan, the best I ever made. . . . It is sure to succeed." The priests won't allow it, warned one critic. A moment of hesitation, then: "So about those Papists. I'll pass the children, and aim for the priests."

"I never drop an idea except for a better one."

Another idea. But still not workable. Baker heard it from a local seaman, who explained:

He has one thousand things on hand. This is a steamboat. No paddle-boxes. Nary screw. It has a belt with paddle-boards on it all along, one

[5] *Ibid,* 111–12.
[6] District Court, Minutes, 1843–45, Galveston County, Texas, 215 Records, E, Galveston County, Texas, 172, 650.

to every two feet. The belt is driven along deck from the stern, over the bow into the water, all along under the keel, up out of the water at the helm, up and along the deck and down over the bow again, and so for ever and ever. . . . He invents. I apply. A dead failure. Not the first. Nor the last. I know it now. He will know it by night. Not a better man alive.[7]

Work for his Lord. Helping raise funds for a Baptist church building. Borden now a deacon—for a while the church's only deacon. A leader of the choir, a leader of prayer meetings, and superintendent of the Sunday school.

As his spiritual influence spread beyond the Baptists, he became Galveston's Sunday-school missionary for poor children and strangers. A member of Baylor University's committee on printing, he urged strongly the establishment of a Texas Baptist newspaper, a recommendation later fulfilled.

Even on religious matters Borden was outspoken, a characteristic that plunged the Galveston church into a small tempest which centered around Borden. The Reverend James Huckins had brought to Galveston a touch of New England liberality which appealed to Borden, especially when Huckins overlooked doctrinal questions to dwell on the brotherhood of all Christians regardless of disparities in doctrine.

Accordingly, when in 1848 a visiting revivalist began to expound Baptist concepts rather forcefully, Borden objected. The revivalist was the youthful Reverend Rufus C. Burleson, and the occasion was a Sunday afternoon baptismal service at which perhaps two thousand Galvestonians were present. To Burleson, "an old Landmark Baptist," the gathering represented a call to proclaim the doctrines he had been taught, especially the doctrine of baptism.

Some of the crowd standing among the pink and white oleanders bordering the little baptismal tank resented Burleson's talk, terming it a "mean proselyting affair." Gail Borden went straight to the minister: "Oh, my dear brother," Burleson quotes Borden as exclaiming, "you will offend the Pedobaptists and ruin our meeting. Brother Huckins never did preach on baptism, and he was the most popular preacher, with everybody, ever in Galveston."

[7] Baker, *A Year Worth Living*, 68, 104, 84.

Burleson replied that as God's witness he must tell the truth as he saw it, and he would tell that truth, though it should carry him "like old John Bunyan, to jail, or Obadiah Holmes, to the whipping post."

A day later Borden was back. Now that Burleson had aired his doctrines, why not turn the revival into a union meeting with the Presbyterian and Methodist pastors also participating? "Preach nothing but Christ, and not say one word about baptism," suggested Borden. Burleson refused. No man could "preach Christ" and not preach baptism, he said; besides, union meetings too frequently ended in strife.

When on the following Sunday evening Burleson held another baptismal service before a large audience, reiterating and elaborating his explanations of the week before, Borden was more wrought up than ever, threatening to call a deacons' meeting. Again Burleson assured Borden that all the deacons on earth could not stop him from preaching the truth.

It was one of those small arguments, important chiefly to the participants, that might have lasted interminably if Burleson's persuasiveness elsewhere had not produced an event which caused Borden's stand to collapse. At a session a few nights later who should come forward to confess publicly and joyfully their sins and their faith and to present themselves for baptism but Henry Lee Borden, age sixteen, Philadelphia Wheeler Borden, age eleven, and Mary Jane Borden, age seven. Gail Borden's animus melted. He gave Burleson his hand and a "carte blanche" to preach just as he pleased.[8]

In the town of Richmond, Texas, near which Thomas H. Borden had tried unsuccessfully to found Bordenton a few years earlier, forty-six persons assembled on June 16, 1845, to "put their hands to the moral plough." Gail Borden, Sr.—"Old Gail," now nearly seventy—presided. The end of the evening brought the formation of the Richmond Temperance Society.

Old Gail Borden had been temperate all his life. His Puritan training would permit nothing else. He taught his sons as he had

[8] *Minutes of the Fourth Anniversary Meeting of the Union Baptist Association The Life and Writings of Rufus C Burleson,* 725–27, 78–81, 244–45. Burleson later officiated at the baptism of Sam Houston into the Baptist church

been taught, and they listened and heeded. The earliest known indication of the younger Gail Borden's predilection for sobriety appeared in the early days at San Felipe, where Godwin Brown Cotten
used to throw many a merry party. "Three-Legged Willie" Williamson would "pat juba" with his wooden leg, Noah Smithwick
would dance jigs and hornpipes, Sam Williams would drop in for a
glass and a joke, but the Bordens, though friends, never attended.

Now that his father had taken the lead, he plunged into temperance work in Galveston, where on May 1, 1848, the same week
in which W. F. Ramsay gave a concert on four kinds of bagpipes at
the Tremont, Gail Borden and others arranged for their local temperance society to distribute pledges throughout the town. At all
times pledge cards could be signed at Borden's office opposite the
Galveston *News* building. A year later the Galveston society invited J. M. Wade of Huntsville to install it as division No. 47 in the
national Order of the Sons of Temperance. Ten officers were
elected, Borden emerging as assistant recording secretary.

The Sons observed all the pomp and ceremony usually associated with fraternal orders. On December 13, 1849, led by a band
and waving banners and followed by their juvenile detachment,
they marched militantly up Tremont Street in regalia, into the
Baptist and Presbyterian churches to receive Bibles and banners from
the ladies, and then back to the temperance hall on the Strand.[9]
Probably looking on, if not actually marching, was little John Gail
Borden. Thirty years later, as a wealthy young man, he would close
up all the grog shops in Brewster, his home fifty miles above the city
of New York.

1846. Only four Borden children left, following the death of
twelve-year-old Morton Quinn Borden on October 21, 1846.

1847. The year of the Mexican War, which left Gail Borden
and Galveston untouched. Galveston's main interest a new disease,
called "Epidemic colic" by the doctors and "Patent Belly ache" by
the residents—whence came the word "patent" is not known. Dr.
John Taylor said excessive drinking of ice water caused the disease.
Its symptoms—abdominal pains, "general uneasiness . . . anxiety and

9 *Telegraph*, July 2, 1845. Smithwick, *Evolution of a State*, 71. Galveston
Weekly News, May 5, 1848, August 27, December 17, 1849.

THE MEAT BISCUIT,

A new and useful preparation of concentrated EXTRACT OF BEEF, baked in flour,

INVENTED AND MANUFACTURED BY
GAIL BORDEN, Jun.
GALVESTON, TEXAS.

Patent secured in the United States Feb 5, 1850   Patent secured in England Sept 5 1851

DIRECTIONS FOR COOKING.

This article is highly concentrated, and is intended as a stock for Soup, and to be combined with other articles of food, to improve the nutrition and taste   It requires attention in cooking, principally in taking right proportions, and for soup, be sure not to scorch it   It should be properly diffused in water, fruit, or other substances, to bring it to its original state in taste or flavor

To MAKE A SOUP—The Biscuit being ground or made fine, stir it into sufficient cold water to form a thin batter, then pour it into boiling water, and boil it until it is thoroughly macerated or decomposed, requiring 20 to 30 minutes; stirring frequently, until it boils, to prevent burning or scorching

Add salt and pepper to suit the taste   Such condiments may also be added as are used in other soups.   The addition of a little sweet milk or good fresh butter makes an improvement, as in oyster soup   The plain soup is improved by the addition of a little sugar, say a tea-spoonful to the pint

The Biscuit batter as above, put into the liquid of well-boiled vegetables, strained through a cullender, or with the whole substance, as may be preferred, makes a soup unsurpassed

One ounce, or two table-spoonsful—spoon moderately heaped—of this Biscuit, will make a pint of rich, nutritious soup   Care must be taken to have it of a proper consistency, if too thick, dilute with boiling water, or if diluted with cold water, let the soup come to a boil again   Care must be had not to have it too thick, as in this case it is strong and unpalatable

To A HASH OR POT-PIE made of salt meat, the addition of the Meat Biscuit is most beneficial   It restores the juices and other qualities of the meat which have been destroyed by curing and boiling

☞ The Biscuit being entirely fresh, a little salt may be added to all of the following preparations —

To MAKE A PUDDING WITHOUT EGGS OR MILK—To a stock of softened bread, or boiled rice, combine the plain Soup, made a little thicker by stirring in more of the pulverized MEAT BISCUIT—add butter and sugar, with some kind of spice, then bake as other puddings

To MAKE A GOOD SAUCE, for puddings or rice, to the soup made plain as first above described, add a little good butter and sugar, with nutmeg, &c simply sweetened, it will then be a good sauce for rice or duff

To MAKE A MINCE PIE—Provide, and make up fruits, and everything usually employed in a good mince pie, except meat, which the Biscuit is to supply, as follows   For every pound of fruit take two ounces of the pulverized Biscuit, which thoroughly mix into the other mass of stock, and bake, as other pies

To IMPROVE A COMMON APPLE PIE, PUDDING, DUMPLING, &c made either of green or dried fruit, add two ounces of Biscuit for each pound of stewed fruit   At Sea this will be found a luxury

To MAKE A CUSTARD OR PUDDING, WITH OR WITHOUT MILK—To each pint of scalding water add two heaping spoonsful of the pulverised biscuit, or to the thick plain soup made as above (with *little* salt) , when sufficiently cool, add eggs and sugar well beat up together, and then bake in a dish or pan, or upon pastry crust, as other custards   Nutmeg or spice can be added to suit the taste

N B—The MEAT BISCUIT, when not kept in a dry place, should be kept in canisters or bottles
FOR SALE BY

J. H. BROWER & Co. General Agents, 45 South st New-York

ALSO AGENTS FOR ITS SALE,

H. W. PRESCOTT, Grocer, 18 Wall street, and 50 Courtland street, corner of Greenwich st. New York
WILLIAM M ABBOTT, Grocer 29 Burling Slip New York
HAMLIN & PERKINS, Centre street New Bedford
PEIRCE & BACON, Corner of Broad and Milk streets, Boston
THOMPSON & GRIFFIN San Francisco, California
WILLIAM BOLLAERT, 2 St. Peter s Alley, Cornhill, London
WADE & OSBORN St Louis Mo
J P BORDEN, Agent of the Manufactory at Galveston, Texas

D Fanshaw Printer 35 Ann street corner of Nassau, New York

Handbill issued in the eighteen fifties

The Borden Company

great muscular prostration"—hurt less than the cure: "Free cupping over the abdomen, general bleeding, calomel & opium succeeded by castor oil and oil of Turpentine and warm baths." When the patent bellyache epidemic eased in late August, yellow fever set in, and again Galveston became a city under siege, with two hundred more residents dying.[10]

Gail Borden had seen Penelope die with yellow fever. Since doctors knew no cure except possibly acclimatization, Borden resolved to find a cure where medical men had failed. He considered: yellow fever left with the first frost of autumn. Why not refrigerate it out of existence? "Since the doctors fail," he told Baker, "somebody must contrive something." He turned to his blackboard.

"Ether would cost . . . two bits an ounce," he explained. "Now it would take, say, one dozen ounces to freeze you down to, say, 30° or 40°—I mean, to keep you for a week as if under a white frost. Twelve twenty-fives is three dollars. Very well, let us grant that four thousand people are left. . . . If we had the refrigerators ready I could lock up every soul in a temporary winter with twelve thousand dollars of ether." According to Baker, the refrigerator was built. But it was to house not Galvestonians but meat biscuits, because by then Gail Borden was pursuing another trail.

At that, he had not been any farther off the mark than had trained scientists of the period. For only fifty years later Walter Reed and others would determine that the mosquito, whose musical message frequently filled Galveston's night air, brought yellow fever. As Borden lay beneath his gauze covering on a summer's night, candle in hand, singeing the feet of mosquitoes who landed on his bar, he did not realize that within his grasp flitted the assassin. By repelling the mosquito, refrigeration could have helped, but that was all. Besides, there would have been risks of exposure.

Once again, Gail Borden was wrong. He had said of himself: "I am terribly practical . . . too much so, that is, I am more rapid than the rest. I always get to a point on the common road long before other people,—always."[11] This time, though, he was using the wrong pair of sights. But he was trying.

[10] Galveston City Company Records, January 26, 1846. Ashbel Smith to A. [Hester], March 10, 1849, in Smith Papers.

[11] Baker, *A Year Worth Living*, 295–98, 117–18.

The year 1848 brought so much early rain that Wager Smith could not get outside to plough or to look for his pigs. Health was bad in Houston and vaccine unobtainable. Yellow fever decreased Galveston's population by five hundred. Peter Delbrell of the San Jacinto House, who claimed to be the first oyster-caterer since Lafitte's days, advertised that he served oysters "RAW, ROASTED, STEWED, FRIED OR BROILED." On the beach pleasure-seekers clustered around the "Gulf Retreat," a combination bathhouse and bar.

In December a young man of good background and excellent prospects landed to find Galveston "a glorious contrast to the disease and filth of New Orleans!"—comparable, he thought, to Cleveland back in his home state of Ohio. And Texans amazed him. They seemed to live on meat—"Pork ribs, pigs' feet, veal, beef (grand), chickens, venison, and dried meat frequently seen on the table at once."

His Texas acquaintances vied to see who could tell the visitor the most outlandish story. His favorite: One man had chickens who regularly came up to the house, where they would cross their legs to be tied. The owner hardly thought their action unusual—just force of habit, he said, from having moved periodically a day's journey at a time all the way from Kentucky to Texas. The young man who listened to these stories was Rutherford B. Hayes.[12]

In the broader world the United States was defeating Mexico under the guidance of Generals Zachary "Old Rough and Ready" Taylor and Winfield "Old Fuss and Feathers" Scott; the breach between North and South over the slavery, tariff, and Congressional-control issues was widening; and militant liberalism was seething in Europe, threatening to overturn dynasties and sending political refugees by the thousands to seek asylum in the New World. But the outer world was as usual of only passing interest to Gail Borden, who with each succeeding year seemed to live more and more in a world of his own. To him, 1848 was the year in which he borrowed three hundred dollars from the Commercial and Agricultural Bank of Galveston. In that year he also paid taxes on 5 Negroes, 10 horses and mules, 350 head of cattle, 2 carriages and harness, 1 dray, 1 watch, and 2 clocks. In addition, he paid on at least eight lots within

12 Williams (ed.), *Diary and Letters of Rutherford B. Hayes*, I, 245, 253, 259.

Galveston and several more just outside the city, on 13,700 acres scattered throughout Texas, and on eight estates for which he was agent.

He went to court again in 1848, once as plaintiff against Joshua C. Shaw, from whom he won a judgment for $293.56 plus 8 per cent interest.[13] Suits were commonplace for the Galveston City Company, and it might have been one of the suits of 1848 to which the Reverend Rufus Burleson referred when he wrote the following about Borden:

> I was his guest for several days when he was a witness in an important suit in which Galveston City Company was largely interested. He trembled under the fearful responsibility. One morning I was walking in a retired part of his large fig orchard and heard a low voice agonizing in supplications. Supposing Brother Borden was at the court house, I drew near to see who it could be, and there, in sweat and tears, was Brother Borden, imploring divine aid to enable him to so give his testimony as to honor God and his profession as a Christian and good citizen.
>
> I was greatly rejoiced, the next day, to hear a lawyer on the opposite side say: "Mr. Borden's testimony, under the critical, trying circumstances, was the clearest and most satisfactory I ever heard."[14]

All this time Gail Borden or his brother Thomas, or both, had been working on the invention considered—at the moment—the greatest of them all. A "terraqueous machine," it was christened, a sort of prairie schooner which should go equally well on land or water. There is fairly good evidence that the invention may have been Tom Borden's, but other contemporary writers credit Gail. Whoever its inventor, it was a machine worth knowing.

The Reverend William Baker thought the terraqueous machine the most wonderful thing on Galveston Island, with the exception of Gail Borden himself. From his book come accounts of two adventures involving the contraption.

This machine was Galveston's most widely known secret. In strictest confidence Gail Borden is supposed to have told virtually everyone he met of the mysterious contrivance that he was building. To him it was the invention of the century, and he intended to keep it secret until he could spring it full-blown on the public. "No

13 Minutes, I, Galveston County District Court, Texas, 392.
14 *The Life and Writings of Rufus C. Burleson*, 728.

one except my sworn workmen . . . has seen it," Baker quotes Borden as saying. "The papers have been full of it, but I keep blood-hounds in that stable yonder."

One night shortly after dark Gail Borden could be seen "speeding . . . in breathless haste" from door to door inviting favored persons to his house for a midnight dinner and "entertainment." All knew that the time for testing the machine had arrived, and they went to Borden's house in high spirits, there to be informed that they were about to take the fastest ride of their lives. To steel their nerves, he demanded that they fortify themselves with food. Being largely young people, the idea of a midnight snack delighted—until they saw the food. Everything on the table had been condensed or extracted or processed or otherwise concocted by their host.

"There are articles on this table," Borden said, "from which, if you knew what they were in their original condition, you would turn with loathing and horror. I have passed them, however, through certain processes by virtue of which they are delicious. Out of the offal of the kitchens and the streets, I have created . . . a food for the poor which will cost almost nothing. I have transmuted even the dirt itself into delicacies."

But who likes dirt, however transmuted? Or butter made from lard churned in milk, or bread from finely ground bones, or bronze jelly from horns and hoofs of oxen, or cakes of hides soaked in acid and cooked in syrup, or custard covered with a brown powder of blood burned to a crisp and pulverized? Only Gail Borden and a small boy thrilled by the prospect of remaining up all night had any appetite. The others tried merely to be polite.

With the horrible meal ended, Borden led his guests outside to the exotic vehicle. All was dark, which was as the inventor wished, for he intended to have the contrivance back in its shed before daylight. Not even the riders were to see it until the inventor was ready, and tonight was only the first test.

As Borden helped his riders aboard, the livery-stable owner tried to make a speech against the trip—"We may all end up in eternity," he warned. But all soon mounted, and horses drew the machine to the beach, where it was faced west, the horses detached, and the sail hoisted. Slowly the machine gathered speed, then faster and faster it ran. Some of the women began to scream. Ten minutes before the party would have reached the end of the island, where Borden intended to run on into the sea, the clamor and fright of the women had grown so loud that the inventor could only apply the brake and halt the trip.

The next day he spent regarding women as obstacles in the way of progress. If they were going to scream and take fright, they should stay home like his wife.

"No man respects women more than I do," he observed, "but no woman since creation ever invented anything, and no female ever will." Now he would have to make another trip to learn whether the machine would work in water. Next time, too, he would go faster—"and not only by land."

"Will you take to the air?" asked one incredulous listener.

"Not with this machine. But I will one day," was the answer.[15]

By the time of the second trip the secret cloak had been shed. This trip would be made in broad daylight so that at least no passengers would be frightened by the dark.

The car that Borden wheeled out of the shed resembled any wagon of the day, except that it had a mast in front on which its inventor-driver hoisted a square sail. Thanks to pulleys designed by the inventor, manipulating the sail was simple—"as easy as eating," in Borden's words. Once the wheels were in water they doubled as screws.

Borden drove. It was a beautiful afternoon, the crowd was gay, and the inventor was happy as the large sail filled and the vehicle moved down the beach before a strong northeast breeze. On this second trip speed had been his object, but the pushing gale caused his machine to exceed even his expectations. An idea began to thrust itself forward: with the trip proceeding so well, why not try the water now?

Under full sail and without warning to his riders he drove the contraption into the Gulf, the very suddenness of his move bringing an instant's silence of utter astonishment before everyone started scrambling.

15 Accounts of this incident appeared in the following Galveston *Daily News*, March 17, 1877 Dyer, "Early History of Galveston, Texas." Brewster, New York, *Standard*, September 23, 1904. *The Life and Writings of Rufus C Burleson*, 729. Baker, *A Year Worth Living*, 118, 157–68, 115, 250.

"Sit still," yelled Borden. "Still, sit still."

As someone let the sail fall, passengers flocked to the landward side, upsetting the boat's balance until it turned slowly over, dumping its human load into the water not more than fifty feet offshore. As soon as everyone had decided the water was too shallow for danger, someone thought of Gail Borden.

"Where is he?"

"Drowned, I do most sincerely hope!" came one fervent reply. "He richly deserves it!"

But Borden was spied asea, astride the top of his capsized car. When someone inquired whether he could make it ashore, he cried in wrath: "Don't want to make it! . . . It can't sink. Part of the invention! There was no danger. What did you make such fools of yourselves for? . . . I told you the wheels are screws! . . . The sail would have driven them. Con-cern you for dropping it."

Outlined against the sky, he floated on, tugging purposefully at some detail or other. For a while the crowd forgot him as it occupied itself with drying out and dreading the long walk home. Suddenly someone remembered. Where was Borden now?

"Why, don't you know?" answered one wag. "My dear sir! It was a contrivance to go through the air as well. . . . If you look you can see him. Yonder!" and he pointed skyward. "See? Just yonder, by the edge of that cloud. Ha! he is taking a bite—look—out of a patent biscuit. See?"[16]

Before the trip Gail Borden had said: "If I miss it in one thing I will hit it in another."[17] With his terraqueous machine he had "missed it." But he wasted no time regretting. The remark about the patent biscuit was prophetic: a fresh enthusiasm was boiling that would lead to temporary fame, world-conquering hopes, a trip abroad, enticing prospects—and debts.

Exit: Terraqueous machine.

Enter: Meat biscuit.

[16] Baker, *A Year Worth Living*, 272–82.
[17] *Ibid.*, 250.

*My friends in Texas   consider me wild if
not absolutely crazy in persisting in this business*
—Gail Borden to Ashbel Smith,
December 19, 1853

XIII

The Good Ship Meat Biscuit
1849-1855

AMONG the early successful merchants of Galveston was Joseph Osterman, a middle-aged little Dutchman. No small part of his success was due to the indefatigability and astuteness of his frontier trader, a cross-eyed hunchback whose last name only, Hyams, is known.

The Comanche Indians were kind to cripples, and Hyams pressed his advantage, invariably returning to Galveston with his burro train laden with bargains. From one drumming trip to San Saba in Midwest Texas, Hyams brought back a large pack of *pinole*, of no marketable value but interesting to him because it was a principal Indian food. *Pinole*, Hyams told Osterman, was compounded of powdered, pulverized, dried buffalo meat, dried crushed hominy, and mesquite beans, and could be eaten dry or moistened and prepared as a cake. When traveling, the Comanche pressed the compound into a buffalo gut, which they then wore as a belt.

Osterman gave some of the *pinole* to his good friend and frequent visitor, Gail Borden, who chewed it and ruminated. Thus, according to one not altogether reliable version, Gail Borden's idea of a meat biscuit was born.

Borden should have been content. Nearing fifty in a land where men weathered quickly, he could look forward to a comfortable decade or two, enjoying the modest affluence which he had labored so assiduously to amass.

All the pieces seemed now to have fitted into the whole. He held an excellent business position in the largest and fastest growing city in Texas—whose dandies, incidentally, still trod barefoot, shoes in hand, through the ankle-deep sand streets and whose leading hotel boasted a sixteen-year-old native Texan barkeep. Borden was a leader in church and civic affairs. His children were growing in a healthful climate—healthful, that is, if one ignored seasonal cholera and yellow fever visitations. He had his home and his sheds and his orchards and his inventions. By canny investment his wealth should grow. What more could a man of meager schooling and log-cabin background expect? Was not his the American success story in miniature?

The entire Borden family seems to have been enjoying tranquillity at the close of the nineteenth-century's fifth decade. At the moment the most successful of the brothers, Tom Borden, was living in New Orleans manufacturing "manometres," or steam gauges, for Mississippi River steamboats. Paschal was a moderately prosperous blacksmith in Fort Bend County, where John P. was finishing a term as county judge. The father, Gail, Sr., apparently was enjoying good health as a farmer in the same vicinity.

But 1849 was a portentous year in which Gail Borden could not remain complacent. The year before, the treaty closing the Mexican War had given the United States all that vast territory containing such compelling names as California, Utah, and New Mexico. Hardly had American excitement from this tremendous acquisition tapered when a fillip was added by the discovery of gold at Sutter's mill. By the tens of thousands people flocked to the golden land by wagon, foot, and horseback—across plain and desert and mountain. Some chose a safer, more circuitous route—by ship to Panama, across the isthmus the best way they could, then by another ship to San Francisco; or by ship all the way around the southern tip of South America.

In Galveston, Gail Borden, always his brother's keeper, heard of these gold-hungry adventurers and was concerned. He probably knew the story of the 1846 Donner party who, trapped by mountain snows when almost to their goal, in desperation turned to the bodies of their dead companions for food. He was enough of a frontiersman to know that as a last resort cannibalism was not uncommon among starving men of the West. He knew that others in these groups would fall prey to Indians because they had no troops for protection. He knew, too, that even the cautious who went by sea would be subject to disease and perhaps to starvation because of the vagaries of weather and the distance of their journey.

He pondered. Men would always dare: immigrants and traders and fortune hunters, soldiers and sailors. Think of the soldiers in the West chasing Indians, their pursuit limited always by the distance from their supply trains. And the supply lines! Wagons and pack-mules, bulky and slow, unable to penetrate much of the rugged Western mountains and valleys.

In the Pacific especially, the sailor faced a similar problem. A few weeks or less from port and every day became a meatless day, while captains worried about scurvy and men became mutinous. An unexpected calm—and trouble.

Here then was a problem[1]—and here too an opportunity. To the man who could solve the problem, to the man who could grasp the opportunity, the pioneering world would shout *laudamus* and cry for his product. Not just America, but England and Russia and France and any other country which believed in expansion and empire. Gail Borden would have to see what he could do about it.

Exactly when Borden began his experiments on the meat biscuit, devised to remedy the travelers' supply problem, is uncertain, but probably by the middle of 1849 he had made some start, for by October of that year he had the invention well enough underway to accept the secretaryship of a committee pushing a Galveston-to-Brazos canal, a post he promptly dropped in early 1850 when the United States Army began to show serious interest in the meat biscuit. Also, in the same month he manufactured several canisters of biscuit for Dr. Elisha Kent Kane to take on his first Arctic expedition. On February 5, 1850, the government granted his American patent. Later Borden said he tested the biscuit eighteen months before placing it on the market. At any rate, by the time the decennial census taker had called in 1850, Borden was listing himself as a

[1] Another problem, of which Borden's later partner, Dr. Ashbel Smith, was aware, was the South's impoverishing dependence on agriculture to the exclusion of home manufactures. A Galveston manufacturing establishment could aid in a movement of industrialization that would increase the South's population, add to its wealth, and enlarge its representation in Congress accordingly—all this being accomplished without modifying the tariff or Southern opinions on free trade and states' rights *DeBow's Review*, Vol. X, No. 5 (May, 1851), 589–90.

manufacturer of meat biscuit, with six native Germans—five laborers and one engineer—in his employ.

To make meat biscuit, Borden boiled meat until the "solid innutritive portions" were separated from the filtered broth. The broth was then evaporated to "sugar-house syrup" consistency, a liquid gauge being used to determine uniform density. Eleven pounds of meat made one pound of extract, which was in turn mixed with flour—two pounds of extract to three pounds of flour—and then kneaded and baked. In the baking, the five pounds of meat dough were reduced to four pounds of biscuit resembling a light-colored sugar cake which could be fried, baked, or made into syrup, potpie, pudding, or mince pie. The addition of flour to the meat extract was Borden's claim to originality.[2]

With the advent of the meat biscuit, Gail Borden, for almost the first time in his life, concentrated on one thing. Aware that if successful he would own a product of international potentialities, he thought of nothing but meat biscuit for the next two years, shunting the biscuit aside finally only because the invention of his life had come upon the scene.

But in early 1850 his problem was how to achieve that evanescent success which dangled barely beyond reach. Probably he was too busy to realize it, but he was tied down in Galveston by the exigencies of production—beef to contract for, machinery to build, and production to supervise. Besides, he was a simple man, limited in background, with the gaucherie which not even leadership in a frontier society could quite smooth out. What he needed was a man with leisure, with some resources, and with influence or the ability to obtain that influence—a cosmopolite. But where to find such a man in Texas?

There was such a man in Texas, and, moreover, a man who at that time was peculiarly responsive to any project which would occupy his considerable talents. And because of an altercation of a dozen years before, he was Gail Borden's friend.

As early as March, 1848, Dr. Ashbel Smith had written Sam Houston from his Evergreen plantation that "my life is passing idly.

---

[2] A bottle of pulverized meat biscuit, handed down from the eighteen fifties, is owned by Mr. Elliott Bronson, Winchester Center, Connecticut. It appears perfectly preserved and is free from odor and discoloration.

... I want something to do." So when Gail Borden approached him with his plans regarding the manufacture of meat biscuits, it was a receptive Ashbel Smith who listened and approved and suggested.

Although there is no actual contract extant, Borden and Smith undoubtedly made some sort of arrangement quickly, for soon the two men prepared a series of letters outlining the merits and uses of the meat biscuit; and Smith wrote a New York firm in Borden's favor, sent samples to the American Association for the Advancement of Science, which was then meeting in Charleston, refuted a claim in the New York *Journal of Commerce* that the idea was not Borden's, and prepared to address the American Medical Association in Cincinnati. Smith definitely was committed to the meat biscuit.

In May, 1850, the results of the army's first test were made known. On hearing them, Borden, just back from St. Louis and Cincinnati, must have wandered off into a rosy dream of cosmic services and international acclaim. Wrote Brevet Colonel E. V. Sumner, First Dragoons, Fort Leavenworth, to the War Department in Washington:

> I have tried the "Meat Biscuit" and find it all, and more than the inventor thinks it is.
> ... I have lived upon it entirely, for several consecutive days, and felt no want of any other food. . . . I am convinced that I could live upon it for months, and retain my health and strength. I thought that altho: it might sustain life, there would be craving for more solid food, but it is not so, my appetite was perfectly satisfied. . . . I found I could dispense entirely with tea and coffee. . . . In my judgement this is a very great discovery, and must lead to important results.
> Think of a Regiment of 500 men cutting loose from all magazines for two months with no other baggage train than 50 or 60 pack mules. At 5 ounces a day for each man, the weight would be 9,375 lbs: which 45 mules could carry.[3]

Other army men added their testimonials to Colonel Sumner's, until by October, 1850, the secretary of war, Charles M. Conrad, was sufficiently impressed to order the commissary general to pur-

[3] E V Sumner to A. B Eaton, May 14, 1850, in Records of the Quartermaster General, War Department, the National Archives, Washington, D C. (hereafter cited as Quartermaster Records).

chase and issue enough meat biscuit to "give the article a fair trial."[4] The first large hurdle had been cleared.

The remainder of 1850 passed with the intoxication of planning and the routine of manufacture. Agents were lined up in St. Louis, New York, New Bedford, San Francisco, New Orleans, and Galveston. The partners attempted to pull political strings in Washington, Borden urging Smith "to have Genl Houston and Col [R. H.] Howard see our establishment before they go to Congress—It will be worth immense to us."

For a number of reasons, however, work did not progress as rapidly as the partners had hoped. The oven did not bake as well as expected; while Galveston's annual autumnal storm wrecked some of Borden's brickwork: "I had to watch and labor until two o'clock in the morning; when I was absolutely tired out, and sick for twenty four hours—." The same storm ruined several wells, Borden's among them, and cistern owners began asking two cents a gallon for water,[5] adding both to the manufacturers' inconvenience and expense, for without water no beef could be boiled.

Most and perhaps all of the financing seems to have been done by Borden, who almost weekly mortgaged another tract of land.[6] His factory was a two-story brick building at Strand and Rosenberg, 55 by 50 feet, with a one-story frame building, 40 by 24 feet, attached. Inside were a ten-horsepower engine and two cylinder-boilers to drive the machinery, consisting of biscuit machines to knead, roll, and cut the dough; a fan to raise the fire in a blast furnace for heating the oven; a grist mill to pulverize the biscuit; and the "guillotine," an invention of J. S. Savage, a Galveston machinist who sometimes worked with Borden, which cut the meat into small pieces to facilitate boiling. In addition there were two wooden cal-

[4] A B Eaton to George Gibson, May 30, 1850, John G. Tod to Charles M. Conrad, October 7, 1850, George Gibson to James Longstreet, November 2, 1850—in Quartermaster Records.

[5] Gail Borden to Ashbel Smith, October 30, 1850, December 23, 1851, in Smith Papers. Unless otherwise noted, all material for this chapter is taken from the Smith Papers

[6] Deed Record Book, F, Brazoria County, Texas, 5–6. Deed Record Book, B, Fort Bend County, Texas, 560–61. Records, I, Galveston County, Texas, 113, 117–18, 227–28, 254–56, Records, J, 304, 489, 540, 551, 577, 608, 738.

drons for boiling and two more for evaporating the caoutchouc-like broth. The two boiling caldrons held 2,300 gallons each of meat and would boil 7,000 pounds of meat in twelve to sixteen hours. The evaporating caldrons held 1,400 gallons each. All the tubs were heated by steam passed through long coiled pipes, supplied either from the escape-steam or direct from the boiler. When distilled water was needed, Borden condensed the steam.

Borden estimated his expenditure at $10,000, exclusive of the cost of the building, an expenditure that had to be made largely on credit, for Borden was very probably land poor. In buying on promise he had to rely heavily on the respect accorded a New York merchant, John H. Brower, who through Smith lent his name as reference whenever Borden bought materials for which he could not pay.[7]

Thus Gail Borden came to the end of 1850 with many debts, few sales, and a promising enough recommendation by several army officers to justify his faith in his product. If the army could ever get through endorsing its recommendations from major to colonel to general to secretary of war and its orders of purchase back down the chain of command, he might realize some of his glowing prospects. Meanwhile, he was faced with stopping operations entirely because of that great deterrent common to so many inventors, "want of means." At his elbow always was Ashbel Smith, urging, "*Manufacture* and *sell—Manufacture* and *sell*. Do not waste a day. *Manufacture immediately and sell*. . . . Public opinion is now alive to the merit of your invention you are in great danger . . . of letting it die away for want of supplying the market.—So haste, haste, haste.—" But how?

In the face of all this, Borden wrote Smith optimistically to "Please keep the stock raisers in good spirits—I have no doubt of success—none."

[7] *DeBow's Review*, Vol X, No. 5 (May, 1851), 590–91. The Dallas *Morning News*, November 18, 1906 Brower was Texas consul at New York from 1841 until the end of the Republic Of him President Anson Jones had written "The government of Texas has never had an officer, who has discharged his duties more ably, faithfully and satisfactorily." George P. Garrison, *Diplomatic Correspondence of the Republic of Texas*, II, 234. Other information on Brower may be found in Garrison, II, 221–24, 297–300, and Alma Howell Brown, "The Consular Service of the Republic of Texas" (unpublished master's thesis, University of Texas, 1928), 63, 67.

Eighteen fifty-one was to be the year—exciting, romantic with hope, promise, and expectations, such things as Gail Borden lived on.

In common with other years to follow, however, it was a year of debts. Between Christmas, 1850, and the following January 31 Gail Borden borrowed nearly $5,000. By October he was detailing his New York commitments in a dirge that sounded unending: "Without money—no sales of Biscuit—One hundred dollars to pay this week, One hundred and fifty next Monday—Seven hundred on the 11th Nov—Five hundred two weeks after & Six hundred two weeks more . . . ." And these were but the debts in New York.

In addition he owed "thousands in Texas" and was paying "a big interest." Small wonder that his "head became light" and at times he "felt dizzy and almost staggered."

Two months later the situation had become even more desperate: "I am entirely out of money. . . . if [my creditors] should take a panic, and begin to press my whole property would tumble like a row of bricks." Yes, 1851 had its nadir.

But the beginning of the year was fair enough. In London there was to be held a world's fair, the Great Council Exhibition of 1851, and Borden's friends and family were urging that he attend with his product. Borden was not sure what course to take, especially after John Brower, the New York merchant, and other business acquaintances advised him to develop the home market before taking on the world. On the other hand, Smith had already gone to London as Texas' representative to the fair, where, Borden said, he acted "like the pole star on the *Magnet.*—Some times there has been 'a variation' in my purposes, but not so great as to mistake the course of my inclinations."

Borden's inclination was to go: "I have struck some 'tall licks,' " he wrote, "and I find I must strike a good many more before I reach the 'highest persimon.' " One of the high persimmons he had in mind was the emperor of Russia, who might attend the fair. "I wish to make a hasty plate of soup for him as well as other Representatives of the world," Borden explained; "then I shall be styled the Worlds Cook,—the acme of my highest asperations for worldly fame."

Getting Borden off to London in time for the fair's May opening proved more of a task than Brower could handle. Arriving in

New York on April 21, a week later than expected, Borden resisted Brower's efforts to place him aboard the next ship for England, insisting that it was "utterly impossible" since he had a dozen things to do before he could shove off. He had to see about agents, go to New Bedford, superintend sales in New York, prepare a brochure for publication in May, purchase steaming apparatus, and attend to many other details. "Oh for two hours of your head and mind to assist," he wrote Smith. "I have spent hours . . . and have hardly begun."

Brower persevered, however, promising Smith that "I will get him off soon as I can." To help speed Borden's departure Brower gave him a letter of credit for £500 and told him that more would be forthcoming whenever necessary, which elicited from the inventor a "thank God. . . . Mr. Brower has always done more for me than he promises or . . . leads me to suppose."

On a cold, somewhat tempestuous May 1, the Great Council Exhibition opened. Queen Victoria, her carriage "still marked by a gracefulness that makes you forget . . . she is dumpy," attended amid a display of international pageantry. Her navy alone could guarantee the success of the meat biscuit. As Her Majesty swept past the red tables, the forests of painted columns, the flags of all participating nations, and the gigantic statues and fountains to the end of the crystal palace where stood the cases housing the modest American exhibits, would she notice the "two very common barrels" of Borden biscuit displayed by Ashbel Smith in the inventor's absence? If she did, Gail Borden was not there to know.

From an exclusively American point of view the meat biscuit display was fortunate, because Yankee ingenuity was rather poorly exhibited at the fair and almost anything from the United States stood out—that is, if the visitor took notice of anything American at all. Americans had sent such curiosities as Cornelius lamps, artificial teeth, Herring's Patent Salamander safe—(£500 to any person picking its lock), Indian embroidery, a four-thousand-pound ox which had been fattening for eight years but could still lumber a mile a day, Colt's revolver, McCormick's "Virginia Reaper," and Gail Borden's "unsightly" meat biscuit. Not a very imposing array, leading Dr. Smith to observe that the United States would have fared better to have sent nothing—"the Americans here are a set of *nobodies.*"[8] And Gail Borden, en route, was hoping to arrive to find his product in international demand.

What Borden did from May until September is not clear. Almost the only records of him appear in a series of five contracts he drew up with Smith, witnessed by Abbott Laurence, the American envoy extraordinary and minister plenipotentiary. These contracts gave Smith 10 per cent of Borden's United States patent, power of attorney, one-half of all profits from sales to any foreign government, and finally, the right to apply "to the Emperor of Russia for a patent or privilege to manufacture and sell . . . Meat Biscuit, within the dominions of His Majesty the Emperor of all the Russias." Apparently Borden also was busy with patent authorities in London, as the English patent on his meat biscuit was granted on September 5.

Meanwhile, Borden was busy exhibiting the meat biscuit, explaining its merits, and obtaining promises from sea captains and prospective explorers to give it a fair trial. Brower cautioned him against impatience, since "those Jno. Bulls, especially the old fellows who live upon the public purse without work, are so slow and fussy that if they know anything (which may be somewhat doubtful), it takes them almost forever to set about doing it." At the same time "doughty Ashbel Smith," as *Punch* labeled Borden's partner, addressed a French agricultural society on the meat biscuit, receiving the warm approval of part of the French press both for the product he represented and for his ability to speak French with such "*grande pureté.*" Russia loomed larger as a potential customer, and a trip to St. Petersburg for Smith must have been seriously considered—though no trip was ever made.

While these numerous activities were going ahead in London, what was happening back in the United States?

For one thing, testimonials. From Louisiana one man wrote that Borden's invention would "undoubtedly place him among the benefactors of mankind." For simplicity and for filling an obvious need he compared the biscuit with another discovery—that to ring a bell you need not toll the ten-ton bell but merely shake the ten-pound clapper. Captain John G. Tod of Texas suggested to the

[8] Galveston *Weekly News*, May 20, August 26, 1851. N S. Dodge in the *Daily National Intelligencer*, January 13, 1852.

At the Great Council Exhibition in London in 1851, Borden's meat biscuit won one of five gold medals awarded American inventors A young Queen Victoria and Prince Albert are shown on one side of the medal

The Borden Company

Secretary of War that if the War Department would order 100,000 pounds, the cost would be entirely saved in the difference in freight charges.[9]

The *Scientific American* called the biscuit "one of the most valuable inventions that has ever been brought forward." Brower told how his packet ship *Benjamin R. Milam* had kept for fourteen months a canister of biscuit that was as fresh as when it was first manufactured. And Dr. Alexander Dallas Bache, president of the American Association for the Advancement of Science, permitted publication of a letter he had received stating that the biscuit "is perfectly free from that vapid unctuous stale taste, which characterizes all prepared soups . . . hitherto tried."[10]

With the bustle of the Great Council Exhibition in London and such expressions of faith in the United States, the future should have looked excellent. But the American army was to have another say. On June 21, 1851, a board of six army officers, acting on orders growing out of Colonel E. V. Sumner's request for a prolonged biscuit trial, submitted its findings, known as the Waco Report.

The report had four parts, each one of them damaging: the biscuit could not be substituted for the ordinary army ration; it did not possess qualities necessary "to sustain life in health and vigor, whilst on active duty. . . . even when increased to . . . 12 ounces per ration" (Borden had prescribed six ounces as more than sufficient); it was "not only unpalatable, but fails to appease the craving of hunger—producing head-ache, nausea, and great muscular depression"; and it "impairs the capacity of the healthy human-system to sustain as much mental or bodily labor as it can be legitimately called upon to perform, . . . it diminishes the power of resisting the extremes of heat & cold." The six officers therefore felt "reluctantly compelled to report unanimously" against the biscuit's adoption.[11]

Reluctant or not, the report was positive in its assertions—the meat biscuit would not do; and all other fine testimonials to the

[9] John G. Tod to Charles M. Conrad, February 25, 1851, in Quartermaster Records. *The Meat Biscuit; Invented, Patented, and Manufactured by Gail Borden, Jun*, 6

[10] *The Meat Biscuit; Invented, Patented, and Manufactured by Gail Borden, Jun*, 17

[11] Report, H. W. Merrill and others, June 21, 1851, in Quartermaster Records. A copy of this report is in the Smith Papers.

contrary notwithstanding, Borden's product was to suffer thereafter. A disappointed Borden denounced the report as "villainous" and "a plot" and the men who made it as prejudiced, maintaining that he knew before the test that these particular officers would report against the biscuit and hinting that outside pressure had influenced their minds adversely. Whether this unsubstantiated charge was true, the report would hound him for the next several years and confront him every time he approached success.

In London the Great Council Exhibition was drawing to a close, and the decision of the jury—three Englishmen, a Frenchman, a Russian, and Dr. Ashbel Smith—was due. The decision: a Gold Medal, top award, one of five awarded to Americans, to Mr. Gail Borden of Texas for his contribution to the foodstuffs industry. As a corollary, honorary membership in the London Society of Arts. "Singular and excellently made . . . quite sound and free from putridity," noted Dr. Lyon Playfair, commissioner in charge of juries. Commented the London correspondent of the New York *Journal of Commerce*:

Of all the "substances used for food," that which attracted most attention, at the Great Exhibition . . . is the "Meat Biscuit" of Mr. Gail Borden, Jun. of Texas. . . . The preservative qualities of the Meat Biscuit are perfect; . . . its high nutritive properties are evinced. . . . Among the various preparations of food presented . . . no one was deemed worthy of the same high approbation as the Meat Biscuit. . . . the only contribution, I believe, from Texas.[12]

Weighing a reception like this against the unfavorable report the army had given, Borden and Smith could hardly have been expected to abandon their expensive product or even to slacken efforts in its behalf. And they didn't.

[12] Extract from the London correspondence of the New York *Journal of Commerce*, ca October, 1851, transcript in the Borden Papers, Borden Company, New York The Borden Company has the gold medal in its archives. Dr. Playfair is perhaps best remembered for having placed Scotland's famous golf course, St. Andrew's, on a firm basis. In all, 170 Council medals were awarded. Besides the meat biscuit, the American inventions winning gold medals were the McCormick reaper, the Dick engine-tools and presses, the Bond device for observing astronomical phenomena, and the Goodyear India rubber. Merle Curti, "America at the World Fairs, 1851–1893," *The American Historical Review*, Vol. LV, No. 4 (July, 1950), 840.

The winter of 1851 passed with no notable success, the Galveston manufactory turning out 34,000 pounds of biscuit and sixty barrels of beef lard, much of which went into stock. Smith made some progress toward interesting the French in using the biscuit in Algeria. Instead of returning to Texas, Borden stopped off in New York, where he turned his thoughts to Congress, thinking that he might carry his fight to the military committees during the next spring session, even to feeding all their members. But a letter from his brother John chilled his enthusiasm:

"I have come to the conclusion," wrote John Borden, "that the chances for getting relief from [Congress] are so few that it will not justify an outlay of the time and money which the experement will cost. Let the matter lie over another year. It seems . . . unreasonable to ask Dr. Smith to leave his own affairs . . . . make some sacrifices to raise money to bear his expenses, and then spend two months besides."

On March 3 Borden wrote his partner, Ashbel Smith, who had returned to Texas: "This answer of brother John, and nothing from you, was an avalanche that came near overwhelming me. . . . I feel that I am almost deserted. To talk about making *some* sacrifices to raise money, and to spend two months, at this stage of the game, after I have spent every thing I have and thirty thousand dollars worth of property, *all* I have, subject to be sold under the hammer, is like comparing a slight *tooth ache* to the *Cholera*."

Continued adversity was bringing a steady worsening of relations between the pair: "I had & have claims on your services to assist in bringing this enterprise forward not only here but *especially* in Europe," wrote Borden. "It may be said that I should not have risked so much in this enterprise,—but I did not purchase my extensive machinery and apparatus . . . until *after* you had urged me . . . to hasten and 'manufacture & sell' 'manufacture & sell'—." He did not blame Smith, he added, for he realized that the invention was ahead of the world and that "like the first diggers of anthracite coal," he was on the "ruined side."

But he had spent $4,000 in England, he owed Brower $9,000, and many other debts were consuming him. Living expenses he had cut to a minimum· his wife was in one place, his daughters in another, his sons in still another, cared for by relatives and friends. And this the man who a scant three years before had been living comfortably in Galveston. Fifteen hours a day, at least, he spent trying to bring the biscuit to the notice of customers, going into ship's galleys and into hospital kitchens to cook the biscuit himself, cornering Horace Greeley and Charles Dana and other men of influence, and writing agents. And still large clippers were sailing out of New York bound for California with hundreds of passengers but not a "pound on board."

Borden went to work on Dr. Elisha Kent Kane, the explorer, who had taken some Borden biscuit on his Arctic search for Sir John Franklin in 1850. On his return Dr. Kane had complained of too much gelatine in the biscuit. Now Dr. Kane was preparing another Arctic expedition, and both he and his assisting physicians were talking of trying pemmican instead. Borden's efforts were partially successful, for in his journal Dr. Kane noted "We took with us . . . a parcel of Borden's meat biscuit" and later wrote of caching forty pounds of the biscuit, in addition to making numerous casual references when talking of dietetics on the voyage.[13] But pemmican seems to have been the principal food.

Hardly a ship left New York in 1852 without Borden's contact. He visited them all, talking to commissary stewards, showing cooks how to prepare the biscuit, and treating the captains to a bowl of his soup. His doubts of eventual success never wavered. "But all this takes time," he admitted, ". . . and in the *mean time* I am starving. I tell you now is the tug."

When Borden ran out of ships, he turned to hospitals and committees of physicians. Everywhere he met indifference. In one hospital the patients liked the biscuit when Borden cooked and served it, but when he turned elsewhere the cooks took no pains in its preparation, one even serving the biscuit with a burned rag in the bottom of the cup. In an effort to get someone—anyone—to like the biscuit, he asked Smith to try it with his Negroes—"give them rice or homony with it. Try it with the farmers."

Despite his continued unsuccess, Borden, encouraged always by friends, persisted in his world-wide dreams. In England Arthur Goodall Wavell, early nineteenth-century military adventurer in Texas, long-time correspondent of Ashbel Smith, and, incidentally,

[13] E K Kane, *Arctic Explorations*, I, 19, 138, II, 21, 169, 174.

grandfather of Field Marshal Sir Archibald Wavell, the British soldier, statesman, and man of letters, recommended the biscuit to a New Zealand friend as invaluable in bush exploration. Wavell cooked some biscuit for scarred, square-built Sir John Ross, another Arctic searcher, who said he liked it. Wrote another English traveler, Thomas Falconer, conscious of the logistics needs of the British in the Crimean difficulty "What a valuable article would it not be in making a Foray among the Cossacs."

The medical officer of the *Tenedos*, a convict hospital ship, wrote the governor of Bermuda of the biscuit's advantages; the *Scientific American* thought the biscuit would be "a great blessing to the British navy."[14] The American consul at Amsterdam wrote favorably; Borden thought Turkey would provide a good market; Brower insisted the European patent rights were worth $25,000; and another Englishman averred that in Australian mining regions "gold dust would be weighed out in ounces for pounds of the biscuit." To all expansive proposals Borden listened eagerly, only to jerk himself back to reality with a sharp "why talk of taking it to the *ends* of the earth before it sells in the two great metropolis' of the Eastern & Western world?"

The year 1853 found Smith and most of Borden's other friends, especially those in Galveston, beginning to despair of the inventor's ever realizing anything from his biscuit. On April 30 Smith wrote Borden that he was canceling his part in the European patent arrangements. Even so, Borden was glad merely to hear from his old friend, for it was the first word out of Dr. Smith in five months. "I had become exceedingly fearful that you was about to abandon me," he complained.

Borden did not, however, share the forlorn views of his friends. "Do not think that I have given up the ship Meat Biscuit. . . . The article is still making slow progress, but gaining a little. It must succeed." Then he predicted· "If I live—if God spares me two years more, Texas if not the whole world, will see that I have not lived in vain, and shall yet perhaps be counted 'worthy to stand before princes.'" God would spare him two years—in fact, twenty years, and he would fulfill his prediction, but not with the meat biscuit.

[14] *Scientific American*, Vol. VII, No. 23 (February 21, 1852), Vol VII, No. 41 (June 26, 1852)

Nathaniel Amory, realtor and sometime government official under the Republic of Texas, came up from Texas for a visit in New York. Like many another Texan he had wondered just what Gail Borden had been doing since he left Galveston two years before, and now, in June, 1853, he could see firsthand. Reported Amory to a friend in Nacogdoches, Texas: "I have just been . . . to see Gail Borden over at Brooklin, found him with a desk in a cellar where he had some of his meat biscuit. he also showed us boiled milk & essence of coffee condensed that ½ a tea spoonful of the *salve* mak[es] a cup full of café au lait or French coffee & milk this boiling down is in vacuum at a temperature so low that the liquid can be held in the hand without burning. He expects a patent shortly the cup of coffee was very good. . . .

"Gail Borden's children are at a Quaker establishment near Troy. He was well dressed altho his place of business was in a cellar."[15]

So Gail Borden had a new toy—boiled, or condensed, milk. Amory's letter is the first evidence that can be definitely authenticated, although in later years the dates for Borden's milk discovery would be placed back as much as a quarter of a century.

Four days after Amory's visit, on July 2, 1853, public announcement of the discovery was made in the *Scientific American*, but although Borden must have applied for a patent as early as May, he did not confide his discovery to his old partner, Ashbel Smith, until just before Christmas, when he wrote: "I am . . . my friend, happy to inform you that I have invented a new process for the concentration and preservation of milk, and its combination with coffee, cocoa etc which will, if I live, render me independent of faint hearted friends. More of this when I see you—I shall most certainly convince you."

As he read of this latest enthusiasm of Borden's, one can almost hear the Sage of Evergreen drop the letter and with an audible exhalation mutter: "Oh my Lord, here we go again!"

This was the period of the Crimean War between England and Russia and its accompanying outbreak of disease among soldiers of

---

[15] Nathaniel Amory to James Harper Starr, June 28, 1853, in James H Starr Papers, University of Texas Archives Actually the Borden children were in a Shaker, rather than a Quaker, community near New Lebanon, New York Borden's

both sides. In this distress an Englishwoman named Florence Nightingale founded her reputation, and in America an alert Borden saw renewed opportunity.

Once again he turned to Ashbel Smith: "I have thought a good deal lately," he wrote Smith from a "steamboat saloon" in late 1854, "how much I would like to take a ton or two of the MB to the *Crimea*. . . . How beneficial it would prove to the poor sick, and wounded, especially in the case of Colera & bowel complaint. . . . But I am powerless—In debt, my creditors . . . would not wait while I took so long a tour. Besides, I am greatly encouraged to embark in the Milk business."

So he stayed in America. Part of 1854 he spent in Texas selling land to pay debts in a last effort to "conquer or die." When one creditor brought suit against him in the Galveston courts, Borden did not even attend in his own defense. He toyed with a plan to mill lumber in Bastrop County, Texas. He drafted instructions to his English agent to close the Bond Street office in London. Surrender, however, he would not consider, not until he found "that *trying* will do no good." Although he was spending more and more effort endeavoring to establish his milk business, his primary object was still to sell meat biscuit.

To the purple hills west of Austin had moved Noah Smithwick, one of San Felipe's pioneer madcaps who had left that early Texas center by invitation of its outraged citizens. One day in 1854, Gail Borden, recent author of a much-discussed newspaper article telling how to fight corn weevils and to build corncribs, drove up to Smithwick's door in the Mormon Mills vicinity, explaining that he had heard rumors there was gold on his Burnet County lands.[16] The rumor was false, but before Borden departed he divulged another side of his many-faceted life.

According to Smithwick, Gail Borden was now a practitioner in homeopathic remedies, with a "Doctor" prefixed to his name, and "Dr. Borden" imparted to Smithwick the "great secret" of his school of medicine. Said Borden: "It is no use to be a doctor unless you put

living and working quarters together were costing him $18.50 a month. In addition, he was limiting his personal expenditures to one dollar a day

16 *Texas State Gazette*, July 22, 1854.

on the airs of one. Nine times out of ten sickness is caused by over-eating or eating unwholesome food, but a patient gets angry if you tell him so, you must humor him. This I do by taking one grain of calomel and dividing it into infinitesimal parts, adding sufficient starch to each part to make one of these little pellets (exhibiting a little vial of tiny white pills), then I glaze them over with sugar. In prescribing for a patient I caution him about his diet, warning him that the pills have calomel in them. Well, the result is that he obstains from hurtful articles of food, which is all he needs to do anyway."[17] Had Borden turned medicine man? Undoubtedly.

"Found brother Paschal in the third stage of Pneumonia, with a bad cough," he wrote a friend. "Stuffed with drugs etc. I commenced the 'Do Nothing' and Hydropathic practice. In 24 hours began to expectorate. . . . he is now convalescent. begins to set up and eats more than many well men. God be praised for his mercies."

He must have believed in his own treatments, for he used them on himself: "I arrived back here [in New York] 12th March [1855] cold as the North pole, sick with the old fashioned ague & fever," he wrote Dr. Smith. "Got well [but] worked too hard, took the ague & fever again adopted the '*do nothing*' practice; got well again, and again pitched into work."

That was Dr. Borden, whose degrees of medicine could have been obtained only in the crude Borden cellar-laboratory of practical experimentation.

There was a period during the spring of 1855 when Borden thought that at last his meat biscuit efforts might attain fruition. Between January and March he received orders from London for 3,600 pounds at twenty-five cents a pound. He also shipped 1,200 pounds to France, and his St. Louis agent asked for a reorder of an unspecified number of large cases. From Providence, Philadelphia, and New London came inquiries. Morton, his London agent, announced he had sent an order to the Crimea, along with directions to Florence Nightingale and the purveyor-in-chief at Scutari. English and French editions of the meat biscuit pamphlet were printed. Maybe the long period of introducing and selling and promoting was ending.

[17] Smithwick, *Evolution of a State*, 311–12.

In April came a summons from Henry Grinnell, the same wealthy philanthropist who had sponsored Kane's second Arctic expedition, for Borden to call to discuss his product. Could this be the break for which Borden had been waiting five years? But though the interview did not produce quite what Borden had hoped, he did come away cheered: another two thousand pounds—$500 worth—had been sold. He also agreed to make pemmican for the same expedition.[18]

That seems to have been the last great effort. Thenceforward sales were sparse, although in June, Morton wrote that "I have cleaned off all the Meat Biscuit on hand—& Could have sold more if I had had it." By September things were going so badly that he wrote Dr. Smith another of his "wet Norther" letters—that is, letters which "not only drench, but chill". "I am becoming utterly discouraged." Brower, his principal creditor, was losing faith in the meat biscuit, this while Borden yet owed him $2,000. Working in Brower's office, Borden saw his benefactor daily, but for weeks now had received from him only the coldest and most formal of "good mornings" in an almost inaudible voice. Nothing, not even Smith's earlier disinterest, struck Borden so hard as Brower's lack of esteem.

Still he was not ready to abandon the biscuit, for now he needed every cent he could lay hands on, not just for living, but for his new enterprise, condensed milk. Since returning to New York he had sold between eight and nine thousand pounds of biscuit and he would continue marketing it so long as sales would pay expenses, but milk was now what really mattered.

The entrance of condensed milk into highest favor with Borden sounded the death knell of the biscuit enterprise. For a while sales continued, but from late 1855 on, condensed milk held the center of his stage, as every thought, every dollar, every ounce of energy went into the fight to sell America on condensed milk. The meat biscuit left the scene more quietly than it had arrived, and it left Gail Borden perhaps $60,000 poorer as he approached the most desperate financial struggle of his career.

[18] Henry Grinnell to [Gail Borden], April 11, 1855, C. Barlow to Gail Borden, May 18, 1855, Thomas H Borden to Gail Borden, May 21, 1855, J. E Johnson to Gail Borden, June 4, 1855—in Borden Papers, Rosenberg Library Gail Borden to Thomas W. Chambers, May 9, 1855, in T. W. Chambers Papers, University of Texas Archives

Why did the meat biscuit fail? Experts of unimpeachable standing testified to its nutritive qualities, its compactness, and its preservative properties. Was the meat biscuit, as most Borden biographers insist, a victim of collusion of high army officials with fresh-meat and preserved-meat producers who recognized a dangerous adversary and resolved to stop its threat at the very beginning?

There is no direct evidence to support this allegation, but probably there would not be. No conniver would have written Borden nor any of Borden's acquaintances of his intentions. Nor is it likely that any such scheme would have found its way into official army records. True, every one of his contemporaries who wrote a memorial to Borden states unequivocally that the meat biscuit failed because of pressure from the established meat interests. How much of this is fact, and how much the desire to blame outside forces for poor results? If the charges are true, then why did not Borden later combat full scale the meat interests when he had means to fight back? That he did not choose to fight is not necessarily an admission that he had an unmarketable product, but it could be.

The simplest fact is that the meat biscuit was not palatable—people did not like it, which is always the best reason for not buying any food. Time after time Borden wrote that no one cooked the meat biscuit correctly except himself.[19] Invariably he blamed the cooks. But if an article is that difficult to prepare, could not that be the fault of the article and not of the cook?

That delightful reporter, Frederick Law Olmsted, faced once with a choice between Borden's biscuit and watery potatoes, prepared a large dish of biscuit for his party: "We all tried it once, then turned unanimously to the watery potatoes. Once afterwards . . . we tried again [and] then left all we had purchased to the birds. It may answer to support life . . . where even corn meal is not to be had, but I should decidedly undergo a very near approach to the traveler's last bourne, before having recourse to it."[20]

---

[19] Similar charges by other inventors are not uncommon, although the reasons and solutions vary. In this same decade Henry Bessemer, using his new converter, could produce a beautiful quality of steel in his London plant, but when he let others use identical models elsewhere in England, the results were uniformly disappointing. In his case the trouble lay in his use of iron with low phosphoric content while others tried to convert iron high in phosphorus.

[20] F. L. Olmsted, *A Journey Through Texas*, 81, 87.

While praising the lasting qualities of the biscuit, naval surgeon Joseph Wilson testified that many persons found its "unusual flavour . . . absolutely disgusting." Borden's agents in New Bedord insisted that although a number of shipmasters had given it a fair trial, the biscuit simply did not "meet their expectations."[21] These are not isolated statements: the complaints equal the testimonials. If people do not like an article, they do not buy it. For that reason, the meat biscuit did not sell; just as for the same reason the later invention, condensed milk, did.

Thus the curtain fell on Gail Borden's meat biscuit adventure. Financially a failure, it proved a long-range blessing, for through it Borden lost his purely Texas stamp and became instead the man of business with contacts among leading scientists and governmental agencies which were to stand him in such good stead when he started over the same uneven road with his milk invention.

Neither influence nor success accompanied the meat biscuit, but prerequisites of those conditions did—perseverance, character, experimentation, and faith.

"I never drop an idea except for a better one."

[21] Joseph Wilson to Gail Borden, February 2, 1855, Hamlin & Perkins to Gail Borden, July 10, 1855—in Borden Papers, Rosenberg Library

I have succeeded in concentrating milk 80 per cent without the use of sugar—and it is soluble either in hot or cold water It is a beautiful article I do not hesitate to say or predict that should I live two years, I shall present to the world an invention of vast import Milk will be as common . . as sugar Stick your memory in that idea and also, that your Uncle Gail will be inventer of the process
—Gail Borden to Ashbel Smith,
September 22, 1855

Brother Gail is some what inthusiastic and is liable to be mistaken
—Thomas H Borden to T S Sutherland,
July 13, 1856

XIV

Door to Door
1851-1857

WHEN GAIL BORDEN was a young schoolteacher in the tall pine woods of southwestern Mississippi, he boarded with Kinchon Webb and his wife, Rebecca. One day he approached Rebecca Webb with a strange request. Would she permit him to have one of her cows for an experiment? Rebecca Webb granted the request, and Gail Borden milked the cow, boiled the milk, and let it cool for several days and then threw it out and started all over again. That, in Amite County, Mississippi, is the traditional story of Gail Borden's quest for a method of condensing milk.

Other communities and other people have their traditions regarding the genesis of Borden's condensed milk.

"The last hobby failed, the last hope of a great invention had fled, and Brother Borden was dying from sheer gloom and melancholy. [An] old and devoted friend . . . simply to preserve the life of a gentle, noble spirit, showed him a slip cut from a French newspaper [detailing how a French scientist was trying to condense milk]. This bare announcement aroused all his inventive genius and restored his vigor. Soon he discovered his wonderful plan."[1]

[1] *The Life and Writings of Rufus C Burleson,* 729

In Galveston, Borden's work brought him into daily contact with overland travelers. Concerned that the children of these immigrant families would face privation, the kind Galveston Sunday school missionary would give them milk as they departed, scalding it beforehand that it might keep longer. Even then it would keep only a little longer. What was the answer? Texas housewives cooked their fruit in sugar syrup to keep fruit from spoiling. *"Why cant I do the same thing with milk?"* he asked himself.[2]

Another story credits Borden's preoccupation for the discovery. Before retiring one night, this story goes, he placed a pan of milk on the stove to heat a sort of warm milk toddy. Then he drifted off into some other world, returning hours later to find a sticky white paste—his first condensed milk.

Baker tells it another way. He was sitting at the Borden table when Gail, reaching for a dish, overturned a glass of milk. Suddenly he shot from the table, "upsetting his chair, and nearly pulling the cloth off the board. 'An idea strikes me!' It was all he said as he disappeared."[3]

The most original and automatic explanation belongs to the Reverend Rufus Burleson, who in all seriousness once wrote that Gail Borden was so filled with the milk of human kindness that three years later he invented condensed milk!

But of all the traditions the one that persists is the account of Gail Borden's return from the Great Council Exhibition in London in the fall of 1851. The sailing ship was slow, the voyage was rough, and the cows in the hold became so seasick that they could not be milked. The cries of immigrant babies wanting milk where there was none upset this Yankee from Texas until he could think of little else. He talked to the captain and the captain laughed in his face. He cornered deck strollers, but they either told him he was crazy or said nothing. Children were suffering, and only he, Gail Borden, cared enough to provide relief.

Those are some of the stories of Gail Borden's conception of his great discovery. None may be true, which doesn't really matter.

2 Miles K Lewis to Arthur G. Clark, July 21, 1918 In the years immediately before and after 1918 Arthur G. Clark of the Borden Company, New York, gathered letters and statements from many persons, now dead, who had known Gail Borden personally These are now in the Borden Company archives

3 Baker, *A Year Worth Living,* 250

What matters is that somewhere, by some means, he had caught another vision, and that this time he had found his Holy Grail. The dreamer of dreams had caught up at last with his due time.

Gail Borden possessed only a raw idea. He wanted to treat milk, that most delicate of foods, in such fashion that it would maintain its normal purity and freshness for weeks or longer while at the same time it lost none of its flesh-forming, heat-producing, life-sustaining qualities.

Between the raw idea and the successful invention lies molding and reconciliation and fusing and development until the idea becomes workable, the commodity producible and marketable. In the case of milk this evolution from conception to birth to full-blown practicality called for a scientist with a laboratory, a man who understood fluidity, composition, thermochemistry, and bacteriology. But Gail Borden was no scientist and his only laboratory was a cellar whose principal tools were trial and error—and that in meat biscuit, not milk.

Although the Tartars are credited with having concentrated milk-pastes in the fourteenth century, scientists did not really begin to work toward milk condensation until the beginning of the nineteenth century when François Appert, Gallic father of modern canning, evaporated and, in a sense, pasteurized milk.[4] In 1813 a vacuum-pan patent was granted; in 1826 another Frenchman was given a patent for concentrating milk with sugar; and in 1835, when Gail Borden was starting *The Telegraph and Texas Register*, William Newton of England was granted a patent on a vacuum pan designed solely for milk evaporation. Others made improvements, culminating in the patenting of powdered milk in 1855. Most of these inventions met the tests of workability and producibility, but lost in the final stage of marketability.

How then did Gail Borden succeed where so many had failed? How did this man whose science had been learned along Indiana deer licks and in Mississippi forests and on Texas scrub-islands, whose science books had been a rifle and a surveyor's chain and an

---

[4] At least a dozen years before Pasteur's birth in 1822. Many authors mistakenly credit the birth of modern canning to François Appert's brother, Nicolas, an important French prison reformer.

editor's quill—how did this man of the woods and plains, this inventor of yellow fever cures which didn't cure, of terraqueous machines that overturned, of meat biscuits that no one ate—how did this plain, weather-beaten man with the Lincolnesque physique and the headlong Whitmanesque vitality attain the mantle of world's milkman where men of science and education and training had been found wanting?

Until he applied for a patent, Borden likely had little knowledge that he had been anticipated, for his entrance on the scientific scene was too recent for him to have gained much familiarity with earlier inventions. Besides, he was too wrapped up in his day-to-day experiments to devote much time to historical research. He had to try, and then try again. Preserving milk was no problem, but maintaining its quality and its palatability was something else. Probably the first milk was boiled in a pan upon a sand bath heated by charcoal, with brown sugar added to the condensed product, giving it a dark color and a molasses odor. Sealed in glass it would keep for months, but no one would buy anything that looked and smelled like disappointed syrup. To prevent discoloration must have been his immediate reason for turning to the vacuum pan.

He consulted everyone. One valuable friend was Dr. John H. Currie of New York, who permitted Borden use of his laboratory equipment. When the inventor placed son John Gail and daughter Mary Jane in school at Mechanicsville, New York, he dropped over to the Shaker colony at New Lebanon where Mother Ann Lee's dancing disciples owned a vacuum pan. By February, 1853, he had ordered a pan for himself.

Characteristically, he was stubborn. When one scientist suggested that Borden deflect his aim—that he would never be able to retain uninjured all the butter in milk, he refused to consider condensing skimmed milk. He would condense it whole or not at all.

When he condensed, the albuminous constituent of the milk adhered to the inner surface of the vacuum pan, which in turn caused the milk to foam and boil over, or be sucked back through the pump. An experienced sugar-boiler whom Borden had induced to advise him pronounced his method completely impractical. But the inventor persisted, finding his solution finally in a housewife's candy-making device: he simply greased the pan.

Although lack of money hampered his efforts, always he found ways. The following story shows one method:

Many years ago in Troy, N. Y. [wrote James Porter Collins in 1903], I started to construct Turbine water-wheels with very little capital. . . . During the second year of my effort a gentleman came to . . . my home. Scarcely waiting for the customary salutation he introduced himself something as follows: My name is Gail Borden. . . . I have discovered a way to keep milk sweet for a very long time and have tried the process by Hand labor, but . . . I find that to make it pay I must have some mechanical power. . . . I have spent all my money and my friends . . . will not lend me any. I have come to ask you to sell me such a wheel as I require and wait a reasonable length of time for your pay. It was a strange proposal for one so poor even to consider for it meant tying up over 1/3 of my capital for some time, but I had been much impressed by the frankness of his face and speech and had almost decided in the affirmative when my wife, an excellent judge of character, gave her verdict in his favor. . . . there was no note or other evidence of indebtedness given. . . . Mr. Borden was a man who carried his letter of credit in his face.[5]

By May, 1853, Borden was sufficiently satisfied with his product to apply for patents in the United States and England. It was then that he learned he had predecessors—only a dozen years before, another inventor had been granted a patent for evaporating milk "in any known mode," including use of a vacuum pan. In London his patent attorney, C. Barlow, after spending weeks tracing the utilization of the various condensed-milk patents, found that the vacuum method had remained theoretical, that no inventor had ever used a vacuum pan for evaporating milk under any patent. With this information Borden disposed of patent-office objections to the lack of novelty in his method.

But the patent officials insisted on other evidences of the importance of condensing *in vacuo*. "New" and "useful" were the key words in Washington and London. Could Borden prove that condensing milk entirely in vacuum contributed anything to previous modes of condensation? Until he convinced the dubious officials, he could consider his patent applications rejected.

5 J P Collins to the Borden Company, October 27, 1903, in Borden Papers, Borden Company, New York

Borden and Milbank During a chance meeting on a
Connecticut-to-New York train, Borden and Milbank
agree to become partners in producing condensed milk

The Borden Company

Into the Washington maelstrom stepped Borden, to be tossed and whirled from official door to official door for three years. Patent commissioners would listen and nod and agree—"We recognize its novelty, but does that mean it's really *new?*" And Gail Borden would make another appointment and write another half-dozen letters and obtain another interview—and receive another rejection. Nevertheless, he refused to quit.

Back and forth between New York and Washington he shuttled, each trip using more of the meager funds remaining from his borrowings. But he had to make the trips, he had to succeed: by any possible means he had to get his patent and his milk on the market. If he had to sell everything but his soul—and his soul Gail Borden would never have surrendered—he would do so, because the goal justified any honorable means. His faith in himself told him that much when friends told him otherwise.

His assault on the patent office assumed the form of a propaganda bombardment. He talked to scientists and publicists, urging everyone who sounded not unfavorable to write to Washington. He sought letters from General Houston, knowing that he required "the longest and strongest lever to reach the dead weight" in the patent office.

Editor Robert Macfarlane of the *Scientific American*, a dye-process discoverer himself, was one of Borden's earliest supporters. In the summer of 1853 Macfarlane devoted a column to this latest improvement in foods by the Texas inventor, pointing out that incipient decomposition was completely prevented, that he had kept a quantity of Borden's milk for three months in a fairly warm place, and that the milk was as sweet after three months as it was when received.[6]

Milk and meat biscuits were not Borden's only interests. He tried all sorts of condensations—coffee, tea, and "other useful dietary matters." A thunderstorm or a week of hot weather need not turn New Yorkers to milkless coffee; Borden would give them milk and coffee that would ever be ready. If he didn't break in pieces, he maintained, he would condense everything that people used—"I mean to put a potato into a pill-box, a pumpkin into a tablespoon, the biggest sort of a watermelon into a saucer. . . . The Turks made

[6] *Scientific American*, Vol. VIII, No. 42 (July 2, 1853), 333.

acres of roses into attar of roses. . . . I intend to make attar of every thing!'"[7]

As the fight progressed, he took on an avuncular outlook. He became "Uncle Gail"—uncle to his friends, uncle to the world, uncle to himself. Even to men of his own age, such as Ashbel Smith, he signed himself "Uncle Gail." And as he neared his midfifties death was constantly on his mind. Would he live long enough to finish?

Despite rebuffs and no funds, he was encouraged. He felt closer to God than at any time in his life, and in addition, "I understand more of human nature, have made some improvement in my manners and address, and in every way, I feel that I am better qualified to carry on, and to succeed . . . than I was when I commenced in 1850. . . . my spirits . . . are yet unbroken."[8]

Gradually Borden's efforts began to be felt. The acting commissioner of patents conceded the superiority of the Borden concentration, but again failed to see any importance in vacuum condensing, crediting Borden instead with more care and superior manipulation in preparation. Borden's application was turned down another time.

A third time the application was made, and a third time it was refused. But now an opening was seen. Wrote Commissioner Charles Mason on May 10, 1856: "Borden claims evaporation *in vacuo* to be the valuable feature of his discovery, and necessary. The Commissioner sees no reason to believe this." But, added Mason, "If it were really a discovery, Borden would be entitled to a patent." If the inventor could prove that the exclusion of air was important and "that milk, taken fresh from the cow, and evaporated in the open air . . . would not answer substantially the same purpose as when evaporated *in vacuo*, I would certainly grant to Mr. Borden the patent he is asking." But until he was persuaded of the superiority of evaporation in vacuum pan, Commissioner Mason would continue to reject all applications.[9]

Borden called in Macfarlane, Currie, and other practical scientists. They studied every known method of condensing milk, and

[7] Baker, *A Year Worth Living*, 106–107

[8] Gail Borden to Ashbel Smith, February 3, 1855, Gail Borden to John G Borden, November 20, 1855—in Borden Papers, Rosenberg Library.

[9] S. L. Goodale, *A Brief Sketch of Gail Borden and His Relations to Some Forms of Concentrated Foods*, 14–15. *History of Borden's Milk Patent*, 14–15.

then condensed by those methods. Test after test was conducted and results tabulated. Charts were prepared and affidavits drawn up. All added to one total: condensing *in vacuo* was unequaled. Evaporating milk must not be allowed to contact air. The results were dispatched to Washington and London.

This time the applications met no argument. On February 28, 1856, Borden's English application received preliminary approval, which was followed by final approval on August 26, 1856.[10] One week earlier, on August 19, 1856—three years and three months after his first application—Gail Borden was granted American patent No. 15,553 for condensing milk in vacuum over low heat.

In the years since 1856 many men have claimed prior discovery of condensed milk and of milk condensed *in vacuo*, charging that Gail Borden discovered nothing and had been granted a patent on other men's ideas. Borden seldom disputed these claims. His discovery was limited to one element alone—that from the time the evaporation process begins until the milk is hermetically sealed in cans, the air must always be excluded. His intense practicality, or perhaps his intuitiveness for correcting wrongs—for "setting the crooked straight"—was the difference. He alone saw that complete exclusion of air was desirable, that, in his words, "milk is a living fluid," like blood, "and as soon as drawn from the cow begins to die, change, and decompose. In no other process . . . with which I am acquainted has any adequate means been adopted to prevent incipient decomposition of the milk and render it preservative and soluble."[11]

The first two milestones had been passed: he had perfected his product and he had obtained patent protection. Now to market he must go.

It was not an especially auspicious time for Gail Borden to be introducing a new product. The country was worked up over the Dred Scott decision, Kansas was still "bleeding" over slavery and John Brown, and extremists everywhere were talking of disunion. The Republican party had just participated in its first presidential election. Around the corner waited the Panic of 1857 to bring to a sharp halt a general business rise that had been underway for a dozen

10 Goodale, *A Brief Sketch of Gail Borden*, 12, 15–16 *History of Borden's Milk Patent*, 16.
11 Gail Borden, Application for Patent No. 15553, June 12, 1856

years. Europeans were chiefly interested in table rapping and spiritualism—even the great Robert Owen became a convert. In Mississippi, a man had invented a mechanical cotton picker which picked twice as much as a slave. In Texas, General Sam Houston was just getting over being a Know-Nothing, a political alliance which may have cost him the Republican nomination for president in 1856, and was just getting used to being a Baptist, which endeared him to his mother-in-law.

Within his own family Gail Borden's affairs were in a turmoil. For a half-dozen years he had neglected his family to pursue meat biscuit sales and then condensed-milk patents. His eldest son, Henry Lee, was a grown man of twenty-four, married and ranching in Texas for himself and his father. John Gail and Mary Jane had been attending school at Mechanicsville, New York. But causing him the most trouble were his elder daughter, Philadelphia, and his second wife, Augusta.

Philadelphia Borden was almost eighteen when she met Captain A. Swift, a thirty-year-old widower with four children. Gail Borden's first knowledge that romance was afoot came when he opened a delightfully ungrammatical letter from Captain Swift himself:

> I with earnest desire write you this asking your consent to the union of your Daughter Philadelphia and myself in Matrimony She have had the subject under consideration for some months past and expresses a desire or gives her consent to our most earnest wishes I would write you more lenghy and give you the particulars relative to my situation but circumstances do not permit and I deem it sufficient for you to know our intentions which on my part I know are based on the purest of motives with full and entire confidence in he that I willing to devote the whole of my existance for.[12]

It was too matter-of-fact a letter to warm Gail Borden's heart toward his daughter's suitor. Probably before her father's permission could be received, Philadelphia Borden and Captain Swift were married in Seguin, Texas, on February 7, 1855. Borden was undoubtedly surprised by the ceremony and no little displeased, and to hear from his brother Paschal that he "was not much surprised at

[12] A Swift to Gail Borden, January 18, 1855, in Borden Papers, Rosenberg Library The spelling and grammar are Swift's.

it, knowing as I do that most females want to marry," probably did not assuage his pique. What annoyed him most was that he heard of Philadelphia's marriage from everyone except Philadelphia herself, who waited more than a month to write her father.

When she did write she knew what to say. She had wanted so to see him that she could not bring herself to write what she really wanted to say in person. Meanwhile she had been visiting Captain Swift's relatives: "They were all acquainted with you by reputation, and . . . I was more highly respected on your account . . . and my dear father you do not know how happy it makes me to hear your name praised, and your goodness of heart extolled."[13] Gail Borden's heart must have flooded with joy as he forgave everything.

On April 13—two months and six days after her marriage—Philadelphia Swift became a widow. She was still not quite eighteen, with plenty of time to make a life, but now she had to care for four children for whom, in John P. Borden's words, "as yet she could have little affection." And Captain Swift's estate was topsy-turvy. Daughter Philadelphia's troubles then were on Gail Borden's mind as he prepared to sell condensed milk.

His other difficulty is obscure. Three letters tell most of the incomplete story, the first from W. F. Smith, who likely boarded Borden's daughter Mary Jane:

Let me hope thee will write Mrs. Borden. . . . If thee could do so under the softening influence of Heavens love I think it could not [fail] to inspire confidence and eventually restore mutual esteem and finally a happy reunion full of happiness and good fruits.[14]

The second letter, to Borden from his friend J. P. Cole, throws a little more light on the problem:

You say, you fear that "trouble is brewing in this quarter"—as to which I can only suggest that you wait until it is done brewing and bursts upon you, at least don't run to meet it half way. I don't think it will be much of a storm after all.

The *separation* I would consider as already made, and strive ever to bring my heart to look upon the whole *connection*, as only an *Episode* in my life—an uneasy dream when one awaketh. "Advertise her" I would *not* do. It would recoil upon yourself and only increase the bitter-

13 Philadelphia Swift to Gail Borden, March 11, 1855, in Borden Papers, Rosenberg Library
14 W. F. Smith to Gail Borden, n d, in Borden Papers, Rosenberg Library

ness of your thoughts and the laceration of your feelings in that regard —*Forget* if you can, at all events remember as little as possible, and only when the unhappy vision is forced upon you as in the present case. As to pecuniary risk, I think *that* amounts to nothing very formidable;—her idiosyncracy in this respect is your safety. It will under any circumstances not likely to amount in all her life, to as much as would be entailed upon you, at one lump, by any "proceedings" at law.[15]

The third letter, from J. Eastman Johnson, adds that "I should be most happy to learn from you that all causes of domestic grief were obliterated."[16]

What had happened? Who had separated from whom? Had Augusta Borden become so weary of her husband's unceasing chase after inventive chimeras, so weary of his being in one place while she remained behind in another, so weary of his spending and spending and then borrowing to spend still more that she had left him? And what became of her? Most likely she died soon, for in 1860 Gail Borden married again, and no man with Borden's literal beliefs in Bible teachings would have married with a living wife.

There seem to be no answers to these questions, but undoubtedly Borden was disturbed until at times he felt every road led him straight to an impasse. Add to his apparent meat biscuit failure, his struggle for a milk patent, his concern for Philadelphia's welfare, and his uneasiness regarding his wife such comparatively minor vexations and disappointments as his father's crotchety, almost senile belief that Gail was against him, his son Lee's refusal to aid him, and his inability to provide properly for his children—he could not even send his adored John Gail a Christmas present in 1855—and it impresses with cold clarity that here was a man almost beside himself at a time when he was embarking on an enterprise that he hoped would sweep him to the very zenith of humanitarianism and fame.

Virginian Thomas Green, landowner, entered Gail Borden's life in the spring of 1854. He was still there in 1872, with Borden having spent at least fourteen of those years trying to rid himself of Green's presence.

[15] J. P Cole to Gail Borden, May 18, 1855, in Borden Papers, Rosenberg Library.

[16] J. Eastman Johnson to Gail Borden, June 4, 1855, in Borden Papers, Rosenberg Library.

The earliest official relationship between the pair appeared in April, 1854, when for one dollar Borden sold Green twelve hundred acres on the west bank of the Brazos. Undoubtedly there was more to the transaction than that. Green must have rendered or promised services which Borden considered equivalent to the value of his lands. By early 1855 Borden had taken a partner,[17] and in the absence of evidence to the contrary it may be supposed that Green was that partner.

While in Washington pressing his patent application, Borden stayed in the Green home for three months, compensating for his lodging by plotting and mapping several surveys of Virginia land belonging to Green and his sons. Between times he poured into Green's ears his dreams and his fears. He had applied and applied to the patent office, adding evidence with each fresh application until now the patent examiner was complaining at the voluminous papers. To aid, Green prepared a compendium which the patent office accepted, thus expediting the successful conclusion of a tedious fight that had nearly exhausted Borden's strength and funds. In return the grateful inventor conveyed to Green three-eighths of his patent rights, providing, however, that Green aid Borden financially in establishing a condensery.

Although Green talked in terms of millions of dollars to be realized from condensed milk, he either would not or could not advance Borden much aid in 1856, leading Borden to look elsewhere for additional money. This he found in the person of James Bridge of Augusta, Maine, who had married one of the eight daughters of Reuel Williams, the wealthy former senator from the Pine Tree state. Bridge agreed to furnish the money in return for one-fourth interest in the Borden patent.

Gail Borden now had two partners,[18] a patent, and funds with which to begin production. And if the business prospered, he would receive three-eighths of the profits.

[17] Deed Record Book, C, Fort Bend County, Texas, 418–19. Francis Kelsey to Gail Borden, February 23, 1855, Gail Borden, Sr., to Gail Borden, May 9, 1855—in Borden Papers, Rosenberg Library.

[18] Goodale, *A Brief Sketch of Gail Borden*, 16 *History of Borden's Milk Patent*, 5, 9-11, 13. Gail Borden to John G. Borden, August 30, 1856, in Borden Papers, Rosenberg Library. *Drews Rural Intelligencer*, Augusta, Maine, October 24, 1856.

For five or six weeks Gail Borden and James Bridge traveled and tramped the countryside north of the port of New York looking for a business site. In the summer of 1856 they decided. Their factory would be at Wolcottville, a village centered in the gentle Naugatuck Valley west of Hartford, Connecticut.

At Wolcottville's Captain Taylor Tavern, where he stayed, Borden soon became one of the town's delights. Always an animated talker, he strewed Texas prairies with miles of dead Mexicans and Indians for the edification of Wolcottville children and poured out figurative silver rivers of pure condensed milk for the grownups. Families vied for the honor of having him to dinner, especially since he always brought his own milk and coffee and "Oh, it is delicious coffee." When he asked Miss Honora Burnes, the tavern cook, where he could experiment while his factory was being readied, she turned over her own kitchen.

Shortly he opened his little factory in an old brick carriage-shop with an outside runway to the second floor. Since paying jobs were scarce in Wolcottville, nearly everyone in town tried to work for him. Miss Burnes quit the tavern, and her two brothers, Richard and Martin, joined her at the condensery on Litchfield Street. In almost no time at all he was operating, and the town awaited eagerly the appearance of this brand-new product which was going to bring money and people to Wolcottville.

Who would get the first can? Its owner would have a keepsake to treasure the remainder of his life. In making the decision Borden showed himself a businessman. To Charles McNeil went the first milk. As owner of the general store and drugstore and operator of the post office and telegraph office, he would be in a position to sell Wolcottville on Borden's product. But the first can McNeil would not sell; and long after Gail Borden had left Wolcottville and Wolcottville itself had changed its name to Torrington, Charles McNeil had hanging in his store a large framed portrait of Gail Borden.

If condensed milk were going to bring its inventor any money, though, he must please customers outside of tiny Wolcottville. At 173 Canal Street in New York, Borden established a city milk depot, chasing back and forth between there and Wolcottville as prospects and necessity dictated. When he was in Connecticut, he left thirteen-year-old John O'Connell in charge of the basement depot. But when the inventor was in New York, he and his teenage companion would walk Manhattan streets, tin pail in hand, canvassing for trade.

Sophisticated New Yorkers considered Borden's condensed milk too revolutionary to buy. The idea of keeping milk for weeks! Most buyers wouldn't even listen. Although the less interest they showed the more pertinaciously Borden insisted, it was useless. If people could not buy milk fresh from the cow, they would rather not buy it at all than to purchase-something some meddling man had worked with.

Since no sales meant no income, Borden besought his partners. Without more funds he could not pay the Connecticut farmers from whom he bought milk, and without milk he could not operate. But his partners, afraid of getting into this project too deeply, suggested that Borden give it up for a while until the market looked more favorable. Bridge had contributed $1,900; that amount, he thought, was enough.

Borden turned to the dairymen. If they would wait for their money, he knew it would be only a little time before sales would commence. But the New England farmer is a thrifty man who does not relish wasting milk or money. If Borden could not pay, the farmers had customers who could.

Reluctantly Borden postponed his dream and prepared to go home to Texas to straighten out his finances there. Many people in Wolcottville genuinely hated to see him abandon his factory, and in gratitude Borden left behind his heating well. Years later the town of Torrington, which was also the birthplace of abolitionist John Brown and of Samuel J. Mills, placed the battered, rusty old tank in its Center Square as a watering trough, where it was endured until after the close of World War I as a reminder that in Wolcottville Gail Borden had known his first condensed-milk failure.[19]

Despite the factory's failure, Gail Borden's friends in Wolcottville remained loyal. The story of Clark S. Weed, ten years old at the time, is in itself sufficient proof:

"Ben Bissell . . . came to the house one day and asked my father to come up the road a ways. . . . They started out and I went along.

[19] W. T Irwin to T B Niles, March 22, 1932, in Borden Papers, Borden Company, New York Statements by John F. O'Connell, New York, 1911, and Clark S Weed, Torrington, Connecticut, May 20, 1918, in Clark Papers *History of Borden's Milk Patent*, 8 The Hartford *Daily Courant*, March 15, 1936

... Bissell ... suddenly turned to father and said, 'Send that boy back.' " When the elder Weed refused, the three continued down the road.

"Father stopped and said if [Bissell] had anything to say he'd better say it as he would go no farther. Well, Ben Bissell then turned on my father and accused him of conspiring to get Borden out of Wolcottville. ... when Bissell said that [my father] said, 'Any man who says I ain't a friend of Gail Borden's has got to fight,' and he landed on Ben Bissell and gave him an awful layin' out. He threw him right down in the road."[20]

To leave Wolcottville with head high and owing no man there, Gail Borden had to have funds from elsewhere. Daniel Winsor, a Milford, New York, friend, sent him one hundred dollars to pay his board and other local bills and his fare to New York. There he borrowed more money, and he and John Gail set out for Texas.

It was a long road to Texas. Only Gail Borden, God willing, thought he'd ever be back.

In the late spring of 1857 Borden returned to the Litchfield country for another attempt. In Texas he had sold lands and visited his children, finding his daughter Philadelphia happily remarried[21] and his son Lee reasonably prosperous. Accompanying him on the trip north were Mary Jane, who at sixteen showed signs of becoming "fleshy," and John Gail, who Borden hoped would learn French so that later he might travel in Europe for his father. Borden's wife was probably dead, for she was never referred to again in any extant papers or documents.[22]

Borden had returned as the result of the beginning of a series of intricate, often confusing contractual changes in the relationship concerning himself, Green, and Bridge. On November 10, 1856, Bridge had sold his interest in the Borden patent to his father-in-law, Williams. Two days earlier Borden had granted Green one-half of

---

[20] Statement by Clark S. Weed, Torrington, Connecticut, May 20, 1918, in Clark Papers.

[21] Philadelphia Borden's second husband, J. W. Johnson, was a founder of the Houston *Post*, which survives today as Houston's only morning newspaper.

[22] At the beginning of 1857 Borden had written son John Gail "You remember how Mother used to say 'run & cut up,' " which could sound as if Augusta Borden had definitely left the Borden household by one means or another.

his milk patent and any further discoveries that he might make in extracts of coffee, tea, and other foods if Green would settle with Bridge. Accordingly, Green prevailed on Bridge to reinvest, the three owners to share expenses and profits in proportion to their patent interests, with Green advancing Borden's part as well as his own. In addition, Borden and Bridge were allowed certain sums for their services.[23]

On May 11 the second condensed-milk factory was begun at Burrville, five miles north of Wolcottville along the Still River. Like its sister town to the south, Burrville was only a hamlet built around the lumbering enterprises of Milo Burr, who had settled at the foot of the hill there about 1825, one of a long line of Burrs who had been associated with Connecticut since the first Burr, Benjamin, had moved into Hartford in the late seventeenth century.

Borden went to live with Milo Burr's son, John, in a white house just below the factory on the hill. For ten days his gear continued to arrive from Wolcottville—furniture, pipes, tanks, milk cans, bags of coal, sugar, and so on until he had everything necessary to renew operations, including even Miss Burnes and her two brothers, who faithfully moved up to join the inventor.

For $7.50 a month Borden rented from Milo Burr the basement and eastern half of the main story of Burr's water building, with privileges of using water from Burr's reservoir, his flume (an overshot attachment to a thirty foot water wheel), and his sawmill. It was not exactly an ideal arrangement—for one thing, the floors were of rough hemlock, very splintery, when Borden with his penchant for neatness would have preferred smooth pine—but for a man with no more to offer than Gail Borden, it would have to do.

When Borden arrived in Burrville, he had one good shirt and one good suit. On June 15, 1857, Mrs. Burr washed that shirt, pressed the suit ever so little, and Gail Borden, moving spirit of the firm of Gail Borden, Jr., and Company, made ready to assail the New York market on the following day.

What success might have attended his re-entry into New York under ordinary conditions can only be conjectured, for the sum-

[23] *History of Borden's Milk Patent*, 5, 8–12. Gail Borden to John G. Borden, January 26, 1857, in Borden Papers, Rosenberg Library. Williams was never active, but continued to be represented by Bridge.

mer and autumn of 1857 was no ordinary time. Banks suspended, insurance companies defaulted, fourteen railway corporations failed, "hunger meetings" were held in the Eastern cities, Western crops lay unsold, and Southern planters lost perhaps $35,000,000 as the panic fell on the country with full fury. And many of these failures were by men and companies with huge assets. How then could Gail Borden, Jr., and Company, operating on tremendous faith and little margin, hope to survive? As money became tighter, sales fewer, and his partners proportionately less interested in advancing money, Borden turned once more down that despairing, now familiar and repetitious path. For want of means he suspended operations[24] and returned to New York to face his creditors. The Panic of 1857 was really only a short, sharp recession in the midst of a long upward trend, but it lasted long enough to eliminate Borden as a businessman once again.

The well-dressed, obviously well-fed young man listened to his voluble companion with more than the usual tolerant interest which one train traveler bestows upon another chance acquaintance who is going the same way. He had never seen anyone quite like this electric yet cadaverous old man who talked with the ebullience of youth of conquering commercial worlds and saving men's souls and showing the way to a fuller life. Not infrequently in the near-monologue the younger man became somewhat confused as his elder companion ran on like a disorganized fugue. "Apparently," the young man must have reasoned, "my companion's brain is racing." So, too, was his tongue.

To other persons sitting near by who could not help listening, the pair presented a study in real contrasts. On one hand the young man, Jeremiah Milbank, not quite forty, showed the suavity of being educated in good Eastern private schools. The passengers could not know, of course, that he was already a successful wholesale grocer on Front Street in New York, or that he would become a successful broker and private banker, a director of the Chicago, Milwaukee, and St. Paul Railway, a stockholder and owner of a box in the Metropolitan Opera, and a founder and president of the board of

[24] *History of Borden's Milk Patent*, 12 Goodale, *A Brief Sketch of Gail Borden*, 17 The foundation of the Burrville factory can still be seen

trustees of the Madison Avenue Baptist Church in New York.[25] South Dakotans would name a town for him. And when he died no less a magazine than *Harper's Weekly* would say of him that he "was one of those merchants whose careers are the true glory of the metropolis . . . farseeing, conservative, and enterprising, a conceiver of large schemes, a financier who did not fail, a friend to wise charities."[26] He was, in short, a man born to comfort and marked for success.

But his companion. Fifty-six years old and looking older, and an obvious failure. Wearing patched clothes that did not fit. Sunken temples, greyhound nose, thin, underfed body, terribly stooped. The trenchant eye of a kindly fanatic. Arms like willow switches and hands that waved like Texas windmills during a blue norther. That was Gail Borden, a man forever ahead of himself, a man born for great purposes—to save the world from hunger, soul starvation, from itself—and a man who had saved so far only his own soul.

For all his inherent conservatism, however, Jeremiah Milbank possessed that gambler's instinct that told him when to place his money on a long shot. And this was a long shot. The old man had failed, failed, and failed. The panic was on, with money so tight it could not be dislodged with a magnet. The old man's affairs were in a tortuous snarl—it was hard to tell whether he actually owned any of his invention and just how many people he did owe.

But to Jeremiah Milbank the old man's eyes were not the eyes of a fanatic but the eyes of a genius, his stooped body not the frame of a used-up man but the body of a man too busy to straighten, his rattling tongue not the tongue of garrulity but of drive and energy. And he looked into the man's lean visage and saw an honest face. That was all he needed.

If this old man's faith were justified, the world would have a product that would bring pure milk to every home, to every ship no matter how long at sea, to every army no matter how dry and hot the desert. It was a vision of catholic service and commercial enormities that Jeremiah Milbank did not feel he could afford to let pass.

Thus, on a chance meeting on a train, Gail Borden got himself another partner. But this was a partner with a difference, a partner

[25] New York *Tribune*, June 2, 1884
[26] *Harper's Weekly*, Vol. XXVIII, No. 1435 (June 21, 1884), 391.

who knew the folly of shoestring operations, who knew that to profit you must be prepared to lose for a while, who knew that faint heart never won fair lady in business any more than in romance, and that to win you must first have the product and then be prepared to invest and push, push, push.

All Gail Borden knew that day was that he had the promise of renewed backing. What he did not know was that he had taken on a hardheaded partner with business acumen that matched Gail Borden's inventive vision. Jeremiah Milbank was Gail Borden's balance wheel, and he was just what Gail Borden had been needing.

And grasps the skirts of happy chance,
And breasts the blows of circumstance.
—Tennyson, In Memoriam

That luscious milk I shan't forget,
'Till taste and Coffee ceases,—
Dear me! for tea and social sett,
It beats the cow to pieces.
February 1, 1865[1]

XV

The Turning Point
1858-1861

BACK TO BURRVILLE went Borden in February, 1858. Assured at last of enough funds to exploit properly the New York market, he was in high spirits. To convince people that condensed milk was their solution to the fresh milk problem might take time, but now he could afford that time. Jeremiah Milbank had settled the $6,000 indebtedness incurred earlier at Burrville, and he was making progress toward settling the patent rights held by Thomas Green and Reuel Williams.[2]

The eighteen fifties were a period of expansion and unlimited faith in America, a period when a normally conservative businessman might gamble on an unproved product because the United States was seeking new goods to purchase. Economically the trend had been upward since 1843 and would continue to rise till after the Civil War. Political disunion might be around the corner, but business was full of plans for growth. Cornelius Vanderbilt was making better than a million dollars a year in shipping, and within five years would turn to railroads to make money even more rapidly. In New England, Eliphalet Dennison was starting to manufacture merchandise tags by machine, instituting a paper-products business whose sales would be running nearly a half-million annually within fifteen years. Religious John Wanamaker would soon open the forerunner

1 From a newspaper fragment in the Borden Papers, Borden Company, New York.

2 *History of Borden's Milk Patent*, 12–14.

241

of his great Philadelphia and New York department stores. In 1859 Henry Baldwin Hyde would organize the Equitable Life Assurance Society, starting with only a thirty-foot sign, some rented office furniture, and a box of cigars; oil would be discovered in Pennsylvania, the finding of the Comstock Lode would start a silver re-enactment of the rush of forty-nine to the West, and Boston would be the scene of a new Shoe and Leather Exchange. In the same year Philip D. Armour would enter the produce business in Milwaukee, starting a business that in later years would be a chief competitor in certain fields of the business Gail Borden and Jeremiah Milbank would leave behind.

If all over the nation expansion was in the air, it was only a natural contagion of the times that Milbank would be willing to take a chance on impecunious Gail Borden's product. And Borden, always an optimist, would almost instantly react by making his own expansive plans. Everything was going to be new and fresh, especially the inventor's outlook. No more grubbing for money. Milbank might be hardheaded and not so freehanded with expenditures as Borden would have liked, but he had assured Borden that there would be enough—all Milbank demanded was a dollar's worth of results for every dollar spent.

Almost gleefully Borden must have set down what he needed to do, totting merrily the cost, knowing that this time it would be paid. He needed a new furnace front—that would be $25. And new grate bars, a steam gauge, steam trap, safety valves to the pan, repairs to cocks and connections, a heater for the milk—that alone would run $100—and, oh, "Sundry repairs & improvements" at $50. All that would total maybe $295.

As long as it's being done, he thought, do it right. Improve the works to handle five thousand quarts. That would take new pumps with fourteen-inch strokes and eight-inch bores. It would require enlarging the air pipe to eight inches also, and new cocks. Another $500. But the old pumps and pipes could be turned in for, say, $200. Why, six or seven hundred dollars would fix up the condensery almost as good as any inventor could ask.

Retain no reminders of failure. Not even the name. What name then? Why not name it after the market? *The New York Condensed Milk Company.* That would sound all right.

Jeremiah Milbank (1818–84), the financier
who made possible Borden's success

The Borden Company

"The New York Condensed Milk Company."
"Gail Borden, president¹"
How full and rewarding those words must have sounded to the tired inventor, especially when he knew that they were words backed by resources. But he had no time to roll words and sounds about. He must be up and doing.³

A generation later Louis Pasteur would make the world bacteria conscious, but untutored Gail Borden anticipated the distinguished Frenchman. As early as February 13, 1856, Borden had written that "My process brings to light some qualities in milk hitherto not understood by scientific men well versed in Organic Chemistry." In his patent application he had called milk a "living fluid." There was, he knew, some relationship between dirt and the freshness and quality of milk.

Out from Burrville circulated Borden to one farmer after another, instructing and explaining and demanding. If the farmers wanted to sell him milk, they would have to comply with all sorts of, to them, silly conditions, for this man was worse than a government worker. He wanted udders washed thoroughly in warm water before milking. He wanted no milk from cows that had calved within twelve days. He did not want cows fed on ensilage or turnips—might make the milk taste. He wanted barns swept clean and manure spread away from the milking stalls. Wire-cloth strainers had to be scalded and dried morning and night. There was no end to what he demanded. One would think that he had nothing better to do than just think up rules for dairymen.

If there were anyone else to sell to in volume, the farmers would show this crazy Texas . . . .

But Gail Borden was laying a foundation for the entire dairy industry, a foundation that helped develop dairying from a hit-or-miss country-crossroads trade to an organized, efficient, and highly profitable American industry. Years later Borden was quoted as saying that "there is nothing manufactured requiring so much care and everlasting vigilance and attention as that of milk. From the time it is drawn from the cow, until hermetically sealed in cans, it requires

---

³ Unless otherwise noted, all material for Chapters XV and XVI was drawn from the Borden Papers and the Clark Papers, Borden Company, New York.

that everything should be done with the utmost integrity."[4] In Burrville in 1858 Gail Borden was already insisting on what by his death was to become accepted practice.

Borden also would one day be partially responsible for a social revolution on a regional scale. Farmers who once made fine cheese, peddled butter, and tried to outstrip their neighbors in the number of local customers would find that life was much simpler if they merely took their entire milk output into Borden's receiving dock and just drove away, awaiting their check at regular intervals. No hours turning cream separators, no days aging and molding cheese in frigid barns, no straining wives' backs over churns. Settle on contracts, meet Borden's standards of sanitation and coolness, deliver, collect, then forget it. Let Borden's make the cheese and the butter and deliver the milk.

And over a half-century the firm of Gail Borden would grow until the farmer decided he must unite to bargain effectively, farmers' co-operatives would grow, and the farmer would no longer hold a primary interest in his relations with Borden, for his union would take care of that. Still Borden's firm and its competitors would grow and the co-operatives would keep pace until finally both outgrew themselves, and it was the government, not Borden or the union, which set milk prices—so much for the farmer, so much for Borden. And as in other aspects of American life, bigness and union would replace that close personal tie between producer and purchaser, that pride in individual craftsmanship, that necessity for being able to do not one but several things fairly well, that fierce competitive feeling; and in their place would substitute efficiency, security, cheaper cost, higher standard of living, more leisure, more enjoyment of the aesthetic, and a virtual elimination of the difference between rural and urban existence. The same revolution had been undergone in the disappearance of the individual weaver and the emergence of the textile factory; the same revolution would shortly eliminate the cobbler and replace him with a specialist at a shoe machine in Lynn, Brockton, and other shoe-manufacturing centers; the same revolution was going on in most of the other industries. It was the American economy at work, the so-called American way undergoing an

When the New York Baptists had not received him cordially because he held slaves in Texas, Borden had moved over to the more tolerant Congregationalists and had become a regular Sunday attendant at Henry Ward Beecher's services.[8] When James Huckins and James Cole and others back in Galveston heard of his defection, they were amazed and alarmed—and a special meeting was held to discuss their straying former deacon and clerk. Wrote Cole: "If I had *caught* you in one of those *comfortable* seats, I would have thundered in your ears 'What doest thou *here* Elijah?' . . . There's too much of the *world* around you . . . for your good!'"[9]

But Gail Borden could have worshiped God in the house of Satan, and he continued to worship with men of all faiths wherever the need or the opportunity might arise.

By 1860 the New York Condensed Milk Company was doing well. Neither Gail Borden nor Jeremiah Milbank was realizing a fortune, but business was steady enough that Borden could envision better things to come and Milbank could feel secure in his invest-, ment.

In Burrville, Borden and the Burrs were not entirely congenial. Borden wanted this addition and that improvement and some other privilege, which sometimes was agreeable with Milo Burr and more often was not. It was still Milo Burr's building, and he saw no reason to accede to the every wish of this man who was forever seeking changes.

One autumn day son John Burr ventured the opinion that since Borden was sometimes running his factory late at night, he should be willing to pay additional rent for using the Burr's water after regular hours. For some reason the suggestion roiled Borden, who turned on the Burrs to announce curtly: "Gentlemen, I quit."

That night Borden had Darius Miner drive him over into New York state to seek a new location. He was through with Burrville and the Burrs. By the time he and Miner had jounced their way in the uncomfortable buggy across the border, he had rationalized his move completely. There just was not enough room for expansion

[8] *The Life and Writings of Rufus C. Burleson,* 729

[9] J. P Cole to Gail Borden, April 8, April 15, May 20, July 22, 1855, in Borden Papers, Rosenberg Library.

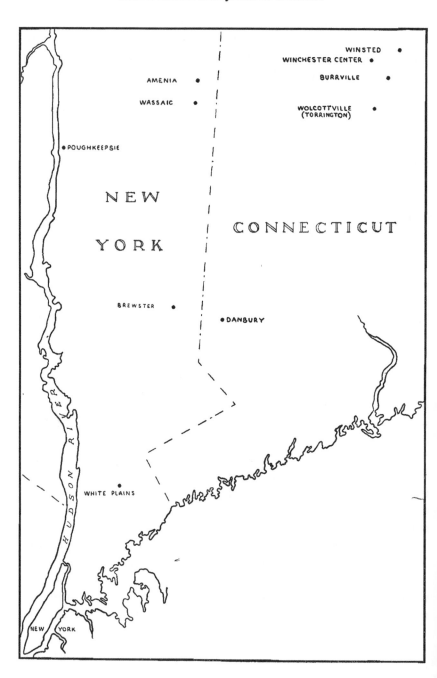

in Burrville. He was itching to enlarge. That was what he needed—
a bigger start in a brand-new place. As soon as possible he would
move. Convincing Milbank of the desirability of quitting an established factory for an undetermined location might require some talking, but next to working and serving, Gail Borden would rather
talk than anything.

Above New York the Harlem Valley winds easily northward
between the tolerant slopes of Hudson hills and western Connecticut mountains. Eighty-five miles up, the two sets of hills converge
sharply on the valley, but lampreylike it eludes the hills to slip
through to wide open fields ahead.

At the crucial, narrow point lies the village of Wassaic, New
York. In 1860 it had only a handful of houses, and today it is little
larger. But at the time it had a newly completed railroad, a branch
of the New York Central, and that was important. It was important,
too, that although at Wassaic there is barely room for a railroad and
village, to the north and south the valley widens into dairying pas-
tures of near perfection.

Because of the railroad and because of the ideal dairy regions
near by, Borden decided on the west bank of Wassaic Creek as the
site for his new factory. In this decision he was acting without the
approbation or financial support of Jeremiah Milbank, who looked
on his elder partner's sudden enthusiasm for changing locations as
evidence of a too frequently indulged capriciousness. Milbank
would have to think awhile on this latest move before sinking any
more of his money into a product that had not yet known much
consumer demand. Knowingly or not, Borden placed himself on
trial.

The big man in tiny Wassaic was dark, burly Noah Gridley,
leading churchman, property owner, and businessman. In a small
way he was a manufacturer himself, turning out ironware that always found an assured market. Gridley owned the town's hotel,
built because Gridley wanted travelers to be able to stay in a place
where no spirits were served.

To Gridley went Borden seeking aid. Would Gridley lease
him a factory site? And if Gridley would lease, would he also erect
a building? It never occurred to Borden to supplicate—he knew he

was honest and right and besides, he would pay Gridley 10 per cent in advance. But what collateral could Borden put up? Only a statement of his intentions and the obvious sincerity of his face. Like Jeremiah Milbank, Noah Gridley looked through this strange man and saw the worth of the risk—and he agreed to Borden's proposals.

Next followed a re-enactment of the Burrville scene, as vacuum pans, tanks, condensed milk, condensed coffee, pipes, and other odds and ends were deposited in a jumble on the Wassaic freight landing. And Honora Burnes and her two brothers, who had followed Borden from Wolcottville to Burrville, followed him now to Wassaic. They were to be his teaching staff, instructing all available Harlem Valley workers in the vagaries of milk condensation and preservation.

While the Borden factory was being constructed, its owner took over the two front rooms in Gridley's hotel to begin remolding Wassaic's life to the Borden pattern. Soon he knew everyone, and the sight of him leaning out of a window to call "Hello" to some townsman became a commonplace. He permitted himself the luxury of an office boy, young Noah Bishop—at five cents an hour—to run his messages to the factory. To young Noah he would hand a hasty memo, clap his hands sharply and command: "Now run, boy, RUN!"

And the youngster would streak all the way to the factory and run all the way back, to be greeted by his employer: "Good, boy, good. Now rest. Rest!"

From time to time he had to borrow additional money from Gridley to meet current debts, Milbank holding back all the while. Once, to meet a pay roll, Borden borrowed $300 from the ironmonger.

Meanwhile he was not wasting time. That not an ounce of energy might be lost, he had developed an ambidexterity that was more nearly equidextrous. When he was gripped in one of his letter-writing phases, he would write for an hour with one hand and then change and write for an hour with the other, invariably with equally mediocre results. When he visited a bank, he reached forth whichever hand was nearer the quill and signed his checks with that hand, and the signature was never questioned.

As usual, he tried educating recalcitrant, often resentful, farm-

ers, who saw no reason for switching to dairying because some out-
land crank told them to. This man did not stop there—he told them
how to milk and how to feed and how to care for their cows and
how to bring in the milk to his factory. And he would accept no
milk on Sunday. But give him his way, he said, and no one would
work at anything on Sunday. Certainly, no one who worked for him.

And then one June day in 1861 the factory was entirely completed, and the farmers brought in their milk loads to find an inspector smelling of covers as they were removed from the cans and
taking the temperature of each batch of milk, turning back any
milk over 58 degrees. There was much for the farmer to see. The
condensery was a long two-story wooden building, 30 by 120 feet,
with outbuildings housing a tin shop, boxmaker's shop, storerooms,
offices, and engines. Most of the power derived from Wassaic Creek,
but in case of drouth three furnaces and boilers were provided. Inside, there were women dressed in white from head to toe—the men
wearing white aprons, everyone wearing white gloves, with the
floors and sideboards and walls whitewashed. A speck of dirt would
stand out like a cat's eyes in the night.

If the farmer's can of milk was accepted, he could see its contents dumped into a tin-lined wooden vat, drawn through a rubber
pipe into a brass open-top can with iron bail, and placed over a
round vat of water. The water was heated by injecting steam until
the milk reached 190 degrees, after which the milk was lifted by
the iron bail and dumped in an open well and boiled once more with
steam. From the well the vacuum sucked the milk into a pan whose
temperature never exceeded 136 degrees.

After the milk was condensed to proper consistency, the vacuum pump was stopped and air directed on the vacuum pan. The
milk was then drawn down in forty-quart cans which were placed
in a round wooden vat of crushed ice to cool. Thus four quarts of
fresh milk were condensed to one quart. Miss Burnes next sealed
the cans, using olive oil as a flux. After the canned condensed milk
was placed aboard the railway cars, the cans were covered with ice
and a large canvas so that the milk might arrive in New York at a
temperature not exceeding 58 degrees.[10]

10 Interviews with William R. Galpin, Norwich, New York, and Arthur G.
Bacon, Bainbridge, New York, August 14, 1946 New York *Daily Tribune*, July
19, 1864.

Around Wassaic the idea of women working for pay was revolutionary, but only one of the men workers ever complained directly to Borden. When Richard Burnes told Borden that he objected to women because of their long hair, the inventor quickly replied: "Oh! the hair, the hair; glad you spoke of it. They must wear caps." Always solicitous, Borden hired three schoolboys, Elijah, Frank, and Noah Buckley, to build the fires for the women before going to school. And on dark nights he would not let the girls walk home alone, sending John Gail with a lantern.

Without forcing, he tried to persuade his workers to know Christ as he knew Him. In smoky, bustling Amenia, three miles north, he held a revival service in a chapel over the Lewis store, assuring each employee that if he would attend, his time would go on at the factory as if he were working. As a result, nearly the entire force turned out to hear Mr. Borden tell of the way of life. Every Sunday morning and night he would load his three-seated rig with workers and, with his Negro, Adam Williams, urging the span of iron-gray horses, drive over to Amenia, where he soon became a church pillar. He was especially pleased with his young people's Sunday-school class, which he built up to a weekly attendance of forty. Denominationalism never entered, and later, when a Baptist church was being built and someone objected to a cross on the steeple as a Catholic device, he stated flatly that no Christian should object to having the crucifixion emblem over the building where he worshiped.

But selling milk was still Borden's business, and although activities around Wassaic and Amenia might make him admirably memorable, they did not capture his original goal—the New York market—and they did not pay bills. And Noah Gridley was chafing under the nonproductivity of playing creditor to a man who seemed to know only how to spend money, not to make it. He began to press Borden for payment.

Just as events presaged a restaging of Borden's previous failures, Jeremiah Milbank returned to the milk scene, prepared to resume where he had left off in support of the always stumbling, never quite succeeding Gail Borden. Milbank paid off Gridley, completed arrangements with Thomas Green and Reuel Williams, and informed Borden that an all out campaign was in order. Borden should recommend what expansions were required, and he could be certain that his recommendations would be followed. Whatever was necessary Milbank would provide. A discerning student of business trends, Jeremiah Milbank was ready to play a hunch—or a bull market. And he was not going to use halfway measures.

Before the Milbank-Borden coalition began to revitalize its plans for wholesale conquest, Gail Borden took off time to marry for the third time. Apparently a marriage had been anticipated for several years, as the Borden children had sued for a division of the estate in 1858.[11]

His bride was Mrs. Emeline Eunice Church, a woman ten years his junior. She had two sons, Alfred B. and Samuel M. Church, who lacked a few years of their majority. To both, Borden became a real father, caring for them, later giving them responsible positions in his company, and at his death making Alfred Church a coexecutor, with his adored John Gail, of his estate. That there was mutual affection is evidenced by the boys' action two decades after Borden's death when they made to Elgin, Illinois, a grant for a city library providing city officials called it the Gail Borden Library.

Details of the courtship are meager. Borden must have met Mrs. Church in Connecticut, where she had returned after the death of her first husband. On the day of the marriage, August 15, 1860, Borden borrowed nearly $1,500 from his father in Texas and on the same day signed a prenuptial contract guaranteeing Mrs. Church $350 a year for the duration of the marriage and the children a minimum of $150 each during the period of their minority in case of their mother's death.[12] Evidently Mrs. Church brought a business head to the marriage altar.

Gail Borden was fifty-nine years old, past the age of romance, especially with condensed milk occupying most of his thoughts, but he had nearly fifteen years ahead of him and he was a man who needed companionship. Mrs. Church seems to have filled the need perfectly.

[11] Deed Record Book, E, Fort Bend County, Texas, 131–35 Minutes, District Court, IV, Galveston County, Texas, 328–31. In the division Borden's estate was valued at $34,550, a two-thirds decrease from the 1850 census estimate.

[12] *The Biographical Record of Kane County, Illinois,* 644. Deed Record Book, F, Fort Bend County, Texas, 670–73. Deed Record Book, L, Bastrop County, Texas, 606–609.

On Sunday, April 14, 1861, after thirty-three hours of bombardment, the Union forces marched out of Fort Sumter, leaving the South Carolina fort to the Confederate States of America. The first engagement of the Civil War had ended, but the war had only begun. When summer brought no Federal victories, it became apparent to more thoughtful men in the North that victory might be no easy task and that conceivably this war could last several years. Jeremiah Milbank, listening to men talk on New York street corners and in New York clubs, began to stir. If this were a large-scale war spread over months, the logistics required by Northern armies would be enormous. That aspect would naturally interest a wholesaler.

What interested Milbank most was that the war would likely be fought in the South, away from centers of population and supplies, in a region whose devastation would increase with time. Food could be taken along. But was food enough for the physical needs of unacclimated men fighting in fierce heat, malarial swamps, and chilling rains? The problem of troop morale alone demanded that men have hot coffee and that men have milk. But even if it could be obtained, how long would milk keep around Richmond? Jeremiah Milbank could answer that question.

It was then that he decided to support Gail Borden to the limit. If the United States government could be persuaded to supply its forces with Borden's condensed milk, was there any ceiling to the heights that could be reached? The potential reward was worth the gamble.

Before Borden could raise his Wassaic production to its eventual five thousand quarts daily, sales had begun. From then on to the close of the war the New York Condensed Milk Company strove to catch up. The problem shifted to supply, not demand—to production, not selling.

The first government order came as Charlie Knight was leaving the New York office for lunch. A man stepped into the office and began asking questions about condensed milk, how it was made, how long it kept, and how satisfactory it was as a fresh-milk substitute. Knight answered the questions, eying the wall clock to see whether the man were going to leave him any lunch hour. When, however, the man said he would buy five hundred pounds, Knight quit watching the clock. Shortly after, when August Klemm, the company secretary, came in, Knight told him of the order. For the next several days the New York staff spent its spare time putting up milk in every obtainable sort of box.

That order was the long-awaited turning point. Never again did Jeremiah Milbank doubt the wisdom of his investment. Never again did Gail Borden, who had always believed in his eventual triumph, have to scrape, borrow, and sacrifice for the sake of his invention and his faith in himself. From 1861 on the story of Gail Borden becomes a story of expansion.

In the three months following June 28, 1862, he sold nearly 50,000 quarts of condensed milk. A year later he would be able to turn out that amount in three days.[18]

18 When Noah Gridley perceived that through his insistence on being paid he had lost any interest in a now successful business, he shut off the water supply, necessitating the building of a reservoir and pipe lines by the company

Moons waxed and waned, the lilacs bloomed and died,
In the broad river ebbed and flowed the tide,
Ships went to sea, and ships came home from sea,
And the slow years sailed by and ceased to be
—Longfellow, *Lady Wentworth*

Let others hail the rising sun
I bow to that whose course is run.
—Garrick, *On the Death of Mr. Pelham*

·XVI

Infinite Pursuit
1861-1874

WITH ELEVEN SOUTHERN STATES, Texas included, waging war against twice as many Northern states and needing every man and brain and physical resource they could lay hold of, what was Gail Borden, a Texan for thirty years, doing in the North during the Civil War? Had this man who had once risked life and property for Texas deserted his state? Had this man who once told a friend that "All I do . . . is for the Master" surrendered to a more immediately alluring master who held forth bags of gold? Had this man who in 1837 had written that the slave Negro of the South fared better than his free Mexican brother below the border,[1] this owner of slaves, turned abolitionist? What was Borden's stand?

The crowd was pushing around the telegraphic bulletin outside the office of the Winsted, Connecticut, *Herald* that mid-April morning in 1861 reading President Lincoln's call for troops, talking excitedly, as men always do, not of what the news meant for the Union or its institutions but of what the news portended for them individually. To one local lawyer the opportunity was ripe to contemn one of his favorite targets, Abraham Lincoln, and he began a harangue. In the midst of his abuse he was halted by a firm voice, while knowing neighbors nudged other listeners, "That's Mr. Borden, used to be over at Burrville."

[1] *Telegraph*, January 3, 1837.

256

"My father [is] in Texas," said the white-whiskered old man, "my brothers are in Texas, my children are in Texas, and the bulk of my earthly possessions are in Texas. But we must have a government. I did not vote for Mr. Lincoln, but I would vote for him today —aye, and fight for him, too."[2]

Like Sam Houston he believed in the Union first, Texas second. There is no refuting the charge that his business interests lay in the North, that economic sagacity dictated his remaining in the vicinity of New York; but two things indicate the integrity of his motives— his past steadfastness in doing always what he thought right regardless of the effect on himself or others, and the fact that after the war all but the most rabid Confederates welcomed him back .to Texas as a brother and not as a profiteering Yankee.

For Borden it truly was a war between brothers—or more accurately, between sons. John Gail was a Union soldier from 1862, when he was only eighteen, until July, 1864, first as a sergeant in the Hundred and fiftieth New York Infantry and then as a second lieutenant in the Forty-seventh New York Regiment; while in Texas, Lee enlisted with the Thirty-fifth Texas Cavalry in April, 1862, to remain until released in September, 1865. Neither son had much opportunity for distinction, John Gail spending most of his time in several Federal hospitals with chronic diarrhea and Lee, who had something of his father's inventive turn, devoting himself to improving products of Park and Dance's pistol factory at Columbia, Texas.[3]

Even with a son on each side, Gail Borden had no desire to be neutral. On April 22, 1861, when the war was only ten days old, he issued a public statement: "I have 'run up my colors.' . . . my best possessions are in Texas, that misguided State, where I had hoped to spend my last days; yet I love my whole country and government more, and wish to do what I can to sustain them."[4]

In a page devoted to Borden on July 19, 1864, Greeley's New York *Daily Tribune*, which, of course, could seldom be accused of

[2] Winsted, Connecticut, *Herald*, April 19, 1861, quoted in Weld, *Historical and Genealogical Record of Richard and Joan Borden*, 189

[3] War Records, Adjutant General's Office, National Archives Brewster, New York, *Standard*, November 28, 1902

[4] Amenia, New York, *Times*, quoted in Weld, *Historical and Genealogical Record of Richard and Joan Borden*, 189.

objectivity, declared that "Those who now hear Mr. Borden express his willingness . . . to give his last dollar and his life, with his gray hairs, to put down the Rebellion and crush out its cause, would not suppose that he was once a large land-owner and slaveholder in Texas. . . . His father has just died, unable to escape from Rebeldom. His brothers, he believes are Union men, though obliged to appear to be Rebels. To all rebels, Gail Borden is opposed, heart and soul, and his greatest anxiety appears to be to live to work for the Union army. He thanks God fervently every day that he is able to work in this cause. He knows that the products of his manufactory are directly aiding the good cause." Since the *Tribune* would not have hesitated to make Borden's printed feelings coincide with those of Greeley, Borden's secondhand statement here must be taken with some caution.

Despite Borden's apparently clear stand, however, *The Houston Tri-Weekly Telegraph*, a paper with definite rebel leanings, on August 30, 1865, spoke proudly of Borden's condensed milk as a "Texas institution [which] the war has not abolished. . . . It is a successful and valuable invention."

During the war, production of condensed milk never caught up with demand. Once convinced of its preservative qualities, the government ordered milk as a regular field ration. Soldiers home on leave told of the milk that was clean and indefinitely fresh; and the demand grew.

Gail Borden found little time, however, to enjoy his wealth. Stepping up production alone required a full day's work, and besides, he wanted to improve his product. It became a common sight to Charlie Knight on arriving at the New York Condensed Milk Company office at 34 and 36 Elizabeth Street to find his employer waiting impatiently in the early morning chill to get inside to work. Often he was at his desk at four o'clock, writing and scheming and figuring without looking up until five hours later, when suddenly he would stop to swallow a couple of quick gulps of food, after which he would go back to his desk to drive himself until both the day and Gail Borden were exhausted.

Although Borden believed there was no better milk in the world than his, he knew he could make it even better. Patent reissue followed reissue, each embodying some improvement by the in-

Borden and his wife, Emeline Eunice Eno Church
Borden, vacationing at Niagara Falls

The Borden Company

ventor: on May 13, 1862, he received a reissue for preparatory milk scalding; on February 10, 1863, for "preparatory coagulating and re-arranging of the albumen"; on November 14, 1865, for coagulating albuminous particles; on April 17, 1866, for further improvements on the vacuum process.

Always he was working on his machinery, trying to by-pass operations, trying to cut down expense, and trying to increase output. He was an inveterate notekeeper. A glance at a day's entry in one of his 1862 notebooks reveals the minuscule details with which he concerned himself: "Get Plank for . . . Press; Wash Cellar Windows; Fix Gate Chains; . . . Hang Grindstone; Sink for bigham; Stand in Manhold cover; Cock wrenches; 10 ft. ⅜ Round packing wanted, Hole through garret floor for Thermometer; . . . Rubbish cleaned out, . . . Road to Pond to be fixed, Sponges wanted."

Sometimes it seemed that only he knew how to correct mechanical faults, and now and then even he was puzzled. With no real engineering background, he found trial and error his most frequent method. His experience perfecting his condenser is typical:

The boiling milk in the vacuum pan was creating such thick fog that neither Borden nor anyone else could see the milk. He tried an eight-inch cast-iron vapor pipe from the vacuum pan to the pumps, running it out fifteen feet from the top of the pan to the elbow where the pipe disappeared through the floor. In the pipe he placed a sprinkler, not unlike a flower sprinkler, except for being made of copper. The results were unsatisfactory.

Next Borden made a condenser out of copper, sixteen inches wide, setting it upright, with a vapor pipe from the pan which ran into a square shoulder connecting twelve inches from the top of the upright pipe, the top foot housing the sprinklers. He tried it: a dead failure. His third attempt was to run a sixteen-inch pipe vertically for fifteen feet from the top of the pan. In conjunction he used a fifteen-foot condenser filled with copper sprinklers. He tried this: better, but still not satisfactory.

A foot at a time he cut off the upright pipe. Each time he found some improvement, but large drops of water from the milk would form in the upper part of the pan and drop back into the milk to be recondensed. Away he cut on the upright pipe until finally he had only enough remaining for a gooseneck. Results with the gooseneck were the best yet, but his sprinklers would not work now. Out came the sprinklers, and instead a pipe with fine holes was placed in the condenser. That worked. Basically, after weeks of toiling and wondering, he was through with his condenser. In more or less time he underwent the same experimentation with his other operations.

By June, 1863, the New York Condensed Milk Company was turning out fourteen thousand quarts of milk daily at Wassaic for "satisfactory" profits, yet, complained Gail Borden, "we do not meet half the orders." There had been lean times in September, 1862, when Robert E. Lee was driving north toward Gettsyburg and the North was becoming truly apprehensive—one day there had been no sales at all—but all that was past, and emphasis was now not on selling but on filling orders.

Extensive repairs to increase production were commenced at Wassaic, but not even these improvements could increase output beyond a daily run of sixteen thousand quarts.[5] And if they did, the company could not take advantage of the expansion, because Harlem Valley farmers were supplying more milk already than had been expected.

Clearly the immediate solution to the production and procurement problems lay in establishing branch factories which could tap new milk-supply centers. Under the Borden patent two independent concerns were licensed—the Baltimore Condensed Milk Company, to operate out of York, Pennsylvania;[6] and the Rokomeka Company in Livermore Falls, Maine, near James Bridge's old home of Augusta. A third company was formed by Borden himself at Winsted, Connecticut, only four miles north of his old Burrville plant. Organization of the company, known as the Borden Condensed Milk Company, was entirely separate from the New York Condensed Milk Company, with Milbank at first having no financial interest. However, the Winsted plant did use the parent company's sales facilities in New York.

[5] At this time fresh milk cost the company between two and three cents a quart, the price running higher always between October and April than for the remainder of the year.

[6] Borden owned $5,000 worth of stock, or one-fifth the total, in John Gail Borden's name, in the Baltimore Condensed Milk Company. His interest in Rokomeka was unspecified

Although the Winsted firm lasted only three years and never exceeded a six-thousand-quart daily capacity, it did realize its object of relieving the pressure on the Wassaic plant during the war years. Borden, of course, was president, with Elhanan Fyler as vice-president and Theron Bronson, with whom John Gail and Mary Jane Borden had boarded on occasion, as secretary-treasurer. Insufficient milk supply forced its closing in 1867.[7]

At Winsted, Borden broke one of his most respected rules—he encouraged work on Sunday. It happened at the close of one Sunday service in Winsted, when Borden arose to ask permission to speak. He had heard, he said, of the terrible conditions under which the Union troops were fighting in the South, especially those with Sherman's army. Dysentery was ravaging whole regiments. If the church people would spend their Sabbath afternoon picking the blackberries lying ripe and abundant in the fields and bring their day's harvest to his factory, he would convert the berries into jelly, which he knew to be a remedy for the scourge, at no cost. By the wagonload the blackberries arrived, and Borden and helpers condensed the juice to a jelly, packed it in small wooden kegs and cans, and shipped it to General Sherman's headquarters, for which action the General reputedly wrote him that he had accomplished more than all the army surgeons in staying the dysentery epidemic.

But the big Borden plant was begun at an unimportant Harlem Railway stop fifty-five miles out of New York called Brewsters Station, later shortened to Brewster. Here Borden began his "perfect" plant, capable of producing twenty thousand quarts of condensed milk daily, surrounded by a rich dairying region, and only four hours by rail out of New York. It soon became the most important plant in the Borden scheme, and in 1864 Borden moved his home to Brewster to be near at hand. He was now prepared to accept any orders from anywhere.

Now that at last his milk products were beginning to be widely used, Borden wanted to broaden his experimentation. In 1862 he was granted a patent for "Improvement in Concentrating and Pre-

---

[7] At the Winsted closing $7,054.45 remaining in the treasury was divided among Milbank, Fyler, and Borden. In addition, Fyler's interest was bought for $12,000.

serving for use, Cider, and other Juices of Fruits," and his decoction of coffee threatened to become as important to him as milk.

He looked westward. Without any particular effort on his part his condensed milk was selling well in Cincinnati, Louisville, and St. Louis. There seemed no reason why coffee and condensed cider should not sell also if pushed properly. He would like to have four more plants—one near Philadelphia; one in Ohio "in back of Cleveland, Toledo, Sandusky and Erie [with] special regard to be had to an apple region"; a third near Chicago and Milwaukee; and a fourth near St. Louis to supply the river trade. Each plant should cost about $25,000, including working capital, of which he would furnish two-fifths.

From the back of his mind he summoned an idea supposedly surrendered a decade before. Never convinced that the meat biscuit was unsound, now that he had capital he wanted to bring it back on the market, as well as an extract of beef on which he had been working. Although he thought of himself as old and feeble, an idea could entangle him as completely in 1865 as it could in 1845; and so it does not surprise to find him in Chicago at the end of summer, 1865, looking over sites for a meat biscuit manufactory.[8] The war was over, the Union had been preserved, America was ready now to come of age, and materialism and expansion were twin rulers. Like a youngster named Rockefeller and an oldster named Vanderbilt, Borden had big plans in his head, and most of them had to do with growth.

In 1835, Hiram Church, a bold American of German extraction, left his pelt trade in St. Louis to follow Indian trails through Potawatomi country into the Fox River valley west of Lake Michigan. Here, forty-two miles west of what later became Chicago, he determined to settle. Others of a like mind had preceded him and still others followed, and before long Elgin, Illinois, was thriving. Later

---

[8] Between August and December, 1862, for instance, Borden purchased more than $5,000 worth of Costa Rican and Santos coffee and chicory from Bynner & Boyce of New York He purchased 18,000 bushels of apples in the autumn of 1863. In 1909 a Nevada woman wrote truculently to the company "During the Civil War . . I boarded at Earles Hotel on Canal St. . . . and Mr Gail Borden sat next to me at table [His] Condensed Cider was most delicious—Is this cider manufactured now? If not—why not?"

In the South, *The Houston Daily Telegraph* on September 19, 1864, had noted without comment that Borden was "going to" make meat biscuit for Federal troops.

Church returned east to Colebrook Centre, Connecticut, where he married Emeline Eunice Eno. After an interlude in Vernon, New York, the couple, grown by now to a family of four, returned to Elgin, where Church remained till his death, after which his widow and her two sons sought to rebuild their lives in Connecticut.

In Connecticut, as has been related, Emeline Eunice Church met Gail Borden. After their marriage she told him of the Fox River country, of its rolling plains, its living springs, and its wide possibilities. To him it sounded like the dairying spot he was seeking in the West, and after an inspection he was convinced. In 1865 he started a factory. Once again he proceeded independently of the New York Condensed Milk Company. Jeremiah Milbank may have held stock but no office. Borden was president; D. M. Cole, treasurer; S. T. Hinckley, director and Chicago agent; and P. Platt, superintendent. Capital stock was $25,000.

By the end of 1866 the Elgin Milk Condensing Company was in full swing, the company purchasing 303,560 gallons of milk at a cost of nearly $49,000 for the year. Seven hundred gallons an hour were being condensed and sent to the company's Chicago depot at 104 State Street. The company also took up cheese manufacturing, its thirty cheese-presses turning out 240,079 pounds in its second year of operation, including some cheeses that weighed more than fifty pounds each.[9]

One day a delegation from the Chicago Medical Society, headed by Dr. H. A. Johnson, visited the plant. It sampled and tested but made no recommendations until January, 1867, when, contrary to society rules forbidding endorsements, it presented to the society a resolution which was adopted unanimously:

Resolved, That the great importance of having milk pure, uniform in quality, and capable of remaining sweet longer than that ordinarily distributed directly from the dairy, makes the condensed milk furnished by the Elgin Milk Condensing Company an article of great value to the community, and one which we freely recommend for general use, and especially for use in feeding children.[10]

[9] *History of the City of Elgin,* 30, 32, 34 *The Elgin Dairy Report,* March 20, 1893

[10] *History of the City of Elgin,* 34.

At Elgin, a thousand miles from Milbank's economic eyes, Borden was putting into operation all his pet schemes. Besides his milk and cheese factories, he had a coffee room, a jelly room (after 1867), a can room which turned out ten thousand cans a day, a cheese-box factory for the general market, a labeling and packing room, and that resurrection from the dismal past, a meat biscuit room in conjunction with an extract-of-beef manufactory.

In Europe, Justus von Liebig, one of the Continent's leading chemists, had augmented his fame by his invention of "Extractum Carnis," or beef extract, which he and others believed retained the "efficacy" and flavor of real beef in the finest possible degree. But, Liebig had admitted, "Were it possible to furnish the market, at a reasonable price . . . a preparation of meat combining in itself the albuminous [and fibrinous substances], such a preparation would have to be preferred to the Extractum Carnis, for it would contain all the nutritive constituents of meat."[11] Borden believed he could work out the combination.

Off and on he had worked at beef extraction for years, until in 1866 he considered his experimentation period terminated. With Dr. John H. Currie, the New York chemist, as his partner, he formed the firm of Borden and Currie, using the Elgin Milk Condensing Company works for his manufactory, where soon he was able to produce two thousand pounds of extract daily.

Borden's beef extract was vacuum-prepared over low heat to prevent coagulation of albumin. The finished product was sold in half-inch thick rectangular packages. Where Extractum Carnis preserved only 3 per cent of the original weight of the meat, Borden's extract purported to retain 5 per cent, the extra amount containing both albumin, fibrin, and creatine, and leaving the muscular fiber of meat so exhausted that after Borden had given farmers the meat residue, the farmers had reported that their swine had exhibited as little interest in it as if the meat had been "so much chips or woody fiber."

As usual, Borden sought the opinion of men who were considered experts. The *American Journal of Pharmacy* added recommendations, and the *Boston Medical and Surgical Journal* announced that "hereafter the physician may be sure of his patient's getting as

11 *Ibid*, 34–36

good essence of beef . . . as the drugs he prescribes."[12] But extract of beef, like the meat biscuit, was an article that promised much and amounted to little. Borden never realized any appreciable profit from the extract. Condensed milk remained the money product in Elgin.

Stuffing two dollars in change in his full pockets, Gail Borden would stride out of the Elizabeth Street office in New York, walk along Bowery and Fourth Avenue, and hand out nickels and dimes to urchins and hobos along the route to the Twenty-sixth Street station where he caught the Harlem train to Brewsters Station. The stretch between Elizabeth and Twenty-sixth was part of his world, and he wanted to contribute.

Once aboard, he was still in his world. Each Harlem Railway coach had a Bible, and though he neither admitted or denied the story, his friends said Gail Borden had been instrumental in placing them there. Occasionally, he would see some of his employees leaving the city for a vacation. Digging into his pockets, he would draw out a roll of bills, divide it among the vacationers, apologize for having no more, and go on to his seat content. But only for the moment.

In Brewster, Borden would putter around his modern factory, instructing little John Pugsley in the horrors of dirt as that young man went from white marble table to white marble table wiping up any spots that the women workers may have left. Here by the banks of the cheerful Croton River the inventor could reflect on the years he had sought to serve mankind and how, now that he was an old man, he was serving in a manner that no one but he—and perhaps Penelope—would have dreamed possible a generation before.

Penelope Borden would have appreciated the style in which he lived—a two-and-one-half story white colonial colonnaded house high above the main road, with double lines of tall, slender cedars— not so tall and not so slender as the Mississippi pines had been, but more impressive—edging either side of the walk in the long front yard. That was his home.

In Brewster he was lord of the manor, a man who could do no wrong. In larger Manhattan he was becoming accepted as a force

12 *American Journal of Pharmacy*, January, 1866, and *Boston Medical and Surgical Journal*, both quoted in *History of the City of Elgin*, 36–38

for good in the world. Some of his friends, such as the two Jays (Gould and Cooke), might have their unsavory sides (the first being blamed for a panic and the other for a major depression), but they were men enough to recognize in Gail Borden a person of integrity and to respect him for that quality.

Happy though he was commuting between Brewster and Manhattan with an occasional long trip to Elgin, pleased though he was to spend comfortable evenings planning with John Gail or reminiscing with John Gail's pretty little blonde wife, Ellen, Borden felt a need for something more. Moving to New York had brought fortune, but he had been too long a Texan and now he wanted to go home. Home to the scenes of his first real triumphs. Home, too, to where Penelope lay buried, where now his father and his brother Paschal lay buried, and where three of his children lay buried. There were his other children, too, Lee and Phila, whom he had not seen since before the war. And there was his brother Thomas, the wealthiest member of the family when Gail had come north in the eighteen fifties, now a grocer stripped of almost everything by the war. How would these, his blood kin who had known the other side of the Civil War and defeat and military occupation, receive their father and brother who had supplied the troops which had overrun their lands?

He had founded an industry—the condensing of milk. A double handful of imitators had sprung up in Europe and in the United States, some licensed by Borden, some working completely independently. In fact, in January, 1866, he had been forced to adopt a new name for his product, since one rival had appropriated the Borden's condensed-milk label. The choice, Eagle Brand,[13] proved a happy one, a name that stuck; and soon Eagle Brand became as well known to consumers as Borden, and many members of later generations would refer to themselves as having been Eagle Brand babies.

He had helped found another industry also—that of modern dairying, for which he shares credit with the perfecters of refrigeration, quick transportation, and pasteurization. He showed American farmers the possibilities of large milk production, and his irritat-

[13] Why *Eagle Brand?* There are the usual contradictions after the Texas eagle which he had often hunted, after Eagle Cove, where lived the Galveston Island Indians, after the American eagle, inspired by a burst of postwar patriotism. Borden himself left no answer.

ing insistence on sanitation opened an understanding of the values of milk cleanliness. But somehow all that paled alongside his wish to go home to Texas.

However, to gratify the wish at this time was out of the question. He had his works at Wassaic and Brewster, where he was listed as active superintendent; his plant at Elgin, where he was president; and the several other firms which he had licensed. And 1866 brought a bad year in which it looked as if his small empire might collapse.

The trouble was a not infrequent outgrowth of war—overexpansion and overproduction in a market that unexpectedly declined, leaving the New York Condensed Milk Company with a huge surplus of milk and more fresh milk arriving daily than could possibly be sold. To cancel the contracts would necessitate larger payments than Borden and Milbank cared to risk, and cancellation without payment would store up ill will among the farmers that would impede co-operation when business grew again, as the two men felt sure it must. The two partners were caught in the beginning of a long downward business trend which would continue until McKinley's election brought an upsurge of confidence in 1897, but like Rockefeller, Armour, and others, Borden and Milbank were going to buck the trend rather than drift with and be victimized by it.

Back and forth flew the letters—between Borden and Milbank; between Borden and George Conklin, his assistant at Wassaic; between Borden and his son John Gail. Meetings with the farmers were held to find a workable basis. Some farmers agreed to withhold milk if the company would pay one cent for each quart not delivered; others insisted on receiving five and one-half cents a quart for every quart they cared to bring in, promising to aid the company by drying off some cows and slacking feed. Small wonder that a person of Gail Borden's excitability should exclaim· "My head! So much to do." Or again: "I wish I could disconnect myself."

By January, 1867, the company's plight was so serious that Milbank wrote Borden to stop the Brewster works if possible. Accordingly production was cut to 6,500 quarts and then to 5,000 quarts for both plants.

In the midst of his worries Borden received word from the

Elgin plant that his partners there had been concentrating on cheese production to the disregard of the other departments and that most of the cheese had been made so hastily and shoddily that it was spoiling. He had poured $17,000 already into that "ugly beast," had lost perhaps $6,000, and stood to lose almost the entire amount unless the company began to prosper soon. But when he told Milbank that a trip to Elgin was necessary, Milbank forbade it: "Do not think of going to Elgin until we shall get a clearer view of things. Let Elgin *adjourn*."[14]

John Gail Borden, who had become his father's assistant superintendent at Brewster and Wassaic, stated that he and several fellow-employees were willing to take drastic pay slashes while the company was in distress; but Gail Borden vetoed this recommendation, counseling his son to "hold steady [and] say nothing."

In February, 1867, business began to increase slightly as the volume of milk accepted from the farmers continued to decrease. Borden then went to Elgin to begin dissolution of the Elgin Milk Condensing Company, paying off some of the other partners and then reorganizing in partnership with Jeremiah Milbank under the title of the Illinois Condensing Company. Alfred B. Church, the third Mrs. Borden's younger son, was named superintendent, and the meat business was transferred to Texas.[15]

Soon after his return to the East in March, Borden received a reinforcement in the arrival of his son Lee from Texas. At once Borden set Lee to learning the intricacies of the manufacturing end of the condensed-milk business. As soon as Lee had served a sufficient apprenticeship, Gail Borden intended to absorb him into the company. He was further encouraged as milk sales began climbing again until in April he could order the Brewster plant to step up production to 5,000 quarts and Wassaic to 5,500 quarts a day. The next month he opened a new market, as Australian merchants placed orders totaling nearly $20,000. The crisis had been weathered. Again the problem would become one of obtaining enough milk.

[14] No statements of profit and loss exist for this period Expenses at Wassaic alone ran $73,432 during the first six months of 1866, $77,809 during the second six months, although 111,319 fewer quarts were handled in the latter period than in the former

[15] Milbank's investment in all the Borden enterprises probably did not exceed $100,000 At his death his half-ownership possessed a market value of $8,000,000. Interview with Albert G Milbank, New York, August 2, 1946

Whether business was good or bad, however, Gail Borden remained the same: worried and convinced that he was ill. His letters are full of physical complaints that he is "laid up," too old to work, or adversely affected by inclement weather. The truth is that although many men of his age are not old, Borden was getting old—sixty-five years was a long time for a man who for decades had worked and fretted sixteen to eighteen hours a day until by habit he could not slow his pace.

Ordinarily not aware of his tired body, whenever something went wrong, he knew that he was aging. When John Gail sent down to New York a load of inferior milk, Borden cried out: "We cant risk thin & grainy milk. it made my back ache all the way down & after I got here." But he did not want to stop and probably would not have known how if he had held such a desire. Always convinced that death lurked close, he could never wait for it but must always drive forward until the day it arrived.

Except for the obvious ravages of war and carpetbag politics Texas had not changed during Gail Borden's ten-year absence. Never prostrated to the extent of some of the other Confederate states, it was picking up rapidly in population and wealth at the end of 1867 and its citizens still held to a notion that some day Texas would be a great empire. Most of her heroes were now dead, Sam Houston among them, but there was no end of former friends to drop around to greet the man whose name had become a household word almost everywhere that American mothers lived. These friends found him little altered, too—still humble, still eager to serve, still ready to talk of plans, still paying scant attention to clothes, still stooped and thin, and still seeking to be a better worker for God.

On this trip he kept a diary in a three-by-five-inch pocket notebook of mock leather. For once his account of his activities is laconic.

It was more than a triumphal home-coming. He had business in Texas. In New York he had formed the Borden Manufacturing Company with its office in White Plains and its factory, including a sawmill, in Bastrop, Texas, and a working capital of $12,000. Products: lumber generally, plus shingles, tubs, cooperware pails, and tanning and dressing of hides. Also he had transferred most of his beef-extract business to a community twelve miles west of Columbus, Texas, where Lee and John P. Borden had homes,[16] which was called Borden in their honor. Gail Borden wanted to check personally on both these enterprises.

At Columbus, seventy miles west of Houston, he was reunited with Philadelphia, mother now of four children[17] he had never seen and expecting another in February. On January 6, 1868, he rode out to his meat-packing factory but found the weather too warm for slaughtering and preparing the beeves. At one o'clock the thermometer stood at 78 degrees, but an hour later he was sharply reminded that the pattern of Texas weather—and Texas always has *weather* and never mere *climate*—never changes, for a norther blew in, dropping the temperature to 48 degrees at two o'clock and to 28 degrees by ten o'clock that night.

At Bastrop he found Lee building a rough cedar house in a brake four miles above town; watched "Hundreds of Freedmen" milling idly; came down with a "Kind of Dumb ague, with fever"; recovered, and relapsed. He rented himself a cottage—three months for $45—bought furniture, and holed up with his correspondence until he could recover his health.

On January 28, with his wife, a worker from his Elgin plant, and a minister friend, he took a carriage to Austin, where he ran into a stiff norther and his old benefactor, impulsive, direct Thomas F. McKinney, once one of Texas' wealthiest men, now a victim of injudicious cotton speculation. At the state capitol he was received by Governor Elisha Pease.

Returning to Columbus in February, he nearly caught up with his chronic forebodings of disaster. Eight miles out of Bastrop his carriage was rolling along briskly when the whippletree broke, sending passengers scrambling. But no one was hurt any more than when the terraqueous machine had overturned in the Gulf two decades ago.

His diary showed only one entry for February 16. No other was necessary: "Attended Sunday School & church with four of My grandchildren.

"Beautiful day—"

16 Draft certificate of incorporation, Borden Manufacturing Company, June 1, 1867, in Borden Papers, Rosenberg Library Julius Schutze, "Die Geschichte von Colorado County, Texas," in *Texas Vorwarts*, July 3, 1896. Deed Record Book, N, Bastrop County, Texas, 722–26, P, 679–80

As a proud grandfather he was having the time of his life. In addition to attending the birth of Phila's fifth child, he was also near by in April when Lee's wife gave birth to a "fine fellow weighed 12 lbs." And two days later he learned that John Gail's wife had a daughter.

From deep in Texas he watched the Washington scene with more than usual interest, for there President Johnson was being tried on impeachment charges. Borden, who seldom mentioned politics, contributed one terse comment after another to his diary. When one uneventful day passed, he recalled the watchword of cautious General McClellan's command, noting briefly, "Quiet on the Potomac."

In May, the Texas idyll drew to a close. In Galveston he lingered, reluctant to leave, enjoying every moment as he "Visited & was visited   Had a good time." Before departing he took time to meet with John Sydnor for a bit of philanthropy, deeding two lots containing a church, parsonage, and other buildings to the African Baptist Church of Galveston. On May 28, he was back in Wassaic.[18] It was time to resume work. The first vacation of his sixty-six years had ended.

The beginning of the nineteenth century's eighth decade found Gail Borden living in his White Plains home on North Broadway, holding morning prayer services and leading songs, stretching his full length in an easy chair to rest his old body while his mind churned with ideas. Except for occasional laxness by some of his workers which permitted inferior milk to slip by, he had his business organized so that routine direction sufficed.[19] But he was still president of the company and he still believed that only he understood the mechanical end of milk condensation, so that he could not release the controls to some subordinate. He felt as responsible for every quart of milk marketed as he had in 1856 when he constituted the entire active personnel of the condensed-milk industry.

17 The third child, Virginia Lee Johnson, married Isaac Milbank, who became a vice-president of the Borden Company
18 Record, Y, Galveston County, Texas, 303–304 The diary is in the Borden Papers, Rosenberg Library.
19 The land for his White Plains home cost $18,000 Record of Deeds, Liber 617, Westchester County, New York, 4–7.

The Elgin plant, where Alfred B. Church was superintendent, continued to give trouble. There the building, a converted tannery of wood, concrete, and brick, was at fault. Every time its old wooden floor was cleaned, the milky water seeped through to the tan bark below, where it stood as if trapped by a sewer. When batch after batch of imperfect milk followed, it was decided that the floor must be ripped up, the tannery vats filled with gravel, and sewers laid to the Fox River.

Borden suspected some farmers of cutting corners at his companies' expense. When on one occasion he threatened to cancel a large contract because the milk had been watered, the dairyman admitted his guilt, adding that if the contract were kept in force he would return the richest milk possible, that heretofore he had never seen Borden's dairying rules and hadn't known his requirements. Assuring the farmer that he would grant a second chance, Borden turned on Noah Bishop, whose duties included tacking contracts in each dairy barn, accusing that discouraged youth of neglect of duty. John Gail, standing by, started to speak.

"No, my son," said Gail Borden, "not a word for that little rascal."

But John Gail persisted until his father heard him say, "I saw a contract in that man's milk house myself."

With that, Gail Borden turned on the dairyman, ordering him from his office, and threatening to "kick him out" personally if he ever returned. Tall talk for a man in his seventies.

Rivalry between the several plants was encouraged as a means of boosting production. In Elgin, John Gail Borden offered Edward S. Eno a wedding suit if he could add a few quarts to the hourly condensing record then held by Brewster.

"Naturally," wrote Eno later, "I was forcing the pan to its limit and a few minutes before the batch was ready to draw off, [John Gail Borden] came into the Pan Room and inquired how I was getting along." When Eno told him that he could not reach the Brewster mark, the younger Borden jokingly said, "I see you are a little afraid," and went out.

Eno resolved to increase his pressure if possible. He was just striking his batch when the "next thing I knew I was picking myself up at the far side of the room with the milk and steam filling the room. The jacket of the pan had been blown all to pieces, the batch of milk had been lost, and I never received the wedding suit." But the Borden pans, which up to then had been equipped with a vacuum gauge but no steam gauge on either coils or jacket, were quickly fitted with new steam inlets and exhausts to restrain overenthusiastic operators from blowing them up.[20] In such ways do trial-and-error manufacturers improve their equipment.

In his beef-extract side line Borden was having only fair success, the firm of Borden and Currie showing a $40,000 cash surplus for the five years of operation previous to May 13, 1871. Neither it nor his meat-packing enterprise would survive him long.

Although he was getting feebler, Borden enjoyed traveling and seeing people, and, as always, talking. He built himself a small house overlooking Harvey's Creek at Borden, Texas, bought another "elegant" home at 60 Division Street in Elgin, and authorized the moving of the New York offices from Elizabeth Street to 60–64 Park Place and the establishment of a Brooklyn branch office at 98–106 Sterling Place.

He lived well but simply, throwing occasional country dinners for New York business associates, summering in the Catskills, running excursions from Lake Mahopac to Brewster so that vacationists there might see firsthand the sanitation and care employed by Borden workers. He loved to tell stories of early Texas—of how, for instance, during the Revolution, Sam Houston had received him outside his tent clad in only a shirt. He loved to give advice, as when he warned Alfred Church that it was not enough to have good milk and good apparatus: "Everlasting vigilance and the most exemplary care; are necessary and indispensable, to success"; and to make small jokes, as at the wedding of Frank Wells, who later matched $8,000 with John Gail Borden's $48,000 to form a Brewster bank. After the ceremony Borden in great spirits told the bridegroom· "Young man, you don't know what you have got yourself into. . . . I know all about it; have been through it three times."

For the first time in his seventy years Borden began to spare his thin body, to seek comfort at the expense of service. Each year the Northern winters seemed more rigorous to him, and so the cold seasons of 1871, 1872, and 1873 found him in his modest Harvey's

[20] Eno became Elgin superintendent in 1882.

273

Creek home in Texas, relaxing in the usually mild weather. His trips to Texas were not all pleasure, for while he lived the meat-packing business thrived, especially after the railroad was extended westward from Columbus.[21] But the sands of time were running out.

On a shady knoll in Woodlawn Cemetery north of Manhattan stood a huge granite milk can easily visible from the New Haven Railway cars. For several years observant passers-by had wondered about its purpose, for no inscription was to be seen. In the second week of January, 1874, those who noticed could discern a change: the milk can was gone. There was a reason.

Gail Borden came to Texas in the early spring of 1873 and again in the fall. Condensed milk required no more of his time than he wished to devote,[22] and since he was not needed regularly, he turned to philanthropy. In two months in Texas he built a school for freedmen, organized a Negro day school and a Negro Sunday school, erected a schoolhouse for white children, and laid plans for a "neat and tasteful Church Edifice," all at Borden. During the same year he also aided in the erection of five other churches, maintained two colporteurs, and supported an unknown number of poorly paid minsters, teachers, and students.[23]

With brothers Tom and John he attended the Texas Veterans Association meeting in Houston. In the Capitol Hotel lobby the veterans talked and mingled, but their talk was more of the recent war and reconstruction than of the Texas fight for independence. Some one asked the opinion of Gail Borden, a man who knew firsthand the Northern point of view. The white-haired inventor closed his eyes meditatively:

"When will the war be over?" he asked his listeners. "Eight years ago Lee surrendered and yet we are in turmoil, when will

[21] In October, 1872, he sold 548 acres of Texas land to the Borden Meat Preserving Company for $35,000. Deed, October 3, 1872, in Borden Papers, Borden Company, New York The first locomotive traversing the twelve miles from Columbus to Borden, Texas, was named "Gail Borden," as was the depot. Joseph J. Mansfield, *Life and Achievements of Gail Borden*, 7.

[22] The New York Condensed Milk Company records for this period are incomplete For the nine months ending March 31, 1873, the Brewster plant sold 1,046,941 cans (probably one pound each) of preserved milk and 1,187,834 cans of plain condensed milk

[23] Gail Borden to W S Griffin, March 20, 1873, typed copy in Borden Papers, Rosenberg Library. Thomas Vassar, *The Divine Ideal of a Christian Life,* 5

Gail Borden (1801–74). This portrait hangs in
the foyer of the Borden Building, New York

The Borden Company

peace be restored between the North and the South? when will the radicals of both sections permit us to return to our former relations? The South has been conquered. That was bad enough. . . . I doubted he wisdom of secession [but] that is ancient history. . . . We have ll suffered from that mistake but the dregs are getting bitter now."[24]

But most of the time he was content to sun himself at his Harvey's Creek home, walking slowly over to Lee's house to play with he children or slipping off to the meat factory to advise some puzzled worker or to check on the quality of beef being slaughtered. On better days he rode into Columbus to see Fannie Baker Darden, Mosely Baker's daughter, who held continuous open house for friends of her soldier father.

Shortly after Christmas he was pottering around the meat factory when he felt a strange weariness. Slowly he picked his way home, impatient that he should tire so easily, lay down on the bed, and acknowledged that he was ill.

Brother John arrived on January 2 to find Gail suffering from pneumonia. In a few days he rallied enough to discuss settling a mortgage he held against Tom and Louisa Borden. It was his last effort.

At sunset on January 11, 1874, Gail Borden died. Fittingly, the day was Sunday, and on a Sabbath he rested for the last time by the banks of Harvey's Creek in his beloved Texas, a humble child of God whose labor was done.

From Columbus a small locomotive chugged the twelve miles to Borden, loaded its shipment into a private funeral car, and headed eastward and northward for White Plains, New York, where on January 21, 1874, the Reverend Thomas Vassar delivered the funeral address, taking a text from Romans 12:11 that St. Paul could have written with Gail Borden in mind: "Not slothful in business; fervent in spirit; serving the Lord."

Interment was at Woodlawn. Gail Borden himself had chosen the site on a knoll that overlooked most of the cemetery and had placed there the granite milk can in one of his rare conceits, with the understanding that the can would be removed when the body

---

[24] Manuscript of a speech delivered by Sam Houston Dixon, Houston, Texas, December 13, 1927, in San Jacinto Museum of History

was ready.[25] Replacing the earthly symbol was a monument with an epitaph that in two lines told the story of a man's life:

> *I tried and failed,*
> *I tried again and again, and succeeded.*

[25] Vassar, *The Divine Ideal of a Christian Life*, 1, 3–5. Interviews with J. J. Mansfield and O. A. Zumwalt, Columbus, Texas, July 17, 1947. *The Texas Baptist Herald*, January 15, 1874

Borden's last recorded act was the purchase of a six-months' subscription to the Galveston *Daily News* on December 5, 1873 The receipt is in the Alamo Museum His will, dated February 4, 1872, was admitted to probate in New York and Texas. Deed Record Book, Z, Brazoria County, Texas, 312–15.

Bibliography

PRIMARY SOURCES

MANUSCRIPT COLLECTIONS: PERSONAL AND ORGANIZATIONAL

Austin (Stephen F.) Papers, 1834–36. The University of Texas Archives, Austin.

Bishop, Noah L. "Some Recollections of Over Fifty Years Service in the Milk Business." Address read at Albany, New York, November 22, 1910. Arthur G. Clark Papers, The Borden Company, New York.

Bollaert, William J. Diary, June 16, 1842–April, 1843. Ayer Collection, Newberry Library, Chicago.

———. Diary, April 20–July 2, 1844. Ayer Collection, Newberry Library, Chicago.

———. "Notes on Texas, 1843–44." Ayer Collection, Newberry Library, Chicago.

———. Private Journals, 1841–49. Ayer Collection, Newberry Library, Chicago.

———. "Residence & Travel in Texas, 1842–43." Ayer Collection, Newberry Library, Chicago.

———. "Texas in 1842." Ayer Collection, Newberry Library, Chicago.

Borden (Gail) Papers, 1805–75. The Borden Company, New York.

———. Papers, 1820–56. In possession of Mr. and Mrs. J. L. Lockett, Houston.

———. Papers, 1837–75. Rosenberg Library, Galveston.

Briscoe (Andrew) Papers, 1826–39. San Jacinto Museum of History, Houston.

Bronson, Elliott B. "An American Nobleman." Address read at Winchester Center, Connecticut, October 19, 1914. The Borden Company, New York.

Bryan (Moses Austin) Papers, 1820–56. The University of Texas Archives, Austin.

Chambers (Thomas W.) Papers, 1854–55. The University of Texas Archives, Austin.

Clark (Arthur G.) Papers. The Borden Company, New York.

Collins, James H. "The Story of Condensed Milk." The Borden Company, New York.

Current Events Club, Madison, Indiana. "Early History of Madison and Jefferson County." Jefferson County Historical Association Archives, Madison, Indiana.

Dixon, Sam Houston. Address read at Houston, December 13, 1927. San Jacinto Museum of History, Houston.

Dyer, J. O. "Early History of Galveston, Texas, 1518–1861." Rosenberg Library, Galveston.

English Manuscripts, Miscellaneous, 1831–32. San Jacinto Museum of History, Houston.

Eno, Edward S. "Some Recollections of the Milk Business." Arthur G. Clark Papers, The Borden Company, New York.

Galveston City Company Records, 1838–54. In possession of Stewart Title Guaranty Company, Galveston, Texas.

Greer, Henry K. "History of The Borden Company." The Borden Company, New York.

Hayes, Gerald Waldo. "Island and City of Galveston." Rosenberg Library, Galveston.

Hayes, Loeb & Co. "History of The Borden Company." The Borden Company, New York.

Heberhart (Charles) Notes. Jefferson County Historical Association Archives, Madison, Indiana.

Heminger (A. L.) Papers, 1817–38. In possession of Mr. A. L. Heminger, Keosauqua, Iowa.

Hill, Mary (ed.). Items from Early Newspapers of Jefferson County, Indiana, 1817–86. Jefferson County Historical Association Archives, Madison, Indiana.

Holley (Mary Austin). Notes Made . . . in Interviews with Prominent Texans of the Early Days. The University of Texas Archives, Austin.

Houston Title Guaranty Company Files, Houston.

Jefferson County, Indiana, First Court Book. Typescript, Jefferson County Historical Association Archives, Madison, Indiana.

Jenkins, W. C. "The Story of Concentrated Milk." The Borden Company, New York.

Old Texas Documents of The Borden Company, 1831–73. Alamo Museum, San Antonio, Texas.

Parker (J. H.) Papers. In possession of Mr. J. H. Parker, Liberty, Mississippi.

Perry (James F.) Papers, 1830–42. The University of Texas Archives, Austin.

Smith (Ashbel) Papers, 1836–73. The University of Texas Archives, Austin.

Starr (James H.) Papers, 1853. The University of Texas Archives, Austin.

Williams (S. M.) Papers, 1830–39. Rosenberg Library, Galveston.

MANUSCRIPTS· GOVERNMENT RECORDS

(Unless otherwise indicated, all governmental records are in Texas)

Bonds and Oaths, Republic of Texas, 1835–40. Texas State Library Archives, Austin.

Comptroller's Letters: Customs, 1836–45. Texas State Library Archives, Austin.

County Records and District Court Records as follows
 Indiana.
 Jefferson County Commissioners Record, A.
 Jefferson County Plat Book.
 Jefferson County Deed Record Book, A–F.
 Mississippi:
 Amite County Conveyance Record, II.
 Amite County Marriage Record, II.
 Amite County Orphans Court Record, I.
 Amite County Probate Record, C.
 New York:
 Chenango County, Book of Deeds, C–U.
 Westchester County Record of Deeds, 617–895.
 Texas·
 Bastrop County Deed Record Book, A–P.
 Brazoria County Deed Record Book, C–Z.
 Brazoria County Record of Marriage Licenses, I.
 Fayette County Deed Record Book, D.
 Fayette County District Court Minutes, A–C.
 Fort Bend County, Deeds, A–J.
 Galveston County District Court Minutes, 1843–45, I–IV.
 Galveston County Marriage License Record, 1838–50.
 Galveston County Records, A–5.
 Guadalupe County Deed Record Book· Gonzales Transcripts.
Domestic Correspondence, 1822–38. Texas State Library Archives, Austin.

Executive Record Book, 1836. Texas State Library Archives, Austin.

Galveston Custom House Record Book, 1835–44. Rosenberg Library, Galveston.

Petitions, 1836. Texas State Library Archives, Austin.

Public Printing Papers, 1835–37. Texas State Library Archives, Austin.

Records of the Quartermaster General, War Department, 1850–68. The National Archives, Washington, D. C.

Source Material for Mississippi History: Amite County. 3 vols. State Department of Archives and History, Jackson, Mississippi.

United States Census Returns. The National Archives, Washington, D. C., as follows:

Third Census, 1810. New York, I.

Fourth Census, 1820. Indiana, II.

Fifth Census, 1830. Mississippi, I.

Seventh Census, 1850. Texas, II.

Eighth Census, 1860. Connecticut, V.

Ninth Census, 1870. New York, CVI.

United States Customs Service Records, Port of New Orleans, 1828. New Orleans, Louisiana.

War Records, Adjutant General's Office, 1862–65. The National Archives, Washington, D. C.

INTERVIEWS

Bacon, Arthur G. Bainbridge, New York, August 14, 1946.

Bronson, Elliott B. Winchester Center, Connecticut, August 6, 1946.

Burr, John. Burrville, Connecticut, August 6, 1946.

Carothers, W. F. Houston, Texas, July 18, 1947.

Galpin, William R. Norwich, New York, August 14, 1946.

Mansfield, Joseph J. Columbus, Texas, July 17, 1947.

Milbank, Albert G. New York, August 2, 1946.

Parker, J. H. Liberty, Mississippi, January 7, 1946; April 11, 1947.

Pugsley, John E. Brewster, New York, August 6, 1946.

Sincerbox, John A. Wassaic, New York, August 6, 1946.

Zumwalt, O. A. Columbus, Texas, July 17, 1947.

NEWSPAPERS

(Unless otherwise indicated, all newspapers listed were published in Texas)

Alamo *News*, April 14, 1932.

Anderson *Texas Baptist*, November 14, 1855.

Augusta (Maine) *Drews Rural Intelligencer,* October 24, 1856.

Austin *City Gazette,* March 4, May 6, 1840.

Austin *Texas Sentinel,* February 5, May 23, June 13, November 28, 1840; June 17, September 9, 1841. (Variant title: Austin *Texas Centinel.*)

Austin *Texas State Gazette,* March 16, April 13, July 13, 1850; November 6, 1852; September 17, October 8, November 1, 1853; July 22, 1854.

Austin *Texas Vorwarts,* July 3, 1896.

Beeville *Bee,* September 23, 1898.

Brewster (New York) *Standard,* November 28, 1902; September 23, 1904.

Charleston (South Carolina) *Courier,* March 13, 1850.

Clarksville *Northern Standard,* August 20, 1842; June 8, 1843.

Columbia *Telegraph and Texas Register,* October 10, 1835–October 29, 1845. (Published also at San Felipe, Harrisburg, and Houston, 1835–45.)

Dallas *Herald,* January 15, 1874.

Dallas *Morning News,* November 18, 1906, April 28, 1929; May 15, 1932; April 11, 1942.

Elgin (Illinois) *Dairy Report,* March 20, April 24, August 21, 1893.

Galveston *Daily News,* August 20, 1873; March 17, 1877; December 11, 1891; October 20, 1901; June 11, 1906, April 11, 1917, October 1, 1920; March 6, September 25, December 18, 1921; April 1, November 18, 1923; July 11, 1936; August 15, October 21, 1939.

Galveston *Weekly News,* April 27, May 5, 1848; October 29, June 11, August 27, October 1, November 5, December 17, 1849; February 4, February 11, 1850, February 18, February 25, March 18, May 20, May 27, August 26, 1851.

Hartford (Connecticut) *Daily Courant,* March 15, 1936.

Houston *Chronicle,* June 1, 1947; February 18, 1951.

Houston *Daily Telegraph,* September 19, 1864.

Houston *Post,* August 18, 1929.

Houston *Texas Baptist Herald,* January 15, 1874.

Houston *Tri-Weekly Telegraph,* August 30, 1865.

London (England) *Evening Standard,* November 25, 1871.

Madison (Indiana) *Courier,* April 8, July 20, 1940.

Middletown (New York) *News,* July 20, 1940.

Newburgh (New York) *News,* September 14, 1939.

New York *Journal of Commerce and Commercial New York,* April 26, 1935.

New York *Leslie's Weekly*, May 8, 1858, April 26, 1906. (Variant title *Frank Leslie's Illustrated Newspaper*.)
New York *Tribune*, November 3, 1851, July 19, 1864, June 2, 1884.
New York *Wall Street Journal*, June 23, 1931.
San Antonio *Express*, October 2, 1921, March 13, 1939.
San Antonio *Light*, February 15, 1944.
San Felipe *Texas Gazette*, January–August, 1830.
Washington (D. C.) *Daily National Intelligencer*, January 13, 1852.
Washington (D. C.) *National Tribune*, March 25, 1926.
Washington (Georgia) *Christian Index*, February 27, March 26, 1840.
Washington *Texas National Register*, December 28, 1844; January 18 February 1, 1845.

BOOKS AND PAMPHLETS

Audubon, Maria R. *Audubon and His Journals*. 2 vols. New York Charles Scribner's Sons, 1900.
Barker, Eugene C. (ed.). *The Austin Papers*. 3 vols. Vol. I, in two parts published as Vol. II of the *Annual Report of the American His torical Association for the Year 1919*; Washington, 1924. Vol. II published as the *Annual Report of the American Historical Associa tion for the Year 1922*; Washington, 1928. Vol. III; Austin, 1927.
Bartlett, John R. (ed.). *Records of the Colony of Rhode Island*. 10 vols Providence, Rhode Island, 1856–65.
Binkley, William C. (ed.). *Official Correspondence of the Texan Revo lution, 1835–1836*. 2 vols. New York, D. Appleton-Century Com pany, 1936.
[Borden, Gail]. *Directions for Cooking Borden's Meat Biscuit*. New York, D. Fanshaw, 1855.
———. *Instructions pour cuire, ou apprêter le Biscuit-Viande de Borden* New York, D. Fanshaw, 1855.
———. *Letter of Gail Borden, Jr., to Dr. Ashbel Smith, setting forth a important invention in the preparation of a new article of food termed meat biscuit; and the reply of Dr. Smith thereto; being letter addressed to the American Association for the Promotion o Science, at their semi-annual meeting, to be held at Charleston n March next*. Galveston, Gibson & Cherry, 1850.
———. *The Meat Biscuit· Invented, Patented, and Manufactured by Gai Borden, Jun*. New York, D. Fanshaw, 1851.
British and Foreign State Papers. 141 vols. London, James Ridgway an Sons (and others), 1841–1950.

Burleson, Rufus C. *The Life and Writings of Rufus C. Burleson.* Compiled by Georgia J. Burleson. [N. p.], Georgia J. Burleson, 1901.

Carter, Clarence E. (ed.). *The Territory of Mississippi, 1809–1817.* (Vol. VI in *The Territorial Papers of the United States.*) Washington, United States Printing Office, 1938.

[Cramer, Zadock]. *The Navigator.* Pittsburgh, Cramer & Spear, 1824.

Dallam, James W. (comp.). *Opinions of the Supreme Court of Texas from 1840 to 1844 Inclusive.* St. Louis, The Gilbert Book Company, 1881.

Dewees, W. B. *Letters from an Early Settler of Texas.* Louisville, Kentucky, Morton & Griswold, 1852.

Documents Connected with the Late Controversy between Gen. T. J. Chambers, of Texas, and Messrs. Wilson & Postlethwaite, of Kentucky. Louisville, Kentucky, Prentice & Weissinger, 1836.

Elgin City Directory for 1881–1882. Chicago, Holland's Directory Publishing Company, 1880.

Flint, Timothy. *Recollections of the Last Ten Years.* Boston, Cummings, Hilliard, and Company, 1826.

Gammel, H. P. N. (comp.). *The Laws of Texas, 1822–1897.* 10 vols. Austin, Gammel Book Company, 1898.

Garrison, George P. (ed.). *Diplomatic Correspondence of the Republic of Texas.* 3 vols. Washington, Government Printing Office, 1908.

Gulick, Charles A., Jr., and others (eds.). *The Papers of Mirabeau Buonaparte Lamar.* 6 vols. Austin, A. C. Baldwin & Sons, 1920–27.

Hatch, Joel, Jr. *Town of Sherburne.* Utica, New York, Curtiss & White, 1862.

Kane, Elisha Kent. *Arctic Explorations.* 2 vols. Philadelphia, Childs and Peterson, 1856.

——. *The United States Grinnell Expedition in Search of Sir John Franklin.* New York, Blakeman & Company, 1857.

Lindley, Harlow (ed.). *Indiana as Seen by Early Travellers.* Indianapolis, Indiana Historical Commission, 1916.

Lubbock, Francis R. *Six Decades in Texas.* Austin, Ben C. Jones & Company, 1900.

Mansfield, E. D. *Personal Memories.* Cincinnati, Robert Clarke & Company, 1879.

Minutes of a Called Session of the United Baptist Association . . . 1842. Washington, Texas, Thomas Johnson, 1843.

Minutes of the Eighth Annual Meeting of the Union Baptist Association. [N. p., 1847?]

Minutes of the Fifth Anniversary Meeting of the Union Baptist Association. Washington, Texas, The Vindicator Office, 1844.

Minutes of the First Session of the Union Baptist Association. Houston, Telegraph Press, 1840.

Minutes of the Fourth Anniversary Meeting of the Union Baptist Association. Washington, Texas, Thomas Johnson, 1844.

Minutes of the Ninth Anniversary of the Union Baptist Association. [N. p., 1848?]

Minutes of the Ninth Anniversary of the Union Baptist Association. Huntsville, Texas, The Texas Banner, 1849.

Minutes of the Sixth Annual Meeting of the Union Baptist Association. LaGrange, Texas, Intelligencer Office, 1845.

Olmsted, Frederick L. *A Journey Through Texas.* New York, Dix, Edwards & Co., 1857.

Parker, A[mos] A[ndrew]. *Trip to the West and Texas.* Concord, New Hampshire, William White, 1836.

Santa Anna, Antonio López de. "Manifesto Relative to His Operations in the Texas Campaign and His Capture," Carlos Eduardo Castañeda (ed. and trans.), *The Mexican Side of the Texan Revolution.* Dallas, P. L. Turner Company, 1928.

Smither, Harriet (ed.). *Journals of the Sixth Congress of the Republic of Texas, 1841–1842.* 3 vols. [Austin], Texas Library and Historical Commission, 1945.

Smithwick, Noah. *The Evolution of a State.* Austin, Gammel Book Company, 1900.

Thwaites, Reuben G. (ed.). *Early Western Travels, 1748–1846.* 32 vols. Cleveland, The Arthur H. Clark Company, 1904–1907.

Trollope, [Frances]. *Domestic Manners of the Americans.* New York, 1832.

Vassar, Thomas. *The Divine Ideal of a Christian Life.* Brewster, New York, Putnam County Standard Print, 1875.

Whitehead, William A., and others (eds.). *Documents Relating to the Colonial History of the State of New Jersey.* 35 vols. Newark and Paterson, New Jersey, 1881–1902.

Williams, Amelia W., and Eugene C. Barker (eds.). *The Writings of Sam Houston, 1813–1863.* 8 vols. Austin, The University of Texas Press, 1938–43.

Williams, Charles R. (ed.). *Diary and Letters of Rutherford Birchard Hayes.* 2 vols. Columbus, The Ohio State Archaeological and Historical Society, 1922.

Bibliography

Winkler, Ernest W. (ed.). *Secret Journals of the Senate, Republic of Texas, 1836–1845.* [Austin], Austin Printing Company, 1911.

PERIODICALS

Barker, Eugene C. (ed). "Journal of the Permanent Council (October 11–27, 1835)," *Quarterly of the Texas State Historical Association,* Vol. VII, No. 4 (April, 1904), 249–78.

Castañeda, Carlos E. (trans.). "Statistical Report on Texas by Juan N. Almonte," *Southwestern Historical Quarterly,* Vol. XXVIII, No. 3 (January, 1925), 177–221.

Flint, Timothy (ed.). *Western Monthly Review.* 3 vols. Cincinnati, E. H. Flint, 1828–30.

Food and Health (December 15, 1881), 6–7.

Harwood, Frances. "Colonel Amasa Turner's Reminiscences of Galveston," *Quarterly of the Texas State Historical Association,* Vol. III, No 1 (July, 1899), 44–48.

"Notes on Texas," *The Hesperian; or, Western Monthly Magazine,* Vol. I, No. 5 (September, 1838), 350–60, Vol. I, No. 6 (October, 1838), 428–40; Vol. II, No. 1 (November, 1838), 30–39; Vol. II, No. 2 (December, 1838), 109–18, Vol. II, No. 3 (January, 1839), 189–99; Vol. II, No. 4 (February, 1839), 288–93, Vol. II, No. 5 (March, 1839), 359–67; Vol. II, No. 6 (April, 1839), 417–26.

Red, William S. (ed.). "Allen's Reminiscences of Texas, 1838–1842," *Southwestern Historical Quarterly,* Vol. XVII, No. 3 (January, 1914), 283–305; Vol. XVIII, No. 3 (January, 1915), 287–304.

——. (ed). "Extracts from the Diary of W. Y. Allen, 1838–1839," *Southwestern Historical Quarterly,* Vol. XVII, No. 1 (July, 1913), 43–60.

Scientific American, Vol. VII, No. 23 (February 21, 1852), Vol. VII, No. 33 (May 1, 1852); Vol. VII, No. 41 (June 26, 1852), Vol. VIII, No. 42 (July 2, 1853), Vol. III, No. 1 (July 2, 1860), Vol. VI, No. 22 (May 31, 1862); Vol. XXX, No. 5 (January 31, 1874).

[Smith, Ashbel]. "Manufacturers for the South—Gail Borden's Meat Biscuit Factory, Texas," *DeBow's Review,* Vol. X, No. 5 (May, 1851), 589–91.

Worth, Gorham A. "Recollections of Cincinnati," *Quarterly Publication of the Historical and Philosophical Society of Ohio,* Vol. XI, No. 1 (1916), 5–48.

SECONDARY SOURCES

THESES

(Unless otherwise indicated, all theses are in the University of Texas Library, Austin, Texas)

Armstrong, Siddie Robson. "Chapters in the Early Life of Samuel May Williams, 1795-1836." M. A., 1929.

Brown, Alma Howell. "The Consular Service of the Republic of Texas." M. A., 1928.

Crane, Robert Edward Lee, Jr. "The Administration of the Customs Service in the Republic of Texas." M. A., 1939.

Mixon, Ruby. "William Barret Travis, His Life and Letters." M. A., 1930.

Muncie, Emery O. "A History of Jefferson County, Indiana." M. A (Indiana University), 1932.

Roy, Addie. "History of *The Telegraph and Texas Register*, 1835-1846." M. A., 1931.

BOOKS AND PAMPHLETS

Albach, James R. (comp.). *Annals of the West.* Pittsburgh, W. S. Haven, 1856.

Ambler, Charles H. *A History of Transportation in the Ohio Valley.* Glendale, California, The Arthur H. Clark Company, 1932.

The American Annual Cyclopedia and Register of Important Events of the Year 1874. Vol. XIV. New York, D. Appleton and Company, 1875.

Armstrong, Zella (comp.). *Notable Southern Families.* 2 vols. Chattanooga, The Lookout Publishing Company, 1922.

Audubon, Mrs. John J. (ed.). *The Life of John James Audubon.* New York, G. P. Putnam's Sons, 1901.

Baillio, F. B. *A History of the Texas Press Association.* Dallas, Southwestern Printing Company, 1916.

Baker, William M. *The Life and Labours of the Rev. Daniel Baker, D. D.* Philadelphia, William S. and Alfred Martien, 1859

———. *A Year Worth Living.* Boston, Lee and Shepard, 1878.

Baldwin, Leland D. *The Keelboat Age on Western Waters.* Pittsburgh, University of Pittsburgh Press, 1941.

Bancroft, Hubert Howe. *History of the North Mexican States and Texas.* 2 vols. San Francisco, The History Company, 1889.

Barker, Eugene C. *Finances of the Texas Revolution.* Boston, Ginn & Company, 1904.

——. *The Life of Stephen F. Austin, Founder of Texas, 1793-1836.* Dallas, Cokesbury Press, 1925.

——. *Mexico and Texas, 1821-1835.* Dallas, P. L. Turner and Company, 1928.

Bayne, Martha C. *County at Large.* Poughkeepsie, New York, The Women's City and County Club with Vassar College, 1937.

Benét, Stephen Vincent. *Western Star.* New York, Rinehart & Company, 1943.

[Berney, Alfred]. *The Mystery of Living.* [N. p.], 1868.

Berry, Thomas Senior. *Western Prices Before 1861.* Cambridge, Massachusetts, Harvard University Press, 1943.

The Biographical Record of Kane County, Illinois. Chicago, The S. J. Clarke Publishing Company, 1898.

Blair, Walter, and Franklin J. Meine. *Mike Fink, King of Mississippi Keelboatmen.* New York, Henry Holt and Company, 1933.

Borden, John G. *Dairyman's Ten Commandments.* Walkill, New York, 1884.

Bronson, Elliott B. *A New England Village Green.* [N. p.], 1914.

Brown, John Henry. *History of Texas.* 2 vols. St. Louis, L. E. Daniell, 1892.

——. *Life and Times of Henry Smith, the First American Governor of Texas.* Dallas, A. D. Aldridge & Company, 1887.

Butler, Mann. *A History of the Commonwealth of Kentucky.* Cincinnati, J. A. James and Company, 1836.

Carroll, J. M. *A History of Texas Baptists.* Dallas, Baptist Standard Publishing Company, 1923.

Cincinnati. (American Guide Series.) Cincinnati, The Wiesen-Hart Press, 1943.

Cist, Charles. *Cincinnati in 1841.* Cincinnati [C. Cist], 1841.

Clark, Hiram C. *History of Chenango County.* Norwich, New York, Thompson & Pratt, 1850.

Columbian Exhibit. Chicago, New York Condensed Milk Company, [n. d.].

Commemorative Biographical and Historical Record of Kane County, Illinois. Chicago, Beers, Leggett & Company, 1888.

Condensed Milk for the Use of Families, prepared by the American Condensed Milk Company. New York, L. H. Biglow & Company, [n. d.].

Dixon, Sam Houston, and Louis Wiltz Kemp. *The Heroes of San Jacinto.* Houston, The Anson Jones Press, 1932.

Dorsey, Florence L. *Master of the Mississippi*. Boston, Houghton Mifflin Company, 1941.

Dutchess County. (American Guide Series.) Philadelphia, The William Penn Association, 1937.

Elgin Today. Elgin, Illinois, Lowrie & Black, 1903.

Ellet, Elizabeth F. *The Women of the American Revolution*. 3 vols. New York, Baker and Scribner, 1848–50.

The Encyclopedia Britannica. Ninth edition. 25 vols. Philadelphia, J. M. Stoddart Company, Limited, 1875–90.

Ford, Henry A., and Kate B. Ford (comp.). *History of Cincinnati, Ohio*. [Cleveland], L. A. Williams & Company, 1881.

Fulmore, Z. T. *The History and Geography of Texas as Told in County Names*. Austin, E. L. Steck, 1915.

Gail Borden, Inventor and Manufacturer. New York, Atlantic Publishing and Engraving Company, [n. d.].

Gambrell, Herbert. *Anson Jones, The Last President of Texas*. Garden City, Doubleday & Company, 1948.

Glenn, Thomas Allen. *Pedigree of Richard Borden*. Philadelphia, 1901.

Goodale, S. L. *A Brief Sketch of Gail Borden, and His Relations to Some Forms of Concentrated Food*. Portland, Maine, B. Thurston & Company, 1872.

Gouge, William M. *The Fiscal History of Texas*. Philadelphia, Lippincott, Grambo, and Company, 1852.

Gray, A. C. "History of the Texas Press," Dudley G. Wooten (ed.), *A Comprehensive History of Texas, 1685 to 1897*. 2 vols. Dallas, W. G Scarff, 1898.

Hall, James. *The West Its Commerce and Navigation*. Cincinnati, H. W. Derby & Company, 1848.

Hansard's Parliamentary Debates. Series 3. 356 vols. London, T. C. Hansard (and others), 1831–91.

Hastings, George E. *The Life and Works of Francis Hopkinson*. Chicago, The University of Chicago Press, 1926.

Hehner, Otto. "Food Preservation," *The Encyclopedia Britannica* (eleventh edition). 29 vols. New York, The Encyclopedia Britannica Company, 1910–11.

Historical and Genealogical Record, Dutchess and Putnam Counties, New York. 2 vols. Poughkeepsie, New York, Oxford Publishing Company, 1912.

Historical Sketch of the First Baptist Church of Galveston, Texas. Galveston, News Steam Job Press, 1871.

History of Borden's Milk Patent. Portland, Maine, B. Thurston & Company, 1872.

History of the City of Elgin. Chicago, Republican Book and Job Office, 1867.

Hogan, William Ransom. *The Republic of Texas. A Social and Economic History.* Norman, University of Oklahoma Press, 1946.

Hogeland, A. (comp.). *Centennial Report of the Mineral and Agricultural Resources of the State of Kentucky.* Louisville, Louisville Courier-Journal, 1877.

Hollingshead, R. S., and H. T. Williamson. *International Trade in Concentrated Milk.* Washington, Government Printing Office, 1928.

Hulbert, Archer B. *The Paths of Inland Commerce.* New Haven, Yale University Press, 1921.

Hunziker, Otto F. *Condensed Milk and Milk Powder.* Lafayette, Indiana, Otto F. Hunziker, 1914.

Indiana. (American Guide Series.) New York, Oxford University Press, 1941.

Industrial America; or, Manufactures and Inventors of the United States. New York, Atlantic Publishing and Engraving Company, 1876.

James, Marquis. *The Raven; a Biography of Sam Houston.* Indianapolis, Bobbs-Merrill Company, 1929.

Johnson, Allen (ed.). *Dictionary of American Biography.* 20 vols. New York, Charles Scribner's Sons, 1928–36.

Johnson, Frank W. *A History of Texas and Texans.* 5 vols. Edited by Eugene C. Barker. Chicago, The American Historical Society, 1914.

Kemp, Louis Wiltz. *The Signers of the Texas Declaration of Independence.* Houston, The Anson Jones Press, 1944.

Kennedy, William. *Texas· The Rise, Progress, and Prospects of the Republic of Texas.* 2 vols. London, 1841.

Kentucky. (American Guide Series.) New York, Harcourt, Brace and Company, 1939.

Kirkpatrick, John E. *Timothy Flint.* Cleveland, The Arthur H Clark Company, 1911.

Konkle, Burton A. *Joseph Hopkinson.* Philadelphia, University of Pennsylvania Press, 1931.

Lloyd, James T. *Steamboat Directory.* Cincinnati, James T. Lloyd & Company, 1836.

Lloyd, W. Alvin. *Steamboat and Railroad Guide.* New Orleans, W. Alvin Lloyd, 1857.

Looscan, Adele B. [Mrs. M.]. "The History and Evolution of the Texas Flag," Dudley G. Wooten (ed.), *A Comprehensive History of Texas, 1685 to 1897.* 2 vols. Dallas, W. G. Scarff, 1898.

McBryde, C. N. "Commercial Methods of Canning Meats," United States Department of Agriculture *Yearbook, 1911.*

McMeekin, Isabel McLennan. *Louisville, The Gateway City.* New York, Julian Messner, Inc., 1946.

Mallary, C. D. *Memoirs of Elder Jesse Mercer.* New York, Lewis Colby, 1844.

Mansfield, Edward D. *Memoirs of the Life and Services of Daniel Drake.* Cincinnati, Applegate & Company, 1855.

Mansfield, Joseph J. *Life and Achievements of Gail Borden.* Washington, United States Government Printing Office, 1930.

Martin, Edward W., and Walter Moeller. "Report on Milk and Its Adulterations," *First Annual Report* of the New York State Dairy Commissioner. Albany, Weed, Parsons and Company, 1885.

May, Earl Chapin. *The Canning Clan.* New York, The Macmillan Company, 1937.

Mercer, Jesse. *A History of the Georgia Baptist Association.* Washington, Georgia, 1838.

Miller, Edmund T. *A Financial History of Texas.* Austin, The University of Texas, 1916.

Mitman, Carl W. "Gail Borden," Allen Johnson and others (eds.), *Dictionary of American Biography.* First edition. 20 vols. New York, Charles Scribner's Sons, 1928–36.

Moore, Ike H. "Early Texas Newspapers, 1813–1846," *The Texas Almanac and State Industrial Guide, 1936.* Dallas, A. H. Belo Corporation, 1936.

The National Cyclopedia of American Biography. 35 vols. New York, James T. White and Company, 1893–1949.

Newell, C[hester]. *History of the Revolution in Texas.* New York, Wiley & Putnam, 1838.

Norton, A. B. "History of Journalism in Texas," F. B. Baillio, *A History of the Texas Press Association.* Dallas, Southwestern Printing Company, 1916.

Redford, A. H. *The History of Methodism in Kentucky.* 2 vols. Nashville, Southern Methodist Publishing House, 1870.

Report of the Federal Trade Commission on Milk and Milk Products, 1914–1918. Washington, Government Printing Office, 1921.

Richardson, Rupert N. *Texas, the Lone Star State.* New York, Prentice-Hall, Inc., 1943.

Robinson, Duncan W. *Judge Robert McAlpin Williamson: Texas' Three-Legged Willie.* Austin, Texas State Historical Association, 1948.

Rogers, Lore A., Associates. *Fundamentals of Dairy Science.* New York, Reinhold Publishing Corporation, 1935.

Rothert, Otto A. *The Outlaws of Cave-in-Rock.* Cleveland, The Arthur H. Clark Company, 1924.

Schilling, T. C. *Abstract History of the Mississippi Baptist Association for One Hundred Years.* New Orleans, J. G. Hauser, [1906?].

Sharton, Alexander R., and Harry W. Stenerson. *Accomplishments of Advertising.* New York, The Journal of Commerce and Commercial New York, 1935.

Smith, James H. *History of Chenango and Madison Counties, New York.* Syracuse, D. Mason & Company, 1880.

Smucker, Samuel M. *The Life of Dr. Elisha Kent Kane.* Philadelphia, J. W. Bradley, 1859.

Spalding, M. J. *Sketches of the Early Catholic Missions of Kentucky.* Louisville, B. J. Webb & Brother, [1844].

Specifications and Drawings of Patents Issued . . . for Week Ending October 29, 1872. Washington, Government Printing Office, 1873.

Specifications and Drawings of Patents Issued . . . for Week Ending November 4, 1873. Washington, Government Printing Office, 1873.

Stefansson, Vilhjalmur. *Not by Bread Alone.* New York, The Macmillan Company, 1946.

Stephen, Leslie, and Sidney Lee (eds.). *Dictionary of National Biography.* 63 vols. London, Smith, Elder, & Company, 1885–1900.

Sweet, William W. *Religion on the American Frontier: The Presbyterians.* New York, Harper & Brothers, 1936.

Thrall, Homer S. *A Pictorial History of Texas.* St. Louis, N. D. Thompson & Company, 1879.

United States Department of Commerce. *Stories of American Industry.* Washington, Government Printing Office, 1937.

Weld, Hattie Borden (comp.). *Historical and Genealogical Record . . . of Richard and Joan Borden.* [N. p., 1899?]

Wells, Levi. "Condensed and Desiccated Milk," United States Department of Agriculture *Yearbook, 1912.*

Wharton, Clarence R. *Gail Borden, Pioneer.* San Antonio, The Naylor Company, 1941.

———. *Wharton's History of Fort Bend County.* San Antonio, The Naylor Company, 1939.

Wilson, James Grant, and John Fiske (eds.). *Appleton's Cyclopedia of American Biography.* 7 vols. New York, D. Appleton and Company, 1894-1900.
Wooten, Dudley G. (ed.). *A Comprehensive History of Texas, 1685 to 1897.* 2 vols. Dallas, William G. Scarff, 1898.

PERIODICALS

Arthur, Dora Fowler. "Jottings from the Old Journal of Littleton Fowler," *Quarterly of the Texas State Historical Association,* Vol. II, No. 2 (October, 1898), 73-84.
Barker, Eugene C. "General Arthur Goodall Wavell and Wavell's Colony in Texas, A Note," *Southwestern Historical Quarterly,* Vol. XLVII, No. 3 (January, 1944), 253-55.
———. "Notes on Early Texas Newspapers, 1819-1836," *Southwestern Historical Quarterly,* Vol. XXI, No. 2 (October, 1917), 127-44.
The Borden Eagle, May, 1922 to August, 1923.
"Borden Milk—Yesterday and Today," *Radford Grocery News* (Abilene, Texas), Vol. IV, No. 10 (May, 1926), 2-9.
Bugbee, Lester G. "The Old Three Hundred," *Quarterly of the Texas State Historical Association,* Vol. I, No. 2 (October, 1897), 108-17.
"Condensed Milk First Made in Torrington," *The Lure of the Litchfield Hills,* Vol. I, No. 1 (May, 1929), 3, 17-20.
Crane, Frank. "The Borden Company," *Current Opinion,* Vol. LXXVII, No. 2 (August, 1924), 233-40.
Curti, Merle. "America at the World Fairs, 1851-1893," *The American Historical Review,* Vol. LV, No. 4 (July, 1950), 833-56.
The Dairy Messenger (April, 1892), 36-37.
Dienst, Alex. "The New Orleans Newspaper Files of the Texas Revolutionary Period," *Quarterly of the Texas State Historical Association,* Vol. IV, No. 2 (October, 1900), 140-51.
Drake, Daniel. "Notices Concerning Cincinnati," *Quarterly Publication of the Historical and Philosophical Society of Ohio,* Vol. III, (1908), 1-62.
Dyer, J. O. "Galveston as Seen in Earlier Days," Galveston *Daily News,* October 1, 1920.
———. "The Pioneer Texas Farmer," Galveston *Daily News,* April 1, 1923.
Franklin, Ethel Mary. "Joseph Baker," *Southwestern Historical Quarterly,* Vol. XXXVI, No. 2 (October, 1932), 130-43.
Frantz, Joe B. "Gail Borden: Amite County's First Inventor," *The Journal of Mississippi History,* Vol. XI, No. 4 (October, 1949), 223-30.

————. "Gail Borden as a Businessman," *Bulletin of The Business Historical Society*, Vol. XXII, Nos. 4–6 (December, 1948), 123–33.

————. (ed.). "Moses Lapham· His Life and Some Selected Correspondence," *Southwestern Historical Quarterly*, Vol. LIV, No. 3 (January, 1951), 324–32, Vol. LIV, No. 4 (April, 1951), 462–75.

Fulmore, Z. T. "The Annexation of Texas and the Mexican War," *Quarterly of the Texas State Historical Association*, Vol. 5, No. 1 (July, 1901), 28–48.

Garrison, George P. "Another Texas Flag," *Quarterly of the Texas State Historical Association*, Vol. III, No. 3 (January, 1900), 170–76.

Harper's Weekly, Vol. XXVIII, No. 1435 (June 21, 1884), 391.

Hendrix, Roberta C. "Some Gail Borden Letters," *Southwestern Historical Quarterly*, Vol. LI, No. 2 (October, 1947), 131–42.

Holsapple, Mildred. "The Disappearance of New London," *Indiana Magazine of History*, Vol. XXXI, No. 1 (March, 1935), 10–13.

Hopkins, J. "A Pioneer's Ambition and a World Benefaction," *The American Monthly Illustrated Review of Reviews*, Vol. XXXIII, No. 6 (June, 1906), 37–44.

The Journal of the Royal Geographical Society, Vol. XLVII (1877), cxlviii–cl.

Kemp, Louis Wiltz. "The Capitol (?) at Columbia," *Southwestern Historical Quarterly*, Vol. XLVIII, No. 1 (July, 1944), 3–9.

Looscan, Adele B. "Harris County, 1822–1845," *Southwestern Historical Quarterly*, Vol. XVIII, No. 3 (January, 1915), 261–86; Vol. XIX, No. 1 (July, 1915), 37–64.

McMurtrie, Douglas C. "Pioneer Printing in Texas," *Southwestern Historical Quarterly*, Vol. XXXV, No. 3 (January, 1932), 173–93.

Molyneaux, Peter. "Borden's Dream Comes True," *The Texas Monthly*, Vol. III, No. 3 (March, 1929), 295–311.

Muir, Andrew Forest. "The Destiny of Buffalo Bayou," *Southwestern Historical Quarterly*, Vol. XLVII, No. 2 (October, 1943), 91–106.

Offord, John A. "A Humanitarian Industry and Its Half Century of Development," *New York Observer* (January 7, 1909), 21–23.

Reed, O. E. "Gail Borden," *Successful Farming* (August, 1929).

Sampson, Francis A. "The New Madrid and Other Earthquakes in Missouri," *The Mississippi Valley Historical Association Proceedings*, Vol. VI (1912–13), 218–38.

Schutze, Julius. "Die Geschichte von Colorado County, Texas," *Texas Vorwarts*, June 19–July 10, 1896.

Sinks, Julia Lee. "Editors and Newspapers of Fayette County," *Quarterly of the Texas State Historical Association*, Vol. I, No. 1 (July, 1897), 34-37.

Steen, Ralph W. "Analysis of the Work of the General Council, Provisional Government of Texas, 1835-1836," *Southwestern Historical Quarterly*, Vol. XLI, No. 3 (January, 1938), 225-40.

Talbot, Gayle. "John Rice Jones," *Southwestern Historical Quarterly*, Vol. XXXV, No. 2 (October, 1931), 146-50.

Winkler, E. W. "Membership of the 1833 Convention of Texas," *Southwestern Historical Quarterly*, Vol. XLV, No. 3 (January, 1942), 255-57.

———. "The Seat of Government of Texas," *Quarterly of the Texas State Historical Association*, Vol. X, No. 3 (January, 1907), 185-245.

Index

[Unless otherwise noted, the Borden referred to below is always Gail Borden]

Abbotts, L., printer. 71–72, 72 n.
Abolition 170
Acadia. see Nova Scotia
Adams, President John: 56
Adams, President John Quincy. 56
Alamo. 64, fall of, 90, 104–105, Santa Anna at, 99, apparent trap, 101
Albany, N Y 11
Aldridge, W B 131
Algeria 213
Allegheny River 24 n., 25
Allen, Augustus C helps found Houston, 122, helps found Galveston City Company, 151
Allen, J M 152, 158–59
Allen, John K. helps found Houston, 122, security for Borden, 131, helps found Galveston City Company, 151
Almonte, Colonel Juan N. 70, 102
Amenia, N Y.: 252
American Association for the Advancement of Science 205, 211
American Journal of Pharmacy, quoted 264
American Medical Association 205
American Revolution· 9 ff., 21, 92, 163
Amite County, Miss. 52, 54, names Borden surveyor, 55, 60, replaces Borden, 58, milk experiments in, 222
Amite River 51 f
Amory, Nathaniel 216
Amsterdam, Netherlands 215
Anáhuac, Texas 63 f, 75, 77
Andrews, Stephen Pearl, abolitionist 170
Annexation of Texas 142, 162, 191
Appert, François 224, 224 n.
Appert, Nicolas 224 n.
Apples, experiments with 262 n, see also Borden, Gail
Archer, Branch T. 142
Arkansas, territory of 150
Armour, Philip D 242, 267
Armstrong, H F, merchant 122

Astor, John Jacob 56
Audubon, John J describes perch, 27 n., visits Galveston, 129 f.
Augusta, Ky 31
Augusta, Me. 233, 260
Austin, Henry 75
Austin, Nat. 22
Austin, Seymour 22
Austin, Stephen F. 89, 95, 97, founds Texas, 51, 58, 60, 152, headquarters, 61, convention of 1833, 67 f , to Mexico, 68, 72, arrest, 69, returns to Texas, 79, committee of correspondence, 80, army colonel, 84, 87; candidate for president, 111 f., certifies Borden petitions, 118, death, 121 f., tribute to Borden, 122
Austin, Texas 158, Borden visits, 161, 270, named Texas capital, 161 n , John P. Borden protects, 162
Australia meat biscuit prospects, 215, milk order from, 268

Bache, Dr. Alexander Dallas 211
Baker, land seeker 75
"Baker and Bordens": 73, 84 f , 88, 90, 94 ff.
Baker, Joseph 86 f., called "Don Jose," 70, contemplates newspaper, 71 ff., 76, joins army, 94, 106, leaves Telegraph, 109 n , see also Telegraph and Texas Register
Baker, Mosely 84, 118, militia captain, 101, 106, helps found Galveston City Company, 151, friends of, 275
Baker, Rev. William Mumford 191, 195, describes Borden, 188–89, terraqueous machine, 197–200, on condensed milk, 223
Baltimore Condensed Milk Company, licensed 260
Baltimore flats 45, 45 n.
Baltimore, Md 22, 45, 147, 183 n
Baptism 22, 166, 192–93
Baptist church 9, 39, 192, in Kentucky, 35, in Indiana, 42 f , in Mississippi,

54ff., Bordens belong to, 162, Silas Mercer joins, 163, Jesse Mercer in, 163–66, Huckins as missionary, 164–66, First Baptist Church of Seneca Falls, N. Y., 165, Texas Baptist Education Society, 167, Union Baptist Association, 167, First Baptist Church of Galveston, 169–70, 192, 194, Sam Houston joins, 193n, 230, Madison Avenue Baptist Church of New York, 239, in New York, 247, objects to cross, 252, African Baptist Church of Galveston, 271

Barlow, C., London attorney 226
Bartlett, Jesse 71
Barton, William 161n.
Bastrop County, Texas 217
Bastrop, Texas 71, 98, Eli Mercer represents, 65, favors peace, 77, sawmill established, 269, Borden rents in, 270
Bates school, Miss 54f.
Bates, William 56
"Battle of the Kegs" 9n.
Baudin, Commodore 160
Baylor Female College 167
Baylor, R. E. B 167
Baylor University 167
Beaufort, No. Car 8
Beaumont, Texas 92
Beaver, Pa. 27
Bedford, Pa. 24n.
Beecher, Rev. Henry Ward 247
Beef extract 262, von Liebig product, 264, success, 265, 273, site transferred, 269f, *see also* Borden, Gail
Bermuda 215
Bernon, Gabriel 11
Bessemer, Henry 220n.
Bexar, Texas *see* San Antonio, Texas
Biddle, Nicholas 151
Binghamton, N. Y 22, 24
Bishop, Noah as office boy, 250, reprimanded, 272
Bissell, Ben 235–36
Blennerhassett's Island 29
Bollaert, William 109n., 110n.
Bonaparte, Joseph 10
Bond device 212n
Borden, Amy 48
Borden, Amye 4
Borden and Currie beef extract plant, 264, success, 273, *see also* beef extract *and* Borden, Gail
Borden and Moore created, 123, leave

Columbia, 125, in Houston, 125, dissolved, 127
Borden, Ann (Nancy) 10f.
Borden, Mrs. Augusta (Azuba) F. Stearns birth, 190, marriage, 190, death, 190, 236n, separation, 230–32
Borden, Benjamin (of New Jersey) 7
Borden, Benjamin (of Virginia) 8
Borden, Catherine Carson 168
Borden Company vii–viii, 223n, 244
Borden Condensed Milk Company 260–61
Borden, Denis Woodward 60, 113
Borden, Ellen· 266, 271
Borden, Mrs. Emeline Eno Church marriage to Gail Borden, 253, marriage to Hiram Church, 263, in Bastrop, 270
Borden, England, parish of 4
Borden, Esther 37, 41, 48, 60
Borden, Gail, events in life ancestry, 3ff, birth, 8, 14, childhood, 15ff, education, 15, 35, 41f., baptism and religious activities, 22, 35f., 42, 162–67, 191–93, as surveyor, 34f., 48, 55f, 58, 60f, 69–71, 74–75, 98, 122, 233, young manhood, 43ff, trips, 48ff, 58, 167, 205, 209ff., 235–36, 263f, 268ff, land sales and purchases, 48, 111, 160, 233, 271n., 274n., militia captain, 49, health, 49, 113, 218, 273–75, teacher, 49, 53–55, 61, 86, description of, 49, 173–74, 188–89, 239, 269, 271, rescues Negro, 50, in Mississippi, 51–59, marries Penelope Mercer Borden, 56f, buys slaves, 57, as farmer, 61, residences in Texas, 62ff, 106ff, 111ff, 124ff, 129ff, secretary citizens' meeting, 64; delegate to convention of 1833, 67f., land office duties, 69–72, 74–75, collections agent, 75, 97f., prepares map, 76, on Austin's return, 79, on committee of correspondence, 80, in Texas revolution, 82–109, on committee of safety, 82–84, secretary Permanent Council, 89, temperance activities, 92, 133, 159, 194, presents flag, 102, pledges land, 104, 112, property loss, 109; advises Austin on candidacy, 111f, helps plat Houston, 122, Galveston collectorship, first term, 129–49, named to collectorship, 131, establishes office, 132, writes Treasury Department, 133ff, collections, 134–35, salary, 141, in new customhouse, 135, 138, in storm, 137,

in Galveston, 138–95, supervision of Galveston activities, 139ff., 160, 202, purchases cattle, 142, 170, quarrels with Ashbel Smith, 143–45, dismissal of, 147–49, tribute to, 148–49, rides bull, 155, Galveston City Company agent, 155f., property of, 156f, 162, 170, 196f., 253n, 265, 273, finds water in Galveston, 156f., builds locomotive bathhouse, 157, alderman, 158–59, directs fortifications, 161, 168–69, court trials, 162, 183–84, 197, reappointed Galveston collectorship, 167, 175–80, executor for Grayson, 167, trustee Texas Baptist Education Society, 167, clerk of church, 169f, exchequer bills returned, 176ff., resignation refused, 177f, obtains revenue cutter, 178, resignation accepted, 179f, characterized by Houston, 181–82, customs funds controversy, 182–87, correspondence with Ochiltree, 185–86, philosophy of, 189, 199, 252, second marriage of, 190f., 231–32, jury duty, 191, yellow fever cure, 195, as doctor, 217f., trouble with daughter Philadelphia, 230–31, third marriage of, 232, 253, 263, in Civil War, 256–58, 274, fights dysentery, 261, comparison with Vanderbilt and Rockefeller, 262, and beef extract, 262, 273, philanthropies of, 265, 271, 274, builds house in Texas, 273, death of, 275, epitaph, 276, last act, 276n, will probated, 276n

——, as publisher of *Telegraph and Texas Register* planned, 71–73, 75–76, press purchased, 76n., editor and publisher, 82ff., comparison with Paine, 92f, Texas Declaration of Independence, 96f., editorial leadership, 96, leaves San Felipe, 106, at Harrisburg, 106ff.; bills Texas government, 110, seeks new press, 110, at Columbia, 111ff, offers for sale, 113, finances, 118–19, joined by Moore, 123ff, sells interest, 126f, tribute by Moore, 127n, 128n

——, inventions of locomotive bathhouse, 157, condensation schemes, 189, 198, 216, 222ff, revolving table, 190, steamboat, 191–92, meat biscuit, 195, 200, 203ff, terraqueous machine, 197–200, condensed milk, 216, 222ff.

——— and meat biscuit mentioned, 195, 200, patented, 203, 210, preparation, 204, 214, partnership, 204ff., factory description, 206f., financing, 207f., 219, debts, 208, 213f, 219, exhibits in London, 209f, contracts, 210, Waco report, 211f, wins gold medal, 212, prospects, 213ff., meets Grinnell, 219, end of, 219, reasons biscuit failed, 220–21

——— and condensed milk experiments, 216, 222ff., discovery, 222–24, financing, 226, 232ff, patent sought, 226–29, patents received, 229, partnerships, 232ff, patent rights, 233, 236–37, Wolcottville factory, 234ff., New York depot established, 234–35, first Burrville factory, 236–38, meets Milbank, 238–40, second Burrville factory, 241 ff, rules for dairymen, 243–45, industry founded, 243–45, first advertisement, 245–46, Wassaic factory, 249ff., preparation, 251, factory description, 251, facilities expanded, 254ff, first army order of, 254–55, patent reissues, 258–59, production problems, 259f, Winsted plant, 261, Elgin factory, 263–64, recession of 1866, 267, Elgin reorganization, 268

Borden, Gail (grandfather) 11, 15, 47
Borden, Gail, Sr 12f, 15, 18, 25, 41; birth, 11, land sales and purchases, 12, 16, 23, homemaking, 16, in Kentucky, 31ff., surveyor, 34f., in Indiana, 38ff, petitioner for tobacco commissioners, 44, writes mother, 47–48, manufacturer, 49n, moves to Texas, 58, blacksmith, 60, at Fort Bend, 105, remarriage, 167–68, temperance activities, 193–94, Texas farmer, 202, relations with Gail, Jr, 232, lends money, 253, death, 258, 266
Borden, Henry 4
Borden, Henry Lee· 266, birth, 66, baptism, 193, ranching, 230, 232, military career, 257, joins father, 268, Texas home, 270, child born, 271, visited by father, 275
Borden, Joan 3, 5
Borden, Joane 4
Borden, John (second American generation) 6f.
Borden, John (third American generation) 7ff.
Borden, John (fourth American generation) 9

Borden, John Gail 232, birth, 171, temperance work, 194, education, 225, 230, 261, return to Texas, 236, accompanies women workers, 252, coexecutor of estate, 253, military career, 257, holds stock, 260 n., father's companion, 266, recession of 1866, 267, assistant superintendent Wassaic and Brewster, 268, inferior milk sent, 269, child born, 271, upholds Bishop, 272, forms bank, 273

Borden, John Petit. 24, 88, birth, 15, education, 48, 70, 72, growth, 60, makes survey, 71, contemplates newspaper, 71, 73, 76, military career, 101, 109 n., 168 n., 274, on vigilance committee, 162, commissioner General Land Office, 162, executor for Grayson, 167, law office, 170, county judge, 202, on meat biscuit, 213, on Philadelphia Borden's stepchildren, 231, home in Texas, 270, visits Gail Borden, 275

Borden, Joseph (of Rhode Island) 7

Borden, Joseph (of New Jersey): 9–11

Borden, Mrs. Louisa R. 165, 275

Borden Manufacturing Company 269

Borden, Mary (of New Jersey). 11

Borden, Mary (of Texas) 59, 66, 69

Borden, Mary Jane· birth, 167, baptism, 193, education, 225, 230 f., accompanies father, 236

Borden, Mrs Mary Knowlton. 11, 47–48

Borden, Mathew (of England). 4

Borden, Mathew (of Rhode Island) 5 f.

Borden Meat Preserving Company 274 n.

Borden, Mercy 7

Borden, Morton Quinn 126 n, 194

Borden, Oliver 9 f.

Borden, Paschal Pavolo birth, 15, childhood, 26, 34, health, 48, 68, 218, blacksmith, 60, 202, at San Jacinto, 109 n., Columbia merchant, 122, on Philadelphia Borden's marriage, 231, death, 266

Borden, Patience 8

Borden, Peace 8

Borden, Mrs Penelope Mercer 66, 87, 265 f, in Mississippi, 56–58, moves to Texas, 59, in Galveston, 152, 161, 173 f., baptism, 162–66, birth of daughter, 167, birth of son, 171, illness and

death, 171–74, 195, characterization, 172–74, 190

Borden, Perry 9

Borden, Mrs. Philadelphia Wheeler. marriage, 11, homemaking, 12 ff, 41, birth of children, 14, 15, 37, health, 48, in Indiana, 49 n, death, 60

Borden, Miss Philadelphia Wheeler 266, birth, 126 n., baptism, 193, first marriage, 230–32, remarriage, 236, family, 270–71

Borden, Richard (first American generation). founds family, 3, 6, 14, ancestry, 4, estate, 4, helps found Portsmouth, 5, surveyor, 5, 8, 34

Borden, Richard (third American generation) 6

Borden, Richard (fifth American generation) 10

Borden, Sir Robert Laird 9

Borden, Samuel 8 f.

Borden, Stephen F. Austin. 152 n, 171

Borden, Texas named, 269 f, Borden house at, 273, philanthropies at, 274, first railroad, 274 n, death of Gail Borden, 275

Borden, Thomas (of England) 4

Borden, Thomas (of Rhode Island) 8

Borden, Thomas Henry 193, birth, 15, childhood, 26, 33 f., travels, 48, 61, 110 f., 119, 132, 134, 274, in Indiana, 49 ff., manufacturer, 49 n., 202, Texas fever, 52, member Austin's colony, 57 f, first wife, 60, 113, land activities, 60, 104, 111–12, surveyor, 60, 122–24, 162, on Texas conditions, 66, names slaves, 68, in storm, 69, *Telegraph and Texas Register*, 72 f, 86–88, 113, 123, kills Jesse Thompson, 73 f, military career, 94, 100, Harrisburg, 108, property losses, 109 f, moves to Columbia, 111, helps lay out Houston, 122–24, buys lumber, 131, home in Galveston, 152, 165, rides bull, 155, terraqueous machine, 197, grocer, 266, mortgage, 275

Borden, William (of England) 4

Borden, William (of Rhode Island) 8

Bordentown, N J 9–10

Boston, Mass. 11, 75, 152, 242

Boston Medical and Surgical Journal, quoted 264

Bowie, James 67

Bradburn, Colonel John Davis 63 f, 129

Brazoria, Texas 64, 72, 75, 76, 112, ships

at, 66, Austin dinner, 79, ball at, 114f, suggested Texas capital, 114, 124, Perry at, 142

Brazos River 61f., 68, 73, 77, 83, 90, 101, 233

Bremond, Paul 135

Brewster, N Y 265–68, grogshops, 194, Borden factory, 261, plight of factory, 267, holds record, 272, excursions to, 273

Brewsters Station, N. Y see Brewster, N Y.

Bridge, James, Borden's partner 233–37, 260

Bridgers, William B 70

Brigham, Asa 133–34

Brightman, Emeline 169

Bristol Ferry, R I 6

British War of 1812, 35, cotton agency at Galveston, 162, navy, 209, 215

Brockton, Mass 244

Bronson, Elliott 204n.

Bronson, Theron 261

Brooklyn, N. Y 246, 273, see also New York, N. Y.

Brower, John H arranges credit, 207 ff., Texas consul, 207n, advises Borden, 208ff., lends money to Borden, 213, 219

Brown, George· 115

Brown, John 229, 235

Brown, John Henry 67

Brownsville, Pa 25

Bryan, Guy M. 161

Bryan, Moses Austin 160

Buckley, Elijah. 252

Buckley, Frank 252 ·

Buckley, Noah 252

Burke, Edmund 21

Burleson, Rev Rufus C, quoted on Borden as a farmer, 61, on Borden's newspaper contribution, 127, on baptism, 192–93, on Borden in court, 197, on condensed milk discovery, 223

Burnes, Miss Honora 234, 237, 250–51

Burnes, Martin· 234, 237, 250

Burnes, Richard, 234, 237, 250, 252

Burnet County, Texas 217

Burnet, David G convention of 1833, 67f., judge in Thompson slaying, 74, president of Texas, 106, 110

Burnett, Samuel 46

Burnham, James G. 167

Burr, Aaron 29

Burr, Benjamin: 237

Burr, John 237, 247

Burr, Mrs. John 237

Burr, Milo 237, 247

Burritt, Rev Blackleach 15 n, 21

Burrville, Conn. 250, 256, 260, first Borden factory, 237–38, second Borden factory, 241ff

Bustamante, Anastasio 62, 64

Butler, Pollard 53

Butterworth, Moses 7

Cade, Jack 4

Caffrey, builder 135

Caldwell, John C 65

Calhoun, John C 153

California 202, 214

Camp Leon, Texas 168n.

Canal project 203

Capitol Hotel, Houston 274

Captain Taylor Tavern, Wolcottville, Conn 234

Carl, Prince of Solms-Braunfels 170

Carrollton, Ky 37

Carson, Catherine see Borden, Catherine Carson

Caruthers, messenger to Borden 71

Caster, Diman 68

Catskill Mountains 273

Cave, W, surveyor 71

Chaffin, John 115

Charleston, So Car 205

Chenango County, N Y 20, 22–23

Chenango River 12, 15n, 18, 22, 24

Chicago, Ill 262

Chicago Medical Society 263

Chicago, Milwaukee, and St Paul railway 238

Childress, George C 104

Cholera 68

Church, Alfred B helps give library, 253, superintendent at Elgin, 268, 272, advice to, 273

Church, Mrs Emeline Eno see Borden, Mrs Emeline Eno Church

Church, Hiram 262–63

Church, Samuel M 253

Cincinnati, Ohio 25f, 32, 34, prospects, 33, celebrates end of war, 35, streets, 35, growth, 36–37, Washington visits, 47, Thomas Borden visits, 111, Gail Borden visits, 205, as milk market, 262

Civil War economy during, 241, first engagement, 254, Borden's position, 256ff, 274–75, effects on Borden, 266–67

Clark, Arthur G 223 n.
Clark, George Rogers 33
Clay, Henry. 56, 57, 153
Clay, Nestor 67
Clear Creek, Texas· 167
Cleveland, Ohio compared with Galveston, 196, possible plant site, 262
Clinton, DeWitt 12
Clinton, George 18
Coahuila y Texas 62, 66f.
Cochrane, James 73–74, 91 n.
Cocke, James H. helps Galveston fortification, 168, suggested by Borden as successor, 180, successor to Borden, 181–82, proposal to Borden, 184, Borden's opinion of, 187
Coffee, experiments with 262 n.
Cold Springs school, Miss. 54
Cole, D. M 263
Cole, James P. 231–32, 247
Colebrook Centre, Conn.· 263
Coles, John P 70
Coles' settlement 84
College of Philadelphia 10
Collins, James Porter 226
Collinsworth, James 146
Colorado River (Texas) overflows, 68, theater of war, 83, 90, surveying site, 98
Colt, Samuel· 153
Colt's revolver 209
Columbia, Texas· 71, 125, peace sentiment, 77, capital of Texas, 111 ff., characteristics of, 113–15, Galveston compared with, 130, pistol factory site, 257
Columbus, Christopher· 115
Columbus, Texas 269–70, 274 n, 275
Commercial and Agricultural Bank, Galveston 196
Committee on Texas Affairs of New Orleans 95
Comstock Lode· 242
Concepción, battle of 114
Concord, Ind. 40
Condensed milk see Borden, Gail and condensed milk
Confederate States of America 254
Congregationalist church 247
Congress, Republic of Texas 114 ff, Borden compliments, 121, members visit Galveston, 142 f., names Borden land commissioner, 160, protection of Galveston, 168, law of July 23, 1842, 176, considers settlement of customs

dispute, 184, opinion of Borden, 186, see also Senate, Republic of Texas
Conklin, George 267
Connecticut 237, 253
Connell, Jesse. 39
Conrad, Charles M. 205 f.
Constitution convention of 1836, Texas 101
Constitution of 1824, Mexico 64, 86, 99
Consultation of 1835. 88
Continental congress 10
Convention of 1832 65–66
Convention of 1833 67–68, 69
Cook, Fred 135
Cooke, Jay 266
Cooperstown, N. Y. 12
Copeland, Fayette 75
Copes, Dr. J. Wilson· 144–45
Cornelius lamps 209
Corpus Christi, Texas 180
Cós, Martín Perfecto de sends messenger to Texas, 77, refuses peace commissioners, 79, lands army, 80, capitulation at San Antonio, 90
Cotten, Godwin Brown, publisher 72, 76 n, 194
Cotton picker, mechanical 230
Cotton press· 170
Covington, Ky. 32 f., 36 ff, platted, 34–35, growth, 37
Cranbrooke, England, parish of 3
Cranston, R. I 9
Crimean War 215 ff.
The Crisis, cited 92–93
Cruger, Jacob W., publisher 126
Cuba 171
Cumberland Gap, route to West 31
Cummings, Miss Rebecca 104
Currency, Texas 162, 176 ff.
Currie, Dr. John H 225, 228 f., 264
Customs collections under Mexico, 63, 77, Department of Brazos, 97–98, 130, at Galveston, 129 f., 161, 176 ff.

Daingerfield, William Henry 179
Dairy industry 243 ff, see also Borden, Gail and condensed milk
Damon, Samuel 71
Dana, Charles 214
Darden, Fannie Baker: 275
Davis, J. J. 170
Declaration of Independence, Texas· 102 ff., 150
Declaration of Independence, United States 10–11

Delaware, colony of 6, 11
Delbrell, Peter, caterer 196
Dennison, Eliphalet, manufacturer 241
Derrick, John 158
Dick engine tools 212 n.
Donner emigrant party 202
Dooley, land applicant 75
Dorsey, Florence L., *Master of the Mississippi.* 47 n.
Drake, Daniel 36–37
Dred Scott decision 229
Duanesburg, N. Y 12
Duck industry in America· 8

"Eagle Brand" label, origin of 266, 266 n.
Eagle Cove, Texas (variant title Eagle Grove) 130, 266 n.
East Jersey, colony of *see* New Jersey, colony of
Eberly, Mrs., quoted 76 n.
Eberly, Jacob 115
Egypt, Texas 126 n.
Ehlenger, Joseph 138, 138 n.
Elgin, Ill Gail Borden library founded, 253, town founded, 262, Hiram Church in, 263, site of Borden activities, 264, 266 ff , Borden buys house, 273
Elgin Milk Condensing Company officers and operations, 263, beef extract plant, 264, cheese losses, 268, dissolution, 268, *see also* Illinois Condensing Company
Elysian Fields, Miss. 51, 55
Emily, Negro slave 110 n
Emmet, Thomas Addis 20 f
England 10, 203, 209, 216, Bordens in, 3–4, immigrants, 8, proposed loan to Texas, 120, grants meat biscuit patent, 210, grants condensed milk patent, 224, 226–29
English Lakes *see* Great Lakes
Eno, Edward S 272–73
Eno, Emeline Eunice *see* Borden, Mrs Emeline Eno Church
Episcopalian church 163, 170
Epidemic colic 194–95
Equitable Life Assurance Society 242
Erie, Pa , proposed plant site 262
Erwin, Dr , at Thompson slaying 74

Falconer, Thomas, on meat biscuit 215
Fannin, James 90
Fall River, Mass. 10

Farish, Oscar 168
Farmers Borden's relations with, 235, rules for, 243–45, education of, 250–51, *see also* dairy industry *and* Borden, Gail and condensed milk
Fayette County, Texas 151, 167
Fink, Mike 28
Fisher, George, collector 63
Fisher, S Rhoads 75
Flack, Elisha 71
Flatboats 26, 29, 51, *see also* keelboats
Flint, Rev Timothy, quoted 26, 30
Food on frontier, 13, 17–18, 43, in Texas, 196, condensed, 198 *see also* Borden, Gail and meat biscuit
Fort Bend, Texas Borden, Sr., at, 105, Bordens flee, 107, destruction, 109
Fort Bend County, Texas 61, 202
Fort Hazard, Miss.· 51–52
Fort Leavenworth, Kansas 205
Fort Sumter, So. Car. 254
Fox River 262 f
France 203, 218
Frank Leslie's Illustrated Newspaper: see *Leslie's Weekly*
Franklin, Benjamin 10
Franklin, Sir John. 214
Fredericksburg, Texas 170
Freetown, R. I 6
French 9
Fyler, Elhanan 261

Gail Borden, Jr., and company seeks market, 237, fails, 238
Gail Borden Library, Elgin 253
Gallipolis (Galliopolis) Ohio 30
Galveston Bay 125, 134, Collinsworth drowned in, 136, storm in, 136–37, buoys, 139 f , Pelican Shoal plat, 160
Galveston City Company 151, 160, 175, Jones resigns, 154, Borden joins, 155, sales, 155–56, 167, pays Borden, 156, Borden petitions, 157, Borden a director, 191, suits in court, 197
Galveston County, Texas records, 156; employs Thomas Borden, 162
Galveston Island, Texas 197, Bordens arrive, 59, proximity to Houston, 124; first permanent building, 129, description of, 130, officials visit, 142–43, granted to Menard, 150, fortification, 161, 168–69, baptisms on, 166
Galveston, Texas customs collections at, 77, 129, 131 ff , 176 ff , refuge in Revolution, 108, description of,

129ff, 135ff., 151–52, 160, 167, 201f, smuggling, 134, 178, weather, 136–38, 141, 167, 178, 196, 206, local government, 138–39, 158f, defense 139, 161, 168–69, shipping at, 140f, 152, as cattle range, 142, favors Lamar, 146–47, population and growth, 151, 155, 196, water found, 156–57, gambling, 159, yellow fever, 162, 171–72, 195–96, spiritual life in, 163–66, 192–93, Penelope Borden in, 173–74, trade averted, 182, Ochiltree visits, 185, romance of, 188, temperance, 194, disease, 194–95, compared with Cleveland and New Orleans, 196, meat biscuit factory, 204, meat biscuit agency, 206, milk experiments, 223, news of Borden, 247, Borden philanthropies, 271
Game in New York, 20, in Indiana, 43–44, in Texas, 57, 129f
Garnsey, Peter B 23
Gazley, Thomas J 75
General Land Office, Republic of Texas 162, see also Borden, John Petit
Georgia 33, 55, 147, 163
Gettysburg, Pa., attack on 260
Gist, Christopher 32
Glasgow, Scotland, death rate 245
Gloucester, R I 11, 47
Gold, discovery of 202, 217
Gold, William 70f.
Goliad, Texas 70, 90, 101, 168
Gonzales, Texas 71, 81, 83
Gooch, Sir William 8
Goodyear India rubber 212n.
Gordon, John, printer 72, 76
Gould, Jay 266
Grand Tier Island, La. 133
Graves, Lewis 165
Gray, F. C. 106
Grayson, Peter W 98, 146f, 167
Great Council Exhibition, London 208, 211, 223, Queen Victoria at, 209, American exhibitions, 209f, closes, 212
Great Kenawha River 30
Great Lakes 23
Great Miami River 37
Greeley, Horace 214, 257–58
Greenup, Ohio 31
Green, Thomas becomes Borden partner, 232–33, 236–37, patent rights, 241, makes patent arrangements, 252
Green Valley, Miss 52
Gridley, Noah aids Borden, 249f,

presses for payment, 252, shuts off water supply, 255n.
Grinnell, Henry 219
Gritten, Edward 102
Groce, Jared 67
Groce's Retreat, Texas 106, Sam Houston at, 108, suggested Texas capital, 124
Guadalupe River 120
Gulf of Mexico 40, 134, 156–57, 165–66, 199

"Hail Columbia," song 10
Halley's comet 91
Hamilton, Governor Andrew 7
Hamilton, James 120
Hamilton's Island, Pa 26
Hamline & Perkins, agents 221
Harlem, N. Y see New York, N Y
Harlem Railway 261, 265, see also New York Central railway
Harman, land applicant 75
Harper's Weekly 239
Harris, Howlong 7
Harris, William P. 131
Harrisburg, Pa 24n
Harrisburg, Texas 83, 125, site of Texas government, 105, *Telegraph and Texas Register*, 106ff, burned, 109, Houston founded near, 122, Borden visits, 131
Harrison, William Henry 37, 49, 167
Hartford, Conn. 234, 237
Hayes, President Rutherford B 196
Heard, Mina 126n.
Hedcorn, England 4
Henderson, Rev. Isaac J 190
Henderson, J Pinckney 126
Henry VI, of England 4
Herring's patent salamander safe 209
Hill, Rufus 21
Hinckley, S T. 263
Hitchcock, Captain L. M. 136–37, 168
Hog Island, R. I. 6
Holley, Mrs Mary Austin, quoted 76n.
Hopkins, Mary 48
Hopkins, Mrs. Mary Knowlton see Borden, Mrs. Mary Knowlton
Hopkins, Richard 48
Hopkinson, Francis 9–10
Hopkinson, Joseph. 10
Horton, A. C: 142
Hotchkiss and Company. 95
Houghton, B. 135
Housing conditions 36, 114

Index

Houston, Sam convention of 1833, 67–68, oratory of, 89, defense of Texas, 105 ff, candidate for president of Texas, 111 f, in Columbia, 114, certifies Borden petitions, 118, Houston, Texas, named for, 122, Borden discusses greatness of, 126, names Borden collector, 131, 167, visits Galveston, 142–43, leaves presidency, 146, governor of Tennessee, 153, names John P Borden land commissioner, 162, president second term, 167, 175 ff, instructs Borden, 168, denounces Commodore Moore, 170, on exchequers, 177, characterizes Borden, 180–82, 185, charges Borden with defalcation, 184, baptism, 193 n, Borden seeks aid from, 227, Know-Nothing, 230, Union sympathizer, 257, receives Borden, 273

Houston, Texas 111, 125 f, 133 f, 143 ff, 270, consumes Harrisburg, 105, platted, 122 ff, capital of Texas, 124, 176, Galveston compared with, 130, public store at, 132, weather, 136, 141, water conditions, 157, ordinances, 158, Capitol converted to hotel, 170, trade averted, 182, scarcity of vaccine, 196, veterans meeting held, 274

Howard, Col R H. 206

Howe, Captain 171

Huckins, Rev. James 164, 167, 192, 247

Hulme, Thomas 27

Hunt, Benjamin 39

Hunt, John 45

Hunter, William 63

Huntsville, Texas 194

Hyams, frontier trader 201

Hyde, Henry Baldwin 242

Illinois 40, 150

Illinois Condensing Company formed, 268, trouble at, 272

Immigration 63, 66 ff., 151

Indiana 28, 32, 37, 41, 45, 58

Indians 6, 18 f, 21, 31, 49, 130, 150, 152, 161 n, 201 ff, 262, 266 n

Industrial Revolution 10, 244–45

Inglis, Mary· 32

Ingram, surveyor 75

Jack, Patrick 64

Jack, William H.· 64

Jackson, Alden A. M 161, 175

Jackson, Andrew 67, battle of New Orleans, 35, 55, seeks presidency, 56, employs S M Williams, 70

James River 8

Jameson, G B 71

Jefferson County, Ind 39, 42, 44

Jefferson, Thomas 56

Jersey City, N. J 246

Johnson and Winburn's tavern, San Felipe 80

Johnson, Andrew, impeachment of 271

Johnson, Frank W. 72, 75, 77

Johnson, Dr H. A 263

Johnson, J. Eastman 232

Johnson, Jehu Warner 236 n

Johnson, Noble 56

Johnson, Philadelphia Borden see Borden, Miss Philadelphia Wheeler

Johnson, Virginia Lee 271 n

Johnston, R. I 9–10

Jones, Dr. Anson 207 n

Jones, David 50

Jones, John Rice gathers Telegraph subscribers, 72, member Milam monument committee, 91 n, seeks customs post, 147

Jones, Dr Levi 154

Jones, Randal 80

Kane, Dr. Elisha Kent, explorer 203, 214, 219

Kansas 229

Karankawa colony, Texas 64

Kaskaskia, Ill 150

Keelboats 28 f, see also flatboats

Kennedy, Francis 33

Kennedy, Thomas 32–35

Kennedy's Ferry, Ky see Covington, Ky.

Kent, England 4 f.

Kenton, Simon 32

Kentucky 28, 30 ff., 35 ff., 42, 63, 196

Kentucky River 37

Kerr, James 76

Kidd, Captain William 7

Klemm, August 254–55

Knight, Charles 254–55

Knowlton, Mary see Borden, Mrs Mary Knowlton

Know-Nothing party 230

Lafitte, Jean 59, 130, 137, 166, 196

Lake Mahopac, N Y. 273

Lamar, Mirabeau B· visits Galveston, 142–43, president of Texas, 146–47, dismisses Borden, 146–49, declining

303

popularity, 153, dismisses Roberts, 161, appoints Jackson, 161, John P. Borden land commissioner under, 162, Santa Fé expedition, 168, sends inspector to Galveston, 175

Lapham, Moses 66, 68, 72, description of San Felipe society, 65, receives account of Thompson slaying, 73–74, description of Columbia, 114, helps plat Houston, 122–23

Laprairie, Canada 150

Lattimore, Dr William, Mississippi congressman 51–52

Laud, Archbishop William 3–4

Laurence, Abbott 210

Lavaca, Texas 64, 67n, 76

Law of April 6, 1830, forbidding immigration 63, 66–67, 69

LeClere, J S 135

Lee, abolitionist 170

Lee, inspector for Borden 133–34

Lee, Ann, founder of Shakers 225

Lee, Robert E. 260, 274

Lee's Landing, Ind 41

Leger, Dr. Theodore 114

Leslie, Frank 245

Leslie's Weekly: 245–46

Liberty, Miss 54f, 57

Liberty, Texas 88, 150

Licking River 31ff.

Liebig, Justus von 264

Limestone, Ky *see* Maysville, Ky.

Lincoln, President Abraham 256–57

Livermore Falls, Me. 260

Liverpool, England, death rate 245

Locomotive bathhouse 157, *see also* Borden, Gail, inventions

"Log Cabin and Hard Cider" campaign of 1840 167

London, England 4, 223, site of fair, 208, orders to close meat biscuit office in, 217, meat biscuit orders from, 218, Borden seeks patent in, 226, death rate, 245

London Society of Arts, honorary membership to Borden 212

Long, Mrs. Jane 114

Louisiana 28, 134, 150

Louisville, Ky . 44n., 47, 262

Louisville, Texas 73–74

Ludlow, Ky. 37

Lynchburg, Texas 125

Lynn, Mass. 244

McClellan, General George· 271

McClung, John 43

McCormick, Cyrus Hall 153

McCormick's reaper 209, 212n.

McDowell, Henry 75–76

McDuffie, Gov George 120

Macfarlane, Robert 227ff.

McKean, Thomas 11

McKinley, Samuel. 44n.

McKinley, President William 267

McKinney, Thomas F 75, 84, security for Borden, 98n., 131, on Borden's dismissal, 147, helps found Galveston City Company, 151, dispute over customs funds, 185ff, services to Texas, 186, 186n., finances of, 270, *see also* McKinney and Williams

McKinney and Williams 154, 156, move business, 135, lose warehouse, 137, agents for Ashbel Smith, 144, securities for Borden, 183

McKnight, James 158

McKinstry, J B. 121

McNeel and Woodson, merchants 66

McNeil, Charles 234

Madison, Ind.. 38ff.

Maine 152, 190

Manchester, Ohio 31

Manhattan, N. Y. *see* New York, N. Y.

Marietta, Ohio 29

Mars Hill, Miss 55

Martin, Wily (Wyly)· 80

Mason, Charles, patent commissioner 228–29

Massachusetts, colony of 41f, 9

Matagorda, Texas 75, 83, 147

Matamoros, Mexico· 77

Maysville, Ky. 27n, 31

Meat biscuits 195, 200, conception of, 201, 203, preparation, 204, in 1950, 204n., army approval, 205f., description of factory, 206f, financing, 207f, at London, 209ff, Waco report, 211–12, wins gold medal, 212, 212n., failure, 219ff., 232, resurrection, 262, 262n., 264, *see also* Borden, Gail and meat biscuit

Mechanicsburg, Ohio. 73

Mechanicsville, N. Y. 225, 230

Medcap, John: 44

Memphis, Tenn 60

Menard, Medard 135

Menard, Michel Branamour to Texas, 150, signer of Texas Declaration of Independence, 150, helps found Gal-

veston City Company, 151, home of, 152, argument with Dr. Jones, 154
Menard, Peter J. 135, 158
Menard, Pierre· 150
Menefee, Thomas 64
Menefee, William 64, 98 n.
Mercer, Rev Asa 56f
Mercer, Eli security for Borden, 56, in Mississippi, 56, 58f, interest in Texas, 58, land grant, 60, Texas farmer, 61, member convention of 1832, 65–66, member convention of 1833, 67–68, at San Jacinto, 109 n, religion, 163
Mercer, Jesse: 55, 163–66
Mercer, Penelope *see* Borden, Mrs Penelope Mercer
Mercer, Reason 74
Mercer, Rev. Silas 163
Mercer, Rev Thomas 55–56
Methodist church 35, 50, 193
Metropolitan opera. 238
Mexican War 194, 196, 202
Mexicans land policy, 57, 60, 62, prospects, 58, halt immigration, 63, rule under, preferred to United States, 69, Texas loyalty to, 79, in song, 90, separation, 96f., 99, 101, and Texas flag, 102, Menard trades with, 150, reinvasion of Texas, 168ff., 178, 180, hold Corpus Christi, 180, in Mexican war, 196
Mexico City, Mexico· 64, 68, 79
Middletown, N J. 7
Milam, Benjamin R. 90f., 91 n.
Milbank, Isaac 271 n.
Milbank, Jeremiah meets Borden, 238–40; positions held, 238–39, settles debts, 241, first milk advertisement, 245–46, success, 247, Borden convinces, 249, Gridley compared with, 250, pays Gridley, 252, plays hunch, 253f., expands facilities, 254–55, Borden Condensed Milk Company relations, 260, Elgin activities, 263–64, recession of 1866, 267, forbids Borden trip to Elgin, 268, value of milk investment, 268n, *see also* Borden, Gail
Milford, N Y. 236
Milk, condensed *see* Borden, Gail and condensed milk
Miller, Dr. James B · 72
Mills, Samuel J., missionary leader 235
Milwaukee, Wis 242, 262
Mina, Texas *see* Bastrop, Texas

Miner, Darius 247
Mississippi 51 ff, 172, 174, 222, 230
Mississippi Baptist Association 55–56, *see also* Baptist church
Mississippi River. 29, 40, 47, 52, 60, 166, 202
Missouri 46, 63
Missouri Compromise 56
Mobile, Ala. 119, 131, 147, 158
Mohawk River 11
Monclova, Mexico 70, 72, 77
Money, John H. 80, 91 n.
Monongahela River. 25
Monroe Doctrine 56
Monroe, George. 48
Montreal, Canada 150
Moore, Commodore Edwin W. 170
Moore, Dr. Francis, Jr 96, *Telegraph* partner, 123, character, 123–24, publishing difficulties, 125, patriarch of Texas press, 128n, visit to Galveston, 142–43, Borden's dismissal, 148–49; Borden's resignation, 182
Morgan, Colonel James 110
Mormon Mills, Texas 217
Morrell, Rev. Z. N. 167
Morris, Robert 86
Morris, William, quoted· 154
Morton, I. T., London agent: 218f.
Muldoon, Miguel 68, 98
Murphree, David 132ff.
Muse, George '33
Muskingum River: 29

Nacogdoches, Texas 84, 124, 150, 216
Napoleon, eating habits· 189
Narbonne, Count de, counterfeiter 167
Nash, James P., teacher 162
Natchez, Miss. 51
Natchez Trace 51
Natchitoches, La. 59
Navidad, Texas 64
Neches River 92
Negro rustling 50
New Bedford, Mass. 206, 209, 221
New Castle, Ky. 50
New England, 3, 9, 16, 43, 235, 241
New Jersey, colony of 5f., 9f.
New Lebanon, N. Y, Shaker community 216n, 225
New London, Conn.: 218
New London, Ind.. 38ff.
New Madrid, Mo, earthquakes· 46
New Mexico 202
New Orleans, La 26, 29, 47 ff, 75,

110ff., Thomas Borden visits, 48ff, 111, 132, Gail Borden visits, 49ff., 58f, battle of, 55, printing materials purchased, 94f, Texas agents in, 117, 147, 206, Borden debts in, 119, comparison with Galveston, 130, 141, 196, gamblers, 159, residence of Thomas Borden, 202

New Orleans Medical Society 114
New Washington, Texas 110
New York Central railway 249
New York Condensed Milk Company 263, named, 242–43, first route, 246, success, 247, problems shift, 254, production, 260, recession of 1866, 267, finances, 268n, sales, 274n, see also Borden, Gail and Milbank, Jeremiah
New York, N. Y. 110, 213f., 216, 225, comparison with Galveston, 130, 141, Williams agency at, 147–48, Borden agency in, 206, Borden in, 208ff., milk depot established, 234, milk market sought, 237f, swill-milk exposure, 245–46, milk routes, 246
Newspapers· Philadelphia *Pennsylvania Chronicle*, 10n., 11n, San Felipe *Texas Gazette*, 61, 72, 76n, Brazoria *Texas Republican*, 72, 80, 106, Troy, N. Y., *Sentinel*, 86, London, England, *Daily Mail*, 87, Houston *Morning Star*, 111n., 126n., Lexington, Kentucky, *Intelligencer*, 120, Austin *Centinel*, 126n., Galveston *Daily News*, 170, 194, 276n., Galveston *Civilian*, 175, New York *Journal of Commerce*, 205, 212, Houston *Post*, 236n, Winsted, Conn., *Herald*, 256, New York *Daily Tribune*, 257f, Houston *Tri-Weekly Telegraph*, 258, Houston *Daily Telegraph*, 262n., see also Borden, Gail, as publisher of *Telegraph and Texas Register*
Nichols, W. B. 158
Nightingale, Florence 217f.
Nimitz, Admiral Chester W.· 170
North Bend, Ohio 37
North Carolina 33, 143, 163
North Norwich, N. Y, trial at 21
Northcliffe, Alfred William Charles Harmsworth, Viscount 87
Norton, Major· 75
Norwich, N. Y.: 12, 20f., 27, 33, 35, 37, 41, population, 12, 23, pantries, 16, Indian resort, 18s., anthracite source, 22
Nova Scotia 9

Ochiltree, William B 185–86
O'Connell, John 234–35, 246
Ohio 24, 28, 262
Ohio River 25, 27–33, Covington boundary, 35, destroys New London, 40, freezes early, 42–43, steamboats on, 46–47
"Old Father George," teacher 42
"Old Three Hundred," Austin's original settlers 58, 80
Olmstead, Frederick Law, writer and landscape architect 220
Orozimbo, Texas 71
Osterman, Joseph, merchant 201
Owen, Robert 230

Paine, Thomas 92–93
Panama, Isthmus of 202
Panic of 1857 229f, 238
Park and Dance pistol factory 257
Parker, Captain William E 129
Pasteur, Louis 224n, 243
"Patent bellyache" see epidemic colic
Patents meat biscuit, 203, 210, 215, condensed milk, 224, 229, reissues, 258–59, improvements, 261–62
Peach Point, Texas 122, 161
Pease, Gov. Elisha M, receives Borden. 270
Pelican Shoal, Texas, platted 160
Pellett, Archibald: 23
Pemmican· 214, 219
Permanent Council 89, 95, 97
Perry and Johns: 170
Perry, James F. 71, 122, aid sought, 72, pays debt, 75, Borden writes, 142, children in Galveston,· 161
Petersburg, Ky. 37
Petersburg, Va. 112
Petroleum 25
Pettus, William 80
Philadelphia, Pa.· 11, 218, 262
Philip (King Philip), Indian leader 6
Phillis, Negro slave: 56
Pinole: 201
Pirates, in New London 40, see also Lafitte, Jean
Pittsburgh, Pa.: 24n., 25–30, 40, 127
Platt, P.· 263
Playfair, Dr. Lyon. 212, 212n.
Plow Handle Point, Ind. 40
Plymouth, colony of 6
Point Bolivar, Texas 133–34
Point Pleasant, W. Va.· 30
Polax, Dick· 68

Polk, President James K 191
Ponaganset River 9
Ponton, Andrew 71
Port Allegheny (Allegany), N Y 25
Portland, Me 170
Portsmouth, Ohio 31
Portsmouth, R I, founding of 5 f.
Port William, Ky *see* Carrollton, Ky
Power, Avery 21
Presbyterian church 8, 190, 193, in
    Kentucky, 36, in Indiana, 42, Galves-
    ton Presbyterian church, 188, 194
Providence, R. I 218
Punch, quoted 210

Quakers *see* Society of Friends
Quintana, Texas 112, Philadelphia Bor-
    den born in, 126 n, McKinney and
    Williams leave, 135

Ramsay, W. F, entertainer 194
"Reannexation and reoccupation," cam-
    paign slogan 191
Recession of 1866 267
Reconstruction in Texas, 269, 274–75,
    Borden's views on, 274–75
Red Fish Bar, Texas 133
Red River 59
Reed and Begain 48
Reed, Rev. Isaac, missionary 42
Reed, Dr Walter 195
Refugio, Texas 168
Republican party 229
Rhode Island, colony and state of 5 ff,
    11, 41
Richmond, Texas 73, 170, 193
Richmond, Texas, Temperance So-
    ciety 193
Río Grande River 120
Ripley, Ohio 31
Rittenhouse family. 33
Roberts, Dr. Willis: 153, named Galves-
    ton collector, 147–49, dismissed, 161,
    175
Robertson, Sterling C, *empresario:* 104
Robinson, William 42
Rochelle, France 11
Rockefeller, John D 262, 267
Rokomeka Company, licensed 260
Roosevelt, Nicholas 46
Rose, Negro slave 56
Ross, Sir John: 215
Rowe, Ellen 57
Rowe, Tom 57
Royall, R. R. 89 f.

Rusk, Thomas J 118, 146
Russia 203, 208, 210, 216

Sabine River 134
St. Andrew's, Scotland 212 n
St Lawrence River 150
St Louis, Mo 40, 150, Borden visits,
    205, agency at, 206, 218, proposed
    plant site, 262, church visits, 262, milk
    sales, 262
St Paul, quoted 275
St. Petersburg, Russia 210
Saligny, Count de, French chargé d'af-
    faires 158
Saltillo, Mexico 69–70
Saluda township, Ind created, 44, Bor-
    den teaches in, 49
San Antonio, Texas John Borden in,
    70 f, Texas Revolution, 83, 90 f, 99,
    recapture, 168, *see also* Alamo
San Augustine, Texas 179
Sandusky, Ohio, proposed plant site
    262
Sandusky, William 167
San Felipe de Austin, Texas 63 f, 73,
    82 ff, 87 f, 91, 94, 101, Borden survey-
    ing activities, 61, *Texas Gazette,* 61,
    Austin's capital, 62, *ayuntamiento* at,
    65, school, 66, Almonte banquet, 70,
    Borden in, 75, agitation for war, 76 f,
    seizure of Cós messenger, 77, com-
    mittee of correspondence, 80, hears
    of Alamo, 104 f, burned, 106 f, de-
    struction and decline, 109, 109 n,
    110 n, Smithwick's residence in, 217
San Francisco, Calif. 202, 206
San Jacinto, battle of 109, 129
San Jacinto day 171
San Jacinto Hotel, Galveston 170, 196
San Jacinto River 157
San Jacinto Veterans Association 109 n
San Luis, Texas 168
San Saba, Texas 201
Santa Anna, Antonio López de cham-
    pions federalism, 64, conciliatory to-
    ward Texas, 65, sends soldiers to Tex-
    as, 77, federalism declines under, 80,
    advance, 90, Alamo, 99, on Texas
    politics, 103, invasion, 104 ff, detained
    at San Jacinto, 110 n, reinvades Tex-
    as, 168
Santa Fé expedition 168
Saunders, Miriam 16
Savage, J S., machinist 206
Scientific American, quoted meat bis-

cuit, 211, 215, condensed milk, 216, 227
Scioto River 31
Scotland 3, 8, 50
Scott, General Winfield 196
Scutari, Turkey, meat biscuit sent to 218
Seguin, Juan N. 113
Seguin, Texas· 230
Senate, Republic of Texas confirms Borden's appointment, 131, 175, Ashbel Smith in, 143, on Borden's dismissal, 148, *see also* Congress, Republic of Texas
Seneca Falls, N. Y. 165
Shakers 216n, 225
Shaw, James on law of July 23, 1842, 180, 182, requests money, 183
Shaw, Joshua C: 197
Shay's rebellion 22
Shenandoah River. 8
Sherburne, N. Y. 21 ff.
Sherman, General William Tecumseh 261
Ships *Ark*, 22, *New Orleans*, 46, *Washington*, 46–47, *Hope*, 58, *Sabine*, 69, *Yellow Stone*, 122, *Rein Deer*, 134, *Tom Toby*, 136, *Perseverance*, 137, *Elbe*, 137, 170, *Columbia*, 142, *Potomac*, 142, *Phaeton*, 160, *Neptune*, 161, 164, *Star of the Republic*, 170, *Union*, 170, *Brilliante*, 171, *Santa Anna*, 178, *Archer*, 179–80, *Benjamin R Milam*, 211, *Tenedos*, 215
Shirley, Gov. William 9
Shoe and Leather Exchange 242
Shreve, Henry 46–47
Sims, Bartlett 71
Slavery· 57, 67 f, 74n., 229, 247, 256
Smith, Dr. Ashbel: description of, 143, visits Galveston, 144, customs quarrel with Borden, 144–45, sends Borden potatoes, 160, on Southern problems, 203 n, Borden partner, 204 ff., in London, 208 ff., addresses French agriculturists, 210, on foods jury, 212, condensed milk, 216, learns Borden's cures, 218, Borden writes, 228
Smith, Henry· 126, 153, death of wife, 68, member Milam monument committee, 91 n, secretary of treasury, Texas, 118 f, 131, 138 ff.
Smith, Major 76
Smith, W. F. 231
Smith, Wager: 196

Smithwick, Noah. 74 n, 194, 217–18
Smuggling, in Texas. 134, 178
Social effects, Borden's milk success 244–45
Society of Friends 5 f., 9, 47, 162
Somervell, Alexander 72, 161
Sons of Temperance, Order of 194
South America 202
South Carolina· 33, 120, 254
Southwick, Stephen. 152
Spain 115
Splane, P. R.: 115
Stamp Act Congress 9
Starr, James Harper 216
Steamboating, Ohio and Mississippi rivers. 46–47, 202, *see also* ships
Stearns, Mrs. Augusta F. *see* Borden, Mrs. Augusta F. Stearns
Steel industry 220n.
Stewart, Charles B. 89, 98n.
Steubenville, Ohio 27
Storms 69, 136–38, 178, 206, *see also* weather, Texas
Summerset, Negro slave 56
Sumner, Colonel E. V. 205, 211
Susquehanna River 22, 24
Sutherland, George 64–65
Swansea, R. I.. 6
Swift, Captain A. 230–31
Swill-milk disclosures. 245–46
Sydnor, John S.: 152, 168, 170, 271

Talbot, Rev. Othniel· 35–36
Tanner's Station, Ky.· *see* Petersburg, Ky.
Taylor, Dr. John 194
Taylor, Gen. Zachary. 196
Telegraph and Texas Planter: see *Telegraph and Texas Register*
Telegraph and Texas Register: 90, 130, 142, 224, first issue, 84–88; advertising, 85, 93, rates, 85, original name, *Telegraph and Texas Planter*, 86, early issues, 88 ff., on patriotism, 89, proprietors, 90, 92; Mexican danger, 91, Halley's comet, 91, on Irish potatoes, 92, on drunkenness, 92, difficulties, 93, 112, labor conditions, 93, 102, tardiness of issue, 94, finances, 94 f, 98, 116 ff., petitions to government, 95, policy, 96, style, 96, Texas flag, 102, considers move, 103, approves Houston's retreat, 105, moves to Harrisburg, 106 ff, San Felipe building burned, 107 n, official news-

paper of Texas, 107, Santa Anna destroys, 108f, in Columbia, 111–24, Bordens offer to sell, 113, on needs of Texas, 115f., public printing, 117ff, free copies, 118, Thomas Borden sells interest, 123, in Houston, 124ff., publishes *Journals of the Senate of the Republic of Texas* and *An Accurate and Authentic Report of the . . . House of Representatives*, 124, Gail Borden sells, 126f., carries Galveston protest, 146f, on Houston water, 157, answers charges against Borden, 184, *see also* Borden, Gail, as publisher *and* Borden, Thomas Henry
Temperance 92, 159, 193–94
Tennessee. 33, 67, 153
Tenorio, Antonio. 77
Tenoxtitlan, Texas 84
Terraqueous machine· 197, first trip, 198–99, second trip, 199–200
Texas 196, Borden returns to, 235–36, 274, Civil War, 256–58, conditions in, 269, weather, 270, Borden dies in, 275
Texas Baptist Education Society 167
Texas, colony of 60, 82, 84ff., 90, 98, prospects, 57f., Borden visits, 58, Mercers and Bordens move to, 59ff, Mexican rule, 69, 77; hails Austin's return from Mexico, 79, talk of independence, 101, flag, 102, Declaration of Independence, 102ff., 150, Menard to, 150
Texas fever· 51–52, 58
Texas, Republic of 153, 216, Declaration of Independence, 102ff., 150, government to Harrisburg, 105, capital at Columbia, 111ff., international status, 113f., needs listed, 115f., customs collections, 129ff., 161, 176ff, medical supplies, 144, quitclaims Galveston, 150–51, capital at Houston, 124, 176, annexation, 142, 162, 191, capital at Austin, 161n., Mexican reinvasion, 168, Penelope Borden in, 172–74, exchequers of, 176ff., funds withheld from, 182ff, services of McKinney and Williams, 186
Texas Revolution 81, 90, 92
Texas Supreme Court 183–84
Texas, University of 188n
Texas Veterans Association 274
Textile industry 244
Thomas, David, trial of 20f.

Thompson, Jesse, slaying of: 73f
Tiley, Lily Barbary 70
Tiverton, R. I. 6
Toledo, Ohio, proposed plant site 262
Toby, Thomas 147
Tod, Captain John G. 210f.
Torrington, Conn. *see* Wolcottville, Conn.
Toy, printer 87
Travis, William Barrett firebrand, 63, arrest, 64, attack on Anáhuac, 77, plea from Alamo, 103, death, 104
Treasury Department, Republic of Texas 133ff., 161, 176ff., *see also* Borden, Gail
Tremont Hotel, Galveston: 167, 171, 194
Trollope, Frances, cited 30n.
Troy, N. Y.· 226
Turkey, as market for meat biscuit 215
Turner, Amasa· residence of, 132, 135–37, builds hotel, 138
Turtle Bayon resolutions 63f.
Tyler, President John 167

Ugartechea, Domingo de 81, 83
Unadilla River 12
Underwood, James 42
Union Baptist Association 167
United States. 63, 64, lack of assistance from, 97, 99, contributes to Texas flag, 102, recognition of Texas, 114, Texas seeks loan from, 120, Texas independence of, 141, Texas annexation, 191, Mexican War, 150, 194, 196, 202, adds territory, 202, patents, 203, 224, 229, 258–59, 261–62, represented at Great Council Exhibition, 209ff., buys condensed milk, 254–55, Civil War, 254ff
United States Army: meat biscuit approval, 205f., Waco report, 211f, evacuates Sumter, 254, condensed milk orders, 254–55
Utah, territory of 202

Vacations workers', 265, Borden's, 269–71
Vacuum pan *see* Borden, Gail and condensed milk
Valley Forge, Pa· 11
Vance, Colonel Robert 57
Vance, Susan 57
Vanderbilt, Cornelius 241, 262
Vassar, Rev. Thomas 275
Vawter, Beverly 43

Vawter, Jesse 42
Velasco, Texas 111f, 125, Texas cannon at, 64, customs collections, 77, Austin at, 79, Borden visits, 110, customs post sought, 147
Vernon, N. Y 263
Victor, P. 171
Victoria, queen of England 209
Virginia, colony and state of 8, 30, 233
Virginia Point, Texas 136

Wade, J. M. 194
Wanamaker, John 241–42
War of 1812 23, 35, 49
Ward, Colonel. 87
Washington, D. C· 206, 226f., 233
Washington, George 10f.
Washington-on-the-Brazos, Texas consultation at, 79, site of constitutional convention, 101, Texas government leaves, 105, suggested Texas capital, 124
Wassaic, N. Y. 260, 267, description of, 249, factory at, 249ff, description of factory, 251, women working, 252, production increase, 254, pressure relieved, 261, return of Borden, 268
Wavell, Field Marshal Sir Archibald 215
Wavell, Arthur Goodall 214–15
Weather, Texas 69, 270, see also storms
Webb, Charles 53
Webb, Kinchon, Borden landlord 54, 222
Webb, Rebecca. boards Borden, 54, assists milk experimentation, 222
Weed, Clark S., quoted 235–36
Wells, Frank 273
Wharton, William H. 142
Wheeler, Philadelphia see Borden, Mrs. Philadelphia Wheeler
Wheeling, W. Va 25, 29
White, David, Texas agent 119
White, W. C 71–72
White Plains, N. Y Borden office in, 269, Borden home, 271, Borden funeral service, 275–76

Wightman, Elias R 75
Wilkinson, Angus 58
Wilkinson, Calista, 58f
William I (William the Conqueror). 4.
Williams, Adam 252
Williams, Esther, Borden's grandmother. 11
Williams, H. H. 183n.
Williams, H. H, and Company 183, 183n.
Williams, Reuel, Borden partner 233, 236, 237n, 241, 252
Williams, Roger. 5, 11, 14, 26
Williams, Samuel M.. 194, colonial secretary, 69–75, offers assistance to Borden, 72, arrest demanded by Mexico, 79, loses navy agency, 147–48, helps found Galveston City Company, 151, residence, 152, named commissioner, 186, letter to wife, 173, brother of H. H. Williams, 183n, given customs money, 185, services to Texas, 186, see also McKinney and Williams
Williamsburg, Va. 8
Williamson, Robert M. convention of 1833, 67–68, arrest demanded by Mexico, 77, "pats juba," 194
Wilson, Joseph, naval surgeon 221
Winchester Center, Conn. 204n.
Winsor, Daniel 236
Winsted, Conn 260–61, 261n
Wolcottville, Conn.: 234ff., 250
Woll, General Adrian 168
Woodhouse, M. P. 177–78
Woodlawn cemetery, N. Y., Borden burial at· 274–76
Woods, John, quoted 31
Woodward, Demis see Borden, Demis Woodward

Yale University· 21, 143
Yeamans, Daniel. 75
Yellow fever 162, 171–72, 195–96
York, Pa., milk factory site 260

Zavala, Lorenzo de 77
Zion Hill, Miss.. 54–56

0023031

CPSIA information can be obtained at www.ICGtesting.com
Printed in the USA
LVOW01s1206021113

359719LV00004B/389/P

9 781258 131265